THE FRANCISCANS IN THE MIDDLE AGES

Monastic Orders

ISSN 1749-4974

Monastic houses – houses of monks, regular canons, nuns, and friars – were a familiar part of the medieval landscape in both urban and rural areas, and members of the religious orders played an important role in many aspects of medieval life. The volumes in this new series provide authoritative and accessible guides to the origins of each of these orders, to their expansion, and to their main characteristics.

Forthcoming Volumes

The Benedictines
James Clark

The Canons Regular
Janet Burton

The Carmelites, Austin Friars and Lesser Orders
Frances Andrews

The Carthusians
Julian Luxford

The Franciscans
in the Middle Ages

Michael Robson

THE BOYDELL PRESS

First published 2006
The Boydell Press, Woodbridge

ISBN 1 84383 221 6

The Boydell Press is an imprint of Boydell & Brewer Ltd
PO Box 9, Woodbridge, Suffolk IP12 3DF, UK
and of Boydell & Brewer Inc.
Mt Hope Avenue, Rochester, NY 14620, USA
website: www.boydellandbrewer.com

A catalogue record for this book is available
from the British Library

This publication is printed on acid-free paper

Typeset in Garamond Premier Pro by Word and Page, Chester

Printed in Great Britain by
Biddles Ltd, King's Lynn, Norfolk

CONTENTS

MAPS

ACKNOWLEDGEMENTS

An immense debt is owed to scholars with whom I have discussed aspects of this project. The thirteenth chapter benefited from discussions on satire with Declan Kiberd, professor of Anglo-Irish Literature and Drama at University College, Dublin, and Donald Logan, professor emeritus of Emmanuel College, Boston, Massachusetts, who also offered guidance on the preface. Micheal MacCraith, OFM, professor of Irish at the National University of Ireland, Galway, and Hugh Lawrence, professor emeritus in the University of London, have taken an interest in the book from the outset and have been a source of encouragement and advice. Discussions with Dr Jens Röhrkasten, lecturer in medieval history at Birmingham University, have been both stimulating and illuminating. Responsibility for any remaining errors is mine. Dr Janet Burton of the University of Wales, Lampeter, and the general editor of the series has been patient, encouraging and helpful throughout the preparation of the manuscript. John Watt, professor emeritus of medieval history at the University of Newcastle upon Tyne, read a draft of some of the early chapters and made valuable comments. For the last decade he has offered me sound advice on several aspects of my research. His encouragement and friendship have not tempered his high standards of scholarship. My debt of gratitude is shown in the dedication of this book to him.

The Franciscan Institute at St Bonaventure's University, New York, the Capuchin Historical Institute, Rome, and Sr Maura O'Carroll, SND, generously permitted me permission to reproduce maps of the Irish and English provinces from Francis Cotter's *The Friars Minor in Ireland from Their Arrival to 1400*, Franciscan Institute Publications, History Series 7, 1994, appendix I, and Maura O'Carroll's *Robert Grosseteste and the Beginnings of a British Theological Tradition*, Bibliotheca Seraphico-Capuccina, LXIX (Rome, 1983), p. 325.

CHRONOLOGY

1181/2	Birth of Francis in Assisi.
1202/4	Francis was captured in the battle of Collestrada and imprisoned at Perugia.
1206	Conversion of Francis.
1209/10	Francis obtained initial approval of his Rule from Pope Innocent III.
1215, Nov.	Meeting of the Fourth Lateran Council.
1219	Francis's third attempt to reach the Holy Land was successful.
1220, 16 Jan.	Execution of the five protomartys of the order in Morocco.
1223, 29 Nov.	The Rule of Francis was approved by Pope Honorius III.
1223, 25 Dec.	Francis celebrated the nativity at Greccio.
1224, c.14 Sept.	Francis received the stigmata at La Verna.
1226, 3/4 Oct.	Death of Francis at the Portiuncula just outside Assisi.
1227, 10 Oct.	Seven friars martyred in Morocco.
1228, 16 July	Canonisation of Francis by Pope Gregory IX.
1228, summer	compilation of Thomas of Celano's *Vita prima*.
1230, 25 May	Translation of Francis's body to the new basilica.
1230, 28 Sept.	*Quo elongati*, the first papal exposition of the Rule.
1231, 13 June	Death of St Anthony at Arcella, near Padua.
1231, 17 Nov.	Death of St Elizabeth of Hungary, tertiary.
1232, 30 May	Canonisation of Anthony and the composition of the first biography, the anonymous *Assidua*.
1236	Alexander of Hales, a regent master in theology, entered the order.
1239	Deposition of Elias of Cortona and election of Albert of Pisa, as minister general.
c.1243	Dissent over levels of observance in some Italian provinces.
1245, June/July	First Council of Lyons.
1245, 14 Nov.	Pope Innocent IV's *Ordinem vestrum* gave an interpretation of the Rule, going beyond the terms of Pope Gregory IX's *Quo elongati*.
c.1246–	The *Scripta Leonis* and Thomas of Celano's *Vita secunda* or the Remembrance of the Soul written in response to a plea from the general chapter for recollections of the founder.
1253, 11 Aug.	Death of Clare of Assisi, foundress of the Poor Clares.
1260	General Chapter of Narbonne published the earliest extant constitutions.
1266	Bonaventure's *Legenda maior* adopted as the official biography.

-1272	*Expositio regulae* by David of Augsburg.
1274, 15 July	Death of Bonaventure at the Second Council of Lyons.
1279, summer	Peter Olivi's *Quaestio disputata de paupertate* on *usus pauper*.
1279, 14 Aug.	Pope Nicholas III, *Exiit qui seminat*.
1281, 2 March	Death of Agnes of Prague, Poor Clare.
1288, 22 Febr.	Election of Jerome Maschi of Ascoli, formerly minister general (1274–9), as Pope Nicholas IV (1288–92).
1297, 19 Aug.	Death of St Louis of Anjou, bishop of Toulouse.
1298, March	Death of Peter Olivi.
1300, 18 Febr.	*Super cathedram* promulgated by Pope Boniface VIII.
1305	Angelo Clareno at the papal court in Avignon.
1308, 8 Nov.	Death of John Duns Scotus in Cologne.
1309, 4 Jan.	Death of Angela of Foligno.
1309–12	Debates and pamphlets about the observance of the Rule at Avignon.
1311/12	Council of Vienne.
1312, 6 May	Pope Clement V's *Exivi de paradiso*.
1317, 7 April	Canonisation of St Louis of Anjou.
1317, 7 Oct.	*Quorundam exigit*, sets obedience above poverty and permits the ministers to coerce zealots for poverty.
1318, 7 May	Five friars executed in Marseilles.
1322, 26 March	Pope John XXII's *Quia nonnunquam*.
1322, 8 Dec.	John XXII's *Ad conditorem canonum*.
1323, 12 Nov.	John XXII's *Cum inter nonnullos*.
1324	Louis of Bavaria calls for a general council to depose Pope John XXII.
1326, 8 Febr.	Papal condemnation of Olivi's *Lectura super Apocalipsim*.
1328, 12 May	Peter of Corvara, a member of the order, crowned as Pope Nicholas V, an anti-pope (1328–30).
1328, 26 May	Michael of Cesena escaped from the papal court at Avignon.
1328, 6 June	Michael of Cesena removed from the office of minister general.
1328, 13 June	Cardinal Bertrand de la Tour appointed as vicar general of the order until the next general chapter.
1328, Oct.	Petition of Prince Philip of Majorca to live by the Rule.
1334	John de Valle's community of strict observance begins at Brugliano.
1336, 28 Nov.	Constitutions promulgated by Pope Benedict XII.
1337, 15 June	Death of Angelo Clareno.
1341	Martyrdom of 16 friars in Persia.
1342, 29 Nov.	Death of Michael of Cesena at Munich.
1343	Twelve friars were restored to the Holy Sepulchre in Jerusalem.
1347 , 9/10 April	Death of the impenitent William of Ockham at Munich.
1347/9	The Black Death sweeps through western Europe.
1354	The General Chapter of Assisi approved constitutions for the order.
1357, 8 Nov.	Richard FitzRalph appeals against the friars at Avignon.

1360, c.10 Nov.	Death of Richard FitzRalph at Avignon.
1367	Paoluccio dei Trinci da Foligno licensed to settle at Brugliano.
1380, 8 Sept.	Birth of Bernardine of Siena.
1390, 14 Sept.	Death of Paoluccio de' Trinci da Foligno.
1392	Martyrdom of four friars in Jerusalem.
1407, 26 April	Incipient Observant houses exempt from the minister general.
1407, 13 May	Thomas de Curte appointed as vicar general of the Observants.
1409, 13 May	Peter of Candia elected as Pope Alexander V (1409–10).
1414	John of Capistrano admitted to the community of the Observance.
1414/18	Council of Constance.
1415	The transfer of Santa Maria degli Angeli to the Observants.
1430	The General Chapter at Assisi espouses reform.
1442, 18 July	Albert of Sarteano appointed as vicar general of the order to celebrate the general chapter of Padua the following year.
1444, 20 May	Death of Bernardine of Siena at San Francesco, Aquila.
1446, 9 Febr.	John de Maubert, vicar general for the provinces north of the Alps, was licensed to found sixteen new friaries for the Observants.
1446, 23 July	*Ut sacra ordinis minorum religio.*
1450, 24 May	Canonisation of Bernardine of Siena.
1456, 23 Oct.	Death of John of Capistrano.

GLOSSARY OF TERMS

Cardinal protector: the cardinal designated by the pope to represent the interests of the order at the papal curia.

Conventual: an abbreviated form of Friars Minor Conventual, the friars who favoured the conventual life with papal interpretations of the Rule. Earlier they were known as the Community.

Cursor: a theologian active in the friars' schools under the supervision of the lector or master of theology.

Custody: a group of friaries in a specified region under the jurisdiction of the *custos* and minister provincial.

Custos (*custodes* in the plural): the friar appointed to supervise groups of friaries in a particular territory under the authority of the minister provincial.

Definitors: friars elected to advise the ministers general and provincial.

Delate: a formal appeal against the teaching or conduct of an official.

Discreets: friars whose function was to advise the guardian on the application of the Rule.

General chapter: the highest authority in the order from 1239 and responsible for the life of its members. The triennial chapters elected the minister general.

Guardian: elected by the provincial chapter, he was responsible for the friars' ministry and welfare in a community.

Friars: designated members of the order, some of whom were priests and others who were not clerics and were known as *fratres laici* in medieval nomenclature.

Friary or **convent**: the friars' home in a city, borough or remote location. It included a range of conventual buildings, many of which were a feature of monasticism.

Laudesi: confraternities who sang the Divine Offices and hymns. They frequently met in the mendicant churches of Italy.

Lector: the friar who taught theology in friaries. The terms *master* and *doctor* were also employed in larger friaries, especially the universities.

Limitatio: the geographical boundaries within which the friars worked.

Martyrology or **necrology**: a book or list of benefactors and others for whom the friars prayed, especially on the anniversary of death.

Michaelists: disciples of Michael of Cesena, the deposed minister general, who continued his campaign against Pope John XXII.

Minister general: appointed by the general chapter. He could be re-elected for further terms and was invested with the authority to remove unsuitable ministers provincial from office.

Ministers provincial: elected either by the provincial chapter or the minister general, they were responsible for the government of the order and visited the friaries within the province.

Novice: someone undertaking a year of probation, after which the novice made profession of vows of poverty, chastity and obedience.

Observants: the successors to the Spiritual friars, who became known as *Fratres minores de observantia*.

Procurator general: a friar who liaised between the order and the papal curia.

Provinces: friaries within a region, often a country. There were several provinces in Italy, France, Germany and Spain.

Provincial chapters: an annual review of the friars' ministry. The minister provincial and his advisers appointed guardians, lectors and other officials.

Second Order: an order of nuns, inspired by St Francis and led by St Clare of Assisi. The movement, known also as the Poor Clares, spread from Assisi to numerous centres in western Europe.

Spirituals: the growing group of friars who wished to bypass papal relaxations of the Rule, which they wished to embrace in a more spiritual manner.

Studium generale: applied primarily to the universities of Paris, Oxford and Cambridge which had faculties of theology. The term was later extended to the universities which opened such faculties in the second half of the fourteenth century.

Third Order: the society founded for lay people who wished to live by St Francis's insights.

Visitation: each province and friary was visited by the minister general and minister provincial, who made a report to the general or provincial chapter.

ABBREVIATIONS

AFH	*Archivum Franciscanum historicum*
ALKG	*Archiv für Litteratur- und Kirchen-Geschichte des Mittelalters*, ed. H. Denifle and F. Ehrle, 4 vols (Berlin and Freiburg, 1885–8)
AP	*Anonymus Perusinus*, in *FF*, pp. 1311–51
BF	*Bullarium Franciscanum*, ed. J. H. Sbaraleae, C. Eubel *et al.*, 7 vols (Rome, 1759–1904), new series 1–4, i–ii (Rome, 1929–90)
BIHR	Borthwick Institute of Historical Research, University of York
BL	British Library, London
CA	*Compilatio Assisiensis*, in *FF*, pp. 1471–1690
CF	*Collectanea Franciscana*
DSBOO	Bonaventure, *Doctoris Seraphici S. Bonaventurae S.R.E. episcopi cardinalis opera omnia edita studio et cura PP.Collegii a S.Bonaventura*, 10 vols.
FF	*Fontes Francescani*, ed. E. Menestò, S. Brufani *et al.*, Medioevo Francescano, Collana diretta da Enrico Menestò, Testi II (Assisi, 1995)
FS	*Franciscan Studies*, new series
MF	*Miscellanea Francescana*
MGH, SS	Monumenta Germaniae Historica, Scriptores
n.s.	New Series
RS	Rolls Series
SB	Spicilegium Bonaventurianum
SC	*Sacrum commercium sancti Francisci cum domina Paupertate*, in *FF*, pp. 1705–32
SF	*Sinica Franciscana*, 1, ed. A. Van Den Wyngaert (Florence, 1929)
StF	*Studi Francescani*
Vita prima	Thomas of Celano, *Vita prima Sancti Francisci*, in *FF*, pp. 275–424
Vita secunda	Thomas of Celano, *Vita secunda Sancti Francisci*, in *FF*, pp. 443–639

For Professor John A. Watt

INTRODUCTION

St Francis of Assisi imitated Jesus Christ, his divine master, as closely as he could, abandoning his possessions for the benefit of the poor. His voluntary poverty was perceived as the recovery of an earlier strand in the Christian tradition, the belief that Christ and the Apostles had lived in simplicity and some physical hardship. As a symbol of this life of sacrifice the friars' badge of identity was the cord around their waist; they were known as the *cordati*.[1] The cord's three knots signified the vows of poverty, chastity and obedience.[2] As the movement spread, friars reached almost every diocese of Christendom; within a century of the founder's death there were 1,421 friaries, with the greater number to the north of the Alps.[3]

Friars left their mark upon the medieval Church and society – their itinerant ministry took them to almost every parish. Their origins coincided with the growth and expansion of cities in western Europe. Their apostolate was attuned to the pastoral needs of the city and they became part of its fabric. They brought the Gospel to the laity in colourful, dramatic and intelligible terms, preaching in both church and *piazza*. This adaptation became a salient feature of their preaching and the allied ministry of hearing confessions. Friars preached peace in the divided cities of Italy, and friars restored peace and harmony, frequently in a public demonstration of reconciliation. Their sermons against usury and their social influence led to the creation of the *monte di pietà* in several Italian cities during the second half of the fifteenth century. The *monte* was a charitable, non-profit organisation which lent money at a low rate of interest. Some cities revered individual friars as the founders of the *monte*.[4]

Innumerable communes supplied the friars with alms and contributed to the construction of their churches. The friars' church was a place of devotion

---

[1] 'Defensio fratrum mendicantium', in *Fratris Johannis Pecham quondam archiepiscopi Cantuariensis tractatus tres de paupertate*, ed. C. L. Kingsford, A. G. Little and F. Tocco, British Society of Franciscan Studies, II (Aberdeen, 1910), pp. 148–91 at 173, v. 301. In Dante's *Divina commedia*, ed. N. Sapegno, La letteratura italiana storia e testi, IV (Milan, 1957), *Inferno*, XXVII, v. 67, p. 314, Guido da Montefeltro introduced himself as a *cordigliero*. The poet and jongleur Rutebeuf refers to the Cordeliers (*Oeuvres complètes*, ed. E. Faral and J. Bastin (Paris, 1959–60), I, pp. 229–37, 325).

[2] Federico Visconti, *Les Sermons et la visite pastorale de Federico Visconti archevêque de Pise (1253–1277)*, ed. N. Bériou, no. 14, p. 780.

[3] G. Golubovich, *Biblioteca bio-bibliografica della Terra Santa e dell'oriente francescano*, 5 vols (Quaracchi, Florence, 1906–27), II, pp. 250–1.

[4] F. L. Tognato, *Legge di Dio e monti di pietà Marco da Montegallo 1425–96* (Vicenza, 1996).

and instruction and the friary was the home of men committed to the dissemination of Christian values. They inspired a new form of architecture designed to accommodate large crowds for sermons and they were decorated by many of the finest artists, from Cimabue to Sassetta, via Giotto, Taddeo Gaddi, Simone Martini and Pietro Lorenzetti and Piero della Francesca. Devotion to the holy name was promoted by Bernardine of Siena whose monogram of YHS, set like the golden rays of the sun, decorated many churches and houses in Tuscany and spread to other parts of Western Europe. The church of San Francesco occupies a central site in many Italian cities to this day; Greyfriars Street or La Rue des Cordeliers are reminders of the suppressed friaries of England and France.

The friars' ranks included preachers and contemplatives, philosophers and ascetics, craftsmen and artists, theologians and musicians, missionaries and scientists, historians and mystics, poets and artisans. They filled many of the highest ecclesiastical offices as well as the most humble and menial. Several friars were renowned for their sanctity and their tombs became places of pilgrimage. While the lives of innumerable friars remain hidden from view, many were lauded by contemporaries. The friary was the home of a large and vibrant religious community which ministered to an urban population. Its members were men possessed of remarkable skills.[5] Friars brought news of events from the surrounding villages, the countryside and overseas, a service underlined by the cosmopolitan nature of the community. Their ranks included a handful of well-travelled men who had served as missionaries and messengers. As a member of a cosmopolitan order the friar inhabited a world which was not circumscribed by a parish, city, diocese or nation. The friary was a place of natural resort, especially for travellers and merchants who found themselves outside the systems of medieval parishes.[6] These men needed confessors and other spiritual ministrations. Men with an attachment to the friars in one city might request burial in the friary nearest to their place of death.[7]

The order's apostolate was grounded in its impressive educational structures. The order and the new universities grew side by side and their histories were closely entwined in the thirteenth and fourteenth centuries. The leading theologians were mendicants, Albert the Great, Bonaventure, John Duns Scotus and Thomas Aquinas. The friars' schools were widely regarded

---

[5]   The order's influence was celebrated by a Majorcan friar, Anselm Turmeda, in 1398. He praised seven friars, one who became a royal confessor and three who became bishops in Malta and Sardinia. Another four taught in the cathedral. A. Turmeda, *Obres menors*, ed. M. Olivar (Barcelona, 1927), pp. 117–19.

[6]   J. Röhrkasten, 'Local Ties and International Connections of the London Mendicants', *Mendicants, Military Orders, and Regionalism in Medieval Europe*, ed. J. Sarnowsky (Aldershot, 1999), pp. 145–83.

[7]   A citizen of York asked for burial in the friars' church at Bruges; his will was witnessed by a member of the Flemish friary on 18 September 1389. BIHR, Probate Register 1, fol. 1v.

as centres of theological excellence. The order pioneered a form of study to equip men for the apostolates of preaching and hearing confessions. Two friars were instrumental in the foundation of Balliol College, Oxford, and Pembroke College, Cambridge.[8] Alumni of the schools contributed to the Church in a variety of ways. The liturgical revisions of Haymo of Faversham acquired an importance and popularity beyond the order. The friars' interest in contemporary events produced several histories of local and international importance. William of St-Pathus, the confessor of Queen Marguerite of Provence, wife of Louis IX, wrote a biography of the canonised king about 1303.[9] The friars' preaching revitalised the western Church and even their critics acknowledged that their message had reached the boundaries of the world.[10] Their preaching and devotional literature provided a boost for the growing use of the vernacular in prose, poetry and hymns. For example, mastery of local languages was reflected in the diocese of Exeter, where their penitentiaries were the only ones who understood Cornish sufficiently well.

Vowed to chastity, obedience and without anything of his own, the friar renounced social and economic status. He was an accessible man in social terms and was a familiar figure in hospitals and the homes of the sick. He was to be seen visiting prisons and the homes of the aristocracy. He was frequently selected as a mediator in urban disputes or between local communes. He could be invited to preach before the king.[11] Equally he might be selected as the ambassador of his community or his country to announce or negotiate peace; he was no stranger to the battlefield. His status as a member of a large international order made him an ideal instrument of the crown, crossing from one territory to another and recognisable by his habit. A further symbol of this global dimension was a ministry to travellers, who moved around the markets. Friars were expressly licensed by the local bishop to hear the confessions of foreign merchants visiting the fairs of western Europe.

Francis's vision was global and his Rule (*regula vitae*) made provision for friars who were inspired to become missionaries in remote lands. He led by example on his pilgrimage to the Holy Land. His boldness in walking into the heart of the Muslim camp during the battle for Damietta in 1219 was breath-taking and betokened his respect for people of different faiths. By

---

[8] William Woodford, *Defensorium fratrum mendicantium contra Ricardum Armachanum*, in Cambridge University Library, MS Ff. I. 21, fol. 120r: *et manifestum est quod unus frater minor confessor unius venerabilis domine movit illam facere Oxonie aulam quae dicitur Baylioli et alius frater minor confessor domine Comitisse Pembrochie movit eam ad constructionem et dotationem aule Pembrochie in Cantebrigia.*

[9] *Vie de Saint Louis par Guillaume de Saint-Pathus confesseur de la Reine Marguerite*, ed. H. F. Delaborde (Paris, 1899).

[10] Matthew Paris, *Matthaei Parisiensis, monachi Sancti Albani, Chronica majora*, IV, ed. H. R. Luard, 7 vols, RS, LVII (London, 1872–83), p. 346.

[11] *Histoire de Saint Louis par Jean Sire de Joinville*, ed. N. de Wailly (Paris, 1868), nn. 11, 132, pp. 20, 235–7.

the turn of the fourteenth century friars were working on missions to the Ethiopians, Indians, Mongols, Persians and Syrians.[12] They were the only Catholic religious or priests ministering in Syria, the Holy Land, Arabia and Egypt. In 1322 James, bishop of Caffa, claimed that the friars had ministered in Morocco and India as well as China for several decades and had given new martyrs to the Church.

St Francis remains one of the most attractive figures of the medieval Church. His exceptional abilities as a preacher soon brought him to the attention of his neighbours. The acceptance of disciples, albeit initially few in number, began to change the nature of this small fraternity, which would soon be transmuted into an international religious order. His was the last Rule to win papal approval before the religious upheaval of the sixteenth century. However, what was permissible and desirable for a dozen friars in Umbria about 1210 was less practicable for the population of more than a hundred at the Cordeliers of Paris a century later. Fidelity to the Rule was a matter of the utmost concern for friars and this caused them much heart-searching. Within four years of the saint's death a crisis of leadership occurred; unable to resolve their doubts about their founder's teaching, friars sought papal intervention in 1230 and this resulted in *Quo elongati*, the first interpretation of the Rule. The controversial conduct of Elias of Cortona concentrated the friars' minds on their vocation and the limitations of the office of the minister general. The general chapter emerged as the ultimate source of authority in the order at the expense of the minister general in 1239. The failings of the ministers during the 1280s and 1290s stiffened the reformers' resolve to seek a measure of independence and therein lay the forces of separation. The desire for a more satisfactory observance of the Rule and the *Testament* stoked opposition. These disputes resulted in two versions of the friars' life.

The accommodation between Francis's vision and the needs of a conventual life for a large community contained the seeds of discord and eventual division. While Francis believed that Christ knew penury and hardship, his followers were required to formulate their own rationale for the order and justify its scriptural and theological bases. The onslaught of the secular masters of the University of Paris in the 1250s was deeply damaging; it also created a durable satire which branded the friars as pseudo-apostles and hypocrites. Although Pope Nicholas III's *Exiit qui seminat* placed the friars on the moral high ground, it proved to be a false dawn and the practicalities of a large number of friars claiming to be living in poverty caused further controversy.

The order's espousal of evangelical poverty, which became the criterion of its fidelity to the Rule and its rationale, brought tensions in its wake.

---

[12] Iacopone da Todi, *Laude*, ed. F. Mancini, Scrittori d' Italia, CCLVII (Bari, 1974), no. 47, pp. 130–2.

David Knowles comments that the friars were 'riven by a succession of acrid controversies over the observance of their founder's conception and command of Christlike poverty'.[13] Even though the Benedictines had groups of monasteries with dependent priories and general chapters, there was nothing comparable to the mendicant centralisation which undoubtedly heightened and exacerbated the bitterness. The impatience, character-assassination and punishment meted out to Ubertino da Casale and Angelo Clareno constituted a black day in the history of the order with a reputation for making peace. Despite currents of reform among the Friars Minor Conventual, there was a remarkable lack of foresight at ministerial level in the 1420s and 1430s when there was still time to preserve the organic unity of the order. Instead of offering decisive leadership and an openness to renewal, many ministers placed the focus on obedience.

Bernardine of Siena personifies the purity and vigour of the Observant reform in the first half of the fifteenth century, when the initiative was passing to the reformers. The two branches of the order co-existed, sometimes in the same city, and were valued by the local Church. On the eve of the dissolution in sixteenth century England many testators gave alms to Observant and Conventual communities alike. The order carried virtually all before it in the thirteenth century. Although the friars' schools produced numerous outstanding theologians in the fourteenth century, it had already surrendered its intellectual dominance. The Observants played a vital role in the preservation of Francis's ideals. Bernardine of Siena, John of Capistrano, James of the Marches and Albert da Sarteano were among the most famous preachers of their epoch. Despite such vigour, new movements of reform appeared and the Observants did not escape criticism, as the *Heptameron* of Marguerite de Navarre (1492–1539) attests. Within fifteen years of Leo X's *Ite vos*, which officially divided the order in 1517, another reform movement, the Friars Minor Capuchin, was born. This book was completed on the threshold of the eighth centenary of the conversion of St Francis. His challenge to respond openly and imaginatively to the Gospel has attracted people since the year 1206. That call is equally fresh and inviting today.

The sources

Hagiography was regulated by its own assumptions and conventions. The hagiographers celebrated the saints, whose virtues and miraculous powers were accentuated. This framework was eternal as well as temporal and Francis's death was unself-consciously reported as his passing from the shipwreck of this world.[14] There were abundant instances of the way in which the saints' conduct was profoundly changed by the grace of God and elevated

---

[13] M. D. Knowles, *Christian Monasticism* (London, 1969), p. 116.

[14] For example BL, MS Add. 14251, fol. 214r.

to a higher level of communion with both their Creator and creatures. The *legendae* were intended to be read in the church and the monastic refectory for the instruction and edification of a religious community. Nonetheless, changing tastes are discernible in the work of Francis's first biographer, Thomas of Celano, who described the character and appearance of the saint:

> he was of medium height, closer to shortness; his head was moderate in size and round, his face a bit long and prominent, his forehead smooth and low; his eyes were of moderate size, black and sound; his hair was black, his eyebrows straight, his nose symmetrical, thin and straight; his ears were upright, but small; his temples smooth.[15]

The *vita* was not a biography in the modern sense because the author was uninterested in the faults of the individual, unless these failings offered an occasion to contrast moments of weakness with the triumph of grace and the resultant conversion. Similarly, parental and sibling ties were of little interest and they constituted a preamble to the work of grace. The act of conversion rendered the family redundant, a fact reflected in the two *vitae* by Thomas of Celano. Hagiography articulates the prevailing values of the Church and this conditions and distorts examples of Francis's contact with women. The *Vita secunda*'s arresting claim that Francis knew only two women by their faces reveals more about the reforming Lateran Councils, which combated clerical marriage and concubinage, than a saint, whose warmth and spontaneity drew people in vast numbers.[16] While the biographers of St Anthony of Padua (†1231) narrate the grace of God at work in the saint who had left the Augustinian Canons to become a friar in 1220, the sources for the life of Francis of Assisi carry an added complexity due to the polemical climate in which they were composed. The sympathies of the biographer and his audience are thinly disguised in the *vitae* compiled from the later 1230s. The biographer thenceforth not only recounts the wondrous virtues of the saint, but also *interprets* them for contemporaries, seeking to offer a reliable and authoritative portrait.

Thomas of Celano, the author of the *Dies irae*, was part of the mission to Germany which was relaunched in 1221, although he was back in Umbria before the death of the saint. His account of Francis is largely derivative. He wrote at the request of Pope Gregory IX for the canonisation on 16 July 1228. This gives the *vita* a wider perspective because the pope wanted to present Francis as a model of the mendicant mission. The *Vita prima* was completed some months later and approved by Pope Gregory IX on 25 February 1229.[17]

---

[15] R. B. and C. N. L. Brooke, *Popular Religion in the Middle Ages: Western Europe 1000 to 1300* (London, 1984), p. 44, *Vita prima*, no. 83.

[16] *Vita secunda*, no. 112.

[17] M. F. Cusato, 'Talking about Ourselves: The Shift in Franciscan Writing from Hagiography to History (1235–1247)', *FS* 58 (2000), pp. 37–75 at 38, n. 3.

This was the first *official* biography and it was located within the traditional models of sanctity culled from the Bible and the Fathers of the Church. The hagiographical influence of the lives of Sts Anthony the hermit, Augustine of Hippo and Martin of Tours provide the context for the radical change which occurs in the life of Francis of Assisi. *The Anonymous of Perugia*, written by John of Perugia between the general chapter of 1239 and before the death of Gregory on 22 August 1241, reflects the new clerical orientation of the order. His account of the history of the order is a partisan one. He endeavours to justify the present orientation of the movement with Haymo of Faversham at the helm. Emphasis is placed on the ministry of preaching and the admission of Sylvester, a priest of Assisi. The friars' relations with members are the hierarchy are underlined.

Conscious that the collective memory of the saint was fading through the death of those who had known him, the general chapter of 1244 invited friars to forward their recollections. Leo, Rufino and Angelo, three of the early friars and companions of the saint, responded with a warm personal recollection. They delighted in anecdotes concerning the simplicity and poverty of the saint and their fresh and spontaneous account is less circumscribed than many of the later biographies. They reflect a primitive view of the order and they emphasise the primacy of the vow of poverty, the Rule and the hermitage. These reminiscences lament the direction which the order was taking in the later 1230s and 1240s. Thomas of Celano produced a revised and expanded biography, the *Vita secunda* or *Memoriale* about 1247/8, incorporating many of the illustrations of the saint's teaching and example and concentrating upon the vow of poverty. He also reaffirms the centrality of the Portiuncula, the scene of a decisive phase in his conversion, as the spiritual focus of the order. The roots of *The Legend of the Three Companions* were also laid in this period. This text offers a full account of the early years of the fraternity and the road to initial papal approbation. The city of Assisi plays a central role in this text.[18]

Bonaventure's *Legenda maior* was conceived as a biography to bring peace and unity to an order. The last part of the prologue sets out the author's credentials as a historian: he had visited Assisi and other places associated with St Francis; the surviving companions of the saint had been interviewed. Despite these lofty claims, the biography contains little new materials. Indeed, substantial portions of the text were derived from Thomas of Celano's *Vita secunda*. What the biography lacks in terms of originality it gains in mystical insights and offers a programme of full conversion. The 1266 general chapter of Paris approved Bonaventure's biography and declared it to be the official *vita*; earlier biographies were recalled and destroyed.[19] This decision, which

---

[18] Cf. ibid., pp. 56–63; R. B. Brooke, 'Recent Work on St Francis of Assisi', *Analecta Bollandiana* 100 (1982), pp. 653–76.

[19] A. G. Little, 'Definitiones capitulorum generalium ordinis fratrum minorum, 1260–1282', *AFH* 7

has provoked historians' wrath, may have been inspired by the general chapter of the Dominicans at Strasbourg in 1260 which enacted similar legislation regarding *vitae* of St Dominic.[20]

The implementation of the decree of 1266 did not extend to paintings of the founder, which supplement the biographical tradition. On occasion, appeal was made to these portraits to settle polemical points regarding the friars' habits.[21] Bonaventura Berlinghieri's dossal in San Francesco at Pescia was executed in 1235 and contains scenes from the *Vita prima*, such as the sermon to the birds, stigmata, as well as different miracle stories. Professor William R. Cook notes that seven Italian dossals were painted before 1263 and were derived from Thomas of Celano. The Siena dossal – from San Francesco, Colle Valdelsa – was painted after 1263 and depends upon the *Legenda maior*.[22] Almost a hundred portraits of the saint survive from thirteenth-century Italy, mainly in Umbria and Tuscany.[23] Artists such as the unnamed master of San Francesco, who was active in the lower basilica, made parallels between the life of Jesus Christ and the founder. While hagiography, art and contemporary references are major sources, they should be used in conjunction with the writings of St Francis, who explains his own conversion and salient features of his piety.

Historians of the order are deeply indebted to the palaeographical skills and patient scholarship of friars, who have supplied critical editions of the major sources. Projects like the Bullarium Franciscanum, Analecta Franciscana, Bibliotetheca Franciscana Scholastica Medii Aevi, Spicilegium Bonaventurianum and the critical editions of the writings of the order's theologians emanating from the Collegio di San Bonaventura offer invaluable assistance. A stream of admirable scholars, from Fr Michael M. Bihl to Fr Cesare Cenci, has produced editions of the decisions of general and provincial chapters as well as constitutions. Frs Celestino Piana, Ignatius Brady and Jacques Bougerol among others have devoted their energies to the publication of texts produced by the friars. Dr Andrew Little, the doyen of historians of the English province, contributed several editions of texts and his commentaries contain enduring insights. Critical editions of chronicles lift the veil on the daily life of the friars and their interests. Historians of the Franciscan movement are indebted to Gratien de Paris, John Moorman, Lazaro Iriate de

(1914), pp. 676–82 at 678, no. 8.

[20] 'Acta capitulorum generalium ordinis praedicatorum', I, *Monumenta ordinis fratrum praedicatorum historica 3*, ed. B. M. Reichert (Rome, 1898), p. 105.

[21] M. Bihl, 'Fraticelli cuiusdam "Decalogus evangelicae paupertatis" an. 1340–2 conscriptus', *AFH* 32 (1939),VI, no. 5, pp. 279–411 at 343.

[22] W. R. Cook, 'The St. Francis Dossal in Siena. An Important Interpretation of the Life of Francis of Assisi', *AFH* 87 (1994), pp. 3–20 at 3–4.

[23] W. R. Cook, 'Fraternal and Lay Images of St. Francis in the Thirteenth Century', in *Popes, Teachers and Canon Law in the Middle Ages*, ed. J. Ross Sweeney and S. Chodorow (Ithaca, 1989), pp. 263–89 at 265.

Aspurz and Duncan Nimmo, who have compiled rich accounts of the order and its distinctive contribution to the medieval Church.[24]

Principle of selection

The present volume begins with the conversion of Francis and concludes with the death of John of Capistrano, a period of some two and a half centuries. The aim is to offer a rather more concise treatment than for example the works of John Moorman and Duncan Nimmo on the Franciscans, and no pretence is made at an exhaustive history of the order. I have continued to use the critical edition of Salimbene de Adam, the chronicler, which was published by Giuseppe Scalia in two volumes at Bari in 1966, and republished in two volumes by the Corpus Christianorum, continuatio mediaevalis series in 1998–9.

---

[24] Gratien de Paris, *Histoire de la fondation et de l'évolution de l'ordre des frères mineurs au XIII siècle*, Bibliotheca Seraphico-Capuccina, XXIX (Rome, 1926); J. R. H. Moorman, *A History of the Franciscan Order: From Its Origins to the Year 1517* (Oxford, 1968); L. Iriarte de Aspurz, *Historia franciscana* (Valencia, 1979), translated from the Spanish by P. Ross, *Franciscan History: The Three Orders of St. Francis of Assisi* (Chicago, 1983); D. Nimmo, *Reform and Division in the Medieval Franciscan Order: From Saint Francis to the Foundation of the Capuchins*, Bibliotheca Seraphico-Capuccina, XXXIII (Rome, 1987).

CHAPTER ONE

St Francis's Vocation to Live and Proclaim the Gospel

> The Rule and life of the Friars Minor is this, that is, to observe the holy
> Gospel of Our Lord Jesus Christ.
>
> St Francis's Rule, c. 1

Francis's early life

Francis Bernardone was born in 1181 or 1182 in the Umbrian city of Assisi to the north of Rome. Steeped in its Etruscan and Roman roots, Assisi is perched on the slopes of Monte Subasio. The cult of various early saints was celebrated in and around Assisi. St Rufino, revered as the first bishop, was martyred not far from the city, beside the river Chiasco, near Costano, around 238. His body was initially buried there, but was brought to the church of San Rufino in Assisi. His cult flourished in the middle of the eleventh century and was stimulated by translation of the ancient sarcophagus, in which his body had once rested, to San Rufino, the recovery of the martyr's *passio*, the account of his ministry, death and miracles, and the miracles which proliferated at his tomb.[1] The rediscovery of the martyr's bones in 1212 and their solemn translation from a hitherto unknown place in the cathedral of San Rufino to their new shrine in the same church occasioned immense celebration in Assisi during 1212. St Vittorino, another martyred bishop of the city, was buried in the Romanesque church of San Pietro; St Savino, also a martyred bishop, was interred at nearby Spoleto. Legends of the local martyrs were part of the religious formation of Francis and Clare di Favorone, the daughter of a local noble family who was to play an influential part in the Franciscan family. The two future saints were baptised in the cathedral. The celebration of the feasts of the local martys may have stimulated Francis's respect for the saints' relics and his desire for martyrdom.[2]

Assisi was not spared the party strife which disrupted the rhythm of life in many Italian cities. Its citizens experienced internal divisions, opposing

---

[1] A. Brunacci, 'Leggende e culto di S. Rufino in Assisi', *Bollettino della deputazione di storia patria per l'Umbria* 45 (1948), pp. 5–91. Peter Damian, sermon 36, in Corpus Christianorum, continuatio mediaevalis, 57, nn. 1–13, pp. 215–22.

[2] Cf. R. Brown, *The Roots of St. Francis: A Popular History of the Church in Assisi and Umbria before St Francis as Related to His Life and Spirituality* (Chicago, 1982).

ideologies and the changes in the balance of power between the papacy and the empire.[3] The Rocca, the fortress which symbolised imperial dominance above the city, was destroyed around 1200, an act expressing the aspirations and growing confidence of the commune. The ancient hostility between Assisi and Perugia persisted and infiltrated the cult of St Rufino towards the middle of the eleventh century. The patron saint of Assisi intervened to restrain the excesses of the Perugians. Friction between the two cities forms the landscape of Francis's early years, conversion and preaching.[4]

Following hagiographical conventions, Francis's biographers were disinclined to heap praise upon his family and its values. Instead, a blistering attack was made upon Francis's parents, Pietro and Pica, by Thomas of Celano, who wrote the first life of the saint. A harsh portrait of Francis's upbringing was painted: he was brought up proud of spirit and imitated his parents' *mores*, becoming vain and proud. Francis dressed in fine garments, as befitted the son of a leading citizen and a prosperous merchant. He was frail and delicate in physique and accustomed to pampering. Small in stature, he was a man of feeble and delicate constitution.[5] Francis was a gregarious and cheerful personality; later in life he castigated friars who were prone to be downcast. He danced and developed a love of music, especially the lute. When he was cheerful, he sang joyfully in French. On occasion he picked up a stick from the ground and placed it over his left arm. While holding a bow bent with a string in his right hand, drawing it over the stick as if it were a musical instrument.[6]

St Augustine recounts his own adolescent folly prior to his conversion. There is a similar emphasis in the biography by Thomas of Celano. Francis's love of music is well attested and there is evidence that he was intent on games. He was no stranger to flamboyant gestures, as his biographers attest. He was a spendthrift and his earnings were squandered by his dining and carousing. Regarding Francis as their leader in vain pursuits, friends invited him to their banquets. Francis had been generous in the past and his reputation for frivolity spread through the city, reaching the ears of the priest at San Damiano.[7]

Francis attended the school attached to the church of San Giorgio, which was staffed by the canons of San Rufino. His education was modest: its aspiration was to equip boys with the necessary knowledge to become

---

[3]   Cf. D. Waley, *The Italian City-Republics*, 3rd edn (London, 1969), pp. 117–57.

[4]   Peter Damian, sermon 36, no. 12, pp. 221–2, *Vita secunda*, no. 4, *CA*, cc. 75, 96, *Vita secunda*, no. 77, Jordan of Giano, *Chronica Fratris Jordani*, ed. H. Boehmer, Collection d'études et de documents sur l'histoire religieuse et littéraire du Moyen âge, VI (Paris, 1908), no. 50, p. 45. Fear that Perugians might snatch the relics of Sts Francis and Clare dictated plans for their death and burial inside the city walls. This material is treated more fully in the last section of Chapter 3.

[5]   *Vita prima*, nn. 1, 16; *CA*, cc. 50, 117.

[6]   *Vita prima*, no. 73, *Vita secunda*, nn. 126–8. *quasi super viellam trahens per lignum.*

[7]   Augustine of Hippo, *Confessionum libri*, II, 4, no. 9, Corpus Christianorum, series Latina 27, p. 22, *Legenda trium sociorum*, in *FF*, pp. 1373–1445, no. 2, *Vita secunda*, no. 7, *Vita prima*, no. 9.

tradesmen and merchants. His knowledge of Latin was not impeccable. Early sources reveal blemishes in his grasp of Latin grammar and spelling He spoke French, which was to become his preferred medium for prophecy.[8] The *chansons de geste* and the Arthurian literature were well known to him. He had some knowledge of the traditions associated with Charlemagne, Roland and Oliver and he styled his friars as knights of the Round Table and divine minstrels.[9]

Francis became a merchant, displaying a remarkable range of skills in communication, a future asset to the family business. He must have accompanied his father to fairs and markets both in Italy and France. A love of France, with its artistic and religious traditions stayed with him. In addition to his attachment to the culture of Provence, Francis believed that the love of sacred things prevailed in France and for that reason he wished to spend the rest of his days there; new forms of eucharitic devotion may have impressed the young merchant.[10]

The launching of the First Crusade by Urban II during the synod of Clermont in November 1095 generated widespread enthusiasm and led to breath-taking success in the recapture of Jerusalem in July 1099. The reverses experienced in the Holy Land led to further crusades; accounts of the vicissitudes of this movement sparked a great deal of interest in Italy. Francis was a child in 1187 when Jerusalem fell to the armies of Saladin at the battle of Hattin. Tales of deeds of bravery and piety in the places of pilgrimage were carried back to Assisi by its citizens who had been on the crusades. Pilgrims from Assisi, including Ortolana, the mother of Sts Clare and Agnes, visited the sanctuaries of the Holy Land. Francis, too, conceived a burning desire to go there, making three attempts between 1212 and 1219.[11]

The ideal of knighthood, with its fame and honour, captivated Francis. An opportunity of earning an admirable reputation came earlier than expected when civil war erupted in Assisi in 1201/2. Francis went into battle against the feudal powers of the city and fought alongside many of his friends and neighbours. The war dealt financial ruin, exile and death to many citizens of Assisi. Francis was captured at the battle of Collestrado in November 1202 and incarcerated in a gaol in Perugia. A prolonged sickness and convalescence gave him time to review his life. A profound change was taking place and new dreams jostled with earlier aspirations of knighthood. A reappraisal of his life liberated him from a partisan attitude towards his neighbours, irrespective of their social standing. The new forces at work in his life made

[8]   *Vita prima*, no. 23, *Vita secunda*, no. 102, Thomas of Eccleston, *Fratris Thomae vulgo dicti de Eccleston Tractatus de adventu fratrum minorum in Angliam*, ed. A. G. Little (Manchester, 1951), p. 32.

[9]   *Vita prima*, no. 16, 2 C, no. 13, *Scripta Leonis, Rufini et Angeli*, ed. R. B. Brooke, p. 22, *CA*, c. 103.

[10]   *AP*, c. 1, no. 3. 'Richeri gesta Senoniensis Ecclesiae', c. 17, in MGH, SS, 25, pp. 249–348 at 306–7, attests that Francis was frequently sent to France by his father. *Vita secunda*, no. 201.

[11]   *Legenda Sanctae Clarae Assisiensis*, in *FF*, pp. 2415–50, c. 1, *Vita prima*, nn. 55–7.

him show compassion and generosity to an unnamed impoverished knight, whom he had hitherto regarded as an enemy in the civil war.[12] This war laid the foundations for the conversion of Francis into a saint devoted to the establishment of peace.

Hagiographical accounts paint a picture of extremes: the rage and anger of the frustrated father, who could not comprehend the inner turmoil of his son, and the innocence of the son who moves slowly but inexorably away from parental expectations and the values of the market place. Shamed and humiliated by the public response to his son's eccentricity, Pietro Bernardone treated Francis as one who had besmirched the name of the family. His harshness and pride were contrasted with the meekness and humility of Francis, who had broken the law and showed no signs of making satisfaction. The biographers emphasise the failings of Pietro while they hurriedly skate over the blemishes in his son's conduct. Hugh Lawrence remarks that twelfth-century hagiography and the monastic world disparaged merchants. Contemporary poets lampooned the merchants's failings.[13] Pietro stood as the antithesis of Francis's desire to embrace the Gospel and build a united community; the merchants' avarice shaped the friars' preaching.

Francis's conversion experiences and the Gospel

In the period following his release from gaol around 1204 Francis suffered a long and distressing illness; his mobility was impaired so that he could move only with the support of a stick. When his strength began to return, he started to take walks in the countryside and became more detached from the values which had previously brought him pleasure. The internal struggle that was taking place is demonstrated by his attachment to his old dreams of attaining fame as a knight. Accordingly, he pursued his plans to accompany a nobleman of Assisi on his military campaign to Apuglia.[14]

Although the process of conversion is cloaked in mystery, the disparate sources point to three stages. First, during this transitional phase Francis entered the rural and ancient church of San Damiano, a short distance from the city walls of Assisi, to pray for a greater sense of direction to his increasingly confused life. He was startled by a voice from the cross commanding him to rebuild the church. His response was to obey in the most literal manner, a trait which would recur. He immediately started to gather stones to repair the church; on occasion stone was purchased from a local priest. The crucifix in that church was treated with greatest reverence because it offered Francis

---

[12] *Vita secunda*, nn. 4–5.

[13] C. H. Lawrence, *The Life of St Edmund by Matthew Paris* (Stroud, 1996), p. 5, Giovanni Boccaccio, *Opere in versi, Corbaccio, Trattatello in laude di Dante, Prose latine, Epistole*, ed. P. G. Ricci, La letteratura italiana storia e testi, IX (Milan, 1965), p. 601.

[14] *Vita prima*, nn. 3–4, 6–7.

direction in his new vocation. Money was given to the priest for the purchase of a lamp and oil to burn before the sacred image.[15] Francis's vocation was not confined to restoring churches with his own hands. He was being invited to renew the universal Church through his preaching and example. The restoration of the rural chapel foreshadowed Francis's apostolate of supporting the universal Church, represented by the Lateran basilica, the cathedral church of Rome.

While the chronology is uncertain, the experience at San Damiano was seminal and it presaged events at the fair in Foligno in 1205. Nothing appeared to be amiss as Francis set out and carried fine cloth to be sold. The illicit sale of his father's merchandise was followed by a hint of the renunciation which would soon place an unbearable strain upon relations with his father. Even his horse, a symbol of wealth, and his clothes were sold. As he walked back to Assisi he pondered his next step. His biographers regarded such conduct as portending a form of renunciation, which was to constitute the foundation of the friars' vocation. The early biographers do not record Francis's act of renouncing his possessions, but there are allusions to the process in the narrative of the events following his return from Foligno; it is clear that he fully divested himself of his possessions. He returned to Assisi with the proceeds of the sale and thrust them into the hands of the impoverished priest of San Damiano. When the priest refused this unexpected bounty, Francis hurled the coins onto the windowsill. There was a subsequent mention of an intention to use the money to feed the poor.[16]

The misappropriation of these materials created a predictable rift, which resulted in Pietro's unsuccessful attempts to bring his son back to his senses. When these measures failed, Pietro sought the return of his money, a decision which brought Francis before the bishop. Guido II, bishop of Assisi (1204–28), was a prelate whom many expected to side with Pietro. Nonetheless, he sensed that the hand of God was at work in this domestic quarrel, although he left Francis in no doubt that dishonesty was no basis for a life rooted in the Gospel. With a typically flamboyant gesture Francis restored both the money and his clothes; his paternal inheritance was rejected in a profoundly symbolic act, which his biographer treated as a fulfilment of the terms of the Gospel, that Christians have one Father who is in heaven (Matthew 23.9–10).[17] The process of conversion was advancing, although Francis manifestly had no blueprint for his future. The wise counsel of Guido, recognised as a divine mouthpiece, was long remembered by Francis, who cited it as a reason for his profound reverence for bishops.[18]

Secondly, Francis was beginning to ponder his future. While there were

---

[15] *Vita secunda*, nn. 10–14, 17.
[16] *Vita prima*, nn. 8–9, 14, *AP*, c. 1, nn. 7–8.
[17] *Vita secunda*, no. 12.
[18] *CA*, c. 58.

several crucial moments in his journey, the dying saint recalled his encounter with a leper about 1206, as he explains in his *Testament*: 'When I was in sin, the sight of lepers made me sick beyond measure. God himself led me into their midst and I had pity on them.' Francis had looked at lepers' houses only from a great distance, holding his nostrils in horror. This unexpected meeting supplied him with an opportunity for self-mastery. Perhaps realising that something momentous was taking grip of him, he behaved with a typical generosity and spontaneity by kissing the leper, the symbol of contagion and rejection, an act which would profoundly alter his outlook. What had previously appalled him became an occasion of grace; horror and disgust yielded to sweetness and delight. He visited the leper hospital of Santa Maria Maddalena in the plain below the city and pressed coins into their hands; he then lived among them and served them. He honoured lepers by addressing them as 'Christian brothers', a clear rebuke of the norms of secular society. When vestiges of his earlier prejudice revisited him, he was absolutely determined not to regress.

As soon as Francis had experienced the force of grace, he employed a conventional term: 'After that I did not wait long before leaving the world.' This moment heralded a new orientation and a lifestyle. Francis distanced himself from the city's social and commercial values. He lived outside the city walls, and that is where his conversion occurred, denoting his determination to give precedence to the Gospel rather than the conventions of his home city. His retreat from Assisi was moral as well as physical. The norms of the New Testament were to prevail over local customs and laws. He would return to his native city as a penitent and evangelist.

Thirdly, when Francis had restored San Damiano, he repaired the churches of San Pietro and the Portiuncula. Thomas of Celano's account echoes the conversion of St Anthony of Egypt, whose life was radically changed by hearing the proclamation of the Gospel.[19] When Francis attended Mass in the tiny chapel, the Gospel assigned to the Mass struck him with a new force and clarity: God was inviting him to live as a disciple. Francis responded in the most literal manner, laying aside his shoes, staff and leather girdle. The habit of the hermit was swapped for the dress of an apostle: bare feet, a single tunic and a small cord.[20] A new form of dress announced the radical change in the life of Francis. The two years of uncertainty gave birth to a new conviction and confidence: the *imitatio Christi* ('imitation of Christ') would illuminate and animate his life. For the remainder of his life Francis displayed the utmost respect for the Bible, the vehicle for his own conversion.

---

[19] Bonaventure, *Legenda maior*, in *FF*, pp. 777–961, II, no. 7, *Vita prima*, no. 21, Augustine of Hippo, *Confessionum libri*, VIII, 12, no. 29, p. 131.

[20] *Vita prima*, no. 22.

The lesser brethren, fratres minores, *and their evangelical Rule of Life*

Francis immediately implemented what he had heard. He did not seek advice from anyone at this stage and relied on his Creator to guide him. Assisi, the city from which he had withdrawn two years earlier, became the theatre of his newly discovered ministry, although he continued to dwell in hermitages and other remote sites. Returning to the city, he began to proclaim the truths of Christianity. The call to conversion and penance was preached fervently and simply; a new spiritual energy and vitality were working in Francis. Neighbours and fellow-citizens were not slow to observe and then comment on the remarkable change in his behaviour; curiosity soon turned into admiration.

Bernard of Quintavalle, a local lawyer, wished to learn more about Francis and invited him to his home in Assisi. Profoundly impressed by what he saw and heard, he became Francis's disciple. Biographers do not allude to any lengthy discussions about the values and practices they would embrace. Francis's response was simple and direct: God would show them what to do. Early the next morning they went to the church of San Nicola to consult the Gospel, opening the sacred text thrice. The first passage counselled those pledged to evangelical perfection to sell their possessions and give the proceeds to the poor (Matthew 19.21), a text which was central to the vocations of Sts Anthony the hermit and Augustine of Hippo.[21] The second focused on the need for the apostles to travel unencumbered (Luke 9.3) and the third underlined the disciples' responsibility to carry their cross (Matthew 16.24; cf. Luke 9.23).[22] The first and third passages occur in the first chapter of the earlier version of the Rule and the second in the fourteenth chapter. Such texts formed the basis of the *regula vitae*.[23] Voluntary poverty, allied to humility and the cross, the symbol of divine generosity, were closely entwined in these passages and in the corrective programme which Francis devised.

Francis's decision to share his spiritual vision with others was a decisive moment, which paved the way for a new form of religious life, reflecting the values of some of reforming spirits in the twelfth century. While some historians argue that Francis did not wish to found a religious order, disciples and companions were accepted from 1208. Bernard and Peter, another early recruit, sought direction and inspiration from Francis.[24] Francis's willingness to communicate his spiritual vision signalled the birth of a fraternity, which others, Peter Catani, who was a lawyer, and Giles, joined. Twice the friars were styled the 'new disciples of Christ' on their return from the papal

---

[21] J. V. Fleming, *An Introduction to the Franciscan Literature of the Middle Ages* (Chicago, 1977), p. 25.

[22] *Vita secunda*, no. 15, *AP*, c. 2, nn. 10–11.

[23] *Vita prima*, no. 32. Cf. G. C. P. Voorvelt and B. P. van Leeuwen, 'L'Evangéliaire de Baltimore. Étude critique sur le missel que saint François aurait consulté', *CF* 59 (1989), pp. 261–321.

[24] Cf. Knowles, *From Pachomius to Ignatius: A Study in the Constitutional History of the Religious Orders* (Oxford, 1966), p. 44, *AP*, c. 2, nn. 10–11, c. 3, no. 14.

court. Recruitment was modest in the first few years. Friars were united in their commitment to Christ and the insights of Francis; they lived by the work of their own hands.[25] Styling themselves penitents of Assisi, they were dispatched in pairs to preach. When their number rose to eight, Francis broadened his pastoral programme to include other cities of Umbria and Italy. Friars went forth in pairs to different parts of the world to proclaim peace and to foster penitence. Bernard and Giles travelled to the shrine of St James at Compostella, enduring penury, hunger, thirst and cold on their travels.[26]

Francis's trust in divine providence was absolute. The Gospel was the context for the last twenty years of his life when he followed the life and footsteps of the apostles and gave himself completely to Christ.[27] The advice to take no thought for the morrow (Matthew 6.34) was obeyed to the letter by friars, who for some time would only accept alms necessary for the day.[28] Francis had such a marked respect for the Scriptures, which had illuminated his vocation, that he exhorted his disciples to show the greatest honour for the sacred text. Whenever they found biblical texts or references to the divine name kept in some inappropriate place, they were to find a fitting place for them. Francis had wished to insert such instructions into the Rule, but had to content himself with its inclusion in the *Testament*.[29]

When the friars were twelve in number, they were keen to secure papal approval for their form of life or Rule, which was based largely on the words of the Gospel. These scriptural passages were interspersed with counsels concerning evangelical perfection. A relatively straightforward account of the process leading to papal approval was supplied by the biographers, who unite in attributing a central role to Guido, the one bishop familiar with the friars' ministry. Moreover, Guido's knowledge of the Roman Curia was placed at the friars' disposal, and this effectively saved the day. While Francis was depicted as persuading the cardinal and the pope, it is more probable that a series of meetings, some of them filled with potential obstacles, was necessary to assuage curial anxieties and papal concern.

Guido vouched for the friars and arranged for Francis to meet John of St Paul, cardinal bishop, a prelate sensitive to the spiritual aspirations of groups seeking new and more satisfying ways of responding to the Gospel. Parrying suggestions that he might become a monk or hermit, Francis through his zeal and integrity impressed the cardinal, who gave him an introduction to the pope. Innocent III, who had already exhibited a greater sensitivity towards groups such as the Humiliati, encouraged the fledgling

---

[25] *Vita prima*, nn. 34, 38, *AP*, c. 3, nn. 14, 17, c. 6, no. 25.

[26] *AP*, c. 4, nn. 18–19, *Vita prima*, no. 30, *Scripta Leonis, Rufini et Angeli*, pp. 322–5.

[27] *CA*, c. 102, *Vita prima*, nn. 84, 88.

[28] *CA*, c. 52.

[29] *Vita secunda*, no. 200, *CA*, c. 108.

community.[30] He gave Francis a favourable hearing, instructed him to return when the number of friars increased and authorised them to preach penance about 1209. At the end of the process the friars received the tonsure. At this time Francis may have been ordained to the diaconate.[31] This initial approbation sheltered the friars from the prohibition on the foundation of new Rules for religious communities, a measure enshrined in the thirteenth canon of the Fourth Lateran Council of 1215. The urgency for the completion of the Rule was illustrated by the disorder and divisions which occurred during Francis's visit to the Holy Land in 1219–20.

When the Rule of 1221 was deemed unsatisfactory by the papal curia, Francis set himself to revise his text; he was advised by Cardinal Ugolino. What began as a fraternity modelled on a family was then changing into an order recognised by the Western Church. Francis was required to compile a text which encapsulated his vision and satisfied the canonists. There was also internal anxiety, voiced by the ministers provincial, that is, the friars responsible for the direction of the order in a particular region. The ministers feared that the Rule might be too severe and exacting. Leo, Rufino and Angelo depict a titanic struggle between Francis and the ministers provincial, who were prepared to enlist the support of Cardinal Ugolino. This tussle sowed the seeds for the gathering momentum of disagreement from the 1240s and the eventual partition of the order. The Rule, which contained elements which had been evolving for some years, was formally approved by Pope Honorius III on 29 November 1223.

The proclamation of the Gospel

From the momentous celebration of Mass at the Portiuncula in 1208 Francis was impelled to preach repentance. Pope Innocent III's licence opened the pulpits of Assisi to Francis, whose first sermon preached was at San Giorgio. His homilies were delivered in several churches within Assisi. The ninth chapter of the Rule enshrined Francis's respect for the jurisdiction of the diocesan bishop, whose permission was required for the friars' preaching; it was the responsibility of the ministers provincial to appoint suitable friars for that office. Similarly, the *Testament* affirms that Francis refused to preach in parish churches without the permission of the parish priest. His learning was derived from the Holy Spirit rather than from books, and he spoke the truth boldly, exposing faults and abuses. His message challenged all Christians.[32] His exhortations and sermons were marked by a fervent spirit; he

---

[30] Cf. F. Andrews, 'Innocent III and Evangelical Enthusiasts: The Route to Approval', *Pope Innocent III and His World*, ed. J. C. Moore (Aldershot, 1999), pp. 229–41.

[31] *Vita prima*, nn. 32–3, *Vita secunda*, nn. 16–17, *Legenda trium sociorum*, XII, nn. 46–52, *AP*, c. 7, nn. 31–6.

[32] *Vita prima*, nn. 23, 36.

was a fearless preacher who refused to remain silent in the face of vices. He was not afraid of publicly confessing his own failings.[33] His preaching was spontaneous in character and, when he did meditate on what he might say, he sometimes forgot what he had prepared. On such occasions he would admit that his memory had failed him. At other times he did not know what to say and accordingly blessed and then dismissed the people. He preached so movingly during the first Mass of Christmas at Greccio in 1223 that those present reflected anew upon the mystery of the Incarnation. The teaching of Christ was applied to urban tensions, when the Perugians were castigated for their lack of humility. The men and women of Greccio, who were plagued by devouring wolves, were exhorted to make amends for their sins lest their assailants return.[34]

Prayer was the context of Francis's sermons, which were reinforced by his example. His homilies at San Rufino were preceded by prolonged prayer in a garden belonging to the canons of the cathedral. Friars, too, were urged to ask for God's guidance upon his words.[35] Francis's preaching was enlivened by his dramatic skills in communicating the Gospel by word and example. His whole body conveyed the truth of the Gospel in deeds and gestures ('he made a tongue out of his whole body'). For example, his homily for the sisters at San Damiano began with a prayer and then he asked for ashes, which he sprinkled around himself, placing some on his head. This was followed by an unexpected silence which was broken by the recitation of the penitential psalm, *Miserere mei Deus* (Psalm 50), in place of a sermon. This symbolic sermon instructed the sisters that they were pilgrims in the world and would return to dust and ashes.[36]

Like many reformers of the twelfth century such as Norbert of Xanten, the founder of the Premonstratensian order, Francis was indefatigable in his travels to disseminate the Gospel. He frequently made a circuit of four or five villages and cities in a single day; the comment that a particular event occurred while he was going through the provinces preaching recurs in the early biographies.[37] When the friars were still few, he made a tour of the churches in the villages and the neighbourhood of Assisi to preach penance. After his sermon he gathered the priests together and preached to them about the salvation of souls and encouraged them to be diligent in keeping their churches clean. Although the figures given by medieval chroniclers and hagiographers do not invariably inspire confidence, Thomas of Celano relates that Francis often preached to thousands of people: crowds flocked

---

[33] Ibid., nn. 34, 52–4, *CA*, c. 80.

[34] *Vita prima*, nn. 72, 86, *CA*, cc. 75, 74.

[35] Bonaventure, *Legenda maior*, IV, no. 4.

[36] *Vita prima*, no. 97, *Vita secunda*, nn. 107, 207.

[37] *Vita prima*, no. 97, *CA*, c. 113.

to hear him each day.[38] The responsibility for presenting the Gospel to people engaged the attention and resourcefulness of Francis, who showed that Christ's teaching should be applied to daily life; it was not a message to be confined to churches only. He was in the habit of addressing people wherever they gathered. While he preached innumerable sermons to the assembled crowds in the *piazze*, his biographers offer a few examples: Assisi, Bologna, Perugia, Poggio, which is probably Poggio Bustone,[39] and Terni. At Alviano he moved to a higher place, where he would be more visible, for his sermon. He seems to have preached in the open at Alessandria in Lombardy and at a hermitage near Roccabrizia.[40]

Francis was divinely inspired to greet people with the words of peace, a salutation which was incorporated into his *Testament* and particularly apposite for Assisi, a city recovering from the scars of civil war. Friars were instructed to bestow peace upon all who dwelled in the houses which they entered; contemporaries noted that no other religious order gave such a greeting.[41] Francis's sermons opened with the greeting of peace to everyone. One of the first fruits of his preaching was urban reconciliation, and his biographers illustrate his capacity to promote peace in a turbulent age. This presages the sterling work of his followers in bringing peace to divided families, neighbourhoods and cities. The dispute between Bishop Guido II and Oportulo di Bernardo, *podestà* of Assisi, the leader of the civic community, saddened the ailing Francis, who knew both men well. A quarrel led to the sentence of excommunication imposed on the *podestà*, who retaliated by imposing a commercial boycott on the prelate. Francis invited the two protagonists to meet at the bishop's house, where two friars sang the *Canticle of Brother Sun*, a hymn in celebration of creation, which moved both men to acknowledge their faults and seek pardon. Thomas, archdeacon of Split, was present at a sermon preached by Francis in the piazza at Bologna on 15 August 1222. He contrasted Francis's clothing and person with the power of his words, which restored harmony and peace. Francis spoke of putting an end to hatred and arranging a new treaty of peace between the contending parties in the city.[42]

Francis's preaching stimulated the birth and growth of the order, and his sermons were sometimes followed by the admission of new recruits.[43] Numerous men of Greccio were brought to the order by his preaching and the friars' good example. A fervent sermon at Ascoli brought about the

---

[38] *CA*, c. 60, *Vita prima*, nn. 72, 91.

[39] *Vita secunda*, no. 131, *CA*, c. 81.

[40] *Vita prima*, no. 59, *Vita secunda*, nn. 78–9, *CA*, c. 114.

[41] *CA*, c. 101, *AP*, c. 5, no. 19, Alexander Minorita, *Expositio in Apocalypsim*, ed. A. Wachtel, MGH, Quellen zur Geistesgeschichte des Mittelalters, I (Weimar, 1955), pp. 469–70, Visconti, *Sermons*, no. 10, p. 788.

[42] *Vita prima*, no. 23, *CA*, c. 84, *Historia pontificum Salonitanorum et Spalatensium*, MGH, SS, 29, p. 580. Visconti, *Sermons*, no. 11, p. 789.

[43] *Vita prima*, nn. 24–5, *CA*, c. 62.

admission of thirty men, laymen and clerics; on another occasion Francis was approached by a man who had heard him preach in the Marches of Ancona.[44] One of those who turned to Francis for guidance was Lady Jacoba di Settisoli, the widow of a Roman nobleman; she was depicted as the fruit of his preaching and example. Nicholas, a Cistercian monk of Casamari and a papal penitentiary, had left the Roman curia to join the friars by 1216. Four years later Jacques de Vitry attests that, following Francis's sermons and exhortations, members of his household became friars. It was feared that others might do the same.[45] Such levels of recruitment enabled the order to spread throughout Christendom.

[44] *CA*, c. 74, *Vita prima*, no. 62, *Vita secunda*, no. 81.
[45] *CA*, c. 8, M. Bihl, 'Nicolaus de Romanis (†1219), fueritne primus cardinalis O.F.M.?', *AFH* 19 (1926), pp. 286–9, *Lettres de Jacques de Vitry*, pp. 76, 131–3.

CHAPTER TWO

The Initial Expansion of the Order

They have so multiplied in such a short time that there is no Christian province where some of these brothers do not reside.

Jacques de Vitry[1]

Recruitment

Francis's vocation reflected contemporary aspirations for a clearer expression of Christian values. His literal response to the Scriptures injected a freshness and vitality into a society which was searching for new ways of giving authentic expression to its Christian vocation. Fidelity to the Gospel, an ascetical life and the pursuit of goodness, which had previously been perceived as the preserve of a spiritual elite residing in monasteries, were brought to the market-place and *piazza* by Francis.[2] The friars' fervour and dedication were rooted in apostolic zeal and a community life whose hallmarks were simplicity and cheerfulness. The striking levels of recruitment between 1212 and 1220 facilitated the spread of the order and caught the attention of contemporary chroniclers.[3] Vocations were drawn from a broad spectrum of society, including on the one hand Leonard, whose parents were of a higher social rank in Assisi than Francis's family, and on the other converted robbers in the region of Borgo San Sepolchro, amongst many others.

Following Francis's first attempt to reach the Holy Land about 1211 he undertook a preaching tour which brought several good and suitable men, both laymen and clerics, to the order.[4] Their diversity is illustrated by Hermann, a chaplain of the Teutonic Knights, and Alexander of Bremen, a scholastic in his local cathedral.[5] The small number of prelates includes Albert, abbot of the Benedictine monastery of St Mary in Stade, who become a friar

---

[1] *'Historia occidentalis' of Jacques de Vitry: A Critical Edition*, ed. J. F. Hinnebusch, Spicilegium Friburgense, XVII (Fribourg, 1972), p. 160.

[2] Fleming, *Franciscan Literature*, pp. 17–18.

[3] Matthew Paris, *Matthaei Parisiensis, monachi Sancti Albani, Historia Anglorum, sive, ut vulgo dicitur, Historia minor*, II, ed. F. Madden, 3 vols, RS, XLIV (London, 1866–9), pp. 298–9.

[4] *Vita prima*, no. 56.

[5] Jordan of Giano, *Chronica*, no. 41, p. 37, A. Kleinhans, 'De commentario in Apocalypsim Fr. Alexandri Bremensis, O.F.M. (a. 1242)', *Antonianum* 2 (1927), pp. 289–334 at 299.

on 20 August 1240, and Stephen of St-Thibéry, abbot of an unnamed Benedictine monastery.[6] Bartholomew, bishop of Skradin in Dalmatia, Rudolf, bishop of Ålborg in Denmark, Benedict d'Alignan, bishop of Marseilles, and Henry de Geniès, archbishop of Bordeaux, resigned their dioceses in 1247, 1252, 1267 and 1289 respectively to don the friars' habit.[7]

Various hypotheses about the friars' social origins have been advanced in recent years.[8] The practice of men changing their names on entering the order frustrates attempts to ascertain their social origins. Elias of Cortona and Francis, the brother of St Clare of Montefalco, were known as Bonusbaro and Damian before entering the order.[9] A will of 24 March 1247 refers to the families of two friars, Tebaldo, the brother of the testator, and John, the son of Uguccione Peccie.[10] Testamentary documents supply the baptismal and family names of friars as well as information about their place of birth.[11] Although Salimbene is sometimes cited as a witness to the friars' social origins, his testimony is to be interpreted in the light of his predilections for the genealogy of the old families of Lombardy and other regions. His sister-in-law, the wife of his eldest brother, Guido, belonged to the Baratti family, which prided itself on its blood relationship with Matilda, countess of Tuscany. The chronicler delights in providing information about friars such as Lord Ghirardo Rangone of Modena and Ubaldino, a noble of Ravenna and brother of Lord Segnorello.[12] In contrast, his silence on the social background of brothers is eloquent; one of the faults laid at the door of Elias as minister general (1232–9) was the admission of several useless (*inutiles*) men to the order. He knew twenty-five non-clerical friars during his two years at Siena and a further thirty during his four years at Pisa.[13]

[6] 'Annales Stadenses auctore Alberto', p. 366, *Chronica XXIV generalium ordinis minorum cum pluribus appendicibus inter quas excellit hucusque ineditus Liber de laudibus S. Francisci Fr. Bernardi a Bessa edita a patribus Collegii S. Bonaventurae*, Analecta Franciscana, II (Quaracchi, Florence, 1897), p. 669.

[7] W. R. Thomson, *Friars in the Cathedral: The First Franciscan Bishops 1226–1261*, The Pontifical Institute of Mediaeval Studies, Studies and Texts, XXXIII (Toronto, 1975), pp. 152, 236, 165–6, 212–17, Salimbene de Adam, *Cronica*, ed. G. Scalia, Scrittori d'Italia, CCXXXII/III (Bari, 1966), republished by Corpus Christianorum, continuatio mediaevalis, CXXV, CXXVa, 2 vols (Turnhout, 1998/99), pp. 806–7, *Les Registres de Nicolas IV*, 5i, ed. E. Langlois, Bibliothèque des écoles françaises d'Athènes et de Rome, 2e série (Paris, 1886), no. 1695, p. 318.

[8] Cf. J. B. Freed, *The Friars and German Society in the Thirteenth Century*, The Mediaeval Academy of America, LXXXVI (Cambridge, Mass., 1977), pp. 109–34.

[9] Salimbene, *Cronica*, p. 137, *Il processo di canonizzazione di Chiara da Montefalco*, ed. E. Menestò, Quaderni del Centro per il collegamento degli studi medievali e umanistici nell' Università di Perugia, XIV, Agiografia umana, IV (Todi, 1984), pp. 266–99.

[10] *Le carte duecentesche del Sacro Convento di Assisi (Istrumenti, 1168–1300)*, ed. A. B. Langeli, Fonti e studi francescani, V (Padua, 1997), no. 27, pp. 42–4.

[11] M. Apolloni, 'Testamenti a favore dei frati minori di S. Lorenzo a Vicenza tra 1280 e 1348', *Il santo* 30 (1990), pp. 181–237 at 210–11.

[12] Ibid., pp. 52–3, 98, 248.

[13] Ibid., pp. 140–4.

The General and Provincial Chapters and the formation of new provinces

Francis was the source of guidance and inspiration for the friars, who were obliged to obey him and his successors, the *caput istius religionis* ('head of that religion'), as defined by the Rule of 1221. The influence and authority of the minister general were noted by Jacques de Vitry.[14] However, the high-handed behaviour of Elias of Cortona concentrated minds on the urgent need for greater precision in defining the powers vested in the minister general. The highest authority was transferred to the general chapter, which appointed ministers provincial.[15] Like the Cistercians and Premonstraten-sians in the twelfth century, the friars speedily developed as an international institution under the authority of the general chapters, which regulated the business of the community.[16] Schooled by the experience of monastic chapters and the legislation enacted in the twelfth canon of the recent Lateran Council, the friars developed the general chapter as a vehicle of government. Local autonomy was subservient to the centralised authority of the minister general, and this was demonstrated by the appointment of Albert of Pisa as minister provincial of England in 1236. Despite the friars' submission of a list of other candidates, the minister general made his own decision.[17]

Francis and the friars discussed expansion to other countries, and for the first time friars were sent over the Alps and across the seas in 1217. Colonies of friars left Assisi for France, Germany, the Holy Land, Portugal and Spain to work as urban evangelists. Friars travelled to minister in remote lands and reached missionary territory; five friars were martyred in Morocco in 1220.[18] Some of the early missions were vitiated by a certain naivety because the friars neglected to study the prevailing conditions and local languages. This lack of preparation exasperated even supportive prelates such as Jacques de Vitry, who regretted that some of the friars had not been tested by conventual rigour and discipline.[19] In France the friars were asked whether they were Albigen-sians and their ignorance of this heretical band raised suspicion about their orthodoxy. When the friars set out for Hungary, they were accompanied by a bishop. Nonetheless, they were derided as they walked through the fields and shepherds set their dogs on them. They reflected on their reception and returned to Italy in disarray. A group of more than sixty friars accompanied John of Penna to Germany. They, too, were suspected of heresy and returned

[14] 'Historia occidentalis', pp. 158–9.

[15] 'Statuta generalia Ordinis edita in Capitulis generalibus celebratis Narbonae an. 1260, Assisii an.1279 atque Parisiis an. 1292', ed. M. Bihl, prol., no. 3, pp. 13–94, 284–358 at 37–8, Eccleston, *Tractatus*, pp. 43, 69.

[16] R. W. Southern, *Western Society and the Church in the Middle Ages* (Harmondsworth, 1970), pp. 272–3.

[17] Eccleston, *Tractatus*, pp. 78–9.

[18] *CA*, c. 108, Jordan of Giano, *Chronica*, no. 3, pp. 3–4, *Vita prima o 'Assidua'*, ed. V. Gamboso, Fonti agiografiche antoniane, I (Padua, 1981), c. 2, no. 1, c. 5, nn. 1–2, pp. 274–5, 286–9.

[19] *Lettres de Jacques de Vitry*, pp. 131–3.

to Italy. Accounts of their treatment conjured up an image of Germany as a place where the crown of martyrdom might be won easily.[20]

There are least at least three hypotheses for the appearance of a more professional attitude to the new missions from 1221: firstly, change may have been the result of Francis's reflection on earlier failures; secondly, it may mirror the growing influence of some of the ministers provincial; thirdly, Cardinal Ugolino was now playing a more prominent role. The new strategy of ensuring that there was fitting preparation was beginning to reap dividends in the general chapter of 1221. At the termination of the chapter Francis called for zealous volunteers for Germany. The volunteers set out in September.[21] The expansion to the British Isles was formally approved by the general chapter of 1223 or 1224. The leadership of the mission was entrusted to an experienced friar, Agnellus of Pisa.[22]

The formation of new provinces was on the agenda of the general chapter in 1230. Rapid progress had been made in Germany, where there were several foundations and plentiful vocations; the province was divided to form the new jurisdictions on the Rhine and Saxony. Similarly, the friars in England soon turned their attentions to Ireland and Scotland. Provinces were established in Ireland in 1230 and Scotland two years later. In each case the authority for the formation of new provinces came from the general chapter and the minister general. Elias's expansionist policies were reversed by the general chapter of 1239, when the number of provinces was reduced from seventy-two to thirty-two. Almost half of the provinces were in Italy, the land in which Francis's ideals were born. The number of provinces, equally divided by the Alps, remained stable and some seventy years later only two more had been added.[23] Friars were already well represented in most parts of western Europe by the middle of the century. While there was a large concentration in Germany, France, Italy and Spain, where they preached in missionary areas, friars reached the distant regions of the British Isles, Denmark, Sweden, Poland, Lithuania and the Holy Land. Friaries stretched from Ireland to the Baltic sea and from the Balkans to Morocco, an Arab land, a cosmopolitan spread reflected in the *Liber exemplorum*, an anecdotal text containing materials for preaching.[24]

---

[20] Jordan of Giano, *Chronica*, nn. 4–6, 18, pp. 4–7, 19–21.

[21] Ibid., nn. 16, 17, 19, pp. 16–19, 21–4.

[22] Eccleston, *Tractatus*, pp. 3–5.

[23] Jordan of Giano, *Chronica*, nn. 57, 67, pp. 49, 58, A. Chiappini, 'Communitatis responsio "Religiosi viri" ad rotulum Fr. Ubertino de Casali', *AFH* 7 (1914), pp. 654–75 and 8 (1915), pp. 56–80 at 662.

[24] L. Oliger, 'Liber exemplorum fratrum minorum saeculi XIII (excerpta e cod. ottob. lat. 522)', *Antonianum* 2 (1927), pp. 203–76.

France

France provided fertile soil for the order and the province of France sired jurisdictions in Aquitaine, Touraine, Bourgogne and Provence. Francis was travelling to join the mission in France when he passed through Florence, where he met Cardinal Ugolino, who persuaded him to remain in Italy and counter opposition from the Roman curia.

The first party of zealous evangelists was led by Pacificus of the Marches, the king of verses. Pacificus was succeeded by Gregory of Naples, one of the vicars appointed by Francis in 1219,[25] who served as minister provincial (1223–41). Pope Honorius III wrote to the bishops on 29 May 1220, observing that some of them had refused to admit the friars. He confirmed that the order had papal approval, and urged bishops to receive the friars.[26] Tradition associates Pacificus with one of the first friaries in France such as La Cordelle close to Vézelay.[27] The friary in Limoges was an early foundation under the year 1221.[28] Under the year 1212 *The Norman Chronicle* reports the conversion of Francis and the birth of the order. It attests that the friars were received with great joy by both the church and the people because of the novelty of their way of life.[29] Expansion began at an impressive rate. A mortuary roll of 1233 lists the friaries at Amiens, Beauvais, Blois, Chartres, Châtillon-sur-Seine, Compiègne, Etampes, Evreux, Meaux, Noyon, Orléans, Paris, Pontoise, Provins, Rouen, Sens, Senlis, Soissons, Troyes, Vendôme and Vernon.[30] By 1282 there were fifty-eight friaries in the province of France, that is the northern region, thirty-three in Touraine, fifty in Provence and seventy-nine in Aquitaine.[31]

There appear to have been 195 foundations before 1275. Although these friaries were distributed throughout the realm, there was a marked concentration in the south. The friaries of all four mendicant orders were so located that no one in France lived more than thirty miles from a convent and the vast majority must have lived within a day's walking distance of at least two friaries. Foundations were predominantly urban, but friars were not without influence in rural areas; there were also some hermitages.[32] Friars maintained smaller communities than the Dominicans. The schools of Paris were fertile sources of recruitment in the 1220s, when 'very many scholars' were entering

[25] *CA*, c. 108.

[26] Jordan of Giano, *Chronica*, no. 4, p. 4. *BF*, I, no. 4, p. 5. Ibid., no. 2, p. 2.

[27] *Monumenta Vizeliacensia*, ed. R. B. Huygens Corpus Christianorum, continuatio mediaevalis, XLII, pp. 66–7.

[28] *Chroniques de Saint-Martial de Limoges*, ed. H. Duplès-Agier (Paris, 1874), p. 131, transferring themselves to another site in 1244.

[29] *Ex annalibus Normannicis*, in MGH, SS, 26, pp. 512–17 at 514.

[30] L. Delisle, *Les Rouleaux des morts du IXe au XV siècle* (Paris, 1866), pp. 407–20.

[31] D. Cresi, 'Statistica dell'ordine minoritico all'anno 1282', *AFH* 56 (1963), pp. 157–62 at 159–60.

[32] R. W. Emery, *The Friars in Medieval France: A Catalogue of the French Mendicant Convents, 1200–1500*, pp. 3, 5, 6, 7, Salimbene, *Cronica*, pp. 322–3.

Map 1. The friars' journeys and a sample of their foundations in the thirteenth century

the two mendicant orders.[33] Some of the English recruits in that university city were named by Thomas of Eccleston; their number included a future minister general of the order, Haymo of Faversham (1240–4). The mendicants' attraction was summed up by Nicholas Trivet, who observes that many men famous for their learning and sanctity renounced material wealth to become friars.[34]

---

[33] A. Callebaut, 'Le Sermon historique d'Eudes de Châteauroux à Paris, le 18 mars 1229. Autour de l'origine de la grève universitaire et de l'enseignement des Mendicants', *AFH* 28 (1935), pp. 81–114 at 111.

[34] Prominent among them was Alexander of Hales, an English doctor in theology. Eccleston, *Tractatus,*

While the French provinces lacked their own chronicler, Salimbene recounts his own visits to cities and friaries in the 1240s, including Aix, Arles, Auxerre, Avignon, Beaucaire, Bordeaux, Marseilles, Montpellier, Paris, Provins, Salins, Sens, Tarascon, Tortona, Troyes and Vézelay. His chronicle teems with homely detail about the provinces and the friars who ministered there, even down to their taste for alcohol; by 1247 there were eight custodies, that is, regional concentrations of friaries, in the province of France.[35] In addition, Eudes de Rigaud, the third regent master at Paris and subsequently archbishop of Rouen (1248–75), recorded his parochial and monastic visitations and offered a valuable insight into the life of the Church in Normandy.[36]

Germany

The friars travelling to Germany, a country whose borders do not correspond exactly to the modern country, in the late summer of 1221 passed through Trent, where Caesar of Speyer preached to the clergy of the city, while Barnabas addressed the laity. The bishop subsequently gave the friars permission to preach in his diocese. The provincial chapters served as the dynamo for the order's settlement on German soil and supervised the formation of communities in various parts of the country. By the middle of October 1221, within a month of leaving Italy, Caesar of Speyer had convened a chapter at Augsburg. The following month he sent John of Piano Carpini and Barnabas to preach in Würzburg; friars later passed to Mainz, Worms, Speyer, Strasbourg, Cologne, Regensburg and Salzburg.[37]

The general chapter of 1223 appointed Albert of Pisa as the second minister provincial. He convened a chapter in Speyer. Custodies were established in Franconia, Bavaria, Swabia, Alsace and Saxony. The party of friars sent to Saxony arrived at Hildesheim, where they were received by the first canon, Henry of Tossem. They presented themselves to the bishop, Conrad II, a noted preacher and theologian, who received them with honour. The bishop invited John of Piano Carpini to preach to a large crowd of clerics. After the sermon the bishop commended John and the friars, whom he licensed to preach and hear confessions in his diocese. John of Piano Carpini, then the first *custos* of Saxony, extended the network of friaries by dispatching several prudent friars to Hildesheim, Brunswick, Goslar, Magdeburg and Halberstadt later that year. The following year Albert of Pisa, monitoring the

---

pp. 27–33, *F. Nicholai Triveti, de ordine frat. praedicatorum, Annales*, ed. T. Hog (London, 1845), pp. 211–12.

[35] Salimbene, *Cronica*, pp. 304–5, 313, 317–23, 430–1, 463, 754.

[36] *Regestrum visitationum archiepiscopi Rothomagensis. MCCXLVIII–MCCLXIX*, ed. T. Bonnin (Rouen, 1852).

[37] Jordan of Giano, *Chronica*, nn. 20–6 pp. 24–9.

friars' progress in Saxony, glimpsed an opportunity for them to pass through Thuringia to the Rhine. Jordan, guardian of Mainz, and seven friars were authorised to obtain houses in Thuringia. In 1225 Jordan sent friars throughout Thuringia to ascertain conditions in the cities and to make reports.[38]

Some of the order's teething troubles appeared at an early stage in this mission. When Caesar of Speyer called for a chapter at Worms in 1222, the local friary was too small to receive the friars who had joined the initial party of volunteers. The canons came to the friars' aid and permitted them to use their church for Mass and preaching. One side of the choir was allocated to the canons and the other to the friars. The following year the order was short of priests to celebrate the sacraments at a time when friars were beginning their retreat from full participation in the life of the local parish. Novices at both Speyer and Worms celebrated Mass and heard the friars' confessions on the great feasts. As in other provinces of the order, the minister provincial's response was to have three friars ordained and a fourth, Jordan of Giano, the following year. Friars were not universally welcomed by bishops, priests and religious. In 1225 the friars at Eisenach encountered the seculars' worries about the loss of parochial revenue on account of the attractive preachers in the order's ranks.[39]

Information on those who entered the fraternity in Germany is provided by Jordan of Giano, who, like Francis's biographers, ascribes vocations to the friars' preaching and good example.[40] Arrivals began early, such as Peregrine, who joined at Trent. By the middle of the next month the number of friars had climbed to thirty-one. Caesar of Speyer admitted Hartmuth, a capable and educated young man, at Würzburg on 30 November of the same year; within a short time he was ordained to the priesthood and became a preacher and later *custos* of Saxony, and he in turn received Rodiger, a brother, who later became guardian of Halberstadt and the advisor to Elizabeth of Hungary.

The rate of expansion continued and there were at least seventy-three friaries in Germany before 1250. John Freed observes that several foundations were made in the cathedral cities, which were often also commercial centres. The most rapid expansion took place in the province of Cologne, which included several cities and was the most urbanised part in the country. Conversely, there were no friaries in the northern lowland between the Zuider Zee and the Weser. There was a slower rate of growth in the province of Strasbourg.[41] By the end of the thirteenth century there was no town of any significance which did not have a Dominican or Franciscan friary, with the exception of Salzburg and Passau.[42]

[38] Ibid., nn. 31–6, 38–42, pp. 32–5, 36–8.
[39] Ibid., nn. 26, 28–30, 41, 48, pp. 29, 31–2, 37, 42–3.
[40] Jordan of Giano, *Chronica*, nn. 20, 23, 25, 35, pp. 24, 27–9, 34–5.
[41] Freed, *The Friars and German Society*, pp. 28–31.
[42] Ibid., p. 52.

As in other provinces, the friars of Germany were keen to extend the network of communities in new regions. John of Piano Carpini sent friars to Bohemia, Hungary, Poland, Denmark and Norway. He accepted a house at Metz and established the order in Lorraine. The German province was divided into new administrations of Saxony and the Rhine. Saxony in turn gave rise to the new provinces of Austria, Denmark, Bohemia with Poland, Dalmatia and Hungary within a decade.[43] There were friaries in Sweden by 1233. Early foundations were made in Croatia, notably at Split and Sibenik Pula, by the middle of the 1220s. The friars reached Kraków[44] and Przemysl, close to the Ukranian border, in 1237. Two years later they formed a province of Bohemia, which included Poland.[45] They had reached the Baltic and formed a community at Riga by 1238.[46]

The provinces in the British Isles

Thomas of Eccleston chronicled the development of the order in England from its inception until the later 1250s. Within eight years the friars founded provinces in Ireland and Scotland. The only Welsh foundations were at Cardiff, Carmarthen and Llanfaes.

English men entered the order before 1224, and some feature in the accounts of the establishment of the order in France and Germany. The decision to cross the English Channel was a logical extension of the friars' work in France. Gregory of Naples, minister provincial of France, sought volunteers for the English mission; one of his recruits was William of Esseby. Gregory was undoubtedly consulted about the appointments of Agnellus of Pisa, the *custos* of Paris, and Richard of Ingworth. Assembling in northern France in the late summer of 1224, the nine friars travelled to the coast of Normandy, where the Benedictine monks of Holy Trinity at Fécamp arranged their passage. Landing at Dover, the friars walked to Canterbury, where they were received by the Benedictines of Christ Church cathedral. They then found accommodation in the Hospice for Poor Priests on Stour Street. The decision to press on was soon taken and four friars set out for London, where Agnellus of Pisa later joined them. The initial group found hospitality with the Dominicans for fifteen days. Before the end of October two friars left London for Oxford, where they were received by the Dominicans once again.[47] Within two months of landing on English soil the friars had formed communities in the leading centres of the Church, education and commerce.

[43]   Jordan of Giano, *Chronica*, no. 55, pp. 48–9, Golubovich, *Biblioteca*, II, p. 259.
[44]   *Annales capituli Cracoviensis et Annales Cracovienses compilati*, in MGH, SS, XIX, pp. 582–607 at 597.
[45]   L. Lemmens, 'Annales minorum Prussicorum', *AFH* 6 (1913), pp. 702–4.
[46]   Freed, *The Friars and German Society*, p. 69. Cf. V. Gidziunas, 'De missionibus fratrum minorum in Lituania (saec. XIII et XIV)', *AFH* 42 (1949), pp. 3–36.
[47]   Ibid., pp. 3–11.

Map 2. Foundations in England, Wales and Scotland in the thirteenth century

Map 3. Thirteenth-century foundations in Ireland

This three-pronged strategy served notice of the order's plans for expansion. Cathedral cities were a magnet for the friars, who settled at Canterbury, Carlisle, Chichester, Exeter, Hereford, Lichfield, Lincoln, London, Norwich, Salisbury, Winchester, Worcester and York before 1240. The only cathedral cities in which they made no permanent foundations were Bath, Ely, Rochester and Durham (where there was a short-lived foundation). Foundations in the vicinity of monastic houses followed hard on the heels of the cathedrals. When the friars had settled in most of the major urban centres, their attention was turned to the larger boroughs, such as Stamford, Beverley, Boston and Lynn. This rapid expansion was facilitated by the arrival of reinforcements from France and Spain and the boom in vocations from the ranks of the secular and religious clergy as well as laymen of diverse social ranks.

Ireland

The friars quickly turned their attention to Ireland and Scotland. It is probable they crossed the Irish Sea before 1230. The first minister provincial of Ireland was Richard of Ingworth, the former vicar of the English province. He was appointed by John Parenti, minister general, at the general chapter of Assisi in 1230 and held office until 1239. He was succeeded by John de Kethene, formerly minister provincial of Scotland (1232–39). Philip, a Londoner and the fifth vocation of the English province, was sent to minister in Ireland.[48] The number of friars was also supplemented by their confrères from England. The minister general appointed the minister provincial of Ireland, who was generally of English stock.[49] The shortage of cities in Ireland gave a different complexion to the new province. Neither did the province have its own chronicler to narrate the lives of the first friars and the sequence of foundations, although later members of the province compiled histories. Historians are dependent upon incidental references to new friaries and these rarely offer information on the friars' arrival. Foundations were being made at major centres such as Dublin and Limerick in the 1230s, and within two decades they were at Waterford, Drogheda, Cork, Athlone, Kilkenny, Castledermot, Carrickfergus, Downpatrick, Dundalk and Tristeldermot. Most of these were towns in which the English influence was strong, some of them ports.[50] The port of Wicklow received the friars in the 1260s. There were already about eighteen earlier foundations by this stage.[51]

The crown was once again a conspicuous benefactor. When King Edward I

48 Eccleston, *Tractatus*, pp. 4, 15, 41–2.
49 C. N. Ó'Clabaigh, *The Franciscans in Ireland, 1400–1534. From Reform to Reformation* (Dublin, 2002), p. 55.
50 E. B. Fitzmaurice and A. G. Little, *Materials for the History of the Franciscan Province of Ireland A.D. 1230–1450*, British Society of Franciscan Studies, IX (Manchester, 1920), p. xvi.
51 B. Millett, 'The Friars Minor in County Wicklow, Ireland, 1260–1982', *AFH* 77 (1984), pp. 110–36 at 111, 113.

increased the alms to the friaries of Dublin, Waterford, Cork, Drogheda and Limerick on 8 December 1293, he confirmed that he and his ancestors were the founders of the house in Limerick.[52] John Watt's map of the province in 1331 demonstrates that later foundations were generally close to the coast, with few friaries in the west and north. The friars received patronage from both the wealthy and the inhabitants of the towns. They settled in all the English towns of any significance and also penetrated the Gaelic world; they were in Ennis about 1240. Foundations were subsequently made at Armagh, Buttevant, Cavan, Killeigh, Nenagh and Timoleague. The province grew at a slower rate than the English province. There were four custodies and twenty-five friaries in the province *c.* 1290.[53]

This development was facilitated by the large number of men who sought admission to the order in Ireland; recruitment in the Gaelic areas seems to have been vigorous. John Kethene's concern for the friars' welfare was renowned and was instrumental in attracting friars who were unhappy in their own provinces; they flourished in Ireland.[54] The anonymous author of the *Liber exemplorum ad usum praedicantium* ('The Book of Examples for the Use of Preachers') was an English friar who had been sent to Ireland.[55] Noble recruits to the order are represented by Maurice Fitzgerald, son of Gerald, the justiciar of Ireland, who was clothed as a friar before his death at Pentecost 1257.[56] John de Kethene promoted scriptural studies among the friars in Ireland and provided books. Irish friars proceeded to Paris, Oxford and Cambridge; the practice continued into the fourteenth century.[57] The author of the *Liber exemplorum* was a student at Paris in the later 1240s or early 1250s and knew Bonaventure and Roger Bacon.[58] On his return to Ireland he was made lector of Cork. Thomas Ufford, a friar of the Irish province, was at Cambridge, probably in the middle of the thirteenth century.[59]

The Anglo-Norman conquest and settlement in Ireland had left an indelible mark upon the country and shaped the formation of the new province of friars. The friary at Kildare, a frontier post of the Pale, was constructed for Anglo-Irish friars.[60] It was a friar of the English province, Nicholas de Cusack, bishop of Kildare (1279–99), whose undated letter to Edward I drew

[52] *Calendar of the Patent Rolls, Edward I, AD. 1292–1301* (London, 1895), p. 56.

[53] J. A. Watt, *The Church and the Two Nations in Medieval Ireland*, Cambridge Studies in Medieval Life and Thought, 3rd series, 3 (Cambridge, 1970), p. 179, Golubovich, *Biblioteca*, II, p. 244.

[54] Eccleston, *Tractatus*, p. 43.

[55] *Liber exemplorum ad usum predicantium, saeculo XIII compositus a quodam fratre minore Anglico de provincia Hiberniae*, ed. A. G. Little, British Society of Franciscan Studies, I (Aberdeen, 1908), p. vi.

[56] R. Flower, 'Manuscripts of Irish Interest in the British Museum', *Analecta Hibernica* 2 (1931), pp. 292–340 at 332.

[57] Eccleston, *Tractatus*, p. 43.

[58] *Liber exemplorum . . . de provincia Hiberniae*, no. 104, pp. 59–60.

[59] Ibid., nn. 38, 62, 66, pp. 22, 38–9, 41.

[60] I. Fennessy, ' The Franciscan Friary at Kildare', *Journal of the County Kildare Archaeological Society and Surrounding Districts* 18 (1992–9), pp. 322–36 at 322.

attention to political elements in the teaching of Irish friars. Magnates and other trustworthy men, assembled at Dublin, remarked that the peace of the land was disturbed by certain religious of diverse orders who were receptive to nationalist aspirations. Nicholas seems to suggest that religious with Gaelic sympathies should be removed from convents in sensitive districts and that only religious of good English stock should be appointed there. A similar suspicion informs comments made by an official of the exchequer at Dublin in 1285, arguing against the provision of Irishmen to bishoprics. Such men, he argued, always preached against the king and elected Irishmen to episcopal vacancies. The friars' attachment to the Irish language was clothed in subversive dress.[61] Discord between the two cultures erupted at the provincial chapter of Cork in 1291, when sixteen friars were killed and others wounded, some of whom were incarcerated by the crown. These shocking scenes necessitated the intervention of the minister general, who was making a visitation of the country at that time.[62]

Scotland

Like Ireland, Scotland had few towns in the thirteenth century. The friars' arrival there was an extension of their ministry in the north of England. When they had reached York, they travelled further northwards, and English friars were appointed to the new foundations. They crossed the River Tweed in 1231 to make settlements at Berwick in 1231 and Roxburgh before 1233.[63] Henry of Reresby was appointed as the first minister provincial in 1232. Death, however, prevented him from taking up that office and he was succeeded by John de Kethene. The friaries to the north of York were drawn into the new Scottish province. Thomas of Eccleston relates that John de Kethene performed his duties laudably and admitted several good and useful men to the order in Scotland. The Scottish friars lost their provincial status at the general chapter of Rome in 1239, probably due to the low number of early foundations.[64] The order was expanding at a quicker rate in both Ireland and England. The friaries in Scotland returned to the jurisdiction of the minister provincial of England until 1329, when they were given their own vicar.[65] The friars' presence grew at a modest rate and houses were later formed at Haddington before 1242, Dumfries before 1264 and Dundee before 1289.

Although royal support and alms enabled the friars to settle in England,

61 Fitzmaurice and Little, *Materials for ... the Franciscan Province of Ireland*, pp. 52–3.
62 *Bartholomaei de Cotton, monachi Norwicensis Historia Anglicana (A.D. 449–1298)*, ed. H. R. Luard, RS, XVI (London, 1859), p. 431.
63 *Chronica de Mailros*, ed. J. Stevenson (Edinburgh, 1835), p. 142. Cf. W. Moir Bryce, *The Scottish Grey Friars*, 2 vols (Edinburgh, 1909), I, pp. 5–6.
64 Eccleston, *Tractatus*, pp. 31, 41–2.
65 *Chronicon de Lanercost MCCI–MCCCXLVI*, ed. J. Stevenson (Edinburgh, 1839), p. 265.

Ireland and Scotland, the connection was a double-edged sword.[66] Towards the end of the thirteenth century King Edward I (1272–1307) faced unrest in Ireland, Scotland and Wales and expected the friars to support his policies. What had hitherto facilitated the friars' ministry later became a disruptive force, causing suspicion, discord and friction in friaries. Indigenous friars receptive to nationalistic interests were eyed with some anxiety by the crown, which was keen to lavish alms on houses which were seen to be supportive of the king. While John Duns Scotus, the most distinguished *alumnus* of the Scottish province, was completing his theological studies at Paris, Oxford and Cambridge, the king lodged at Roxburgh Greyfriars on 7 May 1296 during his campaign against the Scots.[67] Evangelical poverty was the friars' most effective recruitment sergeant, stimulating and supporting the growth of the fraternity.

---

[66]   BL, MS Cotton Nero A. IX, fol. 69r.
[67]   D. B. Tyson, 'A Royal Itinerary – The Journey of Edward I to Scotland in 1296', *Nottingham Medieval Studies* 45 (2001), pp. 127–44 at 139.

CHAPTER THREE

The Poor Followers of St Francis

O love of poverty, tranquil kingdom that knows not strife or hatred ! . . .
You need pay neither judge nor notary and smile at the avaricious man
fretting over his money.

Jacopone da Todi[1]

The novelty of poverty

There was a strong correlation between the order's poverty and its pheno-
menal rate of recruitment. Contemporary ideas about the simple life, rooted
in the Gospel, were incorporated into the Rule.[2] While renunciation lay at
the heart of the traditional forms of religious life, Francis imitated his divine
teacher literally. The virtue which he and his disciples feminised as Lady
Poverty became its most distinctive feature. Francis looked upon poverty
as especially dear to the Son of God, although it was spurned throughout
the world.[3] Dante presents Francis as joined to Lady Poverty, who had been
bereft of her first husband, despised and obscure for 1100 years and more. This
imitation of the poor Christ and the apostles recovered an earlier strand in
the Christian tradition and the friars' decision to adopt evangelical poverty in
the most literal manner distinguished them visibly from other religious. The
adjective mendicant denoted the friars' decision to cast themselves on divine
providence and their reliance on alms. The friars' bare feet, poor clothing and
rejection of money, claimed Albert of Pisa, exalted the order.[4]

Medieval art depicted Christ and his disciples dressed in sandals, as in the
mosaics of the Norman cathedral of Monreale.[5] This message was reinforced
by Jesus's uncompromising words about the perils of wealth, a healthy detachment from material things and the counsel proffered to the rich young man

---

[1] Iacopone da Todi, *Laude*, no. 36, pp. 97–8.
[2] Walter Map, *De nugis curialium*, ed. M. R. James, revised by C. N. L. Brooke and R. A. B. Mynors,
    Oxford Medieval Texts (Oxford, 1983) pp. 126–7.
[3] *SC, Vita secunda*, no. 55.
[4] Dante Alighieri, *La divina commedia, Paradiso*, XI, vv. 64–6, p. 924, Eccleston, *Tractatus*, p. 82.
[5] Salimbene, *Cronica*, p. 369, reports that the apostles were traditionally (*traditio pictorum ab antiquis*)
    depicted with sandals on their feet and mantles on their shoulders.

(Matthew 19.21). Such advice conjured up an image which was out of keeping with the lives of contemporary prelates. The monasteries accumulated property and extensive estates, which produced revenue for their respective communities. The reformers of the later twelfth century focused on the revival of the apostolic life. There was a striking contrast between the success enjoyed by Albigensians in Toulouse and the pompous ineffectiveness of the papal legates; the heretics' life of penance and simplicity impressed the people, among whom they were making inroads. In contrast, the twelve Cistercian abbots and a papal legate carried the trappings of their ecclesiastical office. The legates were advised by the bishop of Osma that their preaching would gain more credence by the adoption of a simpler lifestyle ('a voluntary poverty').[6] These events of 1203 in southern France reflected a change of mood and aspiration, expressing the thirst for more satisfying standards of religious life based on the way in which Christ and his apostles lived.

The friars' literal following of the Gospel and their voluntary poverty struck their urban neighbours. Jacques de Vitry was a witness to their persuasive conduct, emphasising the way in which they injected a new vocabulary into the dictionary of religious life. These truly poor men were lesser and more humble than any contemporary religious in their clothing, poverty and contempt of the world: the religion, poverty and humility of the primitive Church was their goal. Trait for trait they mirrored the lives of the apostles and renounced their own will and their possessions to take up their cross; in their nakedness they followed the naked Christ. They travelled with neither purse nor haversack, neither bread nor money in their belts; they did not wear sandals. Having no gold or silver, they were not permitted to own anything personally or collectively and hence they had no churches, fields, vineyards, animals, houses, property nor any place to lay their head. They had nothing to do with furs, linen, capes, mantles, cowls or other garments. They possessed nothing in the world apart from a habit and cord.[7] The new and global dimensions of the friars' vocation were encapsulated in St Francis's meeting with the personification of the cherished virtue, Lady Poverty, who asked to see his cloister. He led her to a hill and showed her the whole world as far as he could see.[8]

The early friars engaged in a variety of roles. In accordance with chapter five of the Rule, they were required to work in return for their sustenance, money excluded; the vice of idleness was to be eschewed. Their early ministry was not dependent upon a supply of priests because there was a paucity of

6 *Libellus de principiis ord. praedicatorum auctore Iordano de Saxonia*, ed. M. H. Laurent, *Monumenta ordinis fratrum praedicatorum historica*, XVI (Rome, 1935), nn. 19–22, pp. 1–88 at 35–7.

7 'Historia occidentalis', pp. 158–62, 'Jacobi Vitriacensis episcopi et cardinalis (1180–1240): Sermones ad fratres minores', ed. H. Felder, *Analecta ordinis minorum Capuccinorum* 19 (1903), pp. 22–4, 114–22, 149–58.

8 *SC*, c. 30.

them in the nascent German province as early as 1222; similarly, the second chapter of the Rule focuses on the Divine Office rather than the Mass. The six friars who reached Valenciennes about 1225 earned their living by making mats, weaving and copying and binding manuscripts. Two friars at Peschici in the diocese of Siponto were busy in the construction of a church in honour of their founder by the middle of the century. There are abundant examples of friars who persevered in their earlier trades, such as Laurence of Beauvais, who was engaged in mechanical work. This manual work was a fulfilment of the friars' Rule.[9] Friars were regularly identified with the impoverished members of society and worked with those at the edge of society, the paupers, the prisoners and the sick.[10] The care of the sick was not limited to the early friars, some of whom founded hospitals and held the position of master.[11] In accordance with the example of the founder, friars, prelates and princes distributed alms at friaries.[12]

Bare feet and questing for alms

Believing that Christ and the apostles had not used shoes, the friars went unshod even in the midst of bad weather, including mud and snow. Their bare feet became a distinctive feature of their lives and an emblem of evangelical poverty.[13] References to their lack of shoes were abundant. Matthew Paris testifies that the friars were poor and holy, devoting themselves completely to their ministry. Embracing poverty voluntarily, they abandoned revenues and kept no food for the morrow. On their travels they received hospitality and some overnight accommodation.[14] William of Rubruck went barefoot on his journey among the Tartars in 1253, except in severe cold. John Pecham boasted that the friars' naked feet witnessed their rejection of social conventions and values. No winter had ever prevented the unshod friars from making long journeys among the Tartars, Greeks and Saracens; hot soil made

---

[9] Jordan of Giano, *Chronica*, no. 28, p. 31, Iacobi de Guisia, *Annales historiae illustrium principum Hanoniae*, lib. 21, cc. 1–5, in MGH, SS, XXX, pp. 44–334, at 282–5, III Celano, VIII, no. 60, Eccleston, *Tractatus*, pp. 5–6.

[10] Iunctae Bevegnatis, *Legenda de vita et miraculis Beatae Margaritae de Cortona*, ed. F. Iozzelli, Bibliotheca Franciscana ascetica medii aevi, XIII (Grottaferrata, Rome, 1997), p. 375. Cf. E. Doyle, 'William Woodford, O.F.M.: His Life and Works together with a Study and Edition of His *Responsiones contra Wiclevum et Lollardos*', FS 43 (1983), pp. 17–187 at 156, Salimbene, *Cronica*, p. 145.

[11] F. M. Delorme, 'Les Cordeliers dans le Limousin aux XIIIe–XVe siècle', *AFH* 32 (1939), pp. 201–59 and 33 (1940), pp. 114–60 at 117–18.

[12] *CA*, c. 91, *Processus canonizationis et legendae variae Sancti Ludovici O.F.M. episcopi Tolosani*, Analecta Franciscana, VII (Quaracchi, Florence, 1951), p. 47. H. Johnstone, 'The Wardrobe and Household of Henry, Son of Edward I', *Bulletin of the John Rylands Library* 7 (1922–3), pp. 384–420 at 419.

[13] Eccleston, *Tractatus*, pp. 12–13, 27, 82. Roger of Wendover, *Flores historiarum*, II, ed. H. G. Hewlett, RS, LXXXIV (London, 1887), p. 35.

[14] Matthew Paris, *Chronica majora*, V, pp. 194–5, Bonaventure, *Legenda maior*, miracula, III, no. 1 and VII, no. 7.

going barefoot in summer as great a sacrifice as it was in winter.[15] There are several later references to friars walking barefoot.[16] Their bare feet distinguished them from the other mendicants.[17]

While some religious communities solicited donations for particular projects, such as buildings, the concept of a religious order abandoning the traditional forms of financial support was entirely new. The friars were beggars whose life was sustained only by alms. Their practice of begging from religious houses in the locality is illustrated by the friars of Coimbra, who asked for material assistance from the Augustinian canons.[18] They asked only for those alms that were necessary, begging in the streets and main squares.[19] In some instances they appealed for material support in the name of their canonised founder.[20] From the outset they begged alms daily from door to door, a practice which is attested by Solomon, the first recruit in England. He was not even spared the embarrassment of begging at the home of his sister, who gave him bread and then, averting her face, cursed him.[21] The friars quickly organised the collection of alms. The city or town was split into districts in which friars systematically visited. Salimbene with an unnamed companion made the rounds with his baskets, seeking bread from one house to another at Pisa. Following their circuit, which was finished that evening, he had a dream in which he was questing in the quarter of St Michael, the section of the Vicecomiti family. The embarrassed friar avoided the hostel on the other side, the property of the merchants of Parma, where he was castigated for soliciting alms. As he was walking through the quarter of St Michael alongside the Arno, he had a vision of the Son of God coming out of one of the houses, carrying bread and placing it in the basket; the Mother of God and St Joseph were doing the same. It was the custom for the basket to be left below, covered with a cloth, while a friar went up to the houses to seek bread. Donations would then be carried back to the basket.[22]

Gifts of clothing represented one form of alms from at least 1218 when a testator supplied tunics for the friars of Ravenna.[23] Such donations became a feature of the friars' dealings with their benefactors. The only recompense

---

[15] 'Itinerarium Willelmi de Rubruc', *SF*, c. 28, no. 11, pp. 145–332 at 247, F. Tocco, 'Tractatus contra Fratrem Robertum Kilwardby, O.P.', in *Fratris Johannis Pecham . . . tractatus tres de paupertate*, pp. 91–147 at 112, 129.

[16] 'Relatio Fr. Iohannis de Marignoli', *SF*, pp. 513–60, 547.

[17] *Brut y Tywysogyon or The Chronicle of the Princes, Peniarth MS. 20 Version*, ed. T. Jones (Cardiff, 1952), p. 104.

[18] C. N. L. Brooke, *The Age of the Cloister: The Story of Monastic Life in the Middle Ages* (Stroud, 2003), p. 231, *Vita prima o 'Assidua'*, c. 5, no. 4, pp. 290–1.

[19] Eccleston, *Tractatus*, p. 12, Chiappini, 'Communitatis responsio', p. 59, F. M. Delorme, 'Explanationes constitutionum generalium Narbonensium', no. 19, *AFH* 18 (1925), pp. 511–24 at 517.

[20] Bonaventure, *Legenda maior*, miracula, II, no. 3, and VIII, no. 3.

[21] *CA*, c. 74, Eccleston, *Tractatus*, p. 12.

[22] Salimbene, *Cronica*, pp. 60–3, 587.

[23] G. Zinotti, *I francescani a Ravenna. Dai tempi di Dante a oggi* (Ravenna, 1999), p. 12, nn. 5–6.

sought by John of Piano Carpini, when acting as papal legate, was some cloth to fashion a habit for his companion.[24] As an act of piety for the welfare of their souls, donors provided for the friars.

The friars and their benefactors

Supported by benefactors, the friars made their homes in the major centres of population, where they were helped by senior ecclesiastics, monastic communities, urban bodies, the universities and the clergy. Reports of major benefactions should not lead to the questionable inference that these were the only source of material support. It is probable that friars drew limited support from people of modest means, although this is not easy to verify.[25] Because the early friars settled in small numbers, initially groups of three or four, living in ordinary dwelling houses, foundations could be made with comparatively low levels of investment by founders and patrons. One of the first friars in Germany professed that he did not know what a cloister was.[26]

Papal support was vital to the spread of the new order, and this was nowhere more visible than in Assisi. Simon di Puzarello's land, hitherto known as the 'hill of hell' (*collis inferni*), was handed over to Elias of Cortona, who received it on behalf of Pope Gregory IX on 30 March 1228. Further grants of land for the basilica were made on 31 July 1229, 15 October 1241 and an unspecified date in December 1245 or 1246. The new church quickly became a major centre of pilgrimage. It was deemed to be glorious, beautiful and spacious. Pope Innocent IV endowed and enriched it with great privileges and treasures.[27] Pope Gregory IX's *Quo elongati*, promulgated on 28 September 1230, permitted the friars to have an agent to receive and expend money for their immediate needs. This was followed by a reaffirmation that the friars could not hold property either individually or collectively. They were given the use of equipment, books and moveable things at the ministers' discretion.[28] This permission was enlarged by Pope Innocent IV's *Ordinem vestrum* of 14 November 1245. The friars were permitted to have recourse to money through an agent not only for necessities, but also for their convenience. The property used by the friars was taken into the hands of the papacy, with the exception of those cases where the benefactor expressly retained ownership and dominium.[29] Popes and cardinal protectors acted for the friars, as was

---

[24] Salimbene, *Cronica*, pp. 305–6.

[25] Cf. J. Paul, 'La Signification sociale du franciscanisme', in *Mouvements franciscains et société française XIIe–XXe siècles*, ed. A. Vauchez (Paris, 1984), pp. 9–25.

[26] Roger of Wendover, *Flores historiarum*, II, pp. 35–6, Eccleston, *Tractatus*, p. 10, Jordan of Giano, *Chronica*, no. 43, pp. 38–9.

[27] *Le carte duecentesche del Sacro Convento di Assisi*, nn. 6, 8, 17, 26, pp. 10–14, 25–6, 40–2, Visconti, *Sermons*, no. 6, p. 777.

[28] H. Grundmann, 'Die Bulle "Quo elongati" Papst Gregors IX', *AFH* 54 (1961), pp. 3–25 at 20–1.

[29] *BF*, I, no. 114, pp. 400–2.

illustrated when William, procurator of Raynaldo dei Conti di Segni, bishop of Ostia, cardinal protector of the order, purchased a house for the friars of Bologna on 5 July 1245.[30]

Prelates and clerics followed the papal lead in extending a welcome to the friars. The bishops of Trent and Brixen received them enthusiastically. The bishop of Augsburg and his nephew, the vicar and canon of the principal church, charitably welcomed them, the latter accommodating them in his own house. Friars were kindly received by the bishop of Salzburg.[31] John of Bournain, archbishop of Vienne (1218–66), had a particular love for the order and had a stone bridge constructed over the Rhone because he had given them a convent in his lands across the river dividing their friary from the city.[32] Some of the alms were given annually. For example, from 1232 the friars of Chichester received bread and ale on the anniversary of William Durandi, late archdeacon of Chichester.[33] The Benedictine monastery on Monte Subasio provided the friars' with their first home at the Portiuncula. Honouring the principle that the order should not own any property, the friars paid the monks an annual rent, and this became the pattern for foundations such as Nordhausen.[34] The friars received hospitality from innumerable monasteries. This was demonstrated in the previous chapter by the assistance and accommodation provided by the Benedictine monks of St-Denis, Paris, for at least a decade. The friars were granted a new site by the abbey of St Germain-des-Près in the parish of Sts Cosmas and Damian within the walls of Paris and near the porta de Gibardo, afterwards known as St Michael's Gate, in 1230 and the area was enlarged in 1240. Monks not only gave the early friars shelter, but charitably received them on other occasions.[35]

The nobility is represented by Lord Bonaventure, who supplied the friars of Siena with land for their friary. The friars' poverty brought them admiration and innumerable gifts from leading civil figures. Lord Manfred de Cornazano, *podestà* of Lucca, and his wife, Auda, were outstanding benefactors. Merchants became the friars' patrons, providing them with accommodation.[36] The Franciscan author of the *Annales Erphordenses* reports that the friars reached Erfurt on 11 November 1223, while Jordan of Giano attests that they arrived the following year. When Jordan, *custos* of Thuringia, reached Erfurt,

---

[30] *Acta Franciscana e tabulariis Bononiensibus deprompta*, ed. B. Giordani, Analecta Franciscana, IX (Quaracchi, Florence, 1927), no. 13, p. 7.

[31] Jordan of Giano, *Chronica*, nn. 20–2, 24, pp. 24–8.

[32] Salimbene, *Cronica*, p. 334.

[33] *The Chartulary of the High Church of Chichester*, ed. W. D. Peckham, Sussex Record Society, XLVI (Lewes, 1946), no. 542, pp. 140–1.

[34] *CA*, c. 56. Jordan of Giano, *Chronica*, no. 44, p. 39.

[35] A. Callebaut, 'Les Provinciaux de la province de France au XIIIe siècle. Notes, documents, et études', *AFH* 10 (1917), pp. 289–356 at 300, 303–4, Eccleston, *Tractatus*, p. 47, Salimbene, *Cronica*, p. 909.

[36] L. K. Little, *Religious Poverty and the Profit Economy in Medieval Europe* (London, 1978), pp. 205–6.

he received a warm welcome. Plans for the establishment of a community were discussed, but were shelved on account of the winter. On the advice of citizens and some of the clergy, the friars were lodged in the house of a priest, who was in charge of the lepers outside the walls. The following year the friars moved to the deserted church of the Holy Spirit. Lord Henry and Gunther, his assistant, and the citizens were the main protagonists in this settlement, where the friars remained for six years. The citizens appointed a procurator for the friars and he consulted Jordan about the construction of conventual buildings. During this period the citizens were active on the order's behalf and six years later, in 1231, the friars, who had been living outside the walls, moved into the city. The burghers of Nordhausen received the friars in the summer of 1225 and accommodated them in a house.[37]

The friars' refusal to accept ownership was no legal fiction, as some difficulties demonstrated. Firstly, four friars were sent to Mühlhausen at the request of Count Ernest III, who assigned them a new house and garden in 1225. However, after a year he grew weary of the friars' lack of progress with the buildings and withdrew his support; the friars were obliged to leave. Their return to Mühlhausen in 1231 was not entirely uncomplicated. With royal permission they were lodged in a hospital, whose master became perturbed by the alms being diverted to them. Eventually a soldier came to the friars' aid and gave them a plot of land on which they settled. Secondly, the friars were given a house by Jordan of Exeter at Strade, in Mayo, but were ejected at the instigation of his wife and they were replaced by Dominicans in 1252.[38]

The local authorities, corporately and individually, were the friars' benefactors, often making grants for the building of friars' churches. Several cities owned the sites and conventual buildings used by the friars. The land and houses occupied by the friars of England were often vested in the borough or city.[39] The bond between the local authorities and the friars was to find a later expression in the decision of the civic officials to seek burial in the friars' churches and cemeteries. The interest which members of the local community took in the life of the friars is reflected in the opposition which Albert of Pisa, minister provincial of England (1236–9), encountered in his demolition of a stone cloister at Southampton.[40] Later in the century the links between the friars and commune were mirrored by a communal celebration of the feast of St Francis.[41]

[37] 'Annales Erphordenses', in MGH, SS, XVI, pp. 26–47, at 27, Jordan of Giano, *Chronica*, nn. 39, 43, 44, 46–7, pp. 36, 38–9, 40–2.

[38] Jordan of Giano, *Chronica*, no. 45, pp. 39–40, C. Mooney, 'The Franciscans in County Mayo', *Journal of the Galway Archaeological and Historical Society* 28 (1958–9), pp. 42–69 at 42–3.

[39] A. G. Little, 'The Mendicant Orders', in *The Cambridge Medieval History*, VI, ed. J. R. Tanner, C. W. Previté-Orton and Z. N. Brooke (Cambridge, 1929), pp. 727–62 at 733.

[40] Eccleston, *Tractatus*, p. 79.

[41] Cf. R. Goffen, *Spiritualility in Conflict: Saint Francis and Giotto's Bardi Chapel* (Pennsylvania, 1988), pp. 7, 91, n. 53.

Poverty, a virtue to be defended

The circumstances in which the Rule was compiled generated tension, particularly among the ministers provincial. When Pope Honorius III confirmed the text on 29 November 1223, Francis withdrew to the fringes and gave himself to prayer, culminating in the reception of the stigmata the following year.[42] The *Testament* reflects Francis's vision and ideals, many of which were either diluted or omitted from the Rule. It rehearsed the genesis of his vocation, his profound love of churches, respect for the priestly office, deep reverence for the Eucharist, care for the reserved sacrament, and the claim that God was his principal teacher. His vision for the fraternity was unfurled: friars were to be properly engaged in work, generally manual labour. When their supply of food failed, they were to have recourse to begging. They were to dwell only in places consonant with poverty and they were to cultivate a level of detachment befitting strangers and pilgrims in this world. No friar was authorised to seek papal privileges for the order and it was unambiguously declared that the *Testament* was not another Rule; it was, rather, an aid to its proper observance.

The manner of Francis's death at the Portiuncula on the evening of 3 October 1226 offered little comfort to the friars who looked for developments and relaxations. Faithful to his initial inspiration, Francis was placed naked upon the ground and sprinkled with dust and ashes. Despite his burning love for the Portiuncula, there was no question of his burial outside Assisi; his body was solemnly carried back to the city for burial at San Giorgio, which now forms a chapel in the basilica of Santa Chiara. Thomas of Celano's account of the passage from the Portiuncula to San Giorgio discreetly omits any mention of the soldiers who had earlier brought Francis from Siena to Assisi and then escorted him from the episcopal palace to the Portiuncula. The presence of an armed guard, which was re-formed for the death of St Clare some twenty-seven years later, foreshadowed what was to follow.[43] Within a couple of years plans for the construction of a shrine worthy of the remains of the saint were nearing completion. Security was a priority. Friars of different ideological shades were united by the need of safeguarding Francis's body lest it be stolen.

The planning of a tomb for Francis was no domestic matter for the friars alone. The early miracles associated with his death and burial raised the matter of canonisation. The papal court was party to the plans that were taking shape. Following the canonisation on 16 July 1228, Pope Gregory IX laid the foundation stone of the new basilica and lavished gifts and privileges upon it, which he controversially declared to be the head and mother of the order on 22 April 1230, despite the fact that Francis had earlier bestowed that

[42] *Vita prima o 'Assidua'*, c. 7, pp. 302–11.
[43] *Vita prima*, no. 110, *Vita secunda*, no. 214, *Legenda Sanctae Clarae Assisiensis*, c. 47.

title upon the Portiuncula.[44] The perception of papal responsibility for the church and friary finds expression in Salimbene's remark that Pope Gregory IX, a benefactor of the basilica, constructed a 'great palace' as a papal residence. Pope Innocent IV stayed there when he visited the dying Clare at San Damiano on 9 August 1253 and confirmed her Rule.[45] The construction of the church was entrusted to Elias of Cortona. After the ugly scenes at the general chapter of 1230 he was sufficiently rehabilitated to be elected as minister general two years later. The perception of the basilica became so inextricably entwined with him that it was regarded as a symbol of his extravagance and bullying. The ministers provincial were burdened with the expense of having seven great bells cast for the basilica. The king of Hungary sent a golden cup, adorned with a striking portrait of the saint. Although the sanitised biographies of the thirteenth century offer few clues about the friars' view of the basilica, Dr Michael Cusato detects a critical stance in the *Sacrum commercium beati Francisci cum domina Paupertate*.[46] Writers of the fourteenth century knew no such constraints and voiced the frustration, indignation and sense of betrayal felt by many. In the fifteenth century the basilica and the adjacent friary were viewed as a structure unsurpassed in the whole order.[47] The design and immensity of the new building ignited the flames of controversy at a time when there was a vacuum in the moral leadership of the order. It is ironical that the building resembles a vast fortress rather than the final resting-place of the man who wished to be absolutely poor.

Elsewhere the vexed question of how the order should construct friaries and churches divided modernisers and conservatives. Friction between these groups pervades the account of plans for a new friary at Paris which would enable the friars to move from St-Denis into the city. Enthusiasm for this project was expressed by Philip de Grève, the chancellor of the university, whose sermon of 1 September 1228 encouraged people to give alms for the new church at Valvert, near the Luxembourg gardens. The progressives gained the upper hand, but had to contend with the intercession of the saint, who was prone to vent his displeasure with building which flouted the principles of his *Testament*.[48]

The euphoria of the canonisation was short-lived, and within two years the order encountered its first real crisis. The ministers provincial and

---

[44] *Legenda trium sociorum*, c. 18, nn. 71–2. *BF*, I, no. 49, p. 60.

[45] Salimbene, *Cronica*, p. 235. L. Alessandri and F. Pennacchi, 'I più antichi inventari della sacrestia del Sacro Convento di Assisi (1338–1473)', *AFH* 7 (1914), no. 46, pp. 66–107, 294–340, at 78, *Legenda Sanctae Clarae Assisiensis*, nn. 40–2.

[46] Salimbene, *Cronica*, p. 152, Cusato, 'Talking about Ourselves', pp. 42–53.

[47] Enea Silvio Piccolomini Papa Pio II, *I Commentarii rerum memorabilium*, ed. L. Totaro, Classisi, XLVII (Milan, 1984), II, c. 17, pp. 298–301.

[48] D. Vorreux, 'Un sermon de Philippe le Chancelier en faveur des Frères Mineurs de Vauvert', *AFH* 68 (1975), pp. 3–22. Eccleston, *Tractatus*, p. 47.

custodes were invited to Assisi at Pentecost 1230 for the general chapter and the solemn translation. Their mood was not improved by the clandestine transfer of the relics on 25 May at the instigation of Elias of Cortona, who had been the driving force behind the construction of the new basilica and its adjacent friary. The general chapter was marked by scenes of unbridled ambition and scandalous intimidation. Perhaps unnerved by the disorder, the delegates pronounced themselves unable to give authoritative guidance on the interpretation of the Rule and they appointed a group of friars to consult the pope. Pope Gregory IX underlined his friendship with the saint and his knowledge of the latter's intentions. He responded to the friars' scruples in *Quo elongati*. As a lawyer, he set about resolving doubts and displayed no embarrassment in clarifying doubtful passages of the document which he had helped to write. The status of the *Testament* was addressed first. Friars were advised to take its teachings into account, but they were not bound by its contents because the saint had not sought the consent of the ministers; the saint was unable to bind his successors in such a matter. Despite *Quo elongati*'s controversial beginning, it was accepted as a moderate application of the saint's teaching to evolving circumstances.

The events of the 1230s stimulated strong currents of renewal. A particular catalyst was the controversial conduct of Elias of Cortona, minister general (1232–9), whose failings were vented by the chroniclers. The chroniclers' hostility towards Elias was contrasted with the affection and trust which both St Francis and Pope Gregory IX placed in him. Causes of friction were his taxation of the provinces for the completion of the basilica, a refusal to convene general chapters and his capricious removal of ministers provincial. Elias's flagrant contravention of the vow of poverty and his growing ostentation sounded the alarm. He regarded himself at liberty to accept money on the grounds that he had not professed the Rule approved by Pope Honorius III. Nonetheless, this style of government does not seem to have provoked any concentrated opposition, despite rumblings in the province of France.[49] The moral vacuum created by the minister general was filled by friars, several of whom were associated with the schools, who assumed a position of leadership in the dark days of the later 1230s. Haymo of Faversham was a prime mover against Elias and launched the appeal against him from Paris.[50]

The immediate cause of his downfall was the appointment of visitors whom he dispatched to the provinces from 1236/7. Their high-handed behaviour produced howls of protest from different provinces where they made themselves deeply unpopular. Such discontent galvanised the provinces in their protests during 1238 and 1239 and led to a co-ordinated attack on the behaviour and policies of the minister general. One of the chief architects of the general chapter of Rome in 1239 was Arnulph, an English friar and papal

---

[49] Jordan of Giano, *Chronica*, no. 61, pp. 54–5, Salimbene, *Cronica*, pp. 151–2.
[50] Eccleston, *Tractatus*, pp. 29, 67.

penitentiary. He thwarted Elias's plans to pack the general chapter with his own supporters and paved the way for the first papal deposition of the minister general. The chroniclers depict the priests in the order, especially a group of theologians at Paris, as playing a pivotal role in the orchestration of opposition to Elias.[51] It is ironical that Elias's deposition resulted in the election of Albert of Pisa, the first priest to fill the office of minister general.[52] While the removal of Elias ended an unhappy decade, it severed a close link with the founder and triggered the transfer of influence and power from lay members to the priests. This set the order firmly on the road to clericalisation.

---

[51] Cf. *Expositio quatuor magistrorum super regulam fratrum minorum (1241–1242)*, ed. L. Oliger, Storia e letteratura raccolta di studi e testi, XXX (Rome, 1950).

[52] Eccleston, *Tractatus*, pp. 37–9, 67–9, 94–5, Salimbene, *Cronica*, pp. 157, 232–3.

CHAPTER FOUR

The Friars' Ministry of Preaching

Francis said that the friars would preach to nations and peoples, to kings
and princes, and many would be converted to the Lord.

John of Perugia[1]

The Fourth Lateran Council and the friars' ministry

The order's ministry was shaped by the canons of the Fourth Lateran Council,
whose reforms they disseminated widely. The council was concerned with the
extirpation of heresy, the recovery of the Holy Land and the renewal of the
life of the Church at every level.[2] When the prelates assembled in November
1215, they approved remedies for a number of abuses. Heretical propaganda
was to be countered by a reaffirmation of the articles of faith enshrined in
the first canon. There was an urgent need for theologically articulate priests
competent to engage heretics in debate. The link between preaching and
the welfare of the Church was articulated in the tenth canon. A healthy and
vigorous Church was to be nurtured by the exposition of the Scriptures. The
large and scattered nature of some dioceses was compounded by the fact that
prelates were required to shoulder temporal duties in the service of the crown.
Bishops were required to appoint suitable men for the office of preaching,
men who were delegated to visit the churches entrusted to them. Such clerics
were to build up the faithful by word and example; cathedral and conventual churches were obliged to supply men suitable to assist prelates in this
ministry. Just as bishops were required to be theologically astute, so were
their collaborators. Contemporary sources provide abundant examples of
priests who failed to meet these standards. Several priests were berated for
their avarice and usury.[3]

Francis's teaching chided contemporary clerics who were too attached to
material things and his example castigated priests who panted after revenues.
The phenomenon of non-resident rectors and vicars attracted the scorn of
satirists and chroniclers. The defects of rectors who visited their parishes at

---

[1] *AP*, c. 4, no. 18.
[2] Cf. Watt, 'The Papacy', in *The New Cambridge Medieval History, V c. 1198–c. 1300*, ed. D. Abulafia
(Cambridge, 1999), pp. 107–63 at 119–26.
[3] Fr. Rogeri Bacon, *Opera quaedam hactenus inedita*, ed. J. S. Brewer, RS, XV (London, 1859), p. 399.

harvest time to collect their revenues featured in the *exempla* collections.[4] Commenting on Deuteronomy 5.18, Thomas Docking argued that priests who neglected their pastoral duties were thieves (*raptores*).[5] Clerical ignorance became a *topos* and colourful examples were recounted by Gerald of Wales (†1223).[6] The agenda for the renewal of the Church supplied the context and emphases of the apostolate of Francis, who was present at the council. Francis worked closely with the bishop of Assisi, and developed friendships with curial cardinals. At the time of the council the friars were few in number and their preaching was more exhortatory than doctrinal; they were not yet in a position to supply the kind of support to the Church for which they became more famous in later years. After the council, however, the friars' ranks increased and the number of priests grew, paving the way for their work as preachers. The need to prepare men for the apostolate was enshrined in the ninth chapter of the Rule and the correlation between the preachers' message and their conduct was underlined in the *Vita prima*.[7]

The eucharistic piety at the heart of a number of the conciliar decrees was a salient feature in Francis's writings. The twenty-first decree of the council required members of the Church to communicate at least annually during Easter. Summarising Pope Innocent III's contribution to eucharistic piety, S. J. P. van Dijk and J. Hazelden Walker observe that he had no more fervent supporter in these policies than Francis, whose followers promoted higher standards of reverence towards the Body of Christ. The sacrament was to be received reverently by the faithful; this is reflected in the recollections of a Tuscan friar. When he was a child, the friars instructed him to hold the Eucharist in especial reverence; he had fasted for almost the whole of Lent in order to prepare himself to communicate.[8] The same canon of the council yoked the sacraments of the Eucharist and penance, and this twin approach was central in the friars' apostolate. Confession was perceived as a preparation for the annual reception of the Body of Christ and the dovetailing of the two sacraments is visible in the pastoral priorities of Haymo of Faversham. He was so anxious for the people to communicate fittingly that his sermon in a Parisian parish church at Easter 1224/5 was followed by three days of hearing confessions. The friars' pastoral, liturgical, and ascetical writings focused on the two sacraments, while the devout and dignified celebration

4   *Vita secunda*, no. 84, *La Tabula exemplorum secundum ordinem alphabeti: recueil d'exempla compilé en France à la fin du XIIIe siècle*, ed. J. Th. Welter, Thesaurus exemplorum, III (Paris, 1926), p. 135.

5   BL, MS Royal 3. B. XII, fol. 31ra.

6   Giraldi Cambrensis, *Opera*, II, ed. J. S. Brewer, 8 vols, RS, XXI (London, 1861–91), pp. 341–57. Giovanni Boccaccio, *Decameron, Filocolo, Ameto, Fiametta*, ed. E. Bianchi, C. Salinari and N. Sapegno La letteratura italiana storia e testi, VIII (Milan, 1952), VIII, 2, p. 532.

7   *CA*, c. 117, *Vita prima*, nn. 23, 36–7.

8   S. J. P. Van Dijk and J. Hazelden Walker, *The Origins of the Modern Roman Liturgy: The Liturgy of the Papal Court and the Franciscan Order in the Thirteenth Century* (London, 1960), p. 360, Eccleston, *Tractatus*, p. 96.

of the Eucharist stimulated the creative energies of Haymo of Faversham and William of Melitona.[9]

Friars were regarded as supplementing the work of the prelates and the tenth canon was glossed by one metropolitan, who maintained that the friars, proficient in theology, were assigned as 'fellow helpers in the sermons of the prelates' to supply their defects and act as their vicars. His parochial clergy and chaplains were to receive the friars who acted in his name. Contemporaries viewed the impact of the friars' preaching as a providential response to the challenges besetting the Church in western Europe. The sense of excitement occasioned by their arrival is captured by Matthew Paris: on Sundays and feast days the friars emerged from their convents, carrying Bibles, and preached in parish churches and other places where people were accustomed to congregate.[10] The friars' ministry was located within the tradition of the twelve disciples; they were depicted as the apostles' sons through their preaching. The mendicant movement in general is credited with the revival of preaching and this claim was conceded by contemporaries. The friars asserted that preaching had been a rarity prior to their emergence, a view confidently articulated by Bonaventure. Moreover, the friars argued that their Rule alone obliged them to preach, as John Pecham maintained.[11] Friars explained that because the secular clergy had shown themselves to be unfit for the ministry of preaching the responsibility passed to the followers of *il poverello*, who had made the people accustomed to hearing preaching rooted in knowledge and integrity of life.[12]

The content of the friars' preaching

Friars were hailed as an 'order of preachers': this was perceived as a central element in their ministry.[13] Pope Gregory IX's *Cum, qui recepit prophetam* of 12 June 1234 exhorted bishops to receive the friars who travelled through different regions to preach the Word of God for the benefit of souls.[14] The reinvigoration of the Church, attests Jacques de Vitry, owed much to the preaching of the friars, whose one passion was to snatch souls endangered by the vanities of the world and to prevail upon Christians to follow their

[9] Eccleston, *Tractatus*, p. 28, *Sources of the Modern Roman Liturgy: The Ordinals by Haymo of Faversham and Related Documents (1243–1307)*, ed. S. J. P. Van Dijk, 2 vols, Studia et Documenta Franciscana cura fratrum minorum in Austria, Belgio, Germania, Neerlandia edita (Leiden, 1963).

[10] *Roberti Grosseteste episcopi quondam Lincolniensis Epistolae*, ed. H. R. Luard, RS, XXV (London, 1861), pp. 121–2, Visconti, *Sermons*, no. 9, pp. 350–1, no. 9, pp. 777–8, Matthew Paris, *Historia Anglorum*, II, pp. 109–10.

[11] Alexander Minorita, *Expositio in Apocalypsim*, p. 454, Visconti, *Sermons*, no. 2, p. 776, 'Apologia pauperum', c. 12, no. 8, in *DSBOO*, VIII, pp. 233–330, 318–19, Tocco, 'Tractatus contra Fratrem Robertum Kilwardby', p. 127.

[12] Salimbene, *Cronica*, p. 596.

[13] 'Historia occidentalis', p. 158, *ordo predicatorum quos fratres minores appellamus*.

[14] *BF*, I, no. 131, pp. 127–8.

own example.[15] Sent out in pairs as precursors, they prepared the way for the second coming of Christ. Their preaching, example and virtues encouraged people of all social ranks to subscribe to the Gospel.[16] They were itinerant evangelists and their ranks included outstanding preachers, such as Hermann. There was an enthusiastic response to his homilies, which were so popular that people followed him wherever he was due to preach. He announced the places at which he would preach and the entire population of Eisenach would flock there.[17]

Evidence of preaching in the vernacular becomes more common and is exemplified by Archbishop Federico Visconti.[18] The friars preached in the vernacular, even to the extent of apologising for an imperfect grasp of French.[19] Anglo-Norman was used as a medium by some friars in their writings. Some of them such as Nicholas Bozon produced sermons in Anglo-Norman verse.[20] The ministry of preaching, rooted in orthodoxy, was addressed in the ninth chapter of the Rule, where it was ordained that friars' words should be properly weighed and chaste: they should preach for the usefulness and edification of those present, announcing vices and virtues, punishment and glory.[21] Prayerful reflection should precede sermons, whose objective was the conversion of those present rather than a display of erudition.[22]

The Gospel was applied to the urban vices of usury and avarice. The fate of usurers was depicted by Dante in the seventeenth canto of *Inferno*. The friars' assault on usury is illustrated by a member of the order who preached at sermon at Como on a feast day in 1233. When the homily was interrupted by the noise of builders constructing a tower for a local usurer, the friar correctly predicted that the tower would disintegrate within a short time.[23] Paris, Bibliothèque nationale, MS 11560, fol. 138, executed *c.* 1250, shows the Dominicans and Franciscans spurning the usurers' offerings.[24]

Avarice, defined as 'immoderate love of owning good worldly chattels (*temporalia*)' and epitomised in the wealthy man who was indifferent to

---

[15] *Lettres de Jacques de Vitry*, p. 75.

[16] 'Historia occidentalis', pp. 159–62.

[17] Jordan of Giano, *Chronica*, no. 41, p. 37.

[18] Visconti, *Sermons*, p. 782.

[19] N. Bériou, *L'Avènement des maîtres de la Parole: la prédication a Paris à XIII siècle*, 2 vols, Collection des études augustiniennes (Paris, 1998), I, pp. 231–2.

[20] Cf. *Nine Verse Sermons by Nicholas Bozon: The Art of the Anglo-Norman Poet and Preacher*, ed. B. J. Levy, Medium Aevum Monographs, New Series, XI (Oxford, 1981).

[21] Cf. S. Wenzel, *Verses in Sermons: Fasciculus Morum and Its Middle English Poems* (Cambridge, Mass., 1978), pp. 9–10, 93–4. M. W. Bloomfield, B.-G. Guyot, D. R. Howard and T. B. Kabealo, *Incipits of Latin Works on the Virtues and Vices, 1100–1500 A.D.* (Cambridge, Mass., 1979).

[22] *Vita secunda*, nn. 163–4.

[23] Salimbene, *Cronica*, p. 105.

[24] Little, *Religious Poverty and the Profit Economy*. The miniature is reproduced opposite the title page.

the plight of others, was a special target of the friars' preaching.[25] Indeed, the friars' campaign against avarice was cloaked in eschatological language. Apologists for the order confidently affirmed that mendicant preaching was divinely ordained to combat avarice. While God raised up men to extirpate idolatry and heresy in earlier ages, the contemporary vice of avarice was combated by men who voluntarily embraced evangelical poverty.[26]

A remedy for social and spiritual ills of urban centres was supplied by Anthony of Padua, an exceptionally talented preacher, the fruits of whose homilies were summarised by his first biographer. The estranged were brought back to fraternal accord; the imprisoned were liberated; full restitution was made for whatever was taken by violence or usury; many who had mortgaged houses and fields placed the money at Anthony's feet and sought his advice about reparation; the illicit fruits of fraud, extortion and bribery were restored to their legitimate owners; prostitutes were freed from their profession and thieves were restrained. The focal point of the sermon was a display of penitence by large numbers of men and women who confessed their sins to the friars and secular priests, who accompanied Anthony. The friars' preaching resulted in a heightened awareness of the canons of honesty; thus Ugolino Cavaze, a friar at Bologna, stated that his father had accumulated 'a great many things illicitly and dishonestly', as much through usury as any other way, as a mandate of 29 March 1237 explains.

The vexed question of restitution was one of the themes addressed in the friars' sermons.[27] While the parish church or local religious house was a normal venue for homilies, friars preached wherever people were assembled. Preaching in the open air was part of their ministry: many sermons were preached on the piazza, the fields or the sea shore.[28] During the penitential movement, known as the Alleluia movement, with its apocalyptic expectations in 1233 Gerard of Modena preached from a specially constructed platform in the piazza of Parma and elsewhere.[29] Berthold of Regensberg, one of the most talented and inspiring preachers of his generation, climbed into a wooden tower which was built like a bell tower, which he used in the fields as his pulpit. A wind-indicator was fitted to the top of the tower so that those present might ascertain the direction of the wind and select a good place to listen.[30]

[25] BL, MS Royal, 7. E. II, fol. 318ra. Cf. L. F. Sandler, *Omne Bonum: A Fourteenth-Century Encyclopedia of Universal Knowledge, British Library MSS Royal 6 E VI – 6 E VII*, 2 vols (London, 1996), II, p. 60.

[26] 'Quaestiones disputatae de perfectione evangelica', q. 2, a. 2, conc. ad ob. 20, *DSBOO*, V, pp. 147–8.

[27] *Vita prima o 'Assidua'*, c. 13, nn. 1–15, pp. 338–47, *Acta Franciscana e tabulariis Bononiensibus deprompta*, nn. 1165, 1168, pp. 592, 593, Salimbene, *Cronica*, p. 584.

[28] Boccaccio, *Decameron*, VI, 10, pp 455–6.

[29] Salimbene, *Cronica*, p. 108.

[30] Ibid., pp. 805–6, 813–19, Roger Bacon, *Opera*, p. 310.

The breadth of the friars' preaching

Francis preached in the presence of the clergy, cardinals and the pope.[31] Anthony of Padua, preaching at a synod, reproached the archbishop of Bourges for his vices, moving him to tears, contrition and devotion.[32] His sermons at the papal court were heard with the warmest devotion by the cardinals; Pope Gregory IX hailed him as the ark of the Testament.[33] Friars gained an early popularity with the monarchs and were invited to preach regularly at court and on special occasions. For example, Luke of Apuglia in 1233 delivered the sermon at the funeral of Henry, king of Germany, in the presence of the emperor, Frederick II. The friars of Paris quickly integrated themselves in the life of the new university and the city's parishes.[34]

The friars' ministry of preaching continued throughout the year, although it was sensitive to the demands of the harvest.[35] Preaching was intensified during Advent and Lent. Diocesan statutes from the later thirteenth century exhorted the clergy to receive the friars as preachers and confessors during these seasons.

While friars were perceived as an urban phenomenon, their influence was more widespread. They established a systematic programme for making annual visits to the parishes within their *limitatio*.[36] Peter of Cori, a novice at Bologna, accompanied an unnamed friar who was going to the village of Polesio to hear confessions.[37] The friars' ministry in mountainous regions was demonstrated by Humile of Milan. When he was appointed to the friary at Fano, he was zealous in the offices of preaching and hearing confessions during Lent. The people dwelling in the mountains invited him to preach. Accompanied by his companion, he spent many days preaching and hearing confessions. The friars' sermons in villages and remoter regions, even in bad weather, are exemplified by Simon da Collazione (†1250). Undeterred by the cold and snow, he preached in cities and villages.[38]

St Clare of Assisi was converted by the words and example of Francis, who received her vows at the Portiuncula during holy week in 1211 or 1212. She and other nobles of Assisi settled at San Damiano. He had prophesied that the church would one day be rendered famous through the lives of holy women. The community of nuns, living in accordance with Francis's insights,

---

[31] *CA*, c. 60, *Vita prima*, no. 73.

[32] *Vite 'Raymundina' e 'Rigaldina'*, c. 9, nn. 21–3, pp. 590–3.

[33] *Vita prima o 'Assidua'*, c. 10, nn. 1–4, pp. 320–5.

[34] Salimbene, *Cronica*, pp. 122–3, M. M. Davy, *Les Sermons universitaires Parisiens de 1230–1231*, Études de philosophie médiévale, XV (Paris, 1931), pp. 3–6, 349–60. Cf. Bériou, *L'Avènement*, II, pp. 704–13.

[35] *Vita prima o 'Assidua'*, c. 15, nn. 1–2, pp. 350–1.

[36] A. G. Little, *Franciscan Papers, Lists and Documents* (Manchester, 1943), p. 119.

[37] Salimbene, *Cronica*, pp. 837–8.

[38] Ibid., pp. 594–5, M. Faloci-Pulignani, 'Il Beato Simone de Collazzone e il suo processo nel 1252', *MF* 12 (1910), no. 10, pp. 97–132 at 104, 118.

was known as the order of Poor Ladies. Thomas of Celano's warm commendation of St Clare is all the more remarkable because it was circulated during her lifetime. The sisters' conversion and example ennobled and edified the whole order of friars, who were few in number at that time. Many of the early biographers of Francis and Clare were determined to project an image of irreproachable friendship. This produced a rather strained account of the communication between the two saints and nowhere more so than in the *Vita secunda*. A more refreshingly honest account is provided by Leo, Rufino and Angelo, who report that the ailing Francis was nursed for some fifty days at San Damiano, where he composed *The Canticle of Brother Sun*.[39] Between 1226 and her own death in 1253 Clare assumed Francis's mantle as the valiant defender of his ideals at a time when the order was changing. She was also a focal point of unity among the increasingly polarised body of friars, from Elias of Cortona to Giles of Assisi.

Francis's universal call to repentance was heeded by family men and women, who combined their domestic and familial responsibilities with a devotional and penitential life; a norm of life was compiled for them. Reflecting an earlier development among the Humiliati, Francis formed an order of penitents, which became known as the Third Order or tertiaries.[40] These men and women adapted the teaching of the saint to their domestic or social responsibilities. A large number of people at Hyères did penance for their sins. They were devoted to the friars and gladly attended their sermons. Men and women participated in the friars' prayers at Greccio. Numerous women preserved their virginity, wearing the garments of religion while dwelling in their own homes; they gave themselves to asceticism, fasting and prayer.[41] Members of the Third Order had a close spiritual affinity with the order, and many chose friars as their confessors and guides. The broad spectrum of medieval society was reflected in the Third Order.[42] Many members were interred in the friars' churches, such as Blesssed Umiliana de' Cerchi (†1246). There was a formal ceremony of admission. Some members attained the heights of personal sanctity and cults gathered around their tombs; among these were Rose of Viterbo (†1251) and Novellone of Faenza (†1280). The saints of the movement were honoured in the friars' sermons.[43]

[39] *Vita prima*, nn. 18–20, *CA*, cc. 83, 85.

[40] *Vita prima*, nn. 36–7, Cf. F. Andrews, *The Early Humiliati*, Cambridge Studies in Medieval Life and Thought, 4th Series, XLIII (Cambridge, 1999), p. 100.

[41] M. d'Alatri, ed. *Il movemento francescano della penitenza nella società medioevale*, Atti del terzo convegno di Studi francescani, Padova, 1979 (Rome, 1980), Salimbene, *Cronica*, p. 338. *CA*, c. 74.

[42] Cf. M. Bihl, 'Elenchi Bononienses fratrum de poenitentia S. Francisci (1252–88)', *AFH* 7 (1914), pp. 227–33.

[43] G. Abate, 'S. Rosa da Viterbo, Terziaria francescana (1233–51), Fonti storiche della vita et loro revisione critica', *MF* 52 (1952), pp. 133–278 at 239–41, F. Lanzoni, 'Una vita del Beato Novellone Faentino Terziario francescano (†1280) composta nel secolo XV', *AFH* 6 (1913), pp. 623–53, C. Cenci, 'San Pietro Pettinaio presentato da un predicatore senese contemporaneo', *StF* 87 (1990), pp. 5–30.

Francis's spiritual revolution exercised a strong appeal for groups of religious women as well as lay fraternities. Friars had close ties with female religious, such as St Douceline (*c.* 1215–74), the foundress of the Beguines of Marseilles, and St Clare of Montefalco (1268–1308).[44] Lay confraternities attached themselves to the friars and met in their churches.[45] An indulgence of 22 August 1257 for the confraternity of Santa Maria, Montefalco, confirms their weekly use of the friars' church.[46] The friars' preaching generated groups of penitents in numerous cities.[47] The guilds of shoe-makers, tailors, leather-workers and potmakers of Valencia sought the spiritual advice of the friars.[48] There is ample evidence of other confraternities and *laudesi* groups which gathered in the friars' churches to celebrate the divine praises.[49]

The friars' relations with their neighbours

It was not unknown for new religious orders to incur criticism and for fun to be poked at their saints, an experience also visited upon the friars.[50] At first the clergy welcomed the friars.[51] The friars' arrival was not perceived as a threat to the sacramental and liturgical life of the parish and the income of its rector or vicar; few of the early friars were ordained. Their work was of a manual nature or it took them to the fringes of society. They played a full part in the life of the parish, where they attended Mass and participated in the Divine Office.[52] The number of friars, however, increased towards the middle of the 1220s and the percentage of priests grew; one gauge of the growing number of priests is Pope Honorius III's *Quia populares tumultus* of 3 December 1224, permitting friars to erect altars and build domestic chapels.[53] These oratories were initially small and for internal use.

These developments did not escape the attention of the secular clergy, who feared the disruption of their parochial ministry. Moreover, the increase in

---

[44] *La Vie de Sainte Douceline fondatrice des béguines de Marseille*, ed. J. H. Albanés (Marseilles, 1879), *Il processo di canonizzazione di Chiara da Montefalco*, pp. 266–99.

[45] Salimbene, *Cronica*, p. 369.

[46] S. Nessi, 'Storia e arte delle chiese francescane di Montefalco', *MF* 62 (1962), pp. 232–332 at 237–8, 310–11.

[47] Cf. D'Alatri, ed. *I frati penitenti di San Francesco nella società del due e trecento*, Istituto Storico dei Cappuccini (Rome, 1977).

[48] R. I. Burns, *The Crusader Kingdom of Valencia: Reconstruction on a Thirteenth-Century Frontier*, 2 vols (Cambridge, Mass., 1967), p. 201.

[49] Cf. P. Guerrini, 'Gli statuti di una antica congregazione francescana di Brescia', *AFH* 1 (1908), pp. 544–68.

[50] For example, *De nugis curialium*, pp. 78–81, 84–113, A. Vauchez, 'Les Stigmates de saint François et leurs détracteurs dans les derniers siècles du moyen âge', *Mélanges d'archéologie et d'histoire* 80 (1968), pp. 595–625.

[51] As exemplified by the vicar and canon of the main church of Augsburg. Jordan of Giano, *Chronica*, no. 22, p. 27.

[52] As the Parisian sermon of Haymo of Faversham confirms. Eccleston, *Tractatus*, p. 9.

[53] *BF*, I, no. 17, p. 20.

the number of priests disturbed the balance which had hitherto prevailed between the priests and the friars. A parish priest, who might have been assisted by three or four chaplains, was now heavily outnumbered by the rapidly growing mendicant communities, which might include twenty-five or thirty friars, as at Paris in the later 1220s. The incumbent's ministry of the pulpit and confessional might be compared unfavourably with the gifted preachers and theologically articulate friars resident in his parish. Relations were exacerbated by the friars' more ambitious building plans from the later 1230s. There is ample evidence that both the secular clergy and the monks began to feel that their vested interests were jeopardised; both groups took action against the newcomers. The voice of clerical concern was raised before the death of Francis, when Hermann's sermons in Eisenach in 1225 mobilised the local clergy to express their foreboding about the loss of revenue. Six years later the master of a hospital in Mühlhausen, who feared that some of his revenues might be deflected to the friars, began to harass them.[54] As early as the 1240s some priests refused to receive the friars who visited their parishes. Buoyed by episcopal support, the secular clergy began to press their case against the friars.

Potential conflicts of interest with monks were not slow to surface and relations were strained on account of the friars' unwelcome presence in monastic towns. The flames of resentment were fanned by the defection of some monks to the Franciscans and the transfer of monastic churches to the new order. Examples of the friars' arrogance and boasting merely exacerbated relations with the monastic cosmos.[55] The friars' plans to open new houses in monastic towns in the 1230s were a source of friction and brought forth complaints that the friars were brash and arrogant. Caution should be exercised because the sources were monastic and they were inclined to make provocative comments about the newer religious orders.[56] The friars' activities at Vézélay, for example, aroused the monks' ire and relations deteriorated to the point where the monks took the law into their own hands. Pope Gregory IX's letter of 3 June 1233 announced that he had received reports that the monks had destroyed and pillaged the friary; the abbot and monks were excommunicated for this act. Nonetheless, the monks and the friars reached an agreement, which Gregory described as amicable. The friars were permitted to remain at Vézélay and celebrate the liturgy. A comparable new

---

[54] *BF*, I, nn. 41, 45, pp. 37, 40.

[55] Shortly after the friars' arrival at Roxburgh, fears that their popularity might undermine the local burial practices exercised the monks of Kelso, a Tironian community. Anticipating what would become a major bone of contention elsewhere, the monks orchestrated a skilful campaign which limited the order to the burial of its own members. A contract was agreed and the friars' cemetery was consecrated by the bishop of Glasgow on 13 September 1235. *Liber S. Marie de Calchou, Registrum cartarum abbacie Tironensis de Kelso, 1113–1567*, II, ed. C. Innes (Edinburgh, 1846), no. 418, p. 321.

[56] C. H. Lawrence, *St Edmund of Abingdon: A Study in Hagiography and History* (Oxford, 1960), pp. 276–7.

friary was to be constructed in place of the one which had been destroyed. Nonetheless, steps were taken to safeguard monastic revenues and restrictions were placed upon the friars' liturgical activities.[57]

The perception that the friars were attempting to extend their sphere of influence at the monks' expense lay behind more than one dispute. The friction between the abbey of St Martin and friars at Limoges in the 1240s is richly documented. The friars arrived there in 1223 and lodged initially at the church of St Paul. Anthony of Padua arrived about two years later as the *custos* of the group of friaries in the area and in 1226 he transferred the friars from the original site to the land owned by the abbey of St Martin. Peter Coral, abbot of St Martin, reports that Anthony entered into a contract whereby the friars settled on land belonging to the monastery, although certain agreements and conditions were imposed. Within a short time the friars wished to break free and complained that the monks were holding them to the original conditions. They began to build at an early date, between 1227 and 1242; a legal document of 26 May 1239 mentions the friars' church. However, the monks complained that the friars had acted beyond their powers and obliged them to withdraw in 1243. On 21 January 1245 the pope wrote to the bishop of Angoulême, stating that John Pineta and some burgesses of the town had purchased land on the friars' behalf for the construction of a friary with the consent of the abbot and monastery, whose land it was. The name of Christ was invoked by the monastic chronicler to emphasise that the monks were not culpable in this matter; blame was laid entirely at the friars' door.[58]

The complaints of the clergy and monks found support in the writings and example of Francis, who believed that God had appointed him and his followers to supplement the apostolate of prelates and clergy; this is a salient feature of his writings, especially his *Testament*. The concerns of several friars were articulated by Leo, Rufino and Angelo, who appealed to the founder's belief and practice at a time when friars were slipping into conflict with the local clergy. The saint's companions regarded such disputes as a betrayal of his heritage and the order's rationale. They reaffirmed the conviction that evangelical poverty should govern the friars' decisions about the kind of sites offered to them; friars were to live as pilgrims and strangers in small communities, where the virtue of evangelical poverty was to be enshrined; proprietary rights should be eschewed. At a time when the mendicant churches were being built on a larger scale, they protested that the new churches should be small. The friars would give much better example by preaching in the parish churches.[59] The success of the friars' mission of preaching was rooted in the appropriate level of preparation, the focus of the next chapter.

---

[57] *BF*, I, nn. 110, 111, pp. 110–12.

[58] Delorme, 'Les Cordeliers', pp. 215–22.

[59] *CA*, c. 58.

CHAPTER FIVE

Preparation for the Apostolate

Although the friars were vowed to absolute simplicity ... , they were so eager to study the divine law and undergo scholastic training that they did not hesitate to travel to the theological schools daily even in the midst of cold and deep mud.

Thomas of Eccleston[1]

The origins of the friars' schools

Francis shared some of the monastic reservations about theological study in the cathedral schools. There were, nonetheless, important changes taking place which impinged upon him. Friars working in northern Italy and southern France required a solid form of training, one fitted to stemming the tide of heresy. Proponents of heretical views were well versed in the explanation and dissemination of their propaganda. Good will and integrity of life alone were blunt instruments to deploy against such well-organised and highly articulate groups. The differing circumstances in the cities of Italy and France are reflected in the biographies of Francis and Anthony of Padua. While the former was an inspirational preacher, the latter toiled in regions where support was haemorrhaging from the Church. Canons 10 and 11 of the Fourth Lateran Council made a clear connection between theological instruction and the office of preaching. The strength of Francis's links with the papal court left him in no doubt that the Church's mission of evangelisation presupposed a supply of zealous, talented and orthodox preachers. Although it is probable that he took counsel on how best to respond to the demands of the Church, his answer was masterly. The connection between theology and virtue was restored, implicitly harking back to an earlier age in which zealous pastors skilfully expounded the faith, combining this with the search for holiness of life. This union set the tone for theological study in the order.

Monasticism drew both masters and students from the cathedral schools. This is exemplified by Bernard of Clairvaux's celebrated sermon to the masters of Paris, who were exhorted to swap the school for the cloister.[2] The

---

[1] Eccleston, *Tractatus*, p. 27.
[2] Geoffrey of Auxerre, *S. Bernardi vita prima*, IV, 11, 10, in Patrologia Latina 183, 327.

change of mood occurred in the 1220s; one of its fruits was the canonisation of Edmund of Abingdon, who lectured at Oxford until 1222. The perceived incompatibility between virtue and learning was being eroded. The recovery of the link between holiness and life and theological acumen meant that it was no longer necessary to quit the schools in search of personal sanctity, something reflected in the speedy canonisation of Anthony of Padua on 30 May 1232. Anthony began his teaching at Bologna, at the instigation of the founder. Francis's condition – that study should not extinguish the spirit of prayer – echoes chapter five of the Rule. The first lector in the order devoted himself to the preparation of friars for their ministry.[3] His stay in the university city was short and within a year or so he was sent to southern France, where he taught at Montpellier and Toulouse.[4] Anthony's teaching in southern France was conditioned by the pastoral agenda of the beleaguered local church. The threat of heresy and the pressing need to teach sound doctrine were priorities. His theological formation was shaped by the biblical emphasis of the cathedral schools, although some of his masters had studied in the nascent University of Paris.[5] The sermons which he composed for Sundays and feast days offer an insight into his teaching methods. Although in both France and Italy he filled administrative offices, he returned to Padua, where he preached, heard confessions and taught theology.[6]

Francis's decision about schools received encouragement from a small group of prelates. Jacques de Vitry helped to assuage the anxieties of some friars who were troubled by such developments.[7] The advice of Robert Grosseteste, bishop of Lincoln (1235–53), was that, unless the friars embraced theological study, they would certainly fall into the same state as other religious who were living in darkness. This was sound counsel in an era of proliferating religious groups, many of which had a short life. Similar support came from William of Auvergne, protector of the order's privileges and bishop of Paris (1229–48), and Eudes of Châteauroux, chancellor of the university (1228–44) and then cardinal bishop (1246–73).[8] The ministers general and provincial were involved in the supply of lectors. John Parenti and John of Parma provided lectors for Magdeburg in 1228 and Genoa in 1248 respectively.[9] The response of the former offered telling evidence of the heightened place of

3   *Vita del 'Dialogus' e 'Benignitas'*, ed. V. Gamboso, Fonti agiografiche antoniane, III (Padua, 1986), c. 13, no. 2, pp. 496–7.

4   Ibid., c. 17, no. 3, pp. 518–19. *'Liber miraculorum' e altri testi medievali*, ed. V. Gamboso, Fonti agiografiche antoniane, V (Padua, 1997), c. 3, nn. 1–4, pp. 214–15 and appendix II, no. 4, pp. 526–9.

5   *Vita prima o 'Assidua'*, c. 4, pp. 282–7.

6   *Vite 'Raymundina' e 'Rigaldina'*, c. 6, no. 24, pp. 548–9, *Vita prima o 'Assidua'*, c. 11, nn. 2, 7, pp. 326–9, 332–5.

7   Pitra, *Analecta novissima. Spicilegii Solesmensis altera continuatio*, II (Frascati, 1888), p. 403.

8   Eccleston, *Tractatus*, p. 91, 'Jacobi Vitriacensis episcopi et cardinalis (1180–1240): sermones ad fratres minores', p. 121.

9   Salimbene, *Cronica*, pp. 431–2.

theological study by prevailing upon Simon Anglicus, minister provincial of Germany (1227–8), to exchange his office for that of the lector at Magdeburg.[10] The promotion of theological studies was the single virtue attributed to Elias of Cortona as minister general. John of Parma argued that the order rested on the walls of learning and good example.[11] He sent Bonaventure to lecture as a bachelor at Paris in 1248 and Ralph of Corbridge, still a novice, as the second friar to serve as lector at Oxford.[12] Despite powerful support, the order's theologians trod warily and the apologetic tone of their writings implies some deep-seated reservations among their confreres.[13]

One important fruit of the schools was the study of the art of preaching. Apart from the collections of sermons for Sundays and feast days assembled by Bonaventure of Iseo, Thomas of Pavia and Servansanto of Faenza, the friars expended much energy and resources in the production of aids for preachers.[14] The sermons of Anthony of Padua consisted of a series of notes and themes rather than a transcript of the homilies; they were written for the benefit of itinerant friars.[15] *Exemplum* collections were assembled by friars in England, France, Ireland and Italy for the benefit of preachers.[16]

The studia generalia *of Paris and Oxford*

The mendicant vision exercised a strong influence in the schools. The leading school of the order was established at Paris, the first *studium generale* to offer a degree in theology in the thirteenth century. Scholars have speculated on the establishment of a friars' school there before 1236.[17] The arrival of Alexander of Hales brought the friars' school into the heart of the faculty of theology. The new views regarding the compatibility of theological studies and the search for moral integrity meant that Alexander could remain on the banks of the River Seine. During his novitiate year he continued his lectures, which were open to members of the university. He was regarded as

---

[10] Jordan of Giano, *Chronica*, no. 54, pp. 47–8.

[11] Salimbene, *Cronica*, p. 147, Eccleston, *Tractatus*, p. 74.

[12] Salimbene, *Cronica*, p. 435, Eccleston, *Tractatus*, pp. 50–1.

[13] Cf. Eccleston, *Tractatus*, p. 91, F. M. Delorme, 'Textes franciscains', *Archivo italiano per la storia della pietà*, 1 (1951), pp. 179–218, at 214–16.

[14] Salimbene, *Cronica*, pp. 384. 621. Cf. Padua, Biblioteca Antoniana, MSS. 442–7, V. Gamboso, 'I sermoni "De communi" e "De proprio sanctorum" di Servasanto nei codici 520 e 530 di Assisi', *Il santo* 13 (1973), pp. 211–78.

[15] *S. Antonii Patavini, O. Min. doctoris evangelici sermones dominicales et festivi ad fidem codicum recogniti*, ed. B. Costa, L. Frasson, I. Luisetto and P. Marangon, 3 vols (Padua, 1979).

[16] *Le Speculum laicorum: édition d'une collection d'exempla, composée en Angleterre à la fin du XIIIe siècle*, ed. J. Th. Welter (Paris, 1914).

[17] Cf. J. Bougerol, 'Le origini e la finalità dello studio nell'ordine francescano', *Antonianum* 53 (1978), pp. 405–22 at 408–9, I. C. Brady, 'S. Bonaventura alunno della scuola francescana di Parigi', *Incontri bonaventuriani, l'uomo Bonaventura: Atti del XIII incontro al cenacolo bonaventuriano dell' Oasi Maria Immacolata di Montecalvo Irpino 27–9 Settembre 1972*, 9, 1972, pp. 63–74 at 64, n. 1.

the first to have lectured on the *Sentences of Master Peter Lombard*, which became a medium for theological study in the Parisian schools in the 1230s. He was also credited with the subdivision of that text into distinctions for the benefit of scholars.[18] Although the *Summa fratris Alexandri* remained unfinished at his death on 21 August 1245, it was completed by members of the school by command of Pope Alexander IV on 7 October 1255.[19]

Alexander was succeeded by Jean de la Rochelle, Eudes Rigaud and William Melitona, prolific and influential writers on a range of scriptural and theological topics. The *domus Parisiensis* exerted an influence upon the entire order because it trained masters and lectors who returned to lecture in their own provinces. The order's major theologians studied or lectured there. This school was recognised as the most prestigious *studium* in the order. Its unrivalled position was enshrined in the general constitutions of Narbonne, which regulated the appointment and conduct of the friars sent there. Students were required to remain there for a minimum of three or four years, with the exception of those selected for the office of lector. Each province was entitled to send two students without any special provision and such students were to be supplied with books at the decision of the minister provincial and definitory.[20] Bonaventure was the fifth master of theology and one of its most distinguished *alumni*. His successors were Gilbert of Tournai, John Pecham, Matthew of Acquasparta and Walter of Bruges. The theological tradition of the order was shaped by an adherence to the heritage of Augustine of Hippo. It was also marked by an uneasiness about an uncritical application of Aristotle's heritage to the study of theology. The order's focus on the contingency of the Incarnation and the Immaculate Conception reached its apex in the writings of John Duns Scotus, who experienced each of the three *studia generalia* at the universities of Paris, Oxford and Cambridge.[21]

There was a comparable movement at Oxford, whose university conferred degrees in theology from the 1220s. Some of the Oxonian masters were trained in Paris, although English masters, such as Richard Rufus of Cornwall and Roger Bacon, were selected to lecture on the banks of the river Seine. Before the summer of 1225 many impressive bachelors were admitted to the order at the house donated by Robert le Mercer in the parish of St Ebbe. Numbered among the early recruits between 1227 and 1232 were masters who brought lustre to the order: Walter of Burgh, Richard of Normandy, Vincent and Henry of Coventry, Adam of Oxford, William of York

---

[18] *Chronicon de Lanercost*, p. 53. I. C. Brady, 'The Distinctions of Lombard's Book of Sentences and Alexander of Hales', *FS* 25 (1965), pp. 90–116, 115.

[19] Cf. *Summa fratris Alexandri studio et cura PP. Collegii S. Bonaventurae ad fidem codicum edita*, 6 vols (Quaracchi, Florence, 1924–48, 1979). Cf. Roger Bacon, *Opera*, pp. 326–9. V. Doucet, 'The History of the Problem of the Authenticity of the Summa', *FS* 7 (1947), pp. 26–41, 274–312.

[20] Bihl, 'Statuta generalia' (Narbonne), VI, nn. 13–19, p. 72.

[21] *Ioannis Duns Scoti doctoris Mariani Theologiae Marianae elementa quae ad fidem codd. MSS*, ed. C. Balic, Bibliotheca Mariana medii aevi (Sibenik, 1933), pp. 1–10, 17–43.

and Adam Marsh.[22] Encouraged by the recruitment of bachelors and masters of theology, Agnellus of Pisa, the minister provincial, took the step of constructing a small school which came to play a leading role within the nascent university. While the direction of the school could have been entrusted to one of the numerous recruits, Agnellus's seriousness of purpose is evinced by his approach to Master Robert Grosseteste, one of the luminaries of Oxford and a man of encyclopaedic interests.[23]

Agnellus's audacious invitation paid handsome dividends: Grosseteste accepted, and communicated his pastoral vision. Under his tutelage the friars made excellent progress both in dealing with questions and in preaching on difficult moral problems. Grosseteste taught the friars from 1229/30 until his election as bishop of Lincoln on 25 March 1235.[24] This time as lector coincided with a fertile period in which he completed the *Hexaëmeron* and the *De cessatione legalium*, as well as compiling biblical commentaries and increasing his knowledge of and translating from the Greek theologians.[25] His exceptional linguistic ability and command of Greek were praised by Roger Bacon.[26] He and Adam Marsh, the first friar to serve as lector at Oxford (his *Lectura super Genesim* was written before 1248),[27] with whom he collaborated on some scientific projects, were deemed perfect in all wisdom and philosophy, divine and human. Their teaching was rooted in the exposition of the Scriptures, but was combined with a remarkable originality.[28] Andrew Little notes that Oxford seems to have been the only friars' school to engage secular masters, a decision he ascribes to the exceptional abilities of Grosseteste.[29] Another luminary of the school was John Duns Scotus.

The University of Cambridge arose as a result of a secession of masters and students from Oxford in 1209 and became a *studium generale* which began to confer degrees of theology.[30] The friars were also present in the town *c.* 1225 and contributed significantly to the study of theology.[31] The first masters of the new university were generally trained at Oxford and mirror the dif-

---

[22] A. G. Little, *The Grey Friars in Oxford*, Oxford Historical Society, XX (Oxford, 1892), Eccleston, *Tractatus*, pp. 15–18, 22.

[23] Cf. S. Gieben, 'Robert Grosseteste on Preaching, with the Edition of the Sermon "Ex rerum initiatarum" on Redemption', *CF* 37 (1967), pp. 100–41 at 100–7.

[24] Eccleston, *Tractatus*, p. 48.

[25] Robert Grosseteste, *Hexaëmeron*, ed. R. C. Dales and Gieben, Auctores Britannici medii aevi, VI (London, 1982), Robert Grosseteste, *De cessatione legalium*, ed. R. C. Dales and E. B. King, Auctores Britannici medii aevi, VII (London, 1986).

[26] Roger Bacon, *Opera*, p. 91.

[27] Salimbene, *Cronica*, pp. 431–2.

[28] Ibid., pp. 70, 75, 328–9.

[29] A. G. Little, 'The Franciscan School at Oxford in the Thirteenth Century', *AFH* 19 (1926), pp. 803–74 at 807.

[30] Cf. D. R. Leader, *A History of the University of Cambridge, I, The University to 1546* (Cambridge, 1988).

[31] Little, *Franciscan Papers, Lists, and Documents*, pp. 122–43.

fusion of higher studies from the older institution throughout the English province. Although Cambridge remained in the shadow of Oxford for the remainder of the thirteenth century, its stature grew, as is reflected in the appointment of William of Melitona, Thomas of York, Roger Marston and Thomas of Bungay as its masters. Its special position as a *studium generale* was recognised by the constitutions of Pope Benedict XII in 1336.[32] It attracted both masters and students from other provinces.[33]

The network of friars' schools

By the middle of the thirteenth century the order had followed the Dominicans into the schools. The friars' growing ease and confidence in theological matters is reflected in the comment by Hugh of Digne after his lengthy debate with Peter of Apuglia, the Dominican lector, that the followers of *il poverello* could no longer be described as a bunch of ignorant men.[34] The friars committed themselves to theological studies so successfully that they took a position of leadership, which was acknowledged both inside and outside the fraternity. Roger Bacon maintained that from 1230 the secular masters had neglected the study of theology and philosophy, leaving the two mendicant orders to fill the vacuum in the queen of the sciences.[35] On both sides of the Alps friars were devoting themselves to the study of theology.[36] A threefold layer of schools was taking shape by the middle of the century.

First, the smallest communities excepted, each friary had its own lector. Lectors kept their own notebooks for teaching, produced sermons, theological writings and the lives of saints, all of which presupposed some precision and finesse in theology.[37] On occasion guardians and lectors were invited to attend local synods. Writing in 1284, Salimbene affirms that during his first year in the order he attended lectures on Isaiah and Matthew. From that time he had never ceased his studies.[38] The lector was responsible for the theological instruction of the entire community; not even the senior friars were exempt from the lectures. He had a particular responsibility for ordinands and he examined candidates for the office of preaching. The order developed its own equivalent to the *fratres communes* among the Dominicans, that is, the friars who did not attend the custodial schools or the universities.[39] These

---

[32] M. Bihl, 'Ordinationes a Benedicto XII pro fratribus minoribus promulgatae per bullam 28 Novembris 1336', *AFH* 30 (1938), c. IX, nn. 1–3, pp. 309–90 at 346.

[33] Cf. J. R. H. Moorman, *The Grey Friars of Cambridge 1225–1538* (Cambridge, 1952).

[34] Salimbene, *Cronica*, p. 364.

[35] Roger Bacon, *Opera*, p. 428.

[36] Visconti, *Sermons*, nn. 8, 12, pp. 688, 771.

[37] For example, V. Gamboso, '"Franciscanus Paduanus". I quattro sermoni sanfrancescani di frate Luca Lettore da Padova (c. 1270)', *Il santo* 30 (1990), pp. 3–76.

[38] Salimbene, *Cronica*, pp. 580–1, 402.

[39] Ibid., pp. 452–3, L. Boyle, 'Notes on the Education of the "Fratres communes" in the Dominican

friars persevered in their theological studies, which informed and sustained them in the apostolate as preachers and confessors.

Secondly, the more able students were dispatched to the custodial schools for higher studies. At this level there were two lectors, bachelors and others entrusted with various levels of instruction. Friars were designated to teach philosophy and biblical studies as well as theology. Scholastic stratification was evolving as early as 1248 in the experience of Benedict of Colle and Gerard of Prato, who had studied at Pisa for many years before being sent to Toulouse to prepare themselves for study at Paris.[40] The general constitutions ordained that those sent to study at Paris should be assigned to a house of studies in their own or a neighbouring province for two or three years after the novitiate, unless they had already attended the schools.[41] Candidates for the doctorate spent only one or two years lecturing on the Sentences at a *studium* before returning to the university to read the same text.[42] Lectors were in close touch with the *studia generalia* and made decisions about students proceeding to the universities. Many fine lectors functioned at custodial level, which was not much below that of the *studia generalia*.[43]

Thirdly, a smaller number of friars attended the *studia generalia* of Paris, Oxford and Cambridge in preparation for appointments as lectors in provincial schools, but a small number advanced to the baccalaureate or the doctorate, following the same preparation as the lectors.[44] The path to the doctorate was a prolonged one in the thirteenth century, taking as long as twenty-three years.[45] The post of the regent-master in theology was held for relatively short periods, probably on account of the flow of talented theologians who were waiting in the wings. There were two intersecting courses of study available in the University of Paris. One was directly linked to the university, training candidates for graduation as bachelors and masters of theology. The other was internal and prepared friars for the office of lector; it was not governed by the statutes of the university. Friars enrolled for the lector's course greatly outnumbered those selected for degrees.[46] The universal influence of the Parisian school was recognised by the general chapter of 1266, affirming that friars from many provinces received their theological formation.[47] Among the lectors trained in the shadow of the University of Paris were friars of con-

Order in the Thirteenth Century', in *Xenia medii aevi historiam illustrantia oblata Thomae Kaeppeli O.P.*, ed. R. Creytens and P. Künzle, Storia e letteratura raccolta di studi e testi, CXLI (Rome, 1978), pp. 249–67.

[40] Salimbene, *Cronica*, p. 453.

[41] Bihl, 'Statuta generalia' (Narbonae), VI, no. 12, p. 72.

[42] W. J. Courtenay, *Adam Wodeham: An Introduction to His Life and Writings*, Studies in Medieval and Reformation Thought, XXI (Leiden, 1978), pp. 45–53.

[43] W. J. Courtenay, *Schools and Scholars in Fourteenth-Century England* (Princeton, 1987), p. 67.

[44] For example J. A. Sheppard, 'Vita Scoti', *FS* 60 (2002), pp. 291–323 at 297.

[45] J. Marenbon, *Later Medieval Philosophy (1150–1350), An Introduction* (London, 1987), pp. 21–2.

[46] Courtenay, 'The Parisian Franciscan Community in 1303', *FS* 53 (1993), pp. 155–73 at 157–9.

[47] Little, 'Definitiones capitularum generalium', p. 678, no. 1.

trasting fortunes: Rainaldo of Arezzo and Gerard of Borgo San Donnino. Rainaldo was sent by the convent of Siena and served as lector of Rieti before becoming bishop there.[48] Gerard was to go to the province of Sicily, but died in disgrace because of the stubbornness of his apocalyptic views.[49]

The order's early theologians worked initially within the traditional compass of biblical studies.[50] Glosses on the Bible featured among the books used by the friars or donated to them.[51] Friars preparing for the pastoral ministry required a good working knowledge of Canon Law.[52] This dimension of the friars' studies became more prominent from the middle of the century, especially with scholars like the papal penitentiary, Claire of Florence, author of a *Summa de casibus*.

This educational enterprise was sustained by collections of books, which laid the foundations for the formation of impressive libraries. Manuscripts were donated by benefactors and novices while others were copied by the friars.[53] The friars' libraries in the universities were exceptional. M. B. Parkes comments that 'the first signs of organisation or corporate enterprise' in the supply of books for study at Oxford lie in the activity of the Dominicans and Franciscans.[54] As early as 1234 friars were purchasing books. John de Kethene bought a glossed copy of the Bible in the 1240s.[55] The theft of the books from the friaries was frequently reported, and occurs in the *vita* of St Anthony of Padua. Unease about the friars' access to books, and its implications for the observance of evangelical poverty however, are mirrored in the writings of Leo and the early companions of St Francis.[56]

---

[48] Salimbene, *Cronica*, pp. 468–89, 472.

[49] Ibid., pp. 341–2.

[50] Exemplified by Bartholomaeus Anglicus, who lectured cursorily on the whole Bible at Paris. His *De proprietatibus rerum* enjoyed a wide popularity. Alexander of Hales, Jean de la Rochelle and William of Meltiona produced biblical commentaries. Salimbene, *Cronica*, p. 134, I. C. Brady, 'Sacred Scripture in the Early Franciscan School', *La sacra scrittura e i francescani*, Pontificium Athenaeum Antonianum, Studium Biblicum Franciscanum (Rome, 1973), pp. 65–82.

[51] Bartolo of Palmerio of San Gimignano, for example, left five *libras* to the local friary for the purchase of glossed books of the Gospel on 6 June 1282. *Carte dell'Archivio arcivescovile di Pisa: Fondi Luoghi Vari, 3 (1281–1300)*, ed. L. Carratori and R. P. Monti (Pisa, 1997), no. 29, pp. 102–3.

[52] Manfred of Tortona, a disciple of Alexander of Hales and Jean de la Rochelle, compiled a *Summa de casibus*. Cf. B. Kurtscheid, 'De studio iuris canonici in ordine fratrum minorum saeculo XIII', *Antonianum* 2 (1927), pp. 157–202.

[53] Cf. K. W. Humphreys, 'Le biblioteche francescane in Italia nei secoli XIII e XIV', E. Menestò, 'La biblioteca di Matteo d'Acquasparta', in *Francesco d'Assisi, documenti e archivi, codici e biblioteche, miniature*, ed. F. Porzio (Milan, 1982), pp. 135–42.

[54] M. B. Parkes, 'The Provision of Books', *The History of the University of Oxford, II, Late Medieval Oxford*, ed. J. I. Catto and R. Evans (Oxford, 1992), pp. 407–83 at 431.

[55] J. N. Hillgarth, *Readers and Books in Majorca 1229–1550*, Documents, études et répertoires publiés par l'Institut de recherche et d'histoire des textes, in 2 vols (Paris, 1991), I, p. 15, n. 57, Eccleston, *Tractatus*, p. 43.

[56] '*Liber miraculorum*' e altri testi medievali, pp. 214–15, *CA*, cc. 101, 103.

Friars and the local clergy, secular and religious

The fact that John of Piano Carpini, Haymo of Faversham and Peter of Tewkesbury were celebrated as outstanding defenders of the order offers telling commentary on some strained relations with the secular clergy.[57] Salimbene allots a significant amount of space to the disputes between friars and the clergy. He records the six grounds of frustration articulated by Matulino of Ferrara, who asserted that the friars did not support the system of tithes; they buried the dead in their churches; they flouted the will of the secular clergy in hearing confessions; they arrogated to themselves the office of preaching; their conventual Masses deflected people and offerings from the parish churches and they were unduly familiar with women. Another critic was Master Guido Bonatti of Forlì, who debated with Hugh of Reggio. These polemical exchanges point to a context not unlike the public disputations between heretics and friars in southern France, as recounted by Jordan of Saxony. Hugh attacked the enemies of the order, confuting and overwhelming them by his preaching and examples. He convincingly routed Guido before the whole population of Forlì.[58]

The intensification of the complaints of the secular clergy found many outlets. Priests turned away the friars who wished to preach in their parishes and there was some episcopal backing for plans to circumscribe the friars' activities. There was speculation that a move would be made against the friars at the first council of Lyons in 1245.[59] The haemorrhaging of support from the parish church undermined the spiritual authority of the parochial clergy and threatened their revenue. Pope Innocent IV was persuaded to act against the friars and condemned them on eight points. Although he was not disposed to limit access to the mendicant churches, the pope later decreed that the friars should not open their doors from matins until after terce. He took steps to protect the liturgical and sacramental life of the parishes from the friars' encroachments. In contrast, the friars protested against the legislation. They reported that when *Etsi animarum* of 21 November 1254 was read out, Innocent lost the power of speech. They triumphantly announced that the restrictive decree had been abrogated by the new pope, Alexander IV (1254–61), their former cardinal protector.[60] For example, Alexander instructed the archbishop of Milan and the bishop of Imola to protect the friars of Lombardy and Ravenna in a letter of 8 January 1257.[61] The friars parried criticism of encroachment upon the rights of the parochial clergy

---

[57] Jordan of Giano, *Chronica*, no. 55, pp. 48–9, Eccleston, *Tractatus*, pp. 28, 91.

[58] Salimbene, *Cronica*, pp. 610–11, 239.

[59] *Monumenta Franciscana*, I, ed. J. S. Brewer and R. Howlett, 2 vols, RS, IV (London, 1858/1882), pp. 376–8.

[60] Eccleston, *Tractatus*, pp. 94–5, Salimbene, *Cronica*, pp. 607–8.

[61] P. M. Sevesi, 'Documenta hucusque inedita saeculi XIII pro historia almae fratrum minorum provinciae Mediolanensis [seu Lombardiae]', *AFH* 2 (1909), pp. 561–74 at 567.

by asserting that people were attracted to their churches by their dignified celebration of Mass.[62]

Welcomed to the universities in the 1220s, the friars did not easily fit into the structures of an academic community. Their anomalous position was highlighted by their refusal to back the secular masters during the dispute of 1253/4. They were accused of having a semi-detached attitude towards the corporation of masters. The university authorities regarded the friars as availing of its privileges without submitting themselves completely to its governance. The *locus classicus* for this struggle was Paris, where the friars' attitude of aloofness stoked up bitterness.[63] Following a dispute between town and university in 1253, the masters of the university proclaimed a strike and a letter of 4 February 1254 notified the bishops of their grievances against the mendicants. The secular masters complained that the friars were already teaching theology in cities and large towns, a factor which was causing a disturbing decline in the number of students at Paris; this in turn raised questions about the sustainability of twelve magisterial chairs. It was decreed that henceforth mendicant masters would be obliged to swear an oath to observe the university's statutes.[64]

The order's chroniclers underline the efforts of John of Parma to defuse tensions in the university. In response to the flames fanned by William of St Amour, John preached disarmingly in the presence of masters and scholars. He affirmed that the friars had derived their theological instruction from the secular masters, whose servants, sons and disciples they were.[65] The Parisian masters limited the number of chairs of theology occupied by the mendicants. While those enrolled to read theology were graduates from the faculty of arts, the friars claimed an exemption on the grounds that their candidates for degrees had been adequately prepared in custodial *studia*. The appearance of Gerard of Borgo San Donnino's *Liber introductorius ad evangelium aeternum*, however, raised the stakes and played into the hands of the secular masters. The text circulated outside the order and the secular masters exploited the book's thirty-one errors, which stemmed from Gerard's interpretation of the apocalyptic teaching of Joachim of Fiore. Led by William of St Amour, the university sent a delegation to the papal curia at Anagni to seek the condemnation of the book.[66] Gerard's intemperate volume was condemned on 4 November 1255. The masters swapped pamphlets with the friars and what

---

[62] Salimbene, *Cronica*, pp. 607, 615–16, Van Dijk and Walker, *The Origins of the Modern Roman Liturgy*, pp. 56–7, n. 4.

[63] D. L. Douie, 'St. Bonaventura's Part in the Conflict between Seculars and Mendicants in Paris', in *S. Bonaventura 1274–1974*, II, ed. J. Bougerol *et al.* (Grottaferrata, Roma, 1973), pp. 585–612. G. Leff, *Heresy in the Later Middle Ages: The Relation of Heterodoxy to Dissent c. 1250 – c. 1450*, I (Manchester, 1967), pp. 51–68.

[64] *Chartularium universitatis Parisiensis*, I, ed. H. Denifle, 4 vols (Paris, 1889–97), no. 230, pp. 252–8.

[65] Salimbene, *Cronica*, pp. 436–8.

[66] Ibid., pp. 341–2, 663–4.

began as a local dispute gave rise to the first sustained assault on the theological foundations of the order. This dispute about the government of the faculty of theology was broadened to raise numerous issues of discipline and theology, especially the friars' right to preach and celebrate the sacraments.

The death of Innocent IV on 7 December 1254 removed a pope sympathetic to the cause of the secular masters. The pendulum swung in the direction of the friars with the election of Pope Alexander IV. The focus of the debate switched from the procedure for the friars' admission to the faculty of theology to the more fundamental question of the friars' vocation and its scriptural basis. William of St Amour's *Quaestiones disputatae*, delivered in Advent of the following year, opened a debate with Bonaventure. The friars' practice of questing for alms was placed under the microscope, as was the validity of the personal renunciation to live off alms. As in monastic debates about renewal, the spectre of manual work was raised and there were ample scriptural texts to be invoked against the friars on a range of subjects. The friars' link between preaching and the expectation of alms was scrutinised. Moreover, it was pointed out that Christ possessed a purse, a scriptural text which would haunt the friars in 1322/3. These criticisms were amplified and developed in William's *De periculis novissimorum temporum*, which was completed between March and September 1256. He argued that no religious order depending on alms while they preached could be saved.[67] In addition, he exploited the apocalyptic climate to liken the friars to the pseudo-prophets predicted by St Paul. The friars stood accused of hypocrisy. It was argued that the office of preaching should not be exercised by the friars. *De periculis novissimorum temporum* was condemned by Pope Alexander IV on 5 October 1256 and its author was expelled from Paris by Louis IX on 9 August 1257.[68] Such polemics against the friars, however, took their toll on recruitment and provided the basis for anti-mendicant satire, which arose at this time and enjoyed a long life.[69] Anti-mendicant feeling was stirred up by the poet Rutebeuf, who drew upon the arguments of William of St Amour.[70] Pope Alexander IV's support for the friars in this protracted dispute was critical. The nature of the bond between popes and friars forms the basis of the next chapter.

---

[67] *Chronique latine de Guillaume de Nangis de 1113 à 1300 avec les continuations de cette chronicque de 1300 à 1368*, ed. H. Géraud, 2 vols (Paris, 1843), I, pp. 209, 216–17, P. Glorieux, 'Le Conflit de 1252–7 à la lumiere du Memoire de Guillaume de Saint-Amour', *Recherches de théologie ancienne et médiévale* 24 (1957), pp. 364–72.

[68] *BF*, II, no. 241, pp. 160–2.

[69] Salimbene, *Cronica*, pp. 74, 437–8.

[70] Rutebeuf, *Oeuvres complètes*, I, pp. 242–8, 256–66.

CHAPTER SIX

Friars and the Papacy

Above all other religious the Friars Minor, who profess a most profound humility, should show the utmost reverence to the pope.

John Pecham[1]

The order's hagiography and artistic tradition proclaimed Francis's good relations with three popes, Innocent III, Honorius III and Gregory IX. These claims were confirmed by the way in which the friars became instruments of papal reforms throughout Christendom. They emphasised the strength of the partnership between the popes and the friars.

Friars and papal strategy

The friars' preparation for their ministry made them a dedicated and efficient body of men, whose ecclesiology was marked by a strong fidelity to the Church and the pope as the successor of St Peter. Gregory IX and the succeeding popes played a central role in promoting and channelling the friars' ministry. Francis's close relations with the papacy are reflected in his presence at the death bed of Innocent III; his followers attended the dying Honorius III, Gregory IX and Innocent IV.[2] The office of cardinal protector bound the order closely to the heart of the Church, and it was initially filled by men who held key positions in the Roman curia. This reciprocal relationship is reflected in the request of the curial cardinals that Francis should release a friar for each household.[3] Friars were also drawn into episcopal households, serving as chaplains, confessors and theologians. While papal letters facilitated the geographical spread of the order, the popes looked to the order as a band of talented men capable of shouldering various missions. *Ab initio* friars were drawn into the service of the Roman Curia and from the 1220s several served as papal penitentiaries. One of them was Nicholas da Calvi, who was successively chaplain, confessor and biographer of Sinibaldo

---

[1] John Pecham, 'Expositio super regulam fratrum minorum', c. 1, no. 11, *DSBOO*, VIII, pp. 391–437, 396.

[2] Eccleston, *Tractatus*, p. 95.

[3] *AP*, c. 10, no. 42.

Fieschi, cardinal priest, who became Pope Innocent IV (1243–54).[4] Nicholas was consecrated as bishop of Assisi in 1250.

Salimbene maintains that the popes who succeeded Innocent III loved the order, whose ministry was useful for the Church.[5] Innocent IV kept six friars with him throughout his pontificate.[6] Friars were drawn into a number of activities at the Roman curia. John de la Rochelle, Hugh of Digne and John of Parma all preached before the papal court at Lyons.[7] The order's theologians formulated an ecclesiology which supported the centralising tendencies of the pope and exalted the Petrine authority. The friars' theological prowess brought invitations for them to lecture at the papal court. For example, in the later thirteenth century John Pecham, who had lectured at both Oxford and Paris, was summoned to the papal curia to teach theology. He spent two years in confuting the arguments of heretics before being provided to the diocese of Canterbury on 28 January 1279.[8] Among the friars to lecture there in the 1280s and 1290s were distinguished masters of theology, some of whom were subsequently raised to the episcopate and cardinalate, Matthew of Acquasparta, Peter de Falegar, John of Murrovalle and Gentile of Montefiore. Friars were also engaged to teach outside their own cloisters.[9]

One of the priorities of the Fourth Lateran Council was articulated in its first canon, which reaffirmed Catholic teaching. Pope Innocent III was anxious about the dissemination of heresy, especially in southern France and northern Italy. The pressing need to combat such movements and reconcile Catholics with their Church lay at the heart of St Dominic's order of preachers, better known as the Dominicans. Francis was deeply orthodox, and the second chapter of the Rule insists that postulants should be examined on their faith in the Church's teaching and its sacraments. While heretics make only a fleeting appearance in the biographies of Francis, they were central to the *vitae* of Anthony of Padua and Rose of Viterbo. Anthony of Padua spent the greater part of his time as a friar preaching and teaching in regions where the Church was under intense pressure from a cohort of well-drilled preachers. When he found many people at Rimini who had succumbed to theological error, he called the citizens together and began to preach fervently. His sermons were designed to detach people from their erroneous beliefs and

---

4   Cf. L. Oliger, 'I penitenzieri francescani a San Giovanni in Laterano', *StF* 11 (1925), pp. 495–522, F. Pagnotti, 'Vita Innocentii IV scripta a Fr. Nicolao de Carbio', *Archivio della società romana di storia patria* 21 (1898), pp. 7–120.

5   Salimbene, *Cronica*, pp. 421–2.

6   Ibid., pp. 86, 302.

7   J. Bougerol, 'Sermons de maîtres franciscains du XIIIe siècle', *AFH* 81 (1988), pp. 17–49 at 47–8, Salimbene, *Cronica*, pp. 324–34, 433–4.

8   Eccleston, *Tractatus*, pp. 52, 53, *Chronicon de Lanercost*, pp. 100–1.

9   Cf. R. Creytens, 'Le "Studium Romanae curiae" et le Maître du Sacré Palais', *Archivum fratrum praedicatorum* 12 (1942), pp. 5–83 at 55–61. For example, M. Robson, 'Franciscan Lectors at Christ Church Cathedral Priory, Canterbury, 1275–1314', *Archaeologia Cantiana (Kent Archaeological Society)* 112 (1993), pp. 261–81.

were accompanied by disputations with the leaders of the heretical groups. His first biographer sums up the success of this mission in the submission of Bononillo, who had embraced the heresy some thirty years earlier.[10] However, heretical beliefs had sunk deep roots in that territory and this dissuaded his first biographer from making excessive claims that the saint had undermined or eradicated it. Later biographers provide further information on his efforts to arrest the spread of heresy in Rimini, Toulouse and Milan. A celebrated debate and the miracle in which a mule acknowledged the Eucharist were witnessed by a large crowd at the main square of Toulouse. This reveals something of the air of competition between heterodox and orthodox preachers and evokes Jordan of Saxony's description of a debate held at Fanjeaux some twenty-five years earlier.[11]

Anthony of Padua was the most celebrated member of the order engaged in countering heresy. Pope Gregory IX's *Quoniam abundavit iniquitas* of 6 April 1237 acknowledges the order's contribution in stemming the tide of heresy, and this was a constant feature of the friars' ministry in some provinces.[12] Friars in Tuscany were entrusted with the inquisition by Pope Alexander IV.[13] Malcolm Lambert observes that although Francis had no aim of extirpating heresy, his followers played an important role in combating theological deviance through their treatises and their urban ministry, where they attracted lay support through the Third Order.[14] Friars were also drafted into missionary work against members of other world religions and this was exemplified in Spain, where friars were invited to speak in synagogues and mosques. John of Perugia and Peter of Sassoferrato were publicly executed at Valencia, a city in Muslim control, around 1228.[15]

The friars' ranks included many highly talented and theologically astute men who might be recruited to further the work of the Church in varied situations. They breathed fresh air into the life of the Christian community and their pastoral talents were widely recognised and valued. While they did not belong to the diocesan structures, they were employed at parochial level by rectors and vicars of urban churches for the regeneration of the Church and at international level by bishops and popes. Friars were vigorous supporters of the reforms promulgated by the Fourth Lateran Council and they

---

[10] Abate, 'S. Rosa da Viterbo', pp. 239–41, *Vita prima o 'Assidua'*, c. 9, nn. 4–6, pp. 318–21. Cf. ibid., c. 40, nn. 1–4, pp. 486–7.

[11] *Vita del 'Dialogus' e 'Benignitas'*, c. 16, pp. 504–15, 'Libellus de principiis ord. praedicatorum auctore Iordano de Saxonia', nn. 24–5, p. 38.

[12] *BF*, I no. 224, pp. 214–15.

[13] J. N. Hillgarth, *The Spanish Kingdoms 1250–1516, I, 1250–1410, Precarious Balance* (Oxford, 1976), p. 135, Visconti, *Sermons*, no. 5, pp. 991–2.

[14] Salimbene, *Cronica*, p. 633, M. D. Lambert, *Medieval Heresy: Popular Movements from Bogomil to Hus* (London, 1977), p. 97.

[15] *Chronica XXIV generalium ordinis minorum*, p. 669, M. D. Lambert, *The Cathars* (Oxford, 1998), pp. 126–7, 166.

carried such measures into each diocese and virtually every parish of Christendom. In addition, they were adequately equipped for diplomatic work and specialised ministries. Examples of such assistance are explored in the subsequent sections of this chapter.

The province of the Holy Land and the Crusades

The campaign to recover the Holy Land was a priority of the Fourth Lateran Council. Jerusalem was perceived as the centre of the universe, as countless medieval maps attest. Once the queen of the nations and the prince of the provinces, the city of the Law and the priesthood, it was the holy city *par excellence*. Despite the Crusaders' success in capturing the city in 1099, it was recovered by Muslims in 1187. Christians lamented the loss of the holy places. They bemoaned the fact that it was occupied and oppressed, to the great disgrace of Christians; its walls and Temple were overthrown.[16] The friars' province of the Holy Land was celebrated on account of Francis's visit. Having been thwarted on two earlier occasions, he realised his ambition of going to the Holy Land in 1219. His arrival was at a most unpropitious moment, although he did attract some vocations. Despite the conflict between the two armies, he responded with typical directness. Ignoring all advice to the contrary, he and Illuminato walked into the Muslim camp and requested a meeting with the sultan, Malik-al-Kamil. The western accounts, which are prone to exaggeration and propaganda, highlight the poor treatment initially meted out to the friars. Francis was admitted to the sultan's presence and engaged him in religious discussion. Later accounts express Francis's reservations about the conduct of the Crusading forces besieging Damietta and his advice that they should not go into battle. They underline his offer to undergo an ordeal by fire with the Muslim leaders and speak of a trap set to ascertain whether he would walk on a carpet decorated with crosses.[17]

The first friar known to have reached the Holy Land was the pilgrim, Giles of Assisi, who was there about 1215.[18] Once sufficient friars were available, a group set out for the Holy Land, where they laboured under the leadership of Elias of Cortona, the minister provincial. Friaries were established at Acre, Aleppo, Antioch, Beirut, Constantinople, Corinth, Damietta, Galilee Jerusalem, Nazareth, Sebaste, Sidon, Sis, Tebe, Tripoli and Tyre.[19] As elsewhere, recruits followed quickly. The Benedictines at Montana Nigra, near Antioch, retaining their conventual buildings, became friars between 1220 and 1230.[20]

[16] *Itinerarium Symonis Semeonis ab Hybernia ad Terram Sanctam*, ed. M. Esposito, Scriptores Latini Hiberniae, IV (Dublin, 1960), no. 93, pp. 106–7.

[17] *Vita prima*, nn. 55–7, 2 C, no. 30, Bonaventure, *Legenda maior*, IX, nn. 7–9. 'Liber exemplorum fratrum minorum', pp. 209–10.

[18] *Scripta Leonis, Rufini et Angeli*, pp. 324–5, Golubovich, *Biblioteca*, I, p. 105.

[19] Golubovich, *Biblioteca*, II, p. 264.

[20] *De conformitate vitae beati Francisci ad vitam Domini Iesu auctore Fr. Bartholomaeo de Pisa*, Analecta

The rhythm of the friars' ministry was affected by the gains by the Crusaders, as illustrated by Louis IX's foundation of the friary in Jaffa in 1252; friars were provided with missals and other necessary items.[21] Friars in the Holy Land continued their customary ministries. Lectors were mentioned at Constantinople in 1249, Acre in 1255 and Tripoli shortly afterwards. Provincial chapters were celebrated annually. Henry of Pisa, minister provincial, died during the chapter at Corinth in 1247.[22]

Frederick II was welcomed to Jerusalem in September 1228, but he had already been excommunicated by Pope Gregory IX for his delay in fulfilling his vow to take the cross. On 7 May 1228 the papal letter was entrusted to two friars, who delivered it to the patriarch of Jerusalem.[23] The perception that the friars were papal envoys marred their relations with the emperor in the Holy Land and Magna Graeca.[24] One manifestation of this suspicion was the rough manner in which the emperor interrupted the friars' preaching at Jerusalem on Palm Sunday 1229.[25] Papal documents and chronicles refer to the friars' role as missionaries and the pastoral support for the Church in the Holy Land. Pope Gregory IX announced on 15 February 1233 that friars were to be sent to the Holy Land as missionaries. On 4 March 1238 the friars were seeking to win over the Muslims by persuasion, were granted the same remission of sins as was usually promised to crusaders; Gregory referred to their ministry for the conversion of pagans. The friars were at Aleppo in 1238, when Manasserio or another friar was ministering to Christian prisoners.[26] Similar work among prisoners in Egypt was undertaken by Johannino of Ollis of Parma, minister provincial of the Holy Land (1270–9).[27] When the crusaders were beginning to enjoy more success in the 1270s, the Muslims agreed that Christianity should be preached by the Franciscans and Dominicans among others.[28] Many friars, however, lost their lives in the Holy Land, particularly with the fall of Tripoli in 1289 and Acre in 1291.[29]

The province of the Holy Land was located at the frontier of the Christian world and its fragility and instability differed markedly from the provinces established in western Europe. One mark of this is that, despite the admission of Europeans, the evidence indicates that the mission was sustained by other

---

Franciscana, IV (Quaracchi, Florence, 1906), p. 344.

[21] *Vie de Saint Louis*, p. 76.

[22] Salimbene, *Cronica*, p. 468, 'Itinerarium Willelmi de Rubruc', epilogus, no. 1, pp. 329–30, 'Liber exemplorum fratrum minorum', no. 7, p. 215, Salimbene, *Cronica*, pp. 266–7.

[23] *BF*, I, no. 22, p. 41, Golubovich, *Biblioteca*, I, pp. 156–7.

[24] Jordan of Giano, *Chronica*, no. 73, pp. 60–1. *Matthaei Parisiensis, monachi Sancti Albani, Historia Anglorum, sive, ut vulgo dicitur, Historia minor*, II, p. 472. Matthew Paris, *Chronica majora*, IV, p. 256.

[25] Matthew Paris, *Chronica majora*, III, p. 183.

[26] *BF*, I, nn. 87, 249, 266, pp. 93–6, 233, 245.

[27] Salimbene, *Cronica*, pp. 457–8.

[28] Ibid., pp. 702–4.

[29] 'Chronica minor auctore Minorita Erphordiensi', in MGH, SS, XXIV, pp. 178–213, at 207.

provinces, just as it is now.[30] Henry of Pisa, for example, offered a *douceur* to an Italian friar in the form of a Bible 'and many other books' to attract him to the province. The emotional appeal of the Holy Land drew friars from diverse provinces, such as Richard of Ingworth, former minister provincial of Ireland (1230–9), Robert Thornham, *custos* of Cambridge, and James of Iseo, former minister provincial of Rome.[31] Unsatisfactory forms of recruitment, however, moved the general chapter of 1292 to ordain that the Holy Land was no suitable place for misfits from other provinces; the ministers provincial were admonished not to send insolent friars there.[32]

Friars joined the stream of pilgrims to the Holy Land. The friars' preaching in western Europe moved men to join the Crusades. The pope employed the friars to preach the Crusade throughout the world two years later, although they bore the opprobrium for bestowing the cross on unsuitable men, who promptly redeemed their vows through a financial offering.[33] The scene which accompanied Louis IX's departure for the Crusades is vividly recounted by an eye-witness present at the provincial chapter of Sens in the summer of 1248. The king arrived on foot at the friars' church in the attire of a pilgrim with a staff and scrip on his shoulder and was accompanied by his three brothers. Entering the chapter, Louis commended himself, his brothers and his mother, the queen, to the friars' prayers. His words moved some of the French friars to tears. Eudes de Châteauroux, formerly chancellor of the university of Paris and then cardinal bishop, planned to accompany the king on the Crusade. He addressed the friars and a formal response was made by John of Parma, who commended the conduct of the king in taking up the cross for the liberation of the Holy Land.[34]

Latins and Greeks

Friars from the province of the Holy Land, also known as Graecia, Romania, Syria, Terra Promissionis and Ultramarina, made a noteworthy contribution to negotiations with the Eastern Church. Relations between Greek and Latin Christians were soured by the horrendous events of the fourth Crusade and its destruction of the Byzantine state in 1204. Moreover, linguistic and theological gulfs symptomised the uneasy relations between the East and the West and perpetuated the differences and suspicions. This also percolated into the schools and universities, where Bonaventure knew the eastern Fathers only in translation, despite his occasional use of Greek theological terms. His pupil, John Pecham, readily admitted that he knew no

[30] Cf. *The Tablet*, 10 April 2004, p. 38, regarding the staffing of the current custody.
[31] Eccleston, *Tractatus*, pp. 4, 89, Oliger, 'Liber exemplorum', no. 7, p. 215.
[32] Bihl, 'Statuta generalia' (Narbonae), V, no. 17b, p. 69.
[33] Matthew Paris, *Chronica majora*, III, p. 312.
[34] Ibid., IV, p. 9, ibid., V, pp. 73–4, Salimbene, *Cronica*, pp. 317–23, 444.

Greek. Friars who were proficient in Greek were comparatively few and were specifically mentioned by the chroniclers. Benvenuto of Modena, a lector in theology and a graduate of Paris in the later thirteenth century, knew both Greek and Latin.[35] Each of the three papal legations to the Greeks during the thirteenth century contained some friars, generally from the province of the Holy Land. Schooled in both Greek and Latin theology, these friars were ideal emissaries to be sent between the emperor and the pope.

The central theological differences between East and West concerned the theology of the *Filioque*, that is, the procession of the Holy Spirit not only from the Father but also from the Son, a later addition to the Nicene Creed not accepted by the Byzantine Church, the use of unleavened bread in the Eucharist and the authority of the pope. Despite the excesses perpetrated by the Crusaders, a residual bond united the Greek Orthodox and the Western Catholic Church. There was also a level of political pragmatism. Friars in the Holy Land turned to their Greek neighbours for succour against the Turks, just as the Greeks would seek papal assistance in the face of the expansionist policies of Charles of Anjou, king of Sicily. Initially it was the friars' growing expertise in theological matters which made them suitable ambassadors for Pope Gregory IX. Friars of the Holy Land were selected as envoys to foster reconciliation between East and West. Late in 1231 or early in the following year five friars from the Holy Land, who had been imprisoned by the Turks, sought the help of Germanus II, the patriarch at Nicaea. In due course the conversation moved to a discussion of relations between the two Churches and, at the friars' suggestion, the patriarch sent an ambassador to Pope Gregory IX. Having accompanied the friars to Italy, the Greek envoy presented his credentials to the pope at Rieti shortly before 26 July 1232. On that day the pope announced that he would take the matter in hand at once by sending him some religious men to discuss matters of doctrine.

About the middle of the next year four friars left Rome with a letter of 18 May 1233, *Cum iuxta testimonium*, which encouraged the patriarch of Constantinople to seek union with the Roman Church. Two Dominicans of French origin, Peter of Sézanne and Hugh, and two English Franciscans, Ralph of Rheims and Haymo of Faversham, were appointed to represent the western Church. They travelled to Byzantium and from there went to Nicaea, arriving on 15 January 1234; they were officially received by the patriarch the following day. Long drawn-out discussions continued until the end of the month in the presence of the emperor. The departure of the latter put an end to the debate. The friars returned to Byzantium and after Easter they travelled to Nymphaeum in Lydia, where meetings and discussions were held from 27 March to 4 May; the atmosphere deteriorated. Exasperated by delay and subterfuge, the friars walked out of the talks on 21 April. On their return,

---

[35] B. Hughes, '*De numeris misticis* by John Pecham. A Critical Edition', *AFH* 78 (1985), pp. 3–28, 333–83 at 358. Salimbene, *Cronica*, pp. 918–19.

the attitude of the Greeks had not changed and the mission ended in mutual recriminations. On their journey home the friars suffered much inconvenience from imperial and ecclesiastical officials; their baggage was searched and their books were inspected. Van Dijk believes that the account of the friars' travels and theological exchanges was probably written by Ralph of Rheims, who seems to have been the only member of the delegation familiar with Greek.[36]

Secondly, John Vatatzes, Byzantine emperor, recruited friars for his negotiations with Pope Innocent IV. He had heard of the reputation of John of Parma and in 1248 he requested Innocent to send the minister general to Greece to bring the clergy there back into communion with the Church of Rome. Salimbene, the chronicler, met John of Parma at Avignon and together they set out for the papal court at Lyons. The chronicler and John of Parma travelled to Vienne, where they met another friar named Salimbene, the messenger of the emperor, whom they took to Lyons; his parents were Greek and Italian. He spoke Latin very well and had a good command of Greek and Italian, although he was not a very learned man. Thomas, the lector of Constantinople, a Greek friar who spoke Latin well, was also sent to the papal court by the emperor.

The papal court nurtured the hope that through the mediation of John Vatatzes, a theological agreement would be reached. Pope Innocent IV, having recalled John of Parma from Spain, received him warmly. Explaining the news that the Greeks wished to be reconciled with the Roman Church, Innocent asked John to go to the Greeks with a good company of the friars and to take whatever help was necessary. John agreed and appointed an experienced team of friars to assist him: Thomas, the lector at Constantinople, Dudo, minister provincial of Burgundy, and Bonaventure da Iseo, a famous friar who had filled the office of minister provincial in different regions. Many other suitable men were selected, but their names were not recorded by Salimbene. Some time after Easter 1249 the party of friars took their leave of the papal court. Two papal letters of 28 May 1249 indicate that the friars were already active in Greece. The procession of the Holy Spirit was a central topic in the theological discussions. John of Parma impressed the emperor, who sought to shower him with numerous gifts, which the friar declined. The emperor insisted on conferring a sign of imperial power to be carried throughout Greece by the minister general. Salimbene reports that the Greeks met the friars' expenses, but he offers frustratingly little information on the work conducted by the friars during their stay in Greece.[37]

---

[36] *BF*, I, no. 103, pp. 103–5, Cf. H. Golubovich, 'Disputatio Latinorum et Graecorum seu relatio apocrisariorum Gregorii IX de gestis Nicaeae in Bithynia et Nymphaeae in Lydia 1234', *AFH* 12 (1919), pp. 418–70. Van Dijk, *Sources of the Modern Roman Liturgy*, I, pp. 17–18.

[37] *Les Registres d'Innocent IV*, ii, ed. E. Berger, Bibliothèque des écoles françaises d'Athènes et de Rome, 2e série (Paris, 1887), nn. 4749, 4750, pp. 129–30, Salimbene, *Cronica*, pp. 443–4, 467–8.

Thirdly, from 1261 the main enemy of the Byzantine world was Charles of Anjou, the newly enthroned king of Sicily. Michael Palaeologus, the Greek emperor, regarded the pope, Charles of Anjou's feudal lord, as the only power able to restrain this grave military threat. The price of such an alliance was an unappetising reunion with the western Church with all its connotations of submission. The desire for reunion was shared by Pope Gregory X, elected on 1 September 1271. He had spent many years in the Holy Land and his desire for reunion with the Greeks was one of the reasons for the second council of Lyons, which he convened during the summer of 1274. He informed the emperor of his willingness to dispatch delegates to Constantinople to re-open a theological dialogue.

Gregory sent John Paraston, a friar who had been born in Constantinople, ahead of the team of formal ambassadors in order to instruct the emperor in the theological beliefs of the Roman Church. Paraston was not only greatly respected by the emperor but also by the Greek people. He was immensely respectful of the Greek rites and regarded disagreement over the *Filioque* as excessive; he and the friars were happy to attend Greek liturgies. He presented unity as a return to the beliefs and practices of earlier times rather than the acceptance of new dogmatic beliefs or rites. Gregory turned to the order once again for nuncios and applied to Bonaventure, the minister general, for friars suitable for this mission. The pope wrote a lengthy letter to the emperor on 24 October 1272,[38] the day on which Jerome of Ascoli, Bonaventure da Mugello, Bonagratia and Raymond Berengar departed for the Bosphorus. It is thought that Jerome of Ascoli, the chief legate, was the only one to know Greek. Moreover, his somewhat inaccurate remarks about Greek religious practices cast doubt on his mastery of that language. Nonetheless, the minister general claimed some of the credit for the success of the mission, which lasted for fifteen months and paved the way for the reunion effected at the council of 1274.[39]

One exception to this derivative knowledge of the Greek language and theology was Robert Grosseteste. During his time as lector to the friars of Oxford his interest in the Eastern theological tradition was growing. Greek Fathers were cited in his *Hexaëmeron*, where he makes use of the writings of Basil the Great, Gregory of Nyssa, John Chrysostom and John of Damascus. Grosseteste was styled as one of the greatest scholars of the world. The second man to translate John of Damascus, he also translated *The Testament of the Twelve Patriarchs* and many other books. His sermons incorporate the writings of the Greek Fathers and mirror his growing appreciation of the theological heritage of the eastern luminaries. His writings proposed a way

---

[38] *BF*, III, no. 10, pp. 186–92.
[39] D. J. Geanakoplos, 'Bonaventura, the Two Mendicant Orders and the Greeks at the Council of Lyons', *The Orthodox Churches and the West*, ed. D. Baker, Studies in Church History, XIII (Oxford, 1976), pp. 183–211, 185–90.

of exploring the divergence of views on the *Filioque*. During his celebrated visit to the papal court at Lyons in 1250 he berated Pope Innocent IV about the separation of the Greek Church.[40] James McEvoy suggests that Grosseteste may have obtained some of his Greek texts through the friars, who were active in Magna Graeca.[41] His knowledge of Latin, Greek and Hebrew distinguished him from the vast majority of his contemporaries at Paris and Oxford.[42] His interest in Hebrew was also communicated to the friars. These skills are exemplified in William de la Mare's *De Hebraeis et Graecis vocabulis glossarum Bibliae*.

Missions to the Tartars

Rumours about the advances made by the Mongols or Tartars had already reached Rome before the death of Pope Gregory IX on 22 August 1241.[43] A letter of 25 May 1241 from Henry de Tanne, bishop of *Constantiensis*, exhorted the friars of his diocese to preach a Crusade against the Tartars, who were persecuting Christians.[44] The military threat loomed even larger to the Poles and the Germas who suffered greatly from such incursions.[45] A letter of 10 April 1242 announced that two of the Polish custodies of friars had been destroyed by the invading Tartars.[46] Additional reports of incursions wrought havoc in some parts of western Europe; among the victims were Russia, Poland and cities in Austria, Moravia, and Hungary.[47] John of Piano Carpini affirms that people in the west feared that the Church's mission would be endangered by the Tartars. There was widespread concern that such forces would sweep across other countries at a time when the new pope, Innocent IV, and Frederick II, provided no united front for the protection of the mediterranean world. Pope Innocent IV responded by dispatching envoys to the court of the Great Khan and this mission was entrusted to the friars. Some of these friars kept a record of what they had seen and experienced on their lengthy journeys into lands, which were markedly different

[40] Salimbene, *Cronica*, p. 335, S. Gieben, 'Robert Grosseteste at the Papal Curia, Lyons 1250. Edition of the Documents', *CF* 41 (1971), pp. 340–93, 353.

[41] J. McEvoy, 'Robert Grosseteste's Greek Scholarship: A Survey of Present Knowledge', *FS* 56 (1998), pp. 255–64 at 257–8.

[42] BL, MS Add. 14251, fol. 93v.

[43] Salimbene, *Cronica*, p. 302, *Les Registres de Grégoire IX recueil des bulles de ce pape publiées ou analyses d'après les manuscrits originaux du Vatican*, ed. L. Auvray, Bibliothèque des écoles françaises d'Athènes et de Rome, 2nd serie (Paris, 1908), nn. 5022, 6055, 6057–62, 6094, pp. 161–3, 523, 524, 554.

[44] L. Oliger, 'Exhortatio Henrici episcopi Constantiensis ad fratres minores, ut crucem contra Tartaros praedicent a. 1241', *AFH* 11 (1918), pp. 556–7.

[45] P. Jackson, *The Mongols and the West* (London 2005), pp. 58–86, for an account of the incursions between 1241 and 1244.

[46] Matthew Paris, *Chronica majora*, VI, pp. 80–3.

[47] Van Den Wyngaert, ed. 'Fr. Iohannes de Plano Carpini, Ystoria Mongalorum, c. 9, no. 8, pp. 105–6.

from the cities of Germany, France, Italy, and Poland. John of Piano Carpini, a veteran of the missions to Germany and Poland, led the pioneering party in 1245 and he was followed by a succession of his confrères and the Dominicans. He was accompanied by his unnamed companion who fell ill at Kiev and left the mission. Benedict, a Polish friar, was the translator who also compiled a brief memoir. As papal envoys they set out from the papal curia at Lyons and carried Pope Innocent IV's letters of 5 March 1245 to the Great Khan.[48]

Already aged approximately 65, John was unsure whether he was going to find sufficient food or to be imprisoned or sentenced to death. His journey took him more than sixteen months. Before setting out he approached Wenceslas, king of Bohemia, for advice and assistance. The king gave the friars a safe conduct throughout his lands and arranged for them to be supplied with food for their journey through Poland to Russia, as did his nephew, Boleslaus, duke of Silesia, who was already known to the friars. Alms were also provided for the friars' needs on their journey. The bishop of Krakow offered them some hospitality and introduced them to other bishops of Poland before they set out for Kiev.[49] John furnishes additional details of the devastation wrought by the Tartars, who destroyed Russian cities and fortresses, slaughtering men. Tartars laid siege to Kiev and took the city, massacring the inhabitants. The once populous capital city contained the bodies of countless slain. *En route* John fell ill and was so weak that he could hardly ride. Fears for his personal safety persisted and on occasion the friars rode from dawn to dusk with little food.[50]

The eighth chapter offers a full account of the Tartars' military plans to bring the rest of the world into subjection. Christendom was a particular target and western leaders were urged to reject the overtures of the Tartars, whose new emperor had already unveiled his plans to send an army to Livonia and Prussia. John's advice was that the Christian nations should co-operate to resist such invading forces. It is ironical that this follower of the peace-loving *poverello* proffered advice on the type of weapons to be deployed and military tactics. Those who wished to fight the Tartars were advised to deploy good strong bows, crossbows and axes made from strong iron, swords, lances, knives, cuirasses of a double thickness. A strong discipline would be necessary to combat the Tartars in battle. On no account should Christian troops pursue them far, lest they be lured into an ambush and killed. John travelled to Karakorum, where he participated in the enthronement of the Great Khan, Güyük in August 1246. He frequently admits that he does not know the names of the rivers which he had seen or the leaders of the regions which he visited. On their return journey the friars travelled throughout the

[48] *BF*, I, nn. 75, p. 353.
[49] Van Den Wyngaert, 'Fr. Iohannes de Plano Carpini, Ystoria Mongalorum', prol., nn. 1–2, c. 9, nn. 2–3, pp. 27–8, 101–3.
[50] Ibid., c. 5, no. 27, c. 9, nn. 19, 28, pp. 71–2, 111, 116.

winter and often slept in the desert in the snow. When they reached Kiev, they were treated like men who had returned from the dead; the same happened throughout Russia, Poland and Bohemia.[51]

Friars were missionaries to lands beyond the confines of the Roman Church, as Andrew Little notes.[52] Before the end of the thirteenth century the friars reached Armenia, Persia and India.[53] At the heart of the friar's vocation was a missionary impulse, which found recognition in the life of the founder and the twelfth chapter of his Rule. While John of Piano Carpini travelled as a papal envoy, William went among the Tartars as a friar and a missionary. Where appropriate he travelled with bare feet, although sometimes the intensity of the cold obliged him to wear shoes.[54] He recounted his dialogue with potential converts and his wish to preach the Gospel.[55] He received a Bible from Louis IX and a beautiful psalter from the queen, Margaret of Provence. The king gave alms to the friars and there are several references to the letter which vouched for them.[56] This was addressed to the Sartach, a leader of the Mongols incorrectly deemed to be a Christian, and Mangu Chan.[57] William's familiarity with France provides him with comparisons for what he beheld on his travels. His observatation that the river Etilia was four times as wide as the river Seine corrected Isidore of Seville's account. The city of Caracorum was compared unfavourably with Paris.[58] Some rice ale resembled the best wines of Auxerre.[59]

William's desire to preach to the people and to explain the truths of Christianity was hampered by the incompetence of his translator.[60] There were similar limitations placed upon his attempts to inform himself of the religious beliefs of the Yugurs. The dangers which he encountered on the road were just as terrifying as those faced by John of Piano Carpini. Towards the middle of December 1253 the friars passed through a region where it was rumoured that demons were wont to carry men off, seizing horses and leaving the rider behind. At other places the demons had pulled out men's innards and left the corpses on the horses. The fearful friars recited the Creed as they passed such dangerous territory.[61] *En route* William met a number of Christians, including a man who had been baptised by the friars in Hungary and a woman from Metz, who had been captured in Hungary.[62] Nestorians

[51] Ibid., c. 8, nn. 1–15, c. 9, nn. 25, 47, pp. 93–101, 114–15, 126–7.
[52] Little, 'The Mendicant Orders', pp. 727–62, 752.
[53] 'Epistolae Fr. Iohannis de Monte Corvino', *SF*, pp. 333–55, 354, no. 7.
[54] Ibid., c. 28, nn. 4, 11, pp. 245, 247.
[55] Ibid., c. 12, no. 1; c. 28, no. 8, pp. 193, 246.
[56] Ibid., c. 15, no. 5, c. 19, no 10, pp. 201–2, 216.
[57] Ibid., c. 9, nn. 1–2, c. 19, no. 8, c. 28, nn. 2, 16, c. 33, no. 8, pp. 187–8, 215, 244, 250, 292–3.
[58] Ibid., c. 18, no. 4, c. 32, no. 1, pp. 210–11, 285–6.
[59] Ibid., c. 28, no. 1, p. 244.
[60] Ibid., c. 13, no. 6, c. 22, no. 2, c. 27, no. 4, pp. 196, 221–2, 240.
[61] Ibid., c. 25, no. 8, c. 27, nn. 3–4, pp. 232, 239–40.
[62] Ibid., c. 20, no. 4, c. 29, no. 2, pp. 217, 252–3.

lived alongside Saracen neighbours, although William observed that their crosses did not have the figure of Christ on them, and he described their liturgy.[63] Nestorian churches had large bells, like those used by Christians in Russia and the Greeks in Gazaria. William assumed that Christians in the East were unwilling to adopt these because they resembled western practice.[64] Nestorians resided in fifteen cities of Cataia, with a centre at Segin. They were depicted as ignorant. Their scriptures and liturgy were in Syriac, a language which they did not know. William regarded them as usurers and drunkards and some of them dwelling among the Tartars had several wives; episcopal visits were rare. Their priests were more concerned to provide for their families than to preach Christianity. On his way back to the west William celebrated Christmas 1254 in the city of Naxaun, once the capital of a substantial kingdom, which the Tartars had reduced. At one stage there were eight hundred Armenian churches there, but only two remained. There William met an Armenian bishop, who told him about the nearby church where St Bartholomew was martyred.[65]

---

[63] Ibid., c. 26, no. 1, c. 29, no. 19, pp. 233, 258–9.
[64] Ibid., c. 24, no. 5, pp. 228–9.
[65] Ibid., c. 26, nn. 11–12, c. 38, nn. 1–2, pp. 237–8, 321–2.

CHAPTER SEVEN

St Bonaventure

> When I was still only a child, I became seriously ill and my mother made a vow to the blessed father Francis, so that I was snatched from the jaws of death and restored to perfect health...
>
> Bonaventure[1]

Bonaventure personifies the friars' commitment to the ministry of preaching, the study of theology and service to the universal Church. His seventeen years as minister general (1257–74) mark a crucial stage in the order's development. He was the first friar to be raised to the purple on 28 May 1273, becoming cardinal bishop. During the last year of his life he devoted his energies to the preparations for the second council of Lyons, where he died on 15 July 1274.

The scholar

A native of Bagnoregio, Bonaventure, the 'seraphic doctor', enrolled in the faculty of arts in the University of Paris in 1236. After his graduation he joined the Cordeliers in 1243 as a member of the Roman province and began his novitiate. His formative theological studies were spent under the direction of Alexander of Hales, a wealthy archdeacon and master who embraced a life of evangelical poverty. His conversion was presented as an *exemplum*. He was singled out for special praise by Bonaventure, who declared his intention of following the teaching of his father and master.[2] He also studied under Jean de la Rochelle, Eudes Rigaud and William of Melitona. He progressed through the customary *cursus* for theologians and in 1248 he was a bachelor appointed to lecture on the Gospel of St Luke. These cursory lectures on the Bible, spanning two years, were given under the supervision of William of Melitona. There followed another two years of cursory lectures on the books of Proverbs.[3]

---

[1] Bonaventure, *Legenda minor*, c. 7, no. 8.

[2] Delorme, 'Textes franciscains', p. 216, Bonaventure, 'Praelocutio in secundum librum sententiarum', *DSBOO*, II, p. 2.

[3] Salimbene, *Cronica*, p. 435, J. Bougerol, *Introduction à l'étude de S. Bonaventure*, Bibliothèque de théologie, série 1, Théologie dogmatique, II (Paris, 1961), pp. 240–1.

As a master of theology Bonaventure produced the customary *Commentaria in libros Sententiarum*. His *Quaestiones disputatae de scientia Christi*, *De mysterio Trinitatis* and *De reductione artium ad theologiam* breathe the air of the Parisian lecture halls. Perhaps the best-known product of this period is the *Breviloquium*, a compendium of the central questions in theology. The treatise was a distillation of his experience as a master and was intended to assist new members of the faculty of theology. The seven sections encompass salvation history, from the act of creation to the last judgement. The treatise is introductory; its purpose was to guide students rather than to provide an extended treatment of the key questions. Statements are made in brief and students are expected to turn to the *Commentaria in libros Sententiarum* and the *Quaestiones disputatae* for fuller discussion. Bonaventure's favourite writers from the patristic and early medieval world are identified in the *Breviloquium*. Augustine of Hippo, the chief Latin Father, was followed by Ambrose, Dionysius the Areopagite and Gregory the Great. These theological luminaries were joined by eleventh and twelfth-century theologians, Anselm of Canterbury, Bernard of Clairvaux and the Victorines, Hugh and Richard.

Bonaventure's teaching came to an end on 2 February 1257, when he was elected as the seventh minister general. He was required to resign his chair of theology and devote his time and energies to the welfare of the order at a critical time in its history. He gave himself to periods of protracted reflection and compiled a number of devotional treatises on themes which had been dear to the founder. The *De triplici via* and *Itinerarium mentis in Deum* are among the classics of western spirituality. The *Soliloquium*, cast in the form of a dialogue, provided an extended form of spiritual advice and the *De perfectione vitae*, a digest of spiritual counsel, was compiled for Isabelle, the former princess and abbess of the Poor Clares of Longchamp. The *Lignum vitae* draws the reader into the scenes from the Gospel and generates the appropriate dispositions, deploying the traditional method of *excita mentem*. Many of these treatises dwell upon the central points of mendicant piety, the crib, the cross and the sacraments. Their intention was to inculcate higher standards of piety among priests, religious and laity alike.

Continued residence in Paris enabled Bonaventure to keep abreast of current scholastic debates. He had made ample use of the newly available Aristotelian treatises in his lectures and copiously quoted the ancient philosopher. He did, however, detect some worrying trends among some theologians who relied increasingly upon the Aristotelian corpus. Reservations about an excessive dependence on Aristotle's teaching were expressed in Bonaventure's lectures on the *De septem donis Spiritus Sancti* in 1268 and the *Collationes in Hexaemeron* in 1273/4. One of the master's duties was to preach. Bonaventure's homilies breathe the air of the schools.[4] A number of his homilies were

---

[4] His sermons for feast days and Sundays have been edited in the ninth volume of the *Opera omnia* and by Jacques Bougerol in a separate collection.

delivered before the French court.[5]

Bonaventure is celebrated as one of the most influential theologians of the thirteenth century. His scriptural scholarship is belatedly starting to attract more attention. The biblical foundation of his theology finds expression in the lengthy prologue to the *Breviloquium*, which contains an exposition of the appropriate application of the Bible. As a master of theology he was drawn into the polemical exchanges with the secular masters in the University of Paris in the mid-1250s and the later 1260s. He completed his *Quaestiones disputatae de perfectione evangelica* against William of St Amour in 1253 and *Apologia pauperum* against Gerard of Abbeville in 1269. These disputed questions and the treatise developed a rationale for the friars' activities within the schools and a theology of religious life, especially their adoption of evangelical poverty.[6]

Advocates of theological study within the order carefully laid down the guiding principles for lectors and students. Scholastic formation was perceived as laying the necessary foundation for the ministry of preaching and hearing confessions. Following the views articulated by Hugh of Digne's *Commentary on the Rule*, Bonaventure established guidelines for theological study in his letter to an unnamed master about 1254/5. The apologetic tone reflects a division of opinion on the desirability of theological study in the order. Bonaventure presents Francis as a man who learned through prayer and reading; his desire to learn is demonstrated by an anecdote about his dismembering a copy of the Scriptures in order that each friar might have a folio for his own instruction. In a contentious reading of Francis's *Testament*, Bonaventure claims that the saint showed the utmost respect for the clerics whom he admitted to the order and he commanded the friars to show reverence to the lectors of the order.[7]

The prologue to the *Commentarius in evangelium S. Lucae* affirms that the friars' studies were charged with a spiritual dimension and that they should approach the sacred texts in a spirit of humility and openness to divine grace. The last section of the prologue of the *Breviloquium* explores the teleology of theological study. Faithful to the tradition of the order, Bonaventure affirmed that such study was to render the student or master virtuous and to attain salvation. This could not be perceived solely in cerebral terms; neither was it the fruit of mere speculation, but of a disposition of the will.[8] These thoughts shaped the instructions for the selection and conduct of students at

---

[5] Sancti Bonaventurae, *Sermones dominicales*, ed. J. Bougerol, Bibliotheca Franciscana scholastica medii aevi, XXVII (Grottaferrata, Rome, 1977), J. Bougerol, 'Saint Bonaventure et le roi saint Louis', in *S. Bonaventura 1274–1974*, II, pp. 469–93.

[6] Cf. Y. M. Congar, 'La Querelle entre mendiants et seculiers', *Archives d'histoire doctrinale et litteraire du Moyen Age*, 28 (1962), pp. 44–52, Cf. G. Dufeil, *Guillaume de Saint-Amour et la polemique universitaire parisienne, 1250–9* (Paris/Picard, 1972).

[7] Delorme, 'Textes franciscains', p. 216.

[8] F. M. Delorme, 'Breviloquium', prol., V, no. 2, *DSBOO*, V, pp. 199–291, 206.

the *studium generale* of Paris in the sixth section of the general constitutions of Narbonne. Bonaventure embodied his teaching and this commended him to the friars, especially John of Parma, who appointed him to lecture at Paris and nominated him as minister general.

The minister general

John of Parma was a widely admired minister general and he was the first to visit all the provinces of the order. His simple lifestyle, integrity and asceticism attracted much praise. His policies as minister general earned commendation and brought him many friends and admirers. The unanimity about his personal and administrative qualities, however, did not extend to his apocalyptic beliefs. His enthusiasm for the speculations of Joachim of Fiore was well known and it became his Achilles' heel. The condemnation of Gerard of Borgo San Donnino's *Liber introductorius ad evangelium aeternum* endangered John's position. The four accounts of John's removal from office reflect the varied responses to his plight. Thomas of Eccleston maintains that Pope Alexander IV permitted John to resign because he could no longer bear the weight of office.[9] Peregrine of Bologna testified that, following his return from the East, John faced many accusations and the pope secretly commanded him to lay aside his office.[10] Salimbene's view was that John did not wish to remain in office, despite the friars' views. Several members of the chapter had hoped that John might be dissuaded and the business of the order was delayed by a full day before they acceded to his request. He was accorded the rare privilege of nominating his successor and he presided over the remainder of the chapter. The anonymous author of *La Vie de Sainte Douceline* declared that he renounced office and retreated to a mountain for a lengthy period of penance.[11]

John's apocalyptic beliefs cost him the support of Popes Alexander IV and Nicholas III, two former cardinal protectors. He was exposed to criticism, which is attributed to Bartholomew Calaroso de Mantua, formerly a lector and then minister provincial of Milan and Rome. Bartholomew asserted that John had caused a great deal of trouble for himself and the order. Despite his holiness of life and learning, he was compromised by his Joachimism and this turned the ministers provincial against him. Nonetheless, he was held in high esteem by Popes Innocent V (1276) and John XXI (1276–7), who had wished to make him a cardinal; Nicholas III's formal offer of a cardinal's hat was declined. The differences of opinion about John's deposition

---

[9] Salimbene, *Cronica*, p. 434, Eccleston, *Tractatus*, pp. 73–4.

[10] Peregrine of Bologna, *Cronica* (an appendix to Eccleston, *Tractatus*), ed. A. G. Little (Paris, 1909), pp. 143–4.

[11] Salimbene, *Cronica*, pp. 450–1, *La Vie de Sainte Douceline fondatrice des béguines de Marseille*, X, no. 17, pp. 136–7.

stored up trouble for his successor. Angelo Clareno regarded Bonaventure with some suspicion because of his role in championing the friars' presence in the schools. He overlooks the fact that John had been a lector at Naples, Bologna and Paris and his promotion of theological studies. A similar veil was drawn over the abuses which took place in his time as minister general. For example, Lambertinus Cazanimici of Bologna, a novice, compiled his will on the advice of his mother and the *custos* of Bologna on 19 September 1249. The sum of £40 in the currency of his native city was assigned for the purchase of books to be placed at his disposal after his profession of vows.[12]

Bonaventure was the longest-serving minister general in the thirteenth century. Although this period saw continued development, historians now shy away from the concept that he was the second founder of the order. The title might more fittingly be awarded to Haymo of Faversham, who promoted priests at the expense of non-clerical friars.[13] What remains of Bonaventure's correspondence points to the continuation of his predecessors' policies and the perennial attempt to suppress contraventions of the Rule. His first letter as minister general, written on 23 April 1257, opens with the customary assertion of personal unworthiness for the office which had been thrust on him by the general chapter and papal command. Styling himself as the servant of the order, he announced his reliance on the ministers provincial and *custodes* for industry, eagerness and lively zeal in removing evil, promoting good, fortifying weakness and confirming strengths. Officials of the order were invested with the positions of immense responsibility. Had Bonaventure been present at the general chapter, he would have raised matters where correction was required.

Taking advice from colleagues, he presented his diagnosis of the order; he wrote with a sense of urgency. He was aware that the order was still imperilled, that the consciences of some friars were disturbed by matters of fidelity to the Rule, that the order had become a counter-sign and a cause of scandal. Whereas the order should be a sign of holiness, it had become an object of contempt and disgust in various parts of the world. Its problems were laid out in plain terms. It was being brought into disrepute for ten reasons: the multiplication of business transactions in which money was eagerly sought, rashly accepted, and even more imprudently handled; the idleness of certain friars was a cesspool of vices whereby many were lulled to daydream; the rampant wandering of many had become burdensome to those through whom they travelled, especially on account of the friars' love of creature comforts – such friars gave bad example; improper begging which made travellers fear friars as much as robbers; the cost and unusual construction of expensive and pretentious buildings disturbed the peace of the friars, placing heavy

---

12 Salimbene, *Cronica*, pp. 439–43, *Acta Franciscana e tabulariis Bononiensibus deprompta*, no. 28, p. 11. Cf. ibid., nn. 49, 98, 121, 173, 196, pp. 16, 33–4, 43, 66–7, 75.

13 Peregrine of Bologna, *Cronica*, p. 142.

burdens on their benefactors, and greatly exposing the order to criticism; the multiplication of familiarities, forbidden by the Rule, giving rise to rumours, suspicions and many scandals.

The administration of the order was not spared; offices were being bestowed upon friars who were ill-equipped, as their acts of omission and commission confirmed. The thirst for funerals and legacies was an invasion of the rights of the clergy. Frequent and expensive changes of residence, accompanied by some violence and disturbance to the neighbourhood, menaced the ideal of poverty. A certain rise in expenses showed that the friars did not wish to be content with a few things; friars had become more burdensome to all, and would become even more so in the future unless a remedy were to be found quickly. The abuses were inflicting severe damage on the order. Bonaventure wanted the constitutions concerning admission to be observed strictly and in every detail. The durability of some of these abuses, however, is visible in the fact that similar complaints were made after the general chapter of Paris in 1266. Bonaventure complained that the order was losing its lustre, as laxity made inroads. In the context of the building programmes of the 1250s and 1260s, he reiterated the earlier complaint that such projects were the cause of scandal. Moreover, some friars, defying the teaching of Francis, preached against bishops. Abuses concerning burials and the pursuit of legacies had sown the seeds conflict with the secular clergy. Pope Clement IV (1265–8) had sought the assistance of Bonaventure in this matter. The decrees of the general chapter were not being honoured and those who flouted such directives went unpunished.[14] These two letters reveal that Bonaventure was no friend of relaxation. He promoted high standards of behaviour, as Peter Olivi attests.[15]

One of the tasks over which Bonaventure presided was the production of general constitutions. Salimbene reports that, following the deposition of Elias of Cortona, several general constitutions were instituted, although they were not ordered. They were later codified by Bonaventure, who added a few of his own.[16] His first general chapter was held at Narbonne in 1260, when he regulated the government of the order. The twelve rubrics or sections of the constitutions, largely incorporating the legislation of the previous eighteen years, provided guidance on the observance of the Rule. As *Quo elongati* was recognised as a moderate interpretation of the Rule, so these constitutions offered the friars a high level of fidelity. Despite the fact that Angelo Clareno pilloried Bonaventure for his treatment of John of Parma,

---

[14] 'Epistolae', *DSBOO*, VIII, pp. 468–71.

[15] D. Burr, *The Persecution of Peter Olivi* (Transactions of the American Philosophical Society, n.s., LXVIv) (Philadelphia, 1976), p. 15, n. 28.

[16] Salimbene, *Cronica*, pp. 232–3. Cf. C. Cenci, 'De fratrum minorum constitutionibus praenarbonensibus', *AFH* 83 (1990), pp. 50–95 and 'Vestigia constitutionum praenarbonensium', *AFH* 97 (2004), pp. 61–98.

these constitutions were invoked by Ubertino da Casale in his criticism of levels of observance in friaries at the beginning of the following century. The constitutions form almost a commentary on the Rule and are closely associated with the *Legenda maior*.

The figure of St Francis in the Legenda maior

As the general constitutions regulate the lives of the friars and bind them to an appropriate level of observance, so the *Legenda maior* offers both an encomium of the founder and guides friars in the changing circumstances of the 1260s. This official biography was approved by the general chapter of 1266 and it established a level of observance for the whole order. What the biography lacked in originality, it gained in theological and mystical insight. The casual reader may miss the deft arrangement of the chapters, which is based on Bonaventure's purgative, illuminative and perfective way. This threefold course provides the framework for the life of the saint. The portrait holds up the values of the order and depicts St Francis as the personification of the threefold way.[17] Francis was the one in whom right order was restored. The excesses of God's mercy were to be contemplated in the saint, whose example encourages the friars to forgo irreverent thoughts and worldly appetites and to live like their divine master. Francis's purpose was to withdraw people from the road to ruin and to stimulate an evangelical renewal in their hearts. He was divinely inspired to profess the life of Gospel perfection; he was appointed as a leader and an apostle. Just as St John the Baptist opened the way for the first coming of Christ, so Francis heralded the second coming.

Anticipating Dante's judgement, Bonaventure contrasts the brilliance of Francis, like a morning star, with the gloom of secular society.[18] *Il poverello* was not merely a saint of local importance or one whose cult was to be confined to his growing band of followers. Bonaventure wrote in a context of a global cult and affirmed that the saint was worthy of admiration throughout the world. Francis, the imitator of angelic purity, received the mission to summon all to mourn, lament and embrace penance (Isaiah 22.12). His penitential habit was conformed to the cross and the seal of truth itself was impressed on his body, which made him like the Christ crucified. The wounds inflicted upon him, the stigmata, were not the work of nature's powers or of any human agent. This becomes all the more important at a time when there were many who cast doubt upon the reality of the wounds borne

---

[17] E. Cousins, translation and introduction, *Bonaventure: The Soul's Journey into God, The Tree of Life, The Life of St. Francis*, The Classics of Western Spirituality (New York, 1978), pp. 37–46.

[18] Dante Alighieri, *La divina commedia, Paradiso, XI*, v. 50, p. 922, Jordan of Giano, *Chronica*, no. 50, pp. 45–6. Cf. M. Michalczyk, 'Une compilation parisienne des sources primitives franciscaines, Paris, Nationale ms. lat. 12707', *AFH* 74 (1981), pp. 3–32, 401–55 at 403: Francis was *quasi sol oriens mundo*.

by Francis. The thirteenth chapter of the biography assembled the miracles associated with the stigmata, including those who doubted this special mark of divine favour.

Bonaventure's profound admiration for the saint was tinged with personal thanksgiving, which permitted him to overcome his innate diffidence. He wished to pay his debt of gratitude to the saint whose intervention had been so decisive and beneficial in his life. As a boy he fell sick and was healed through the intercession of the saint, who snatched him from the jaws of death. Had he deflected the friars' petition for him to write a biography, he would have been deemed guilty of ingratitude towards the saint. Another account confirms that he was restored to full health as a result of a vow which his mother made to St Francis. It is probable that Bonaventure was healed shortly after the canonisation of the saint, whose intercession was felt throughout the world. His vocation as a friar was the fulfilment of the vow made by his mother.[19]

Francis's love of evangelical poverty is primarily treated in chapter seven in the *legenda*, although its content derived largely from Thomas of Celano's *Vita secunda*. The virtue of poverty was located at the centre of Francis's life and it was a defining character of the order. A paean of praise for the virtue stands at the beginning of the chapter. In language which echoes the beginning of the constitutions of Narbonne, Bonaventure affirms the place of this pivotal virtue as the foundation of the order. The friars' lives were founded on evangelical poverty. Provided that such a foundation remained, the order would stand firm; its opposite was also true. Thus, evangelical poverty, the criterion of the friars' fidelity to the Gospel, was a special route to salvation. Francis's love for absolute poverty was a special privilege which enabled him to grow rich in spiritual wealth. Evangelical poverty pointed unerringly towards a firm trust in divine providence and denoted a reliance upon the mandate of the Gospel not to worry about the morrow. Francis saw that this virtue, scorned by contemporaries, had been the constant companion of the Son of God; accordingly he embraced it in undying love.

Love of evangelical poverty led Francis to abandon his home, parents and commercial profession. Exploiting the monastic imagery of the sacred exchange, Bonaventure argues that no one was as greedy for gold as Francis was for poverty; no treasure was guarded as jealously as he protected this Gospel pearl (Matthew 13.45–6). Francis placed his imitation of the poor Christ above everything else and subverted the values of society in order to pursue this virtue. The memory of the poverty experienced by Christ and his mother often reduced Francis to tears; he called poverty the queen of the virtues because it was so evident in the life of the king of kings and of the queen, his mother. Poverty was the special way of salvation and the source

---

[19] Bonaventure, *Legenda maior*, prologue, nn. 1–3.

of humility. It was conceived as the root of all perfection and it was the treasure hidden in the field in the Gospel. In order to purchase it the friars were required to sell everything - and anything that cannot be sold should be abandoned for love of it.

The poverty of Christ and his mother provided the blueprint for the friars' perfection. It occupied a special place among the friars, whose emblem it became. In keeping with the first chapter of the Rule, the friars were required to renounce their possessions and to open themselves to the needs of others. Divested of these goods, they should offer themselves naked to the embrace of the naked Crucified. In contrast, those who adhered rigidly to their own opinions in the depths of their hearts had not renounced the world perfectly. Echoes of the *Testament* occur in the statement that Francis gave orders that the friars' houses should be small, like those of the poor. Similarly, the sixth chapter of the Rule shapes the founder's advice that the friars should live as strangers and pilgrims in a house which was not their own. It was the pilgrim's lot to shelter under another's roof and pass on peacefully, longing for home. On a number of occasions Francis had ordered the friars to leave a house, or even had it pulled down because it offended poverty.

Francis was particularly offended if he ever saw anything contrary to poverty among the friars. His poverty established the norm for his followers, even down to details of dress and the type of habit. From the first moment of his religious life until his death, his sole wealth consisted in a habit, a cord, and a pair of trousers, and he was content with that. Some parallels between the constitutions of Narbonne and the *Legenda maior* appear on a variety of subjects such as clothing. Echoing II, n. 7 of the constitutions, Bonaventure stated that throughout his religious life the founder's wealth consisted of a habit, cord and a pair of trousers. Those in search of a relaxed level of observance drew little comfort from the *Legenda maior*. The evangelical counsel to leave home and everything in order to follow Christ (Matthew 19.21) stood at the heart of the renunciation demanded by the saint. Bonaventure had no truck with those who entered the order in a more calculating manner, reserving books and other items for their use after profession. As already stated, such evasions can be traced back to the 1240s. Francis admitted only those men who gave away all their possessions and retained nothing. Among those rejected by the patriarch of the poor was a young man from the Marches of Ancona who left his goods with his family. The suggestion that the aspirants' goods should be converted to meet the friars' material needs was similarly rejected by the saint.[20]

[20]   Ibid., c. 7, nn. 1–4.

Devotional writings: De praeparatione ad missam

The account of Francis's conversion in the *Legenda maior* is couched in a eucharistic context in which the saint was open to the movement of grace and receptive to the Word of God. It exemplifies the way in which materials gleaned from Thomas of Celano were invested with bonaventurean emphases. The verbal parallels are striking. Bonaventure presents Francis as the exemplar of eucharistic piety. The saint was attentive to the movement of the sacred liturgy in which he heard the divine call and responded appropriately. He was attended Mass on the feast of an apostle, probably St Matthias, and his disposition was described as devout (*devotus*). The Gospel reading for the day described how the apostles, unencumbered by material possessions, were sent out to preach (Matthew 10.9–10). His participation at Mass on the feast of an apostle revealed his new vocation to perpetuate the apostles' ministry.

The inculcation of eucharistic devotion was a salient feature of Francis's writings and conduct and formed the basis of his respect for the office of the priesthood. The *Legenda maior* shows that he communicated reverently and fruitfully, associating himself with the sacrificial process of transformation. The promotion of higher standards of reverence towards all that pertained to the Mass was a defining characteristic of the order and a central feature of its programme of preaching. Following in the footsteps of Haymo of Faversham and William of Meltiona, Bonaventure made his own contribution to eucharistic piety as a preacher and devotional writer, especially in his *De praeparatione ad missam*. This treatise was conceived as an aid for priests in the discharge of their sacred office. Advice was dispensed to priests on a dignified, devout and fruitful celebration of this sacrament. This tract inculcated a spirit of reverence to combat indifference, neglect or routine in the celebration of Mass and it reflects the friars' apostolate to the secular and regular clergy. The treatise, completed around 1260, represents Bonaventure's devotional writings in the years following his election as minister general and it mirrors his efforts to foster reform among the priests, including members of his own order. It was the fruit of an emphasis which had been germinating in his academic and devotional writings for the previous decade, especially in his *Breviloquium* and *De regula novitiorum*; similar advice is contained in the constitutions of Narbonne, where special preparations were to be made for the reception of the Eucharist.

The five sections of the *De praeparatione ad Missam* examine the celebrant's faith, intention, disposition, charity and fervour, the rationale for celebrating the sacrament and the immediate preparation. The meditations were devised to guide priests in their preparations for Mass and to draw fully upon the graces contained in the sacrament. A sample will be taken from the second stage of that preparation whereby the celebrant is invited to consider his intention and disposition in celebrating Mass. In earlier comments on the reception of the Eucharist the Bonaventurean focus moves towards the dispositions of the celebrant and communicant. His approach is particularly concerned with combating and correcting those priests ensnared by inadequate dispositions. At the end of this section he calls for a spirit of repentance and reconciliation. The celebrant is urged to consider his motives in offering Mass, which results in a penetrating reflection:

> what are your plans and dispositions in approaching the altar? Examine and search the house of your conscience, lest some impurity remain in your mind, or some stain in the flesh offensive to the eyes of the Holy of Holies.

The mind and flesh have been distorted by original and actual sin and the process of recovery or penance should take place at both levels. Sin begins in the mind and then proceeds to infect the body, which rebels against the natural order. Hence, the mental processes were to be realigned with revelation and grace. In this treatise the penitent is concerned with the process of healing. Hence, the self-examination must be thorough-going and the sacrament must be celebrated with the purest motivation.

First, the celebrant is instructed to look inwards and consider his own shortcomings. He is to ponder the number of sins which he had perpetrated from his youth. Sins of commission and omission are to be recalled. The frailty of human nature was contrasted with the source of goodness contained in the sacrament; the Eucharist was instituted for the full restoration of humanity. The traditional reflection on the brevity of life and the uncertainty of the hour of death ensue. The celebrant is invited to meditate on the values which regulate secular society and their imperfections, recalling the medieval belief that sin was rooted in the world, the flesh and the devil. He should be guided by the teaching of Christ, who provides insight and strength. Above all, the celebrant is required to ask himself whether he has committed or intended any mortal sin since his last confession and penance.

Bonaventure deals not only with the looming sacramental encounter with Christ but also with the celebrant's state of mind. Any future attraction towards sin is to be expelled. Elsewhere he refers to the concept of continuous contrition for sins as an aid to the working of grace.[21] This was underlined by the links between the sacraments of penance and the Eucharist at the Fourth Lateran Council. The individual is exhorted to move towards a fuller commitment to the Gospel. He is not merely concerned with meeting the minimum conditions for the reception of the sacrament. He is left in no doubt that any attachment to disorder would vitiate his celebration and lead to further deterioration in his relationship with his Creator:

> for the bread of life, the divine food, procures no vital flow, provides no nourishment for members that are cut off and dead, as confirmed by the Scriptures: 'into

---

[21] Bonaventure, 'Regula novitiorum', c. 4, no. 1, *DSBOO*, VIII, pp. 475–90, 480.

a soul that plots evil wisdom does not enter, nor does she dwell in a body under the debt of sin' (Wisdom 1.4).

The distinction between the reception of the sacrament and its fruitfulness governs the advice dispensed to a negligent celebrant, who was counselled that he may receive the sacrament, but not its content, that is, the grace of Christ and the divinity of his love. He may take the sacrament into his mouth, but he would not be spiritually fed. The Body of Christ may go down to the stomach, but it does not reach the soul. In such cases it would be swallowed as by a brute animal: the sacrament itself remains unimpaired, but it brings no life to the soul. Such conduct evokes the treacherous image of Judas, the ultimate figure of betrayal (John 13.27).

Elsewhere the betrayer's perfidy is contrasted with the generosity of Christ. The celebrant is admonished to be careful lest he be compromised in his vital ministry of grace. He is admonished to ensure that no reason or necessity impairs his approach to the altar. Due contrition, a firm intention to amend and a proper confession of his sins are to be his companions. The dangers of celebrating the Eucharist without due attention to the preparatory steps or dispositions are spelled out in unambiguous terms.

Clerical defects, ambition, avarice, simony and other failings were at the forefront of Bonaventure's mind in the preparation of this treatise.[22] The defective motivations that brought people to the priesthood are deplored and the failure to use occasions of penitence and renewal:

> alas, how many today are those wretched priests who, unmindful of their salvation, partake of the Body of Christ at the altar as if they were eating the flesh of a mere animal.

Priests who neglected to avail themselves of sacramental confession and subscribed to the erroneous belief that the daily celebration of Mass alone would free them from their sins, were castigated, branded as heretics and corrected in the strongest terms. If they were possessed of an appropriate faith, they would desist from such illicit celebrations. Echoing the teachings and example of *il poverello*, Bonaventure urges that the necessary purity of mind must be accompanied by cleanliness of body and everything else that is used for the celebration of Mass. A thorough examination should lead the priest to penitence. The spirit of the recent Lateran Council informs the exhortation that the Eucharist is to be celebrated with the maximum reverence and devotion. Hands and all other parts of the body must be kept as clean as possible and the celebrant is to recollect himself lest he become distracted during the celebration of Mass. The cleanliness of altar vessels symbolised an inner purity of spirit:

---

[22] Bonaventure, 'De praeparatione ad missam', c. 1, no. 14, *DSBOO*, VIII, pp. 99–106, 104.

furthermore, take good care of the cleanliness and neatness of the altar linens and holy vessels, so that He who is feared and honoured by the angels and archangels may be treated with all due honour and attention.[23]

The second chapter proffers advice on the moments immediately preceding the celebration of Mass and the reception of the Body of Christ. The need for a good confession and the cultivation of a spirit of recollection and charity are reaffirmed. Bonaventure's deep indebtedness and profound gratitude to Francis shaped his vocation and conduct as a friar and the leadership which he brought to the order. He was canonised by Pope Sixtus IV on 14 April 1482 and declared to be a doctor of the Church by Pope Sixtus V on 14 March 1588. The *via media* which he fostered came under heavy strain during the last quarter of the century, especially in the face of the first fragmentation of the order in the 1290s, which now invites consideration.

[23] Ibid., c. 1, nn. 5–7, pp. 100–1.

CHAPTER EIGHT

The Order's Role in the Church

It will not be from Casale or from Acquasparta where such readers come to
the Rule which the one shirks and the other narrows.

Dante[1]

The Florentine poet here recognises that, despite Bonaventure's endeavours
as a theologian, legislator, biographer and mystical writer, internal reflection
and debate persisted among the friars. Lapses from the high standards of the
order stimulated the clarion call for a radical renewal.

Friars and the local community

The friars dispatched by the general chapter of 1217 to form new missions
were more mobile than those who assembled forty years later to elect Bonaventure. The second and third generations of friars took their place within
the constellation of religious communities, many of which were well established in the principal cities. They were beginning to settle on new sites close
to the heart of the cities, where they constructed sizeable conventual friaries.
The constitutions of Narbonne project an image of an order, whose life was
governed by evangelical poverty, sinking roots in the new and expanding
urban centres. The friars' vocation, however, was changing almost impercep-
tibly. Francis withdrew from society, practised self-abnegation and devoted
himself completely to prayer and the propagation of the Gospel. His vision
of religious life differed sharply from those of Augustine and Benedict, as his
confrères delighted in recounting. His first followers were missionaries in
their own towns and cities and their bases were outside Assisi, at Rivo Torto
and the Portiuncula.

A quasi-monastic stability of place was becoming the norm for some friars.
As the order expanded the friars were welcomed to the cities and towns,
where they developed a mutually beneficial relationship with their neighbours. Their spiritual ministrations were warmly welcomed and their contribution to urban life was not confined to the pulpit and the confessional.
One tangible sign of this transition lay in the fact that friars were perceived

---

[1]   Dante Alighieri, *Paradiso*, XII, vv. 123–6, pp. 943–4.

as ideal mediators and were drawn more and more into the affairs of the local commune. Salimbene provides countless examples of friars who mediated in local disputes. Friars were appointed as papal legates and invested with authority to act for leading ecclesiastics.[2] From 1286 Louis, son of Charles II, the king of Sicily, came under the influence of friars, when Francis le Brun of Apt in Provence was attached to his household and became his confessor.[3] Although such appointments might have appeared to confirm the success of the friars' mission, they were symptomatic of a subtle change. Although they were espoused to humility, individual friars were invested with power by the civic authorities. However much the friars might have wished to safeguard high standards, a variety of factors militated against that. The pope and layman found the friars useful and drew them into activities which inadvertently undermined the very features which made the order so attractive.[4]

Friaries were coming to resemble other religious institutions by offering employment as early as the middle of the thirteenth century.[5] What Francis had founded on the rock of humility and poverty was being transmuted into a cohort of highly talented and professional men who exercised wide-ranging influence. Friars' churches were being enlarged to house the large numbers wishing to attend sermons. They began to resemble and rival the monastic and collegiate edifices and offered burial to all, including members of royal families. King Béla IV of Hungary (†1270) and his wife Maria were buried at Esztergom and Peter III, king of Aragon (†1285) at Villanuova. Adrian V (†1276) was laid to rest at Viterbo, the first pope to be buried in a friars' church.[6] This development, which amounted to a change of focus, brought friars into competition with the secular clergy for alms, donations, Mass stipends and the quest for burials in their cloisters and churches. The new duties clothed them in positions of power from which their founder would have recoiled in horror. Membership of the order now offered an opportunity for a successful career in the Church.[7]

Professor Richard Southern observed that the gifts bestowed upon the friars by testators were small in comparison to the endowments of monastic houses.[8] In the early wills there is a stark contrast between the number of

---

[2]   This is exemplified by the appointment of Mansuetus da Castiglione Fiorentino, a papal penitentiary. In the spring of 1257 he lifted the sentence of excommunication which had been imposed upon Pisa. Visconti, *Sermons*, pp. 797–803.

[3]   *Processus canonizationis*, p. 106.

[4]   D. Burr, *Olivi and Franciscan Poverty: The Origins of the Usus Pauper Controversy* (Philadelphia, 1989), p. 16.

[5]   Salimbene, *Cronica*, pp. 372–3. The friars at Parma had a servant named Robert.

[6]   Nicholas Glassberger, *Chronica Fratris Nicolai Glassberger ordinis minorum observantium edita a patribus Collegii S. Bonaventurae*, Analecta Franciscana, II (Quaracchi, Florence, 1887), p. 82, L. Lemmens, 'Chronicon provinciae Argentinensis. O.F.M. circa an. 1310–27 a quodam Fratre Minore Basileae conscriptum (1206–1325)', *AFH* 4 (1911), pp. 671–87 at 678, Salimbene, *Cronica*, p. 868.

[7]   Burr, *Olivi and Franciscan Poverty*, p. 5.

[8]   Southern, *Western Society and the Church*, p. 289.

bequests to monasteries and those to friaries. The friars received alms from a range of sources in local society. Although the amounts were small, they made a valuable contribution to friars' economy in food and clothing. Wills reveal the level and type of material support for the friars. The *Acta Franciscana e tabulariis Bononiensibus deprompta* contain some 1,663 documents regarding the friars of Bologna in the thirteenth century. This collection is a treasure trove and yields abundant information on the friars' church, the requests for burial there, revenue for the celebration of Masses and the friars' links with the poor.

A string of indulgences fostered donations for the construction of San Francesco, Bologna. Wills offer a glimpse of the financial arrangements for the building and the addition of side altars. The high altar was dedicated to *il poverello* and there were at least 13 side chapels; there were also oratories in the friary, the infirmary and the second cloister.[9] Michael of Ugolini of Riosto left £300 for the construction of a new altar in the church and provided the necessary vestments, missal and a silver chalice on 23 June 1269.[10] Albert di Oddofredi, a doctor of law, donated £500 for three altars to be built close to the one dedicated to St Clare; the terms of his will of 22 February 1299 state that the three altars were to be constructed in honour of Sts Peter, Paul and John the Evangelist. Vestments for the use at these altars were provided.[11] The beginnings of family chapels are glimpsed in the will of Philip of Aldrevandini of Sala who requested burial close to the altar of St Agatha, where his parents had been laid to rest. He also gave £700 for the construction of a new altar between the altars of the Lord and St Mary Magdalene on 17/9 October 1299.[12]

Friars served as the commissaries or executors of wills and dispensed advice on ministering to the poor, identifying the actual paupers, although some testators specified the friars as the poor.[13] Zerra Romei left £900 to satisfy his debts; mention was made of his illicit gains through usury and injustice. His wife, Juliana, and his son, Arpinellus Zerre Romei of Castiglione, a friar, were appointed as his commissaries in his will of 8 October 1251. His son was left £60 to dispose of as he saw fit. Hemma Drudi of Aquabelli of Tomaruola left £16 to the friars for a good chalice on 17 May 1255. She assigned amounts of money for her funeral, including wax, candles and the

---

[9] *Acta Franciscana e tabulariis Bononiensibus deprompta*, p. 792, where the index lists the chapels of the church and friary.

[10] Ibid., no. 112, p. 39.

[11] Ibid., nn. 851, 1151, 1507, pp. 429–30, 583, 701–2.

[12] Ibid., no. 900, pp. 454–7.

[13] Ibid., nn. 9, 36, pp. 5–6, 13, *Le carte duecentesche del Sacro Convento di Assisi*, no. 84, pp. 156–8, C. Cenci, 'Costituzioni della provincia toscana tra i secoli XIII e XIV', *StF* 79 (1982), pp. 369–409 and lxxx (1983), pp. 171–206, at 386, n. 47, injects a note of caution because some testators regarded the friars as the poor, such as one on 11 February 1297 which stipulated that the poor were the friars at Santa Croce.

funeral pall. Money was to be distributed among the poor at the discretion of the guardian. Gasdia, wife of Boateris of Bologna, left £100 to Lambertinus Chazanimicis, her son and a friar, to spend on works of charity on 21 January 1273. Joanna Galvani of Perthorellis appointed friars as commissaries of her will of 6 December 1283 to distribute goods among the poor of Christ at the judgement of Gundulf, a friar and a relation.[14]

The teaching of the Rule

The order's success ultimately led to divisions because the lifestyle of the founder was ill-suited to an army of followers.[15] The management of that institutionalisation and interpretation of Francis's teaching were matters of the utmost concern to the friars. Beginning with *Quo elongati*, the popes intervened in the internal affairs of the order and monitored its fortunes. Pope Nicholas III (1277–80), as John Gaetano Orsini, served his apprenticeship as cardinal protector from 1261 and the friars described him as devoted to the order; his private chapel contained a picture of the saint.[16] Shortly after the general chapter of Assisi in 1279 he met the newly elected minister general, Bonagratia of San Giovanni in Persiceto, and called for an authoritative commentary on the Rule. He appointed a commission which included the minister general, the ministers provincial of Ireland and France and two friars who had been elevated to cardinals, Bentivenga da Bentavengi and Jerome Masci of Ascoli. Among the other members were Benedict Gaetani, the future Boniface VIII, and Peter Olivi, whose *Quaestiones disputatae* on the adoption of poverty (*usus pauper*) were completed shortly before the promulgation of *Exiit qui seminat*.[17]

Published on 14 August 1279, *Exiit qui seminat* reflects Nicholas's close relations with Bonaventure.[18] The prologue of this constitution explains the bitter attacks on the order, whose contribution to the Church was warmly commended by Pope Gregory X during the second council of Lyons. Nicholas had received the capitulars of the recent general chapter and been given their assurances that they wished to observe the Rule fully and vigorously.[19] Moreover, countless men had lived the Rule, including some enrolled in the catalogue of saints. The pope acknowledged his long and fruitful links with the order in the years before his appointment as cardinal protector. He

[14] *Acta Franciscana e tabulariis Bononiensibus deprompta*, nn. 36, 50, 138, 273, pp. 13, 16–17, 49, 104–5.

[15] Moorman, *A History of the Franciscan Order*, pp. 3–4.

[16] Salimbene, *Cronica*, p. 727, *Chronicon de Lanercost*, p. 99.

[17] *Chronica XXIV generalium ordinis minorum*, p. 369, *Peter Olivi's Rule. Commentary, Edition and Presentation*, ed. D. Flood, Veröffentlichungen des Instituts für europäische Geschichte Mainz, LXVII (Weisbaden, 1972), p. 159.

[18] V. Maggiani, 'De relatione scriptorum quorumdam S. Bonaventurae ad bullam 'Exiit' Nicolai III (1279)', *AFH* 5 (1912), pp. 3–21.

[19] *Chronicon de Lanercost*, p. 99.

had taken a close interest in the Rule and intentions of Francis. Nicholas's declaration that the Rule encapsulated the Gospel was of crucial importance and would be reviewed by Pope John XXII in 1321/2. The last two chapters of the constitution provided a defence of the Rule, which was deemed to be permissible, holy, perfect, observable and open to no apparent danger. Conscious of the controversies in the schools, where the friars' views were coming under fire, Nicholas stipulated that the constitution was to be expounded there. Masters were instructed to explain the text accurately and faithfully, lest their interpretations deflect men from entering the order. The penalties for flouting the constitution were the loss of clerical offices and benefices. Similarly the pope forbade anyone infringing what he had clarified about the Rule and its interpretation. This warning was accompanied by an injunction that those who tampered with the text or opposed it would incur the wrath of God and the apostles, Peter and Paul.[20]

The opposition to the friars, mentioned more than once in *Exiit qui seminat*, flickered from the later 1260s until the end of the century, with the initiative frequently changing hands. Simon de Brion, afterwards Pope Martin IV (1281–5), was favourably disposed towards the friars. As papal legate on 20 December 1268 he annulled measures which the mendicants deemed restrictive.[21] His *Ad fructus uberes* of 13 December 1281 gave the friars the privilege of preaching and hearing confessions freely, despite chapter nine of the Rule.[22] The constitution was addressed to the minister general and the ministers provincial and gave friars permission to exercise their apostolate both in preaching and hearing confessions; no one must try to stop them. But it also stipulated that the faithful must observe canon 21 by confessing their sins once a year to their parish priest. *The Lanercost Chronicle* reports that the papal bull was promulgated at a time when some twenty-one bishops had prohibited the friars of different provinces from preaching and hearing confessions.[23] Martin's bull provoked French bishops to take action against the sacramental and pastoral intrusion of the friars in the later 1280s.[24]

The tension between the Church's pastoral needs and the integrity of the order arose in the discussions which Cardinal Ugolino held with Sts Dominic and Francis. Although the cardinal recognised the potential for the rejuvenation of the episcopal ranks through zealous and theologically gifted friars, he was slow to comprehend that such a status and responsibility would be in conflict with the concept of the friars as the lesser brethren, men rooted in humility. It is to Ugolino's credit that he was respectful of Francis's wishes in

---

[20] *BF*, III, no. 127, pp. 404–16.
[21] H. Lippens, 'La Lettre de Simon de Brion, en faveur des mendiants (1268) et le soi-disant concile provincial de Reims (1267)', *AFH* 29 (1936), pp. 79–97.
[22] *BF*, III, no. 16, p. 480, Salimbene, *Cronica*, pp. 595–6.
[23] *Chronicon de Lanercost*, p. 107.
[24] A. G. Little, 'Measures Taken by the Prelates of France against the Friars (c. 1289–90)', in *Miscellanea Francesco Ehrle*, III, Studi e testi, XXXIX (Rome, 1924), pp. 49–66.

this matter. The change occurred in the next pontificate and within fifteen years of Francis's death, a friar occupied the seat of St Ambrose. The offices of bishop, cardinal, confessor, inquisitor, master of theology, papal legate and royal envoy were open to the friars before the 1270s. Leo of Vavassori of Perego, the minister provincial in Milan (1233–9) and Lombardy (1239–41), was provided to the diocese of Milan by Gregory of Montelongo, the papal legate, on 15 June 1241, but was not consecrated until 13 April 1245.[25] Thereafter the steady increase in the number of friars raised to the episcopate awakened anxieties, which were articulated following the election of Rainaldo of Arezzo, as bishop of Rieti in 1249.[26] By the later 1270s friars were represented among the college of cardinals and Nicholas IV, Jerome Masci of Ascoli, minister general (1274–9), was the first friar to sit on the chair of St Peter.

Popes from Gregory IX onwards made pronouncements about how the Rule should be applied to the evolving conditions of the order. *Quo elongati* won broad acceptance among the friars, who regarded it as a moderate statement of the order's lifestyle. That same confidence was not extended uncritically. Following the precedent of the general chapter of Metz in 1254, the order decided to be sparing in its use of *Ordinem vestrum*, particularly where it exceeded the terms of *Quo elongati*. The suspension of that papal bull was reaffirmed by the general chapter of 1260.[27] Similarly, the general chapter of Strasbourg in 1282 declared that the friars should not make use of the privilege granted by Pope Martin IV's *Ad fructus uberes* in cases reserved to the bishop, unless they enjoyed the blessing of the bishop. No confessor should use the privilege granted by the pope if it was a matter of a reserved case. The friars should exhort the laity to confess annually to their own priests and they should do their utmost not to offend prelates.[28] The range and nature of dispensations, sometimes in express contradiction to the Rule, led Rosalind Brooke to conclude that at around 1250–60 the popes were inclined to be extraordinarily callous and cavalier in their treatment of the friars' concerns about poverty.[29]

The genre of the commentary of the Rule arose in the early 1240s. There are at least four extant commentaries on the Rule from the last quarter of the century, an indication of vigorous debate and the desire for fidelity to Francis. Friars engaged in the instruction of their confrères were to the fore. David of Augsburg, who was master of novices in Regensburg between 1235 and 1250,

---

[25] *Vita secunda*, no. 148, *CA*, c. 49, Thomson, *Friars in the Cathedral*, pp. 94–101.

[26] Salimbene, *Cronica*, pp. 468–9, 471–8.

[27] Eccleston, *Tractatus*, p. 42, Delorme, 'Diffinitones capituli generalis O.F.M. Narbonensis (1260)', no. 13, *AFH* 3 (1910), pp. 491–504, at 503.

[28] G. Fussenegger, 'Definitiones capituli generalis Argentinae celebrati anno 1282', *AFH* 26 (1933), nn. 1–2, pp. 127–40 at 135.

[29] R. B. Brooke, *Early Franciscan Government: Elias to Bonaventure*, Cambridge Studies in Medieval Life and Thought, n.s., VII (Cambridge, 1959), p. 265.

compiled his exposition of the Rule before 1272.[30] The commentary by John Pecham circulated under the name of Bonaventure and belongs to the period between 1276 and 1279.[31] John of Wales's *Expositio regulae ordinis fratrum minorum* was completed about 1283–4.[32] Peter Olivi's *Expositio regulae fratrum minorum* has been assigned to the 1280s.[33] Echoing the words of Pope Nicholas III's commentary on the Rule, Olivi comments that the old enemy continued to stir up trouble against evangelical poverty. He adds the telling detail that certain religious were claiming that the Rule was neither evangelical, apostolic, nor perfect, but rather dangerous, unobservable and blameworthy. Burr identifies these religious as the Dominicans.[34]

Signs of unrest and division

The desire to live by the Rule assumed various forms. In the last quarter of the century currents of renewal surfaced in different regions and gathered momentum, especially in some provinces of Italy and France. One manifestation of concerns about levels of observance was the provincial legislation of a chapter in Aquitaine.[35] Another was the establishment of a community where a more rigorous interpretation of the Rule obtained. An unidentified community of twenty-two *fratres minores de regula* received alms from Edward I at La Réole or Bordeaux in Gascony on 12 May 1289.[36] A full account of the experiences of reformers in the Marches of Ancona is supplied by Angelo Clareno.

About 1275 the zeal of Angelo and Peter de Macerato, later known as Liberato, earned them gratuitous condemnation to perpetual imprisonment as schismatics and heretics. They were deprived of the sacraments, even at death's door, and were forbidden to have any conversation with their confrères who brought them the necessities of life. The other friars were not permitted to express any critical views about their treatment; Thomas and Mark may also have been incarcerated along with them. The weekly reading of the sentence at the domestic chapter angered one friar, Thomas of Castromili, who refused to be intimidated and questioned such punishment. His honesty consigned him to perpetual imprisonment until his death. The punishment

[30] *Peter Olivi's Rule*, p. 101. Cf. *De exterioris et interioris hominis compositione* (Quaracchi, Florence, 1899).

[31] C. Harkins, 'The Authorship of a Commentary on the Franciscan Rule Published among the Works of St. Bonaventure', *FS* 29 (1969), pp. 157–248, *Peter Olivi's Rule*, p. 100, n. 116.

[32] D. Flood, 'John of Wales's *Commentary on the Franciscan Rule*', *FS* 60 (2002), pp. 93–138 at 93.

[33] *Peter Olivi's Rule*, p. 103.

[34] Burr, *Olivi and Franciscan Poverty*, pp. 49, 55, n. 39.

[35] M. Bihl, 'Statuta provincialia provinciarum Aquitaniae et Franciae (saec. XIII–XIV)', *AFH* 7 (1914), pp. 466–501.

[36] B. F. Byerly and C. R. Byerly, eds., *Records of the Wardrobe and Household 1286–9* (London, 1986), no. 2526, p. 284.

of these friars was a matter of common knowledge throughout the province and it reached the ears of the minister general, Raymond Gaufredi (1289–95). When he presided over a provincial chapter in 1289, he investigated the plight of the imprisoned friars. On the evidence of the minister provincial and the friars of the Marches of Ancona, Gaufredi learned that Angelo and companions had not been punished for any offence or sin: their sole crime was their desire to live in accordance with the Rule and the intentions of the founder. Gaufredi rebuked those responsible for such unjust treatment and absolved the incarcerated friars.[37]

Acting on what looked like a groundswell of support for the imprisoned friars, Gaufredi had them released. Angelo makes no mention of any discussion regarding their reintegration in the life of the province, but the option was undoubtedly considered. The ultimate decision was momentous in its implications: the minister general decided to separate the small band of reformers. Perhaps he feared that the breach was already irreparable. Did Gaufredi consult his confrère, Nicholas IV, about so critical a policy? Their lukewarm personal relations may have militated against such a search for salutary advice. Gaufredi's momentous judgement paved the way for the independence which the reformers would enjoy in the second decade of the fourteenth century. He sent Thomas, Mark, Liberato and Angelo Clareno to Hayton II, the king of Armenia, with special authority and permission. The friars earned the respect and praise of the king, princes, clergy and religious in Armenia. Their lives edified the king, who in turn vouched for them to the general chapter of Paris in 1292. The king was so impressed by the friars that he abdicated and joined them in 1294.

Despite such commendations, the friars were maligned by their confrères in Syria. Relations were bad and such a commotion was raised against the small band of zealots that the minister provincial and others became hostile towards them and denounced them to the king. They alleged that the zealots were apostates and warned the king and his barons against them. The king then summoned the friars, investigated the charges and was happy with their explanation; this episode merely increased his respect for the friars. Nonetheless, in 1294 the hostility of the friars in Syria was such that Angelo and companions returned to Italy, where they encountered renewed opposition in their own province. Mundaldo, the vicar provincial, left them in no doubt that they were unwelcome. The two friars proceeded to Gaufredi, who counselled them to seek help from the new pope, who was known to be supportive of efforts to renew religious life. Celestine V, who would resign the papacy on 13 December 1294, received the friars and investigated their claims.[38]

Having examined their case, he invited them to observe the Rule fully in

---

[37] Angelo Clareno, 'Epistola excusatoria ad papam de falso impositis et fratrum calumniis', *ALKG*, I, pp. 521–33, 523–4.

[38] Ibid., pp. 524–5, Dante Alighieri, *La divina commedia, Inferno*, III, v. 60, p. 35.

accordance with the teaching of their canonised founder. Angelo and companions were removed from the jurisdiction of the order and given papal protection. Dressed as hermits, they were commanded to preserve the teaching and spirit of their founder but without the name of Friars Minor. Liberato, who became the head of the Poor Hermits, was authorised to absolve his companions from any censure and to admit recruits.[39] The new hermits were recommended to Cardinal Napoleon Orsini, the nephew of Pope Nicholas III. Although he was a benefactor of the order, he was to become one of the chief protectors of the reformers. He arranged for them to be received by an abbot of his own order and to dwell in their hermitages. When the friars of the Community, a term which came into vogue in the early fourteenth century, heard that the pope had dispensed them, they disregarded his authority and persecuted and tried to capture Angelo and his companions.[40]

Angelo claimed that he, Liberato and the others were cast out of the order and their reputation was smeared by lies disseminated by the friars of the Community, who also menaced them and sought their death.[41] The band of zealots continued to be harassed by the Community, which made different attempts to capture them in defiance of the mandate of Celestine. The resignation of the pope emboldened the Community's attempts to apprehend the zealots, who moved to a Greek island. Their whereabouts at Sevastocrator of Epirus in southern Thassaly were ascertained by the Community two years later and they redoubled their endeavours to discredit their former confrères, bringing forward a series of false allegations, including that of heresy. In their refuge Angelo and companions were approached by Jerome, a friar who purported to be a messenger of Peter Olivi.[42]

Peter Olivi's appointment as lector at Santa Croce in Florence (1287–9) gave him links with the Tuscan reformers.[43] His ideas about the observance of poverty, especially his concept of *usus pauper*, expressed a sympathy for the ideals of the reformers. At Florence he taught alongside Ubertino da Casale, whose passion for the reform of the order would make him a powerful advocate at the papal court of Avignon. He was the focus of another movement of renewal in Provence, where his views attracted growing support. This task of imposing discipline and uniformity among the friars required good relations with the minister general. Already in 1290 Raymond Gaufredi, himself a Provençal and formerly minister provincial there, had reluctantly initiated disciplinary proceedings against those who regarded themselves as more spiritual than their confrères in Provence by virtue of their witness to

[39] V. Doucet, 'Angelus Clarinus, Ad Alvarum Pelagium, Apologia pro vita sua', *AFH* 39 (1946), pp. 63–200, 99, no. 17.

[40] M. F. Cusato, 'Whence "the Community"?', *FS* 60 (2002), pp. 39–92, at 64–7, Angelo Clareno, 'Epistola excusatoria', pp. 525–7.

[41] Doucet, 'Angelus Clarinus', no. 41,p. 108.

[42] Angelo Clareno, 'Epistola excusatoria', pp. 528–9.

[43] Ehrle, 'Zur Vorgeschichte des Concils von Vienne', *ALKG*, II, pp. 353–416 at 389.

poverty, to the dismay of his critics.[44] Two years later he skilfully orchestrated a defence of the teaching of Peter Olivi. Frustrated with Gaufredi's patience with such groups, Pope Boniface VIII attempted to remove him by promoting him to the bishopric of Padua. When the offer was declined, Boniface deposed him in October 1295. The following summer John of Murrovalle was elected at the general chapter of Anagni. John was more sympathetic to papal viewpoint and was already known to be hostile to Peter Olivi.

In 1299 the minister general prevailed upon the general chapter of Lyons to condemn the teachings of Peter Olivi, who had died the previous year. An ecclesiastical council at Béziers complained that certain religious were stirring up the Beguines with apocalyptic expectations. The minister general responded by initiating an enquiry among the friaries of Provence to ascertain the extent and character of Olivi's influence, particularly on the question of the *usus pauper* controversy. The commission was headed by Vital du Four, lector of Toulouse, and Arnold of Olibé, minister provincial of Aragon. Their findings were disturbing: that Olivi's followers were numerous and he had many adherents among the laity. In a series of letters Morrovalle called for the confiscation and destruction of Olivi's writings, the punishment of those who clung to such books, the extinction of the so-called sect of brother Peter John and the dispersal of his followers, beyond the province if necessary.[45]

Jacopone da Todi

The abdication of Pope Celestine V, the suppression of the Poor Hermits by Pope Boniface VIII and worries about the orthodoxy of Peter Olivi plunged the order into a period of turmoil. While poverty was the emblem of the order, the reformers' discontent centred on a number of questions. These broader grounds are reflected in the witness of Jacopone da Todi, a reformer and an important figure in the evolution of Italian poetry. One of the two sons of Iacobello Benedetti, Jacopone was born between 1230 and 1236. This author of powerful religious poetry (the *Stabat mater* is attributed to him) had studied at Bologna before marrying Vanna di Bernardino di Guidone between 1265 and 1267 and settling down as a notary. Her tragic death was followed by an itinerant period before he became a friar in 1278. His sympathies were drawn towards the reformers, a group which was comforted by the unexpected election of Pope Celestine V on 5 July 1294. He appealed to the new pope and was granted protection against the friars of the Community. His doubts about Celestine's strength to eradicate the corruption surrounding the curia are expressed in *Que farai, Pier da Morrone? Ei venuto al paragone*.[46] These anxieties were confirmed within six months by the

---

[44] *Chronica XXIV generalium ordinis minorum*, p. 420.
[45] Ibid., p. 431.
[46] Iacopone da Todi, *Laude*, no. 74, pp. 218–20.

historical resignation. Jacopone was one of the three friars who signed the Longhezza manifesto of 10 May 1297, which denounced the election of Boniface VIII and called for a council to elect a new pope. He joined Cardinals James and Peter Colonna in their rebellion. Boniface excommunicated the two cardinals, who were sympathetic to the reformers' aspirations, as well as the signatories of the declaration. He called for a crusade against the heretics who had taken refuge in the Colonna fortress in Palestrina.[47]

Palestrina fell in September 1298 and Jacopone was handed over to the order to be disciplined. His sentence was incarceration in the Umbrian friary at Todi. *Que farai, fra'Iacovone? Ei venuto al paragone* recounts the punishment received for his part in the rebellion and then opens an extended criticism of the life of the friars and the ways in which they compromised their vocation. Pouring scorn on the friars who were drawn to the papal court in search of privileges, Jacopone muses that the only benefice which he received from the Roman court was the loss of his good name. His new prebend was the removal of his capuche, as well as the chain which held him like a lion. His underground prison opened to a latrine, whose putrid odour infested his cell. Like Lord's Byron's *Prisoner of Chillon*, he was kept in solitary confinement, with the exception of one friar, his attendant, who was obliged to report his remarks. Whenever he was lying down, the chains became entangled as he moved his legs. A basket containing some pieces of bread was dangled into the cell at a level above the rats. The bread was left over from the previous day and meanly sliced, scarcely enough to satisfy a piglet; there was also an onion to add flavour. The meal arrived when the friars had sung nones or terce. Some soup was dumped into a pail along with an apple.[48]

The figure of *il poverello* represented the ideals pursued by the reformers. *O Francesco, da Deo amato, Cristo en te ne s'è mustrato* commences with a summary of the drama of salvation. Long after his defeat the devil made a further attempt to ensnare humanity, but divine providence sent Francis to lead the Christian forces. The order's policy on admissions came under fire with the observation that the saint admitted only those men who had despised and rejected the world. Poverty, chastity and obedience were the three horses which carried Francis into battle. The sight of the saint, who so closely resembled his divine master, struck fear into the ancient enemy of the human race. Francis wished to dress in rags and beg for his bread. He persevered on the true path in absolute poverty; he had instructed his followers never to touch money. The devil acknowledged that his powers would be blunted by the good work of the friars. When he turned his gaze first upon women and then married people, Francis informed him that he had established a Second Order of sisters and a Third Order of married penitents.

---

[47] *BF*, IV, no. 122, pp. 440–1.

[48] Iacopone da Todi, *Laude*, no. 53, pp. 146–52. Jacopone da Todi is the normal English translation of Iacopone, the Italian form. This is used by the translators, Serge and Elizabeth Hughes.

The devil was equally thwarted when he cast his designs upon heretics. There, too, the saint pledged himself to combat heresy.[49] At the very beginning of *O Francesco povero, patriarca novello* the saint was saluted as truly poor and the patriarch of the present age. The poet enumerates the seven visions of the cross experienced by the saint and one of them featured the call to restore the Church which had lost its way; he set the Church on a salutary path. The sacred wounds of the Crucified were interpreted as a sign of Francis's close union with Christ and that bond steadied and sustained the saint and showed him how to conduct his life.[50]

Povertat' ennamorata, grann' è la tua signoria! provides the poet with a platform for his views about the wholesome nature of the virtue so beloved of the founder. The first salutes the theological virtue of charity. The domain of poverty was immense, sweeping through western Europe and including unknown kingdoms, where the missionaries had laboured. The result of their toil was that the universe was united in praise of the Creator.[51] *O amor de povertate, renno de tranquillitate!* identifies the love of poverty as a tranquil kingdom which knows no strife, hatred, thief or storm. The truly poor die in peace and have no need of a last will or testament, judge or notary. Jacopone smiles at the avaricious man who frets over his money. Evangelical poverty represents the deepest wisdom, which enjoys the detachment and freedom to gain everything. The paradox of poverty was fully exploited whereby those who have contempt for things possess them without risk. In contrast, those who who crave possessions are themselves possessed.[52]

Jacopone's observation that some friars travelled to the papal court and returned clad in mitres is a comparatively mild comment about the growing band of friars consecrated as bishops. An incomplete list of friars raised to the episcopate in the 1280s identifies twenty-three bishops, a number which climbed to thirty-six in the next decade. Some of these friars had already served as ministers provincial, papal penitentiaries, inquisitors or lectors. One of the new prelates was James Thomas Caeitano, nephew of Pope Boniface VIII, who made him cardinal priest on 17 December 1295. Few friars took poverty as a spouse and loved it as a virtue; some were more inclined to swap their vow of poverty for a mitre without a second thought. The poet contrasts his own dealings with the Roman Curia which brought him prison, with the experience of other friars raised to the episcopate. Some friars leave the world and then reject it, while others who firmly reject it are drawn back into secular ways. The friars who resist the world are opposed by it.[53]

The growth of theological study among the friars was perceived by some

[49] Ibid., no. 71, pp. 206–12.
[50] Ibid., no. 40, pp. 113–19.
[51] Ibid., no. 47, pp. 130–2.
[52] Ibid., no. 36, pp. 97–102.
[53] *BF*, V, nn. 109–45, pp. 613–14, Iacopone da Todi, *Laude*, no. 53, pp. 146–52.

as a cause of malaise. *Frate Ranaldo, do' si andato?*, addressed to a deceased doctor of theology, personifies the ills of the order and the threat to the friars' eternal salvation. The *mores* of the *studia generalia* are probed and Jacopone pointedly asks the dead friar where he had gone and what philosophical points he had recently made. The expense of theological study in the universities was high and generated debts for the friars; with studied ambiguity the poet inquires whether Rinaldo's debts had been settled before asking whether he was in heaven or hell. The doctor of theology was asked whether he had attained eternal glory or disgrace. Although he had died with meekness and a confession of his sins, the poet questions his contrition and unction. The doctor of theology had passed to the veritable school of truth rather than the limited academic exercises of the university. The school of eternal truth would examine the words and expose the thoughts of those learned in terrestrial terms. Before the eternal judgement all facts would be clear, unlike the schools where the masters made innumerable distinctions and were capable of distorting the truth. The rules of logic, prose and rhyme would be of no avail before the tribunal of eternal assessment. Rinaldo had attained his doctorate in the University of Paris and had enjoyed honour and prestige. This process had cost the order vast amounts of money, which might have been better employed in charitable causes. The poet wonders whether the doctor of theology's academic labours would be sufficient to release him from his debt to his Creator.[54]

Jacopone was numbered among those who suffered hardship on account of his religious ideals.[55] He was released in 1303 by Pope Benedict XI and spent the last years of his life in the friary of San Lorenzo in Collazzone, dying in 1306. Despite the voices of reform, the order's pastoral contribution was valued by the Church and its remarkable missionary vitality and heroism were displayed in the mission to China, which was begun in the closing years of the thirteenth century and then flowered for a time in the fourteenth, largely through the influence of John of Montecorvino, to whom we now turn.

---

[54] Iacopone da Todi, *Laude*, no. 88, pp. 278–9. Ranaldo is translated as Rinaldo.
[55] *Liber chonicarum sive tribulationum ordinis minorum*, V, 380, pp. 554–7.

CHAPTER NINE

The Mission to China

> For eighty years the Franciscans have preached the Gospel among the Tartars and founded forty churches there; most recently the order has been crowned by nine [new] martyrs.
>
> Jerome, bishop of Caffa[1]

Jerome emphasises the order's contribution to missions in Morocco, India and China. The audacious enterprise of seeking to evangelise China, a region which would be sprinkled with the friars' blood, was launched at a time when more information about the orient was reaching the west. Increased trade took Greek and Italian wines to China, a country visited by Venetian merchants during the thirteenth century.[2] Marco Polo reached China in 1271 and spent many years in the imperial service. The noble conduct of the Chinese entered popular literature.[3] These contacts created opportunities for new initiatives by the western Church in general and the order in particular.

John of Montecorvino (1247–1328)

A native of southern Italy, John of Montecorvino participated in the missions to Armenia and Persia about 1279–83; he returned to Rome in 1289 with a letter from King Hethum II of Armenia to the pope, who replied on 14 July 1289.[4] Pope Nicholas IV wrote a series of letters to the leaders of the Tartars and focused on the opportunities for evangelisation. John was entrusted with a letter to Dionysius, bishop *in partibus orientis*, on 7 July 1289, and a letter to Kubilai Khan on 13 July 1289; the second of these announced that John was being sent with his companions to evangelise the Tartars.[5] On 15 May 1296 Pope Boniface VIII wrote to the friars *in orientalium Tartarorum*

---

[1] Golubovich, *Biblioteca*, III, pp. 38–58, 48.
[2] A. C. Moule, 'Textus duarum epistolarum Fr. Minorum Tartariae Aquilonaris an. 1323', *AFH* 16 (1923), pp. 104–12 at 110–11, 'Martyrium fr. minorum Almaligh an. 1339', *SF*, pp. 507–11.
[3] Boccaccio, *Decameron, Filocolo, Ameto, Fiametta*, X, 3, pp. 679–85, which was purportedly based on the reports of Genoese merchants.
[4] *BF*, IV, nn. 133, 135, pp. 87–8.
[5] Ibid., nn. 129–31, 138, pp. 84–6, 89–90.

partibus.[6] John was revered as *primus apostolus* of the Tartars.[7] This papal legate was the mainstay of the mission, which his fellow missionaries deemed to be hard and demanding.[8] His corresponence illuminates the conditions in which he toiled.

The letter of 8 January 1305 was written when John was aged 58. He entered India in 1291 and remained in the church of St Thomas where he baptised about 100 people in different places. He left India for China, where the hardships of his mission had turned his hair white. Accentuating the theme of isolation, he announced that he had been alone in Beijing for 11 years; he had lacked a confessor until the arrival of Arnold, a friar from the province of Cologne, a year earlier. For twelve years there had been no news about the Roman Curia, the order and western society. John observed that no apostle or disciple of such had preached the Gospel in China.

The imperial authorities were generous towards John and his converts. John preached openly and built several churches, including one with a tower and three bells; this church was completed *c.* 1300. He baptised about 6,000 people and observed that he was constantly administering this sacrament. The number would have reached 300,000 had he not been slandered by the Nestorians, whose duplicity and hostility were a *topos* of the friars' reports. A second church was constructed for the use of the slaves whom he had purchased. One of his early converts was named George, a Nestorian king and a descendant of the celebrated Prester John. George took minor orders and, clad in sacred vestments, assisted John at Mass. This conversion moved the Nestorians to accuse John of apostasy and other crimes, including murder. Despite this, John converted many and built a fine church in honour of the Holy Trinity with financial assistance from the emperor. George died as an exemplary Christian, leaving a nine-year old son and heir, John, whom he named after the missionary friar. Much of the good which he had accomplished was reversed by his children, who were committed to Nestorianism. Additional information on George's contribution to the mission was supplied by Peregrine of Castello, bishop of Zhangzhou (Zayton), on 30 December 1318.[9]

John translated the New Testament, Psalter and Divine Office from Latin so that it might be sung throughout George's territories. He announced that he had successively purchased forty boys of pagan families; they were aged between seven and eleven years and had had no religious instruction. He baptised them and taught them Latin and the liturgy. Another church was being

---

6   Ibid., no. 68, p. 394.
7   'Relatio Fr. Iohannis de Marignoli', I, c. 1, no. 3, p. 526.
8   'Epistola Fr. Peregrini episcopi Zaytunesnsis', *SF*, no. 2, pp. 357–68, 365.
9   Ibid., nn. 1–2, pp. 365–6. G. M. Bastianini, 'Fra Pellegrino da città di Castello, O. Min. Il vescovo di Zayton in Cina (†7 iuglio 1322), e l'autenticità della sua "lettera" (30 dic. 1318)', *MF* 47 (1947), pp. 152–99.

constructed for the boys whom he divided among several places. He wrote thirty psalters with hymnaries and two breviaries for the use of the boys, who were accustomed to keep the choir. The Divine Office was celebrated, regardless of John's presence or absence and the bells of the church announced the hour of prayer. Several of the boys transcribed psalters and other useful things. Two years earlier a doctor from Lombardy unsettled John with his reports about the state of the Church and the Franciscan order. John, who wished to verify this information, expatiated on the opportunities for evangelisation and urged the order to send out missionaries to assist him and to inform the pope about the progress of the mission. Advice about the best route was imparted as well as information about the length of the projected journey.

The letter of 13 February 1306 was addressed to the vicars general of the Dominicans and Franciscans and the friars of both orders in the province of Persia. It opens with a renewed complaint about the lack of communication and the claim that until that year he had been forgotten by his confrères; rumours of his own death had reached friars in the west. The prolonged silence was broken only in the January of the previous year when John took advantage of the travels of a friend, who carried messages to the vicar and friars in the custody of Gazaria in the Crimea. The previous year John had begun a new building before the gate of the imperial residence, thanks to the generosity of Master Peter of Lucalongo, a Christian merchant, who had accompanied him from Tauris. Peter purchased the land for the friary and presented it to John, who marvelled at this ideal site for the construction of a church, which was received in August 1305 and decorated in good time for 4 October. The new buildings included a chapel with a capacity for two hundred people and a red cross stood on top of it. The two churches built by John in the imperial city were separated by two and a-half miles and the boys were divided between them. Mass was normally celebrated there on alternate weeks. Six scenes drawn from the Old and New Testaments were painted in the churches for the instruction of the indigenous population and accompanied an inscription in Latin, Turkish and Persian. As the papal legate John had a right of access to the imperial court and was honoured above all other prelates by the emperor, who wished to receive more western envoys. There were many people in that land given to idolatry, but there were monks, whose discipline and asceticism surpassed levels of observance in the Latin Church.

Towards the end of the letter John painted a positive picture for would-be helpers and emphasised that there was much in the region that was ripe for zealous missionaries. His knowledge of India indicated that it would be a good place for friars to preach. A stately embassy from Ethiopia had approached him with an invitation to preach there himself or to arrange to have others sent there, where no one had expounded Christianity since the time of St Matthew and his disciples. If friars were to be sent there, they would convert the people and instruct them in Christ and the Scriptures; there were many nominal Christians in that region, but they lacked preachers to educate them. Hearing that friars of both orders had reached Gazzaria and Persia, John exhorted them to preach fervently for the salvation of souls. Since the feast of All Saints John had baptised more than 400 people. He was insistent that only *viri solidissimi* should be sent as missionaries.[10]

The missions among the Tartars received an injection of new life in 1302 when James de Monte, the vicar of the Orient, and 12 friars set out from Rome.[11] This initiative on the part of the minister general, John of Murrovalle, may have been sent to another part of that mission, although it is conceivable that Arnold, who became John of Montecorvino's confessor, was one of them. John's letters were digested by Gonsalvo of Spain, minister general, and his definitors and the missionary's recommendations were communicated to the papal court. Friars were received by Pope Clement V to discuss the mission, which was on the agenda of the general chapter of Toulouse in the middle of May 1307. The decisive response was twofold, one on the part of the Roman Curia and the other by the general chapter, which called for volunteers.

The advent of new missionaries in 1307

Gonsalvo and his general definitory were invited to nominate seven friars suitable for the episcopal office in northern Tartary.[12] Privileges which Pope Alexander IV had granted to the friars working in diverse missionary fields were renewed by Pope Clement V on 23 July 1307.[13] A new metropolitan see was established at Beijing, whose first archbishop, John of Montecorvino, was to be invested with jurisdiction over the whole kingdom. The bull of provision referred to John's long years as a missionary. On the same day John was provided with six suffragan bishops: Andrew of Perugia, Nicholas of Banzia (Bantia, Baucia) of Apuglia, minister provincial of Umbria, Gerard Albuini, Ulruic of Seyfriedsdorf, Peregrine of Castello and William of Villanova. They were to be consecrated by their former minister general, John of Murrovalle, cardinal bishop. On 1 May 1308 the pope instructed William to receive consecration and to proceed to China without delay. These friars were instructed to make arrangements for episcopal consecration and travel to Beijing, where they were to consecrate John and invest him with his pallium.[14] Andrew of Perugia travelled with Peregrine. They faced innumerable hardships on their journey and were robbed of everything. Having consecrated John, they

---

[10] 'Epistolae Fr. Iohannes de Monte Corivino', *SF*, pp. 333–55.
[11] Angelo Clareno, 'Epistola excusatoria', pp. 529–30.
[12] Golubovich, *Biblioteca*, III, pp. 93–4.
[13] *BF*, V, no. 84, pp. 35–7. The same mandate was addressed to the Dominicans.
[14] Ibid., nn. 85, 86, 87, pp. 37–9, and no. 112, p. 51.

remained with him for five years. Throughout that period they received the *alafa*, an imperial grant for envoys, for the sustenance and clothing for eight people.[15] Three more friars, Thomas, Jerome the Catalan and Peter of Florence, were appointed as suffragans on 19 February 1311.[16]

During the general chapter the minister general enlisted the support of the ministers provincial in the search for volunteers for the mission. Internal reports mention friars from England, France, Germany, Hungary, Italy and Spain. The friars embraced the missionary policies recommended by John: preaching in various centres, the cultivation of good relations with the emperor and the purchase of slaves to be schooled in Christian ways, a decision which evoked the strategies of Gregory the Great to evangelise the Anglo-Saxons.[17] In a letter of 15 May 1323 the friars reported that since 1306/7 the Gospel had been preached in that region, often to the great cost of the friars and members of other orders. Friars followed the military camps and scarcely had time to eat before nightfall. A German friar snatched ninety-three idols from the hands of idolaters and baptised all the families, who were instructed as fully as possible; the friars appealed for help, especially in view of their limited resources. Their ministry resulted in the conversion of more than a hundred princes, barons and chiliarchs and their families.

Those zealous for Christ were encouraged to reflect on the benefits for the whole of Christendom, if God permitted the continuation of the grace of conversion to nullify the military threat so feared in the west. The tensions and wars between the Tartars and the Saracens were emphasised. The friars visited the camp of the Tartar forces and preached to them many times daily, even in the circumstances of warfare. Some friars learned the appropriate languages, while others preached through interpreters. The Hungarian, German and English friars were proficient; in contrast, the French and Italian friars rarely mastered the language. Each day the friars baptised many. Alms were deployed for the purchase of children of either sex. These children were instructed in the principles of Christianity and were taught how to read. The boys were made clerks and some of them became friars. Pagans came willingly to the Divine Office and behaved with an admirable reverence which some Christians would do well to copy. The friars asserted that such progress had not been made since the time of Gregory the Great.[18]

---

[15] 'Fr. Andreas de Perusia, Epistola', *SF*, no. 7, pp. 369–77, 377.

[16] *BF*, V, no. 176, p. 74, Clement V appointed them as suffragan bishops to John of Montecorvino. Cf. Angelo Clareno, 'Epistola excusatoria', pp. 528–9.

[17] S. Gregorii Magni, *Registrum epistularum* (Corpus Christianorum, series Latina, CXL), VI. 10, pp. 378–9. In September 595 Gregory had ordered his administrator in Gaul to purchase English boys aged 17 or 18 in the slave markets so that they could be brought to Rome and taught in the city's monasteries. Cf. *The Earliest Life of Gregory the Great by an Anonymous Monk of Whitby*, ed. B. Colgrave (Lawrence, Kansas, 1968), c. 9, pp. 90–1.

[18] Moule, 'Textus duarum epistolarum', pp. 106–12. 'Epistola Fr. Peregrini episcopi Zaytunesnsis', no. 3, p. 366, confirms that some friars preached with the assistance of interpreters.

Friars active in the northern part of the mission to the Tartars, an area which incorporated parts of China, gave a report on their apostolate to the general chapter of the order and the papal curia in two letters of 15 May 1323. The letter to the general chapter supplied details of the martyrdom of various friars. The second letter, addressed to Pope John XXII, the cardinals, prelates and the members of the order gathered for their general chapter, announced the successes of the mission, especially the gains of the last seventeen years. The friars' belief that they had converted nearly a third of the population of the empire should be considered alongside their admission that they occupied scarcely a tenth of the land. During the wars between the Tartars and the people described as Saracens, the friars followed the camps and worked with little food and rest. Each day they baptised many and confirmed them. A German friar snatched ninety-three idols and prepared their owners for baptism. The religious devotion of the Tartars impressed the friars, who received food and clothing from them. The friars reflected that the salvation of souls would depend on the work of those who were coming. An indulgence was granted to the friars, who were permitted to perform many episcopal functions. While they could not ordain clerics, dedicate churches or bless chalices, they were licensed to dedicate cemeteries because there were too few bishops. Opposition to the friars' work led to the martyrdom of some Christians and religious. Further progress was, however, hindered by the paucity of friars for the celebration of the sacraments. This created a spirit of contraction, a feature of later letters, in which the friars were obliged to surrender twenty-two stations. St Francis's missionary endeavour was invoked in the hope of attracting more volunteers from the provinces of the order in western Europe. The friars write away from the environment of China's great cities. They speak of rural settlements where most people generally lived in felt tents and dressed in skin with linen and silk garments. The fear of the emperor, whom the friars planned to convert, had brought an end to attacks on missionary stations and churches. For the first time since 1312 the friars were assembled to hear news from their general chapter and a response to their request for more volunteers. The letter closes with a plea for prayers for the support of the mission and for others to join them. Three friars, Anthony of Milan, Monaldo of Ancona and Francis de Petriolo, were martyred on 15 March 1314.[19] After 1321 the mission to northern Tartary had eighteen friaries, including two in Beijing and one at Zhangzhou and Armalech (Saray); there had been two friaries at Zhangzhou when Odorico of Pordenone was making his way to Beijing.[20]

The large city of Zhangzhou, a journey of some three months from Beijing, was the seat of a bishopric.[21] A rich Armenian lady built the church, which

[19] Moule, 'Textus duarum epistolarum', pp. 106–12.
[20] Golubovich, *Biblioteca*, II, p. 72.
[21] 'Epistola Fr. Peregrini episcopi Zaytunesnsis', no. 7, p. 368.

she bequeathed to Bishop Gerard Albuini and the friars;[22] she provided for the material needs of the friars present and those to come. Peregrine of Castello succeeded Gerard as bishop and lived there with three friars, John of Grimaldi, Emmanuel of Monticulo and Ventura of Sarenza, who became a friar in China. The virtues of these friars were praised and Peregrine who lamented that he did not have a hundred such with him. They had a house outside the city with a wood, where they wished to make cells and a chapel. While the friars were supplied with ample material goods, they needed, above all else, more personnel for the mission. With a touch of pathos Peregrine predicted the end of the mission:

> we are in need of nothing so much as friars, whom we seek. Brother Gerard the bishop [of Zhangzhou] is dead, and we survivors cannot live for long; no other missionaries have come. The Church will be left without baptism and without inhabitants.[23]

The aged missionary's plea for assistance on 3 January 1318 did not result in any significant injection of new blood. The major crisis followed the death of John of Montecorvino about a decade later.

Peregrine's comments about an ageing community which had not received an infusion of new life were reiterated in a letter from other missionaries on 15 May 1323. Peregrine died on 7 July 1322 and was succeeded by Andrew, the companion of his pilgrimage, who had resisted earlier attempts by John to appoint him to Zhangzhou. Andrew's letter of 9 January 1326 to the guardian and community at Perugia announced that he had been living in his diocese for four years and was still supported by the imperial *alafa*. He had a church built with accommodation for some twenty friars and with four chambers, while Peregrine was still the bishop. After his succession to the diocese he spent his time in the city or in a hermitage. He comments that, although many idolaters were baptised, they failed to adhere strictly to Christian traditions. He sent his greetings to the minister provincial and to the friars in general and excused himself for not writing to his friends on the grounds that he did not know which of them were alive and which dead. He supplied information on the fate of his fellow bishops who had been appointed to assist John. Nicholas of Banthra (Banzia), Andrutius of Assisi and another unnamed bishop died on their entry into lower India in an exceedingly warm country, where many other friars had died and been buried.[24] Andrew of Perugia, the last of the group of bishops appointed by Pope Clement V, went to his grave in 1332. Archaeological evidence, including a photograph of his tombstone, confirms that he was buried in his own diocese.[25]

22 'Fr. Andreas de Perusia, Epistola', *SF*, no. 3, pp. 374–5.
23 'Epistola Fr. Peregrini episcopi Zaytunesnsis', no. 6, pp. 367–8.
24 'Fr. Andreas de Perusia, Epistola', *SF*, nn. 3–5, 7, pp. 374–7.
25 J. Foster, 'Crosses from the Walls of Zaitun', *Journal of the Royal Asiatic Society of Great Britain and*

Odorico of Pordenone (c. 1270–1331)

Formerly a missionary in Armenia and Russian Mongolia, Odorico of Pordendone left for India and China in 1317 or 1318 and travelled with two friars, James of Ireland,[26] who probably communicated a legend about trees in his native land,[27] and Michael of Venice, his interpreter.[28] His journey was missionary in character because he expressly states that he crossed the sea to visit the countries of unbelievers in the search for souls.[29] He travelled largely along the coastline of India and then into China, whose vast cities captured his imagination. The great cities of China were compared to those in Italy, especially those in the Veneto; Zhangzhou was twice the size of the university city of Bologna.[30] Odorico's narrative enjoyed a wide popularity, which is reflected in the strength of the manuscript tradition and an early translation of the Latin text into Italian.[31]

The text is rich in detail, but disappointing in its lack of information about the friars' heroic mission. Peculiar omissions are the name of John of Montecorvino, the lynchpin of the first mission and settlement in China, and the chronic shortage of missionaries in the 1320s. It is curious that he does not speak of the friars by name, apart from James and Michael, his two companions, especially since he met so many of the missionaries who had ministered there since 1307. He crossed from Venice and landed at Trabzon in Turkey.[32] He reached Soltaniyeh (Soldania), which is south-east of Zanjan and one of the principal cities of the region, where the emperor of the Persians resided during the summer. It was a great city, which housed a market where many costly items were on sale. Odorico does not mention the community of friars there; the friary may have been formed after his visit. A metropolitan had been established on 1 April 1318 and entrusted to the care of a Dominican. Odorico eventually reached Zhangzhou (Zayton), a noteworthy port and the seat of a Catholic bishop. There were two friaries there at that time. The city was the home of varied religious practices.[33]

Entering China, Odorico passed to the former imperial city of Hangzhou (Camsay), where four friars lived. He lodged in the home of one of the friars' converts, a man of authority, who acted as his guide in the city. The city's topography is described and comparisons are made with Venice, Padua and Ferrara. His next port of call was the large city of Yangzhou (Çançay), which

---

Ireland 26 (1954–5), pp. 1–25, 17–20.

[26] 'B. Odoricus de Portu Naonis, Relatio', *SF*, c. 8, no. 22, pp. 379–495, 383, 436, n. 2.

[27] Ibid., c. 31, no. 1, p. 483.

[28] Ibid., c. 8, no. 22, pp. 383, 436.

[29] Ibid., c. 1, no. 1, p. 413.

[30] Ibid., c. 21, no. 1, p. 460.

[31] *Libro delle nuove e strane e meravigliose cose. Volgarizzamento italiano del secolo XIV, dell' Itinerarium di Odorico da Pordenone o. min*, ed. A. Andreose, Centro studi Antoniani, XXXIII (Padua, 2000).

[32] 'B. Odoricus de Portu Naonis, Relatio', c. 1, nn. 1–4, pp. 413–16.

[33] Ibid., c. 3, no. 5, c. 21, no. 1, pp. 418, 460.

had a community of friars and three Nestorian churches.[34] Marco Polo had spent three years there as governor. The immensity of the ancient city of Beijing (Cambelec) and the splendour of its imperial court were described at some length. The four principal feasts kept by the emperor were his birthday, his circumcision and two others which are described in great detail. Guests went forward and offered presents, a ritual in which the friars participated. Odorico spent three years in the capital city and attended a number of the emperor's celebrations. He noted the friars' presence at court, which should be understood either as the financial support of the court for the friars or for their friary close to the palace.[35]

The one aspect of the friars' apostolate to be reported at some length was that of exorcism. The friars in great Tartary expelled devils from the possessed so much that they thought no more of it than to drive a dog from the house. In those regions there were many men and women thus possessed, who were bound and brought to the friars; some travelled a journey as long as ten days to reach the friars. The evil spirits departed from these people on the invocation of Christ. Those so liberated were baptised by the friars, who confiscated their idols made of felt, and carried them to the fire in the presence of a growing crowd. The friars cast the gods into the fire, but they leapt out again. They then took holy water and sprinkled it upon the fire to expel the demons. When the friars cast the idols into the fire again, they were consumed. This policy led to the baptism of large numbers in that region.[36] Odorico witnessed a meeting between the emperor, who was returning from his travels, and the friars, who joined the procession to meet him. He himself carried a thurible which was used when the *Veni, Creator Spiritus* was sung; one of the friars was an unnamed bishop. The friars placed the cross on timber so that it could be seen openly. While the friars were intoning the hymn, the emperor called them forward. The bishop imparted his blessing. In accordance with the custom of that court, no one ventured into the imperial presence empty-handed. Odorico presented a small dish full of apples. The emperor took one and ate it.[37]

The friars admired and lauded their confrères who earned the martyrs' crown. The narration of such heroic deeds added to the lustre of the order, particularly at a time of immense uncertainty over its future in the wake of Pope John XXII's decisions about the observance of the vow of poverty. Odorico produces a lengthy account of the martyrdom of four friars, three Italians and one Georgian, on 9 April 1321. Earlier reports of the martyrdom were circulated by one of their colleagues, Jordan Séverac, a Dominican, on 12 October 1321, by the friars in northern Tartary, who on 15 May 1323

---

[34] Ibid., c. 23, nn. 1–8, c. 25, no. 1, pp. 463–7, 469.
[35] Ibid., c. 25, no. 7- c. 29, nn. 1–7, pp. 471–82.
[36] Ibid., c. 36, pp. 490–1.
[37] Ibid., c. 38, nn. 1–4, pp. 492–4.

notified the pope, cardinals and general chapter, and by Andrew of Perugia, bishop of Zhangzhou, who compiled an account for the friars of his native city in January 1326.[38] Odorico's narrative incorporates many of the classical elements of a saint's passion. Scriptural imagery pervades the narrative. There was a titanic struggle between the forces of good and evil; there were ubiquitous echoes of the passion and miraculous prodigies. The friars' conduct was exemplary and their virtue produced miracles. The four friars, Thomas of Tolentino in the March of Ancona, James of Padua, Peter of Siena and Demetrius, a Georgian brother and linguist, left Ormes for Quilon, not far from the southern extremity of the Indian peninsula. They were captured on board the ship and carried to Tana, near Bombay. There was a small Christian community in that city; fifteen houses were occupied by the Nestorians and the friars found hospitality in one of them. However, during their stay they witnessed a domestic dispute between husband and wife. The matters reported to the cadi, a position which Odorico compared to that of the local bishop. The cadi asked the complainant to corroborate her allegations. Three of the four friars were summoned as witnesses, but the matrimonial alteration was quickly dropped from the scene which followed.

The cadi took the opportunity to discuss matters of religious belief. Odorico, whose purpose was to glorify the friars, suggests that there was a disputation in which the friars prevailed. What began as the friars' interview with the cadi, acquired some of the trappings of a public disputation. The friars' confident affirmation of their beliefs routed the cadi. The friars were prompted to give their views about the Prophet Muhammad. The friars' words angered the Muslims, who called for their death on the grounds of blasphemy. Odorico presents the exchanges as a tussle between Christianity and Islam and his account glorifies the friars and celebrates their heroic martyrdom. The friars were taken and bound in the intense heat to die a most terrible death. The heat was so strong there that anyone who stood bare-headed for the space of thirty minutes would die most horrendously. From the third hour until the ninth hour the friars gave themselves to the praise and glorification of God; they remained cheerful and unscathed in the scorching heat. The executioners then informed the friars that they intended to pitch them into a great fire to ascertain the truth of their comments, a trial by ordeal. A defiant reply was made by the friars, who declared that they would endure imprisonment or death for their faith. James of Padua emereged unscathed from his ordeal in the flames. The cadi then approached the melic, the equivalent to a *podestà* or leading civic official, and expressed his concern lest the friars should detach the populace from Islam. He invoked an ancient law whereby those who kill a Christian obtain the equivalent merit to that of one who goes on pilgrimage

---

[38] A. C. Moule, 'Cathay and the Way Thither', *The New China Review* 3 (1921), pp. 216–28. Cf. Golubovich, *Biblioteca*, II, pp. 69–70, Moule, 'Textus duarum epistolarum', pp. 105–6, 'Fr. Andreas de Perusia, Epistola', no. 6, p. 376.

to Mecca. This persuaded the melic who gave him full licence.

The cadi took four armed men to slay the friars. Arriving at night, they were initially unable to find the friars. The melic caused all the Christians in the city to be seized and imprisoned. When the friars rose at midnight to celebrate matins, they were detected and led to a tree where they were questioned by the soldiers and willingly agreed to go to their deaths as martyrs. Thomas, making the sign of the cross, was the first to be beheaded; he was followed by James and Demetrius. The following morning the cadi and his entourage went to collect the friars' belongings and found Peter, whom they also executed. As a result of a dream in which the martyred friars appeared to him, the melic made his peace with the Christians in the city and had four churches built in honour of the friars.

Odorico had heard of the friars' martyrdom and not long afterwards he visited the graves in which the Nestorians had reverently placed them. He opened their tombs and devoutly took up their bones. Accompanied by a friar and servant, he set out for a friary in upper India. Lodging at a home, he kept the relics under the pillow. The bones protected him from a fire which devoured the house. As soon as he escaped from the building the entire house fell. The two friars arrived at Zhangzhou, where they deposited the sacred relics. Numerous miracles were wrought there. Those afflicted by disease went to the place where the friars were martyred and washed the earth in water, which they then drink and were cured.[39] Odorico may have left Beijing prior to the death of John of Montecorvino. His life was drawing to its close, when he reached the shrine of St Anthony in Padua in the early summer of 1330. He made a solemn deposition of his experiences to the minister provincial, Guidotto. He confirmed that he was either an eye-witness to the events which he recounted or he was drawing upon the experiences of trustworthy witnesses. William of Solagna, a friar, faithfully recorded Odorico's narrative in May 1330. Odorico died at the friary of Udine, Friuli, on 14 January 1331 and thereafter his tomb was associated with numerous miracles.[40]

John of Montecorvino died in 1328, probably at Beijing. Further missions were launched in the 1330s, 1340s and 1350s. The martyrdom of Thomas of Tolentino, an earlier companion of Angelo da Clareno, illustrates the different views among the friars and these informed the polemical exchanges in the first quarter of the century. The writings of Ubertino da Casale and Angelo da Clareno reveal the growing divisions among the friars.

[39] 'B. Odoricus de Portu Naonis, Relatio', c. 8, pp. 424–39.
[40] Ibid., c. 38, nn. 6–8, pp. 494–5.

CHAPTER TEN

The Growing Clamour for Reform

The Rule imposes the same austerity in clothing and poverty upon both novices and professed alike.

Ubertino da Casale[1]

The increasingly fragile unity of the order was placed under a heavy strain in the 1290s when the first fissures appeared with the withdrawal of friars who placed themselves under the protection of Pope Celestine V. Two of the most influential spokesmen for the reformers were Ubertino da Casale and Angelo Clareno.

Ubertino da Casale (1259 – c. 1330)

Ubertino da Casale, who enjoyed contact with Angela of Foligno and Margaret of Cortona, was the leader of the reformers in Tuscany and Umbria. He had served as lector at Santa Croce in Florence alongside Peter Olivi for two years. His nine years in Paris gave him an international outlook on the order and its practices; this global perspective countermanded his critics' claim that he was unfamiliar with life in the vast majority of provinces.[2] His *Arbor vitae crucifixae Jesus* and his *Super tribus sceleribus* reflect the deepening tensions within the order regarding the observance of the Rule.[3]

Ubertino's *Rotulus*, delivered in a polemical context at Avignon, laid out the case for far-reaching reforms under twenty-five headings and influenced aspects of Pope Clement V's *Exivi de paradiso* of 6 May 1312, the last significant papal attempt at a compromise between the two wings of the order. A historical model permitted Ubertino to contrast the halcyon days of the founder with the decline of contemporary friars. The saint and the unnamed 'our fathers' established the appropriate level of observance for friars. Contemporary excesses were pinpointed and areas where the Rule was not satisfactorily observed. The constitutions of Narbonne and Bonaventure's *Legenda maior* created a yardstick for observance, which the ministers at general, provincial, custodial and domestic levels failed to safeguard. What was

---

[1] Ubertino da Casale, 'Rotulus', *ALKG*, III, no. 5, pp. 93–137 at 100.
[2] Chiapini, 'Communitatis Responsio 'Religiosi viri' ad Rotulum Fr. Ubertino de Casali', pp. 662–3.
[3] A. Heysse, 'Ubertini da Casali opusculum "Super tribus sceleribus"', *AFH* 10 (1917), pp. 103–74.

worse was the ministers' harshness and hostility towards those who wished to follow the Rule literally. Zealous friars in the provinces of Tuscany, Umbria, the Marches, Genoa and many other places were unjustly treated; for example, the minister provincial of Provence expelled two friars, Peter Aychi and Raymond de Falgueriis, for this reason.[4] The Rule, Ubertino argued, should be lived 'in spirit' (*spiritualiter*) rather than 'in body' (*carnaliter*).[5]

The early friars lacked buildings, clothes and books, and often went without the necessities of life, an experience unfamiliar to contemporary friars. The latter retreated from the high standards set by the founder by countenancing a situation in which most aspirants donated their possessions to the friary or particular members of the community, or reserved them for use after profession for the purchase of books and other items. Both the *Legenda maior* and the example of the first fathers proclaimed that novices should give their possessions to the poor rather than to rich relatives or the friars.[6]

The novices' inauspicious beginning persisted after the profession of vows: a spirit of 'common laxness' (*communis relaxio*) obtained in friaries, where the Rule was scarcely observed in matters of austerity, dress and poverty. There were abuses regarding the habit, which had been a feature of polemical exchanges between the Benedictines and Cistercians in the twelfth century. The habit, the symbol of the friars' commitment to a penitential lifestyle, instead advertised their ostentation and infidelity. Injunctions about the choice of habit featured in contemporary provincial ordinances.[7] The employment of the noun *curiositas* adroitly evoked images of unease, which were buried deep in the medieval consciousness. The prohibition on the wearing of shoes was flouted by many for no adequate reason. Penitentiaries in the Roman curia were singled out as particular offenders. There were similar failings on the part of friars who lived with prelates and other magnates and the masters of theology. Many of these were accused of routinely wearing shoes without sufficient reason in the winter in defiance of the Rule.[8]

The observance of the Rule was a natural development of the appeal to earlier standards of exemplary conduct. The increasing use of horses by friars, either undertaking long journeys or acting as messengers for others, was deplored internally and externally.[9] Dispensations were granted too readily because the friars abused the exemptions envisaged by the Rule. While

---

[4] Ubertino da Casale, 'Rotulus', nn. 21–2, pp. 122–3, 126.

[5] Ibid., no. 16, p. 118.

[6] Ibid., no. 2, pp. 96–7.

[7] C. Cenci, 'Ordinazioni deï capitoli provinciali umbri dal 1300 al 1305', no. 7, *CF* 55 (1985), pp. 5–31 at 26. The provincial chapter of Spoleto in 1301 reflects diversity of practice and consequent unease among the friars, no. 7: *nec habeant deformitatem in longitudine vel latitudine, artitudine vel notabili brevitate, tam tunicarum quam capputiorum et manicarum; ita quod in habitu exteriori fratres communiter conformentur.* Cf. Boccaccio, *Decameron*, III, 7, p. 234.

[8] Ubertino da Casale, 'Rotulus', nn. 5–6, pp. 100–1.

[9] W. A. Pantin, *The English Church in the Fourteenth Century* (Cambridge, 1955), pp. 267–8.

the infirm were dispensed from this prohibition, some friars rode with great pomp and incurred no small expense. Their ostentatious conduct betrayed the Rule. Ministers offended greatly in this matter, as did inquisitors. Moreover, they rarely took action against friars who travelled on horse back without a good cause.[10] The precept that the friars were to devote themselves to prayer, the celebration of the Divine Office, contemplation and pastoral duties had become onerous for contemporary friars. Instead, they gave themselves to useless discourses, wasted words, vain and other poor uses of their time. Such behaviour fostered the deeply engrained image of the idle and mischievous friar. Ubertino reminded these friars about the words of Bonaventure on the vice of laziness. There was a correlation between the deviation from high standards and the indolence of some friars. Prayer and devotion, which once rose from an army of friars, were rarely to be found in friaries.[11]

The conservation of perishable goods for large communities was a vexed question which had exercised the mind of Peter Olivi and stimulated his concept of *usus pauper*. This matter was raised once again under the exhortation that the friars should be strangers and pilgrims in the world. Beginning with the teaching of the four Parisian masters and the general constitutions, Ubertino considers the question how much food and drink might be legitimately stored by a community. The fathers of the order had ordained that there should be neither granaries nor cellars; goods should not be kept for long periods. The concept of such conservation horrified Francis, who regarded it as a breach of the highest poverty and dependence upon divine providence. Because he had wished only to provide for the day, his example was invoked. Nonetheless, there were granaries and cellars; in some instances they were large enough to store wine and grain for a whole year.[12] The size of gardens and vineyards was deemed to be excessive and food and wine were sometimes converted into money for the friars' use. Friars were permitted to have gardens so that they might grow vegetables for their own needs, but such permission did not extend to the sale of items grown there.[13] Large amounts of money were kept in friaries for the writing of books and the construction of buildings.[14]

Breaches of the prohibition on the receipt of money were numerous and a level of resourcefulness was displayed in finding ways of circumnavigating the Rule and the constitutions. At the basilica of San Francesco and the Portiuncula, where the order began and which the founder had wished to

---

[10] Ubertino da Casale, 'Rotulus', no. 9, pp. 103–4.

[11] Ibid., no. 12, pp. 109–10.

[12] Ibid., no. 14, pp. 114–15.

[13] *BF*, V, no. 195, pp. 80–6, 84. Clement V's *Exivi de paradiso* instructed the friars to correct the practice of having extensive gardens and large vineyards which produced large quanitities of vegetables and wine to be sold. Friars were instructed not to lay aside stores in granaries or wine cellars out of fear.

[14] Ubertino da Casale, 'Rotulus', no. 10, p. 107.

set up as a model of religious observance, money was continually received in the form of offerings. The two convents accepted money in contravention of the Rule, in accordance with a dispensation issued by Pope Nicholas IV; this practice had prevailed before the privilege had been conferred. The bad example given by the two prominent friaries was spreading to other cities and provinces. Money was accepted for the celebration of Masses and candles. Such questionable practices evoked images of the market-place for Ubertino, who recalled the cleansing of the Temple by Christ. Contempt for the Rule led many friaries to quest for alms in the piazza and market place.[15] In many provinces money was received for the celebration of Masses and the friars attended the anniversaries of the deceased; on such occasions they received money like any other priests. Similarly, friars were accustomed to take part in the festival of the dead, when they gave absolution over the graves of the deceased and received a stipend in return. On feast days their practice was to seek alms from those entering and leaving the more important churches in a city. The example of 'our fathers', who were intent on the spiritual welfare of those who approached them for advice or help, chided contemporary friars intent on material benefits.[16]

The friars' desire to build in accordance with the spirit of the founder exercised their minds from the time of his death. Some new projects were perceived as a breach of the principles of the highest poverty and there were lapses into the curiosity and excess proscribed by the general chapter of Narbonne. The dimensions and the decoration of the friars' churches had become a *topos* of domestic debates about fidelity to the Rule. Signs of opulence and curiosity were represented by the excessive amounts of gold and silver in chalices, crosses, thuribles and tables. The friars' churches were so well stocked and furnished that they exceeded the great churches, cathedrals and the richest monasteries. Such ornamentation contradicted the statutes laid down by 'our ancient fathers' on the matter of the curiosity of pictures, books, vestments and other items.[17] Similar comments were echoed in Pope Clement V's *Exivi de paradiso* on 6 May 1312.[18] The late thirteenth century saw the rise of large new conventual churches in the Tuscan cities of Florence, Lucca, Pisa, Pistoia, Prato and Siena; there were two or more cloisters in some of the larger friaries. Leonardo Bruni contrasts the narrowness and smallness of the first chapel at Santa Croce with the magnificent basilica begun in 1294.[19] Ubertino complains that many of these structures appeared more

15 *BF*, V, no. 195, p. 83. Friars to accepted offerings of money in their churches.
16 Ubertino da Casale, 'Rotulus', no. 10, pp. 104–7.
17 Ibid., no. 15, pp. 115–17.
18 *BF*, V, no. 195, pp. 83–4, where the pope echoed some of the complaints articulated by Ubertino. Clement censured the excessive buildings of the friars and the sumptuousness of their decoration. Many of the friars' churches rivalled the great churches and cathedrals in the locality. Such observations were also noted by the order's external critics.
19 L. Bruni, *History of the Florentine People*, edited and translated by J. Hankins, The I Tatti Renaissance

like the palaces of kings than the homes of the poor. There were multiple infringements in such matters.

Articulating the reformers' predilection for the hermitage rather than life in the centre of a city, Ubertino was more contentious in his claim that the founding fathers of the order ordained that friaries should be away from the large centres of population. Instead, he observed that friaries were not only built in the suburbs, but even at the heart of heavily populated cities. The friars in Italy were disposed to accept new sites, which were enlarged for their new structures to the disadvantage and discomfort of both local clergy and laity. They purchased beautiful and expensive houses which were then demolished to make way for their new buildings, which cost large sums of money. Churches, too, were destroyed to make way for the new conventual complexes. There were plans to have cemeteries, vineyards and vast cloisters such as the wealthy citizens could scarcely afford. The conventual buildings included dormitories, kitchens, refectories, chapter houses, schools, libraries, archives, cloisters, stores and other rooms. Such structures neither bore witness to evangelical poverty nor demonstrated that friars were pilgrims in this world. The *Legenda maior* confirms that Francis displayed the greatest zeal in defending his ideals. What was decreed by both the general constitutions and 'our ancient fathers' was being contravened. The decoration of these churches generated similar abuses.[20]

Special scorn was reserved for Paris's *studium generale*, Ubertino's *alma mater*. Ubertino echoes the profound concerns articulated by Giles of Assisi (†1261), Jacopone da Todi (†1306) and Angelo Clareno (†1337).[21] One of the recurring themes of the malaise afflicting the order was the level of ambition among the friars. The observation that the Parisian *alumni* dominated the order as masters and lectors draws much support from an analysis of the key members of the provinces in the thirteenth century; many of the lectors and ministers provincial had been groomed in the *studium generale*. Despite the example of lectors renowned for integrity, devotion and miracles, Ubertino associated academic attainment with a life of exemptions from conventual rigour and discipline. In many provinces, whether they were lecturing or not, the lectors were excused from attendance at the Divine Office and other

Library, 2 vols (Cambridge, Massachusetts, 2001), I, lib. IV, 39, pp. 378–9. Cf. Giovanni Villani, *Nuova cronica*, ed. G. Porta, Biblioteca di scrittori italiani, 5 vols (Parma, 1991), II, lib. IX, c. 7, p. 21.

[20] Ubertino da Casale, 'Rotulus', no. 15, pp. 115–17.

[21] *Dicta beati Aegidii Assisiensis*, Bibliotheca Franciscana ascetica medii aevi, III (Quaracchi, Florence, 1905), p. 91: *item dicebat frequenter in fervore spiritus: 'Parisius, Parisius, ipse destruis ordinem sancti Francisci.'* Iacopone da Todi, *Laude*, no. 91, pp. 293–4, complained that masters of theology received special treatment in the wing of the friary reserved for guests. They did not share the common table with the friars in the refectory, but enjoyed a more delicate menu. They passed new rules in chapters which they flouted. Angelo Clareno, *Liber chronicarum sive tribulationum ordinis minorum di Frate Angelo Clareno*, ed. G. Boccali, I, nn. 214–15, pp. 208–9. Francis predicted that masters from the universities would destroy the order.

common activities. In addition, they ate and drank outside the refectories, just as they pleased. They travelled across territories and the houses of a province, accompanied by a friar who took care of their arrangements and everywhere they were received like secular lords. Few of the ministers or guardians had the courage to deny them anything. Immediately after novitiate these friars were dispatched to study philosophy and they explored vain and arid questions.

The pursuit of devotion and prayer was alien to the younger friars. When they become lectors, they lacked the foundation of virtue and could not rest unless they held sway over others. The matter of study was the cause of friction in several provinces, producing divisions and factions. A carnal spirit and ambition were discerned in both lectors and masters and this cleared the way for relaxations of the Rule and its observance. Such flagrant abuses deterred some friars, the *fratres spirituales*, from study. The conduct of some lectors vindicated the founder's reservations regarding theological study; the saint predicted that some friars would lose their vocations and their love of poverty in this manner.[22] A corollary of higher studies was the formation of large libraries, especially at the *studia generalia*, which were maintained at considerable expense, although the extant catalogues of libraries belong to the fourteenth century.[23] Ubertino expostulated at the growth of personal libraries, which friars transported from one friary to another. He affirmed that it was not the intention of the founder that friars should have vast libraries for their exclusive use; friars should not purchase a Parisian library for themselves and move it with them from one friary to another.[24]

Angelo Clareno (c. 1245–1337)

Born as Peter of Fossombrone, Angelo Clareno was given the name by which he is known by Pope Celestine V in 1294. Four texts recount his ideals and the heavy price that he paid for them. The first, a lengthy *apologia* addressed to the pope and cardinals, was already featured in the Chapter 8. The second was a commentary on the Rule.[25] A third, another *apologia*, was compiled for Alvarus Pelagium, a friar and papal penitentiary.[26] The fourth was a book of chronicles, which explains the genesis of the tensions and divisions within the order and is discussed here. It is a valuable resource for the evolution of the reform movement and its theology of history.

Angelo's chronicle was written in the middle of the 1320s, perhaps in 1326, and describes seven periods of tribulation or persecution endured by those

---

[22] Ubertino da Casale, 'Rotulus', no. 16, pp. 118–19.
[23] Cf. Humphreys, *The Book Provisions of the Medieval Friars 1215–1400*, Studies in the History of Libraries and Librarianship, I (Amsterdam, 1964).
[24] Ubertino da Casale, 'Rotulus', no. 13, p. 111.
[25] *Expositio super regulam fratrum minorum di Frate Angelo Clareno*, ed. G. Boccalli, Pubblicazioni della biblioteca francescana, Chiesa Nuova-Assisi, VII (Assisi, 1994).
[26] Doucet, 'Angelus Clarinus'.

who remained faithful to the vision of the founder.[27] He is a witness to the vicissitudes of the order in the last quarter of the thirteenth century. His longevity enabled him to meet some of the early friars, a factor which confers a particular authority on his chronicle.[28] He had heard Giles and Angelo, the companions of Francis, as well as a friar who had been present at the sermon preached by the saint at Bologna on 15 August 1222.[29] Contact with older friars gave him access to an invaluable oral tradition. Unlike Ubertino da Casale, who mentions Peter Olivi only once in his articles concerning infringements of the Rule, Angelo incorporates a full account of the punitive measures taken against the friar from Narbonne and his followers.[30] Moreover, this chronicle provides a solid foundation for the historical development of the reform movement among the friars. The starting point of his chronicle is that Francis was divinely called to imitate the humility and poverty of Christ. His Rule and *Testament* were divinely inspired; as such they were not to be glossed by the friars.[31] The Rule was equated with the Gospel and Francis was divinely instructed about the details of the friars' lives and living arrangements. For example, friars should accept dwellings only with the permission of the bishop and parochial clergy.[32]

Angelo's interpretation of the history of the order is skilful, although he sometimes finds himself in chronological difficulties with his list of ministers general.[33] He argues that the fraternity was subverted at an early stage by those whom the founder had trusted. Images of betrayal were conjured up with connotations of Judas Iscariot. The persecution of the more zealous friars began with the installation of the two vicars by Francis, when he was about to leave for the Holy Land in 1219. Angelo suggests a more widespread disturbance than Jordan of Giano does and shows that the two vicars regarded the zealous friars as disobedient. Thereby he placed the roots of the reform movement in the lifetime of the founder rather than depicting them as a late thirteenth century group. Informed of the state of the order through a vision, Francis returned to Italy and reasserted his authority. While Francis's return from the East resolved one problem, it placed another in sharper relief. Some friars listened attentively to his divinely inspired teaching, but the more learned adopted a strategy of patience until they could gain control of the order; the image of the friars from the schools seeking to assert themselves in opposition to the founder was a salient feature of the reformers' literature:[34] Angelo differs from Thomas of Eccleston and Jordan of Giano,

---

[27] Angelo Clareno, *Chronica*, pp. 22–5.
[28] Ibid., II, no. 31, pp. 292–3.
[29] Ibid., II, no. 168, pp. 320–1. Ibid., I, no. 158, pp. 198–9.
[30] Ubertino da Casale, 'Rotulus', no. 21, p. 124.
[31] Angelo Clareno, *Chronica*, prol., nn. 58–64, 150, pp. 102–5, 118–19.
[32] Ibid., prol., nn. 88–109, pp. 108–11.
[33] Ibid., II, nn. 156–7, 220–5, pp. 318–19, 328–31.
[34] Ibid., I, nn. 1–38, pp. 168–77.

who credit scholastic figures with the downfall of Elias of Cortona.

The account of the tension regarding the completion of the Rule reflects the writings of Leo, Rufino and Angelo. The ministers provincial were cast in the role of undermining the spiritual heritage of the founder and opposing the final redaction of the Rule of 1223. Seeking the support of both Elias and Cardinal Ugolino, they made representations to the founder because they were worried lest he should insert new and more exacting conditions for his followers.[35] Like Elias of Cortona, they were accused of a preoccupation with the growth and the aggrandisement of the order. They were so intent on increasing the number of friars and provinces that they forgot the wisdom and discernment of their founder.[36] Special vitriol was reserved for Elias, whose failings as minister general were vented by Angelo, just as they had been by earlier chroniclers. Elias's term as minister general occasioned the second tribulation, in which he railed against the saint's companions, whom he persecuted. The harsh treatment meted out to Caesar of Speyer reflected the way in which faithful friars were abused in the later 1230s. Despite the fact that he was the biographer of Francis and Anthony and a widely respected friar, Caesar was arrested, incarcerated and went to his death at the hands of an excessively jealous and cruel friar, his jailer.[37] Elias isolated the early companions of Francis and began to persecute them, that is, Caesar of Speyer, Bernard of Quintavalle, Anthony of Padua and other friars of a more spiritual disposition.[38] Angelo's account, however, derives no support from the early biographers of Anthony, who would scarcely have omitted any persecution of their subject, who had also filled the offices of *custos* and minister provincial before 1230. Some later texts, which are not without chronological difficulties, link Anthony and Adam Marsh in their vigorous defence of the Rule against Elias.[39] In addition, Anthony died on 13 June 1231, that is, one year before Elias's election as minister general.

Haymo of Faversham's four years as minister general were described in brief and positive terms. Perhaps his pivotal role in the deposition of Elias in 1239 blinded Angelo to the English friar's promotion of clerics to the detriment of the non-clerical friars, as Peregrine of Bologna attests. Haymo's successor, Crescentius da Iezi from the Marches of Ancona, attracted much criticism. Although his spent only a single triennium as minister general (1244–7), he followed the tastes and habits of Elias and was blamed for unwelcome developments in the life of the order. He unleashed the period of the third persecution.[40] The surviving companions of the founder discussed

---

[35] Ibid., I, nn. 32–57, 139–57, pp. 176–81, 194–7.
[36] Ibid., I, nn. 298–305, pp. 224–7.
[37] Ibid., I, nn. 1–219, 361–96. II, nn. 74–219, pp. 168–211, 236–45, 300–29.
[38] Ibid., II, nn. 36–149, pp. 294–317.
[39] *Liber miraculorum, e altri testi medievali*, appendix 1, c,73, vii, nn. 1–4, pp. 354–69.
[40] Angelo Clareno, *Chronica*, II, nn. 225, III, nn. 1–3, pp. 330–3.

the condition of the order and a party of seventy-two friars was nominated to bring these causes of disquiet to the ears of the pope and the college of cardinals. When this plan reached the ears of the minister general, he drew upon the skills of his confrere, Bonadie, a lawyer, to discredit the appeal. Asserting that there were friars in different provinces whose reputation for holiness of life was not matched by their deeds, Crescentius presented his case and misled the pope, who authorised him to punish and correct these friars. The delegation of reformers was trapped *en route* for the papal court and the friars were treated harshly as schismatics and heretics; they were exiled to the most remote provinces.[41] Conrad of Offida had been persecuted by the Community for fifty years. Angelo showed that the order dealt sternly with dissident friars, some of those who had enjoyed familiarity with the founder; luminaries of the order were not spared such cruel treatment, which led to some deaths. Several friars had been persecuted, including Leonard, a Joachite and former companion of John of Parma, Gerard of Borgo San Donnino, Poncius, a disiciple of Peter Olivi, Peter de Nubili, Raymond Arioli and Thomas de Castro Mili.[42]

The election of John of Parma gladdened the hearts of the surviving companions of Francis. John was widely respected, but the perception that the abuses were already too deeply rooted was expressed by the celebrated *dictum* of Giles of Assisi that John had come late (*tarde*). John corrected many of the abuses of the previous administration, but was defeated by some deeply engrained scandals.[43] Similar observations were made about Bonaventure. No attention was paid to abuses which prevailed in this period. The fate of John of Parma was cleverly exploited by Angelo, who incorporated the vision of James of Massa. James saw a huge tree at whose summit was John, who was beginning his term as minister general. The branches were filled by friars arranged according to their provinces. Christ gave Francis a chalice brimming with the spirit of life and directed him to give it to the friars. John was the first to drink and afterwards he became luminous. Only a few of the friars followed his example; some even rejected the cup or spilled its sacred contents. Observing the dangers, John vacated his place at the top of the tree for a place of safety. Bonaventure, who had imbibed little, ascended the tree to begin his assault on his saintly predecessor.[44] Angelo articulated the resentment of those friars hostile to Bonaventure for his part in the trial of John and his companions. Reports of the trial come from the group opposed to Bonaventure and they depict the ungrateful disciple maltreating the minister general who had promoted him in the schools.[45]

[41] Ibid., III, nn. 18–76, pp. 336–53.
[42] Doucet, 'Angelus Clarinus', no. 91, pp. 133–4.
[43] Angelo Clareno, *Chronica*, III, nn. 92–104, pp. 356–61.
[44] Ibid., IV, nn. 157–215, pp. 422–35.
[45] Ibid., IV, nn. 114–11, pp. 414–17.

Several values which the founder communicated to his companions and the founding fathers passed into oblivion.[46] Francis's vision of the Son of God was recounted by Angelo, who presents it is a critique of life in contemporary friaries. Francis was advised to adhere to the divine footprints of poverty and humility. His followers should be dead to the world. Their Rule was based on the poverty and nakedness of the cross. The name *minores* denotes that friars should above all be humble of heart and they would find the gates of heaven open to them. Angelo, writing at a sensitive period in the relations between the papacy and the friars, sees an explicit correlation between the Gospel and the Rule. This should govern the places in which the friars reside. They should live in vile, poor and little buildings, which were made of mud and wattle; they should be set apart from the vanities and tumult of the world; they should not own the property or have any rights over it. The foundation of friaries should be made with the permission and blessing of the bishops and local clergy.[47]

Manifestations of this decay were an excessive interest in knowledge, the acquisition of things, the abandonment of solitary and poor places, the transfer to new and larger sites, the pursuit of legacies and burials to the detriment of the secular clergy. The term 'salvation of souls' (*salus animarium*) was adroitly deployed against advocates of change because the more conscientious friars protested that such unwelcome changes effectively endangered souls. Such friars insistently voiced their misgivings to the ministers and their confrères at chapters and regional meetings, but to no avail.[48] The disedifying scramble for alms, Mass stipends and burials were symptoms of decline. A further manifestation was the fact that the friars began to copy other religious.[49] Echoing the parable of the sower (Matthew 13.24–32), Angelo attributes to Christ the prediction the order would become defective. It was prophesied that many would take the habit and live for themselves rather than for the Gospel. They would shamelessly hurl themselves into law suits to acquire money, bequests and legacies.[50]

The uncompromising attitude of the saint lay behind the anecdote about his visit to Bologna. A friar who had been present was Angelo's source. The friary had offended the principle of poverty and, retreating, Francis had lodged with the Dominicans. Moreover, he cursed the stubborn attitude of Peter Stacia, who had been a doctor of law before entering the order. Even at the end of his life the saint refused to lift the curse he had pronounced upon Peter.[51] The predictions which Angelo placed on the lips of Francis echoed

---

[46] Ibid., III, nn. 146, pp. 368–9.
[47] Ibid., prol., nn. 68–109, pp. 104–11.
[48] Ibid., III, nn. 4–17, pp. 332–7.
[49] Ibid., prol., no. 303, pp. 146–77.
[50] Ibid., prol., nn. 190–219, pp. 126–31.
[51] Ibid., I, nn. 158–76, pp. 198–201.

complaints made by earlier reformers. The marriage between the urban centres and the friars was deemed to be irregular and the cause of scandals and abuses. While the first friars preached in the city by day, they were accustomed to spend the evening at a hermitage or an isolated retreat. It was predicated that the friars would abandon hermitages and rural friaries, poor and little places, worthless and small, located far from the world, and exchange them for beautiful and luxurious places inside villages and towns under the pretence that they were designed for preaching and the benefit of the friars.[52] Angelo complains that academic achievement was attained at the expense of prayer and reflection, a claim which he reiterates.[53] He laments that friars in the schools preferred verbs to virtues and science to sanctity.[54] Francis had foreseen that the acquisition of books would supplant prayer and devotion. Learning, wisdom and eloquence would not draw people to Christ.[55]

The criticisms made by Ubertino da Casale and Angelo Clareno are measured and they are echoed by friars and the order's critics. Caution should be exercised in the interpretation of their complaints. Some well-documented failings do not show that the whole order was in decline. Abuses were tackled at chapters and many friars strove to live by the Rule in its purity. As chaplain to Cardinal Napoleon Orsini, the former protector of the Poor Hermits, Ubertino was a persuasive spokesman for renewal at the papal court. David Burr observes that these discussions gave the reformers a temporary equality with the administration of the order.[56] These increasingly polarised debates formed the context for Pope Clement V's judgement about the friars' discipline, *Exivi de paradiso*. The seriousness of these complaints was central to the decisive intervention of Pope John XXII in the 1320s.

---

[52] Ibid., I, nn. 113–29, pp. 190–3.
[53] Ibid., prol., nn. 208–9, pp. 128–9.
[54] Ibid., prol., nn. 316–17, pp. 150–1.
[55] Ibid., I, nn. 116–29, pp. 190–3.
[56] D. Burr, *The Spiritual Franciscans: From Protest to Persecution in the Century after Saint Francis* (Pennsylvania, 2001), p. 113.

CHAPTER ELEVEN

The Crisis under Pope John XXII

Ad conditorem had turned the friars into possessors; *Cum inter nonnullos* now looked like turning them into heretics.

J. R. H. Moorman[1]

This quotation captures the friars' changing relationship with the successor of St Peter and the vicar of Christ and summarises an extraordinary phase in the history of the order.

The Gospel and the friars' Rule

Divisions within the order formed the prelude to the bitter struggle between the pope and the Michaelists, the followers of Michael of Cesena, in the 1320s. The repression of groups of reformers brought together Bertrand de la Tour, minister provincial of Aquitaine, and Michael of Cesena, the new minister general. The partnership between Pope Clement V (1305–14) and successive ministers general, improved the conditions and the aspirations of the Spirituals. The deaths of Clement and Alexander of Alexandria in 1314 created a vacuum in which the initiative was seized by those opposed to the climate of diversity. Michael of Cesena was elected at the general chapter of Naples in 1316 and John XXII emerged from the conclave on 7 August 1316. Early in 1317 John was beginning to train his sights on the reformers, a group whom he viewed as dissidents. On 15 March he wrote to Frederick of Austria, one of the claimants to the imperial throne, urging him to expel Tuscan friars from Sicily.[2] While Pope Clement V had accorded the zealots of Provence a measure of independence, relations deteriorated while the see was vacant from 20 April 1314 to 7 August 1316 and the persecutions were renewed. The reformers assembled at the friaries of Narbonne and Béziers. By March and April 1317 these two friaries were being held against the Community; such public divisions were a source of scandal. On 27 April orders were given for the compilation of a list of recalcitrant friars from the two convents to be

---

[1] Moorman, *A History of the Franciscan Order*, p. 317.
[2] *BF*, V, no. 256, pp. 110–11. Cf. C. R. Backman, 'Arnau de Vilanova and the Franciscan Spirituals in Sicily', *FS* 50 (1990), pp. 3–29.

cited to appear before the papal court.[3] Shortly afterwards a group of sixty-four friars left for Avignon; their sufferings there were narrated at some length by Angelo Clareno. One of their spokesmen was Bernard Délicieux, already well known in Provence for his opposition to the Inquisition. His past record discredited him at the papal court, where he was imprisoned.[4]

John XXII's *Quorundam exigit* of 7 October 1317 was the first in the series of judgements that faced the friars bluntly with the necessity of some kind of dispensation from the literal provisions of the Rule. He explained that an excess of scruple was threatening to destroy obedience. His wish was to restore peace to the order by removing such scruples. He referred to two decisions made by *Exivi de paradiso* on the words of precept in the Rule. In the first Clement had interpreted the command to wear vile clothing as a precept. In the second he had declared that the Rule forbade friars to have cellars or granaries for the storage of food and wine. Again the prohibition had the force of precept: the responsibility for deciding about dispensations was left to the ministers' judgement. John noted that disputes had arisen about the matter of vile clothing. For example, the reformers insisted on wearing mean-looking habits. When asked to exchange them for the habit normally used in the order, they had appealed to Clement's ruling. Although John wished to clarify the situation, he took the opportunity of affirming his own hierarchy of spiritual values, setting integrity over poverty and exalting obedience. He reiterated his predecessor's ruling that friars should follow the ministers' decisions about clothing. Nonetheless, he urged the ministers to be discreet in this matter and their subjects to obey such decisions.[5]

Within a week of the promulgation of *Quorundam exigit* Michael of Cesena took action against the friars of Narbonne and Béziers. He summoned those detained at the Cordeliers of Avignon and showed them the papal bull in the presence of a notary and witnesses. He questioned them about whether they would obey its provisions. In addition, he asked them whether they believed that the pope had the power to make such precepts. By 6 November more than half the friars had made their submission and were returned to their guardians. The remaining twenty-five were handed over to Michael le Moine, the inquisitor of Provence.[6] Under his care the number was drastically reduced; a further twenty submitted and made a public abjuration. A commission was appointed to decide whether their denial of papal authority in this matter was heresy. An affirmative answer was returned and the inquisitor proceeded against the friars, one of whom recanted and was

---

3 Angelo Clareno, *Chronica*, VI, nn. 314–15, pp. 704–5, *BF*, V, nn. 266–7, pp. 118–20.

4 Angelo Clareno, *Chronica*, VI, nn. 389–453, pp. 720–37, *Processus Bernardi Delitiosi: The Trial of Fr. Bernard Délicieux, 3 September – 8 December 1319*, ed. A. Friedlander, Transactions of the American Philosophical Society, LXXXVI, pt. 1 (Philadelphia, 1996). Cf. *BF*, V, nn. 372, 388, pp. 171–2, 180–1.

5 Ibid., no. 289, pp. 128–30.

6 Ibid., no. 293, pp. 132–3.

condemned to perpetual imprisonment. The remaining four were burned in the market-place at Marseilles on 7 May 1318 because they were unwilling to obey the papal constitution. The Beguines of Provence maintained that these friars were unjustly condemned for defending the truth of their Rule. Far from being heretics, they were catholic martyrs.[7]

This spectacle and its repercussions perturbed John XXII, stimulating his reflection on the legacy of St Francis. The case of the reformers was further complicated by their enthusiasm for Peter Olivi's writings, which were being scrutinised by a papal commission.[8] There was deep anxiety about his identification of the Gospel and the Rule, but his adversaries conceded that aspects of his thought were in tune with *Exiit qui seminat*. The writings of Olivi were considered as a source of the theological deviancy of the Beguines of Provence.[9] John XXII found that some of his predecessors' decisions frustrated the condemnation of Olivi. Josef Koch sees the beginning of the new controversies in the condemnation of sixty errors extracted from Olivi's *Lectura super Apocalipsim*, which already existed in a vernacular translation.[10] Using the two extant early reports of the commission on Olivi, Thomas Turley believes that the Dominicans convinced the pope about the dangers inherent in the Franciscan beliefs.[11]

The General Chapter of Perugia in 1322

The debate about the poverty of Christ at the curia from 1321 was ignited by a Dominican inquisitor, John de Beaune, who accused a Beguine of Narbonne of asserting that Christ and the apostles possessed nothing individually or in common. The fuller report of this exchange was recorded by Michael of Cesena, and an abbreviated form was incorporated into a chronicle compiled in that circle and attributed to Nicholas of Freising. Before passing sentence John de Beaune summoned an obligatory council of local notables, clerics, lectors and other prudent figures. When he read out the proposition about the poverty of Christ, he was challenged by Berengar Talon of Perpignan, lector of the Cordeliers of Narbonne, who objected that this doctrine was consonant with *Exiit qui seminat*. Berengar Talon was then accused of heresy. Both friars then appealed to John XXII, who circulated the charges. A public consistory was held in the papal presence and this prompted the pope

---

[7]   *Practica inquisitionis heretice pravitatis auctore Bernardo Guidonis*, ed. C. Douais (Paris, 1886), V, IV, no. 5, pp. 268–70.

[8]   Cf. Burr, *The Spiritual Franciscans*.

[9]   M. D. Lambert, *Franciscan Poverty, The Doctrine of the Absolute Poverty of Christ and the Apostles in the Franciscan Order, 1210–1323* (New York, 1998), p. 230.

[10] J. Koch, 'Der Prozess gegen die Postille Olivis zur Apokalypse', *Recherches de théologie ancienne et médiévale* 5 (1933), pp. 302–15.

[11] T. Turley, 'John XXII and the Franciscans: A Reappraisal', in *Popes, Teachers, and Canon Law in the Middle Ages*, ed. Sweeney and Chodorow, pp. 74–88 at 74, 80.

to solicit the advice of the prelates and theologians at the curia.[12]

A group of contemporary manuscripts contains the exchanges during the consistory of March 1322. A key witness is Biblioteca Apostolica Vaticana, MS lat. 3740, which was annotated by John XXII during this debate. The members of the order who contributed to this debate were Cardinals Vital du Four and Bertrand de la Tour, along with several prelates at the papal court, Bonagrazia da Bergamo; Ubertino da Casale was no longer a friar. Anfroid Gontier, Monaldo Monaldeschi, an anonymous master who was probably John of Reading, and Francis of Meyronnes were consulted. The two Franciscan cardinals were invited to respond to objections made against their positions. The replies in favour of the order were significantly outnumbered by those who took a critical view; Dominican prelates and masters were prominent in that group.[13] There was vigorous debate in the consistory, although some written contributions arrived at a later date. Papal bullying, already mentioned in relation to Berengar Talon, was a *topos* for Michael of Cesena, who recounts John XXII's impatience and irascibility with Cardinal Vital du Four, the archbishop of Salerno and the Franciscan bishops of Lucca and Caffa.[14] Dr Patrick Nold argues that the Michaelist view is not corroborated by the texts in the manuscript already mentioned.[15] Was Michael of Cesena invited to make a formal response on behalf of the order? He had clearly canvassed the views of masters and bachelors of theology at the *studia generalia*, as the chapter's letter of 7 June attests.

Quia nonnunquam of 26 March 1322 lifted *Exiit qui seminat's* ban on further discussion of the theological basis of Franciscan poverty.[16] The friars viewed the new constitution with horror because they believed that the matter, which Pope Nicholas III had resolved once and for all, was now reopened. The Michaelist chronicler reports that some cardinals and several other notable figures petitioned the general chapter of Perugia at Pentecost 1322 to affirm its teaching on the matter of evangelical poverty and to com-

---

[12] Nicolaus Minorita, *Chronica. Documentation on Pope John XXII, Michael of Cesena and The Poverty of Christ with Summaries in English. A Source Book*, ed. G. Gál and D. Flood, The Franciscan Institute (New York, 1996), pp. 62–3, 309–11. P. Nold, *Pope John XXII and His Franciscan Cardinal: Bertrand de la Tour and the Apostolic Poverty Controversy*, Oxford Historical Monographs (Oxford, 2003), pp. 1–24, questions this attribution and points out that none of the manuscripts of the chronicle employ the name Nicholas. Cf. Flood's review of Nold's book, *FS* 62 (2004), pp. 225–35.

[13] K. E. Spiers, 'Four Medieval Manuscripts on Evangelical Poverty: Vaticanus Latinus 3740 and Its Copies', *CF* 59 (1989), pp. 323–49 at 330–5. Cf. F. Tocco, *La quistione della povertà nel secolo XIV secondo nuovi documenti* (Naples, 1910), C. T. Davis, 'Ubertino da Casale and His Conception of "Altissima Paupertas"', *Studi medievali* third series, 22i (1981), pp. 1–56 at 41–56, L. Oliger, 'Fr. Bonagratia de Bergamo et eius "Tractatus de Christi et apostolorum paupertate"', *AFH* 22 (1929), pp. 292–335, 487–511, Nold, *Pope John XXIII*, pp. 28–30, 38.

[14] Nicolaus Minorita, *Chronica*, pp. 310–11, F. Zambrini, *Storia di Fra Michele Minorita con documenti riguardanti i fraticelii della povera vita* (Bologna, 1864), pp. 92–139.

[15] Nold, *Pope John XXIII*, pp. 26–7.

[16] *BF*, V, no. 464, pp. 224–5.

municate it throughout Christendom.[17] Although there is no extant evidence that the pope requested the order to articulate the theological bases for its practices, it was not unreasonable that the friars should be encouraged to make a statement. Cardinals Vital du Four and Bertrand de la Tour supported their confrères' cause at the chapter.[18]

The chapter issued three extant texts. The first, *Ab alto prospectans*, was a letter of protest on 4 June, expressing the friars' fears in the face of renewed criticism and hostility. They petitioned John XXII to restore the ban on discussion.[19] Secondly, they produced a declaration regarding the poverty of Christ and his apostles on the same day.[20] Thirdly, they wrote an encyclical letter to all the faithful in the name of ministers provincial and masters and bachelors of theology. The brief declaration announced that the matter of the poverty of the Son of God was being debated at the papal court and the question of whether it was heretical to believe that Jesus and the apostles had nothing personally or communally. It concluded that Christ, showing the way to perfection, lived in poverty; this teaching was orthodox and catholic. The traditional view was reiterated in the terms of *Exiit qui seminat*, which had been ratified by subsequent popes and incorporated into canon law by Pope Boniface VIII. The chapter quoted the council of Vienne and *Exiit qui seminat*; its tone was measured and restrained.

Thirdly, three days later, 7 June, the same group of ministers provincial and theologians delivered a fuller judgement and invoked several patristic authorities, from both East and West, beginning with Sts Augustine of Hippo and Jerome. The members of the general chapter reported that they had been invited to address the matter of the poverty of Christ and his apostles. They could not find any statements in the Scriptures or the fathers of the Church to show that Christ and the apostles had owned anything. They reaffirmed that the poverty of Christ and his apostles was catholic teaching and they appealed to the papal declarations on the Rule. The theologians' support for the chapter's declaration offers some evidence that the order wished to contribute to the debates at Avignon. The declaration by the general chapter, whose ranks included theologians, was confirmed by the order's forty-one masters and bachelors of theology at the *studia generalia* of Paris, Oxford and Cambridge, who appended their seals, although they were not present.[21]

One Franciscan chronicler attests that the matter of evangelical poverty, which was being discussed in the curia, was aired at the chapter. The friars'

---

[17] Nicolaus Minorita, *Chronica*, p. 67.

[18] Heysse, 'Duo documenta de polemica inter Gerardum Oddonem et Michaelem de Caesena (Perpiniani, 1331 – Monachii, 1332)', *AFH* 9 (1916), pp. 134–83 at 167.

[19] F. M. Delorme, 'Descriptio codicis 23. J. 60. bibliothecae fratrum minorum conventualium Friburgi Helvetiorum', *AFH* 10 (1917), pp. 47–102 at 100–2.

[20] F. Bartoli-Langeli, 'Il manifesto francescano di Perugia del 1322 alle origini dei fraticelli "de opinione"', *Picenum Seraphicum* 11 (1974), pp. 204–61.

[21] Nicolaus Minorita, *Chronica*, pp. 67–82, 83, 185, 919–20.

declaration, however, infuriated the pope, as was subsequently made clear by his numerous references to it.[22] More than a hundred copies of the friars' letters were circulated before December 1322.[23] John XXII turned his energies to the solution of the controversies and his reply to the friars' encyclical was twofold: to assert the papacy's freedom of action and to undermine the friars' beliefs regarding the poverty of Christ.[24] William of Ockham added that the chapter of Perugia had been under pressure and had acted through fear but in good conscience.[25]

John XXII's interpretation of evangelical poverty

An accomplished lawyer, John XXII responded to the general chapter with *Ad conditorem canonum* on 8 December 1322. It opens with a confident affirmation that the pope reserved the right to amend statutes which were in need of clarity or which were having a harmful effect unintended by the author; this right extended not only to his own decisions, but also those of his predecessors. The papal ownership of goods used by the friars, save where the donor retained his rights, was explained along with the mechanics of the system. In the formulation of the bull *Exiit qui seminat* Nicholas was seeking to defend the friars from their critics. Experience convinced John that the matter of papal ownership was not a suitable solution to the question of the friars' use of things; this arrangement was becoming a legal technicality and the situation was in effect harmful to the order and its reputation. He declared that perfection consisted in charity and that the contempt and renunciation of material goods constituted a path to that theological virtue. This act of abandonment was intended to remove the anxiety to acquire and amass things. John's knowledge of the order showed that this laudable intention was not invariably confirmed by the friars' lives and this posed a question about the nature of the friars' renunciation. For example, he was not the first pope to observe that the friars were more frequently involved in litigation regarding items of value than the other mendicant orders, who held things in common.[26]

From this foundation John proceeded to question the theoretical nature of

[22] *Chronica XXIV generalium ordinis minorum*, pp. 480–1, Nicolaus Minorita, *Chronica*, p. 179.

[23] D. L. Douie, *The Nature and the Effect of the Heresy of the Fraticelli* (Manchester, 1932), p. 155, n. 7, M. Bihl, 'Formulae et documenta e cancellaria Fr. Michaelis de Cesena, O.F.M. ministri generalis 1316–28 (disseritur de aliquibus actis eiusdem)', *AFH* 23 (1930), pp. 106–71 at 123–4.

[24] A. Maier, 'Annotazioni autografe di Giovanni XXII in Codici Vaticani', *Rivista di storia della chiesa in Italia* 6 (1952), pp. 317–32 at 325.

[25] Guillelimi de Ockham, *Opera politica*, III, ed. H. S. Offler (Manchester, 1956), pp. 6–17, 16, claims that John XXII was *in sacris litteris idiotae*.

[26] *BF*, V, no. 195, pp. 83, 84. Clement V had noted that the friars were appearing in court and dealing with lawyers. He forbade the friars to become embroiled in lawsuits in order to preserve the purity of their vow.

the friars' use of material goods which were owned by the papacy. He argued that the papal ownership was, in fact, an obstacle because it enabled the friars to boast about their renunciation of ownership and their profession of the highest poverty.[27] The friars regarded themselves as superior to the other mendicant orders due to their lack of possessions. While they protested that they had the *usus nudus* ('bare use') of material things, John pointed out that it was the holy see which had such usage because it derived no benefit from the items placed at the friars' disposal. Virpi Mäkinen explains that John was employing contemporary legal ideas, which presupposed that ownership brought some temporal advantage.[28]

Pope Nicholas III permitted the friars to exchange some items, such as books, with the permission of the appropriate ministers. Inexpensive items were changing hands within friaries and friars were authorised to make presents to their confrères or laymen. Such conduct bore all the hallmarks of ownership, John argued, because use and dominion were inseparable. Moreover, it was absurd to hold that the practical ownership of items of food consumed by the friars belonged to the papacy, which derived no benefit from such arrangements. This was not the intention of Nicholas. Thus, it was the papacy's ownership of such things that was fictitious. In this the friars were effectively no different from people who owned the things which they ate. Their control of consumable goods could not be described as *usus nudus*. In practice, this vitiated the friars' espousal of the highest poverty, a propaganda tool which they arrogantly wielded against their fellow mendicants.

John concluded that the inherited practice regarding ownership was injurious to the order, which was continuing to experience dangerous divisions. Moreover, the *status quo* was damaging for the papacy, whose representatives were reduced to appearing in the ecclesiastical and civil courts to deal with relatively trivial matters. The order's procurators were continually active in disputes concerning property and were under increasing pressure to act in more cases. This redounded to the discredit of the Roman Church to whom such goods were said to belong. *Ad conditorem canonum* closes with the observation that there had been several complaints about the friars. Acting on advice from prelates, John provided a remedy for an anomalous situation, harmful to both the papacy and the order. Henceforth the papacy would no longer accept the ownership of the goods given for the friars' use. Thereby he reversed a policy established some eighty years earlier and turned the order into one of the 'possessioners', robbing them of their distinctive claim to follow Christ in a literal manner. The office of the papal procurator, who

---

[27] *The English Works of Wyclif Hitherto Unprinted*, ed. F. D. Matthew, Early English Text Society, Ordinary Series 74 (London, 1880), pp. 5, 490, where the friars claimed to follow evangelical poverty more strictly than other religious.

[28] V. Mäkinen, *Property Rights in the Late Medieval Discussion on Franciscan Poverty*, Recherches de théologie et philosophie médiévales. Bibliotheca, III (Leuven, 2001), pp. 162–73.

acted for the friars, was abolished. The constitution closed with a statement of respect for the order.[29]

This bull, posted on the doors of Avignon cathedral, was partially framed in response to the declaration made by the chapter of Perugia. Bonagrazia of Bergamo, a doctor of both civil and ecclesiastical law before joining the order, was entrusted with the appeal. He was a veteran of the campaign to suppress the groups of reformers in the previous decade. He was a non-ordained friar and the procurator at the papal court. It was he who launched a protest against *Ad conditorem canonum* on 14 January 1323 in the presence of the pope and cardinals. He began with a historical introduction of the Rule and papal commentaries on it.[30] John responded by taking the bull down, altering it and strengthening its arguments before enlarging the text, which bore the same date and place of origin as the first.[31] The Michaelist chronicler credits Bonagrazia with the amendments to *Ad conditorem canonum*. In contrast, Bonagrazia was in fact cast into prison for a year.[32]

Having dealt with the matter of the friars' possessions, John proceeded to adjudicate on whether it was true that Christ and the apostles had nothing. The constitution *Cum inter nonnullos*, promulgated on 12 November 1323, was another hammer blow for the friars. John took the ultimate step of considering the theological foundation for the friars' vocation and their claims to imitate Christ. He returned to the cause which had precipitated the dispute at the papal court two years earlier and the kernel of the mendicant controversies. In the 1320s there was a larger band of theologians prepared to espouse the belief that it was heretical to maintain that Christ and the apostles lacked possessions both individually and in common. John noted that theologians held different views on this matter, a fact which was corroborated by the views presented by prelates and theologians at the papal court the previous year.

One of the principal weaknesses of the friars' case, which had been exploited in the polemics of the middle of the thirteenth century, prompted John to examine afresh the nature of the life and ministry of Christ and the apostles. *Cum inter nonnullos* decreed that the friars' position was heretical on the grounds that it contradicted the Scriptures. John ruled that Christ and the apostles had the right of using those things; it was erroneous to maintain that they had no right of selling things, giving them or exchanging them. Taking counsel from the prelates, John declared that such assertions would henceforth be wrong and heretical.[33] Both Michael of Cesena and

---

[29] *BF*, V, no. 486, pp. 233–46.

[30] Nicolaus Minorita, *Chronica*, pp. 83, 89–117.

[31] *BF*, V, no. 486, pp. 233–46.

[32] Nicolaus Minorita, *Chronica*, pp. 118, 118–27.

[33] *BF*, V, no. 518, pp. 256–9. L. Duval-Arnould, 'La Constitution "Cum inter nonnullos" de Jean XXII sur la pauvreté du Christ et des Apôtres: rédaction préparatoire et rédaction définitive', *AFH* 77 (1984), pp. 406–20.

John of Winterthur, another friar, attributed John XXII's views on poverty to Dominican influence.[34]

The deposition of Michael of Cesena in 1328

Louis of Bavaria, the emperor, vented his own grievances against the pope and aligned himself with the friars. At the friars' instigation, he appealed to the judgement of a general council. *Ad conditorem canonum* and *Cum inter nonnullos* featured among the charges brought against the pope. Louis's appeal at Sachsenhausen on 22 May 1324 accused the pope of a number of heresies and with having fomented trouble in Italy and Germany, inciting prelates and princes. One of his advisers was Marsilius of Padua. John XXII had refused to confirm Louis's election, favouring Frederick, duke of Austria. He attempted to play off one candidate against the other to augment his own influence. John responded to Louis's criticism of *Quia quorundam* on 10 November 1324.[35]

For four years John XXII busied himself with other matters. He promoted Bertrand de la Tour to the suburbicarian see of Frascati in the summer of 1323. On 8 June 1327 he summoned Michael of Cesena to discuss the order's business. On his recovery from sickness Michael reached Avignon on 1 December and was kindly and graciously received by the pope on the following day. From 2 December 1327 to 8 April 1328 his stay appears to have been agreeable. However, Louis of Bavaria was solemnly crowned emperor by four syndics of the Roman people on 17 January in St Peter's basilica. This coronation and subsequent menaces may explain the change in the papal mood by 9 April 1328. John was aware of events taking place in Rome and of Louis of Bavaria's machinations against him. Michael describes the way in which John roughly corrected him in the presence of Bertrand de la Tour and three friars. While John criticised the chapter of Perugia's declaration, branding it heretical, Michael stood his ground theologically.

The exchanges degenerated into personal insults, especially the charge that the minister general promoted heresy (*fautor haereticorum*). Michael's stout defence of the order earned him imprisonment; he was confined to the city; failure to honour these terms would incur excommunication. Fearing that the pope would compel him to renounce the declaration of the general chapter of 1322, Michael appealed against the sentence and expressed his apprehension about making an appeal alone in the presence of the pope. His appeal of 13 April 1328 from the Cordeliers of Avignon rehearsed the circumstances of his summons. The pope had wished to discuss reports of maladministration in some provinces of the order; Aragon and Umbria were singled out and

---

[34] *Die Chronik Johanns von Winterthur*, ed. F. Baethgen, MGH, SS, n.s., III (Berlin, 1924), pp. 93, 95, 98, Nicolaus Minorita, *Chronica*, pp. 309–10.

[35] Ibid., pp. 59–60, 130–71.

matters of leadership were discussed. Michael protested that the pope had earlier endorsed *Exiit qui seminat*.[36]

Two sources affirm that Michael of Cesana sought permission to travel to Bologna for the general chapter and one of them reports papal suspicions that Michael wished to act as pope in Lombardy.[37] On 18 April 1328 Louis of Bavaria deposed John XXII on account of the erroneous teaching in his encyclicals concerning evangelical poverty; the friars were not slow to follow the lead given by the emperor.[38] Events moved quickly. On 23 April 1328 the pope appointed Bertrand of Poietto, cardinal bishop-elect of Ostia, to attend the chapter and six days later he notified the friars that Michael was needed at Avignon. The letter gave no hint that Michael was confined to the city, omitting any mention of the recent disputes. Despite the papal moves against Michael, the chapter was in rebellious mood and re-elected him by a large majority.[39] Moreover, the chapter affirmed the order's traditional beliefs about evangelical poverty.[40] The dispute was raised to a higher level when Louis of Bavaria prevailed upon a group of Roman clergy to elect Peter Rainalducci as Nicholas V in place of John on 12 May 1328. Thus, the order which prided itself on its close links with the successors of St Peter now supplied an anti-pope, who began to make his own appointments.

Perhaps fearing for his personal safety, Michael fled Avignon on 26 May 1328 with Bonagrazia and William of Ockham. They reached the imperial city of Pisa, where Michael publicised his appeal. John XXII responded at once and a letter of 28 May announced the illicit flight of the friars. Ominously Michael was styled one-time minister general and the friars were charged with heresy. The pope enlisted the help of princes in seeking the return of the three friars. He deposed Michael on 6 June and a week later he appointed Bertrand de la Tour as vicar general until the next general chapter.[41] Michael of Cesena defiantly wrote to the order as its minister general on 9 July 1328. His *apologia* recounted his treatment at the papal court, the theological errors of the pope and the reasons for his own flight.[42] Rainalducci, the anti-pope, joined the emperor at Pisa on 19 February, where he excommunicated John XXII and burned an effigy of him. The following year the Michaelists had moved to the friary of Munich whence they continued their campaign. They

---

[36] Ibid., pp. 177–89.

[37] Ibid., p. 528. C. Langlois, 'Formulaires de lettres du XIIe, du XIIIe et du XIVe siècle', *Notices et extraits de manuscrits de la Bibliothèque nationale et autres bibliothèques* 34 (1891), pp. 1–32, 305–64 at 322.

[38] Nicolaus Minorita, *Chronica*, pp. 191–200.

[39] *BF*, V, no. 706, pp. 341–3. Nicolaus Minorita, *Chronica*, pp. 528–30, Directio periodici, 'Compendium chronicorum fr. min. scriptum a Patre Mariano de Florentia', *AFH* 2 (1909), pp. 92–107, 305–18, 457–72, 626–41, and 3 (1910), pp. 204–309, 700–15, Bihl, 'Formulae et documenta', p. 126.

[40] *Chronicon de Lanercost*, p. 264.

[41] *BF*, V, nn. 711–16, pp. 345–50. Nicolaus Minorita, *Chronica*, pp. 203–7.

[42] Ibid., pp. 207–11.

compiled reports of errors contained in John's recent sermons, particularly on the themes of the beatific vision, the Trinity and the divine power.[43] It was by chance that William of Ockham happened to be in Avignon during this dispute and was drawn into the controversy, perhaps as early as April/May 1328. He was invited to analyse *Ad conditorem canonum*, *Cum inter nonnullos* and *Quia quorundam*. Examining them one by one and exposing their errors, he concluded that John XXII was a heretic.[44]

Opposition to John XXII was not limited to a small circle of Michaelists. Its leaders included secular forces, prelates and friars as well as subjects.[45] The ministers provincial of Slovenia and Abruzzo were dismissed early in 1329.[46] Ripples of this dispute were felt in many provinces. While Bertrand informed the ministers provincial and *custodes* that a general chapter would be held at Pentecost in 1329 to elect a new minister general, Michael commanded the opposite. Despite Michael's prohibition of 27 November 1328, the chapter was well attended. Capitulars deposed Michael and elected Gerald Odonis in his place.[47] Michael of Cesena was the fourth minister general to be removed by a pope. A dwindling band of Michaelists kept up the dispute until the 1340s, when it petered out.

---

[43] Ibid., pp. 624–866, 879–95.

[44] Cf. G. Knysh, 'Ockham's First Political Treatise? The "Impugnatio constitutionum Papae Johannis" [April/May 1328]', *FS* 58 (2000), pp. 237–59. Guillelimi de Ockham, *Opera politica*, III, pp. 5–17, 6, 16. Cf. G. Gál, 'William of Ockham Died *Impenitent* in April 1347', *FS* 42 (1982), pp. 90–5.

[45] 'Chronicon provinciae Argentinensis', p. 685.

[46] *BF*, V, no. 754, p. 370, C. Cenci, 'Ministri provinciali abruzzesi dei secoli XIV–XV', *StF* 78 (1981), pp. 189–94 at 190.

[47] Nicolaus Minorita, *Chronica*, pp. 520–3.

CHAPTER TWELVE

The Friars and Their Neighbours

This solidarity between the mendicant orders and the cities which sheltered them depended on a balanced exchange of services: the municipality granted them regular subsidies in the form of gifts . . . In exchange, it often took advantage of their services as messengers, mediators or diplomats.

André Vauchez[1]

Urban integration

Civic authorities featured prominently among the friars' friends and benefactors; some friaries regarded the local commune as their founders.[2] Such partnerships are illustrated by Louise Bourdua, who explains that the building of the basilica in Padua arose from collaboration between the friars, the commune, nobles, confraternities and the people of the city.[3] One link between friary and commune was the celebration of St Francis's feast, a day connected with gifts of alms. The civic statutes of Treviso ordained that the feast should be celebrated communally and that the *podestà*, bishop and his senior clergy should attend Mass at San Francesco.[4]

Friars ministered to the local population, which supported them in material terms. Their contribution to the city or borough was not confined to the spiritual realm. They were pleased to promote the cities and regions in which they dwelled. For instance, in 1288 a friar of Milan wrote a brief account in praise of that city and its civic and religious institutions.[5] The friars' promotion of local interests is reflected in Richmond, Yorkshire, where they supplied the town with drinking water.[6] In many English towns and cities friars

[1] A. Vauchez, 'The Religious Orders', in *The New Cambridge Medieval History, V, c. 1198 – c. 1300*, pp. 220–55 at 250.

[2] Corporation of London, Records Office, Letter Book M, fol. 224r.

[3] L. Bourdua, 'Friars, Patrons, and Workshops at the Basilica del Santo, Padua', in *The Church and the Arts*, ed. D. Wood, Studies in Church History, XXVIII (Oxford, 1992), pp. 131–41 at 132.

[4] *Gli statuti del comune di Treviso (sec. XIII–XIV)*, ed. B. Betto, Istituto storico italiano per il medioevo, fonti per la storia d'Italia, CIX (Rome, 1984), pp. 110–12, 594.

[5] F. Novati, 'Bonvicinus de Ripa de magnalibus urbis Mediolani', *Bullettino dell'Istituto storico italiano per il medioevo* 20 (1898), pp. 7–188.

[6] J. Hatcher, *The History of Richmond North Yorkshire: From Earliest Times to the Year 2000* (Pickering, 2000), pp. 39–40.

were conspicuous in the provision of the water supply. They were instrumental in compensating people who had been wronged by deceased testators.[7] Neighbours appreciated the friars' ministry and sought their prayers. Intercession for the dead was a strong feature of medieval piety and the friars were soon drawn into that role. Friars were conspicuous at funerals and regularly accompanied the corpse from home to the church for the requiem Mass. Each convent kept a necrology or martyrology to record the benefactors' names, which were read out during the domestic chapter.[8] Anniversary prayers were prescribed for recitation at the tombs in the friars' churches. The necrology of San Francesco at Udine in Friuli (Udine, Biblioteca comunale, MS 1361) incorporates the names of both benefactors and friars as well as rubrics for the celebration of anniversaries and prayers to be recited at the place of burial. The names of benefactors are frequently followed by details of their gifts.[9]

Alms were not only received at friaries but also dispensed there. The friary was associated with a range of charitable activities and these initiatives were carried out by the friars. The crowds of poor people who received alms at friaries find a mention in contemporary literature.[10] The works of the hospital and hospice attracted friars, as they had in the previous century. Peter d'Assisi, an Umbrian friar, preached in the Veneto about 1335. There he began a project to relieve the sufferings of abandoned children, whom he collected near the church of San Francesco de Vinea until such times as a hospice might be constructed. He was an influential figure in the establishment of the Ospedale della Pietà in Venice.[11] The friars' concerns about usury paved the way for the emergence of the *monte di pietà*. The first *monte* was founded at Perugia in 1462 and others followed in cities throughout Italy. The Observant reform of the order, which flowered in the fifteenth century, was prominent in promoting these institutions, especially Bernardino of Feltre (1439–94).[12]

Friaries were suitable venues for a variety of activities. The friary was perceived as a place associated with the local community, which gathered there for civic as well as religious purposes. The Greyfriars of Dumfries was the scene of an event which had powerful repercussions for Anglo-Scottish relations. Robert Bruce, earl of Carrick, arranged to meet Sir John Comyn at the friars' church on the pretext of discussing matters of mutual interest.

[7] L. Bourdua, *The Franciscans and Art Patronage in Late Medieval Italy* (Cambridge, 2004), p. 76.

[8] Bihl, 'Ordinationes a Benedicto XII', c. XIII, nn. 1–2, p. 360.

[9] A. Sartori, *Archivio sartori, documenti di storia e arte francescana, II/2, La provincia del Santo dei frati minori conventuali*, a cura di P. Giovanni Luisetto (Padua, 1986), nn. 1–34, pp. 1732–6.

[10] Boccaccio, *Decameron*, I, 6, pp. 55–6. Louis of Anjou, bishop of Toulouse, fed the poor at the Cordeliers of Paris. *Processus canonizationis*, p. 47. Alms were distributed to the poor at the principal Mass in the London Greyfriars on the anniversary of Queen Isabella, who was buried there in 1358. National Archives, E101/397/7.

[11] L. Ranzato di Chioggia, 'Cenni e documenti su Fr. Pietro d'Assisi, O.F.M. (Fr. Pietruzzo della Pietà) 1300–49', *AFH* 8 (1915), pp. 3–11. Cf. Cecchetti, 'Documenti riguardanti Fr. Pietruccio d'Assisi e l'Ospedale della pietà', *Archivo Veneto* 30 (1885), pp. 141–7.

[12] A. Parsons, 'Economic Significance of the *Montes Pietatis*', *FS* I (1941), pp. 3–28.

When he realised that Comyn was not going to help him, he killed him and his uncle on 10 February 1310 and had himself crowned king of Scotland on 25 March.[13]

Friars and times of crisis in the locality

The friars followed the example of their Benedictine neighbours and kept annals and fuller chronicles of events at local, national and international levels. One hypothesis is that each friary compiled its own chronicle. Numerous friars of various provinces compiled historical accounts of international and local interest.[14] The *Annales Gandenses* were kept by an anonymous friar of Ghent, who explained that he was writing for the friars' pleasure and entertainment as well as the common welfare.[15] He was an eye-witness to the fortunes of his people. Much of the material was devoted to the wars between the Flemish and French forces. He witnessed the measures taken by his people against attacks from the French, describing a bridge built over five boats for the passage of the army in 1302.[16] Political turmoil and warfare disturbed the life of the local communities and its friars; the ministry of preaching and provincial chapters were among the casualties.[17]

Chroniclers supply details of attacks on friaries and instances of friars being killed. Edward Bruce landed at Larne on 25 May 1315 to launch his invasion of Ulster. His army burned Dundalk on 29 June 1315 and robbed the friary of books, altar hangings, chalices and vestments; many of the friars were killed.[18] The following year the friaries of Ulster were despoiled. The friary at Castledermot was destroyed during Lent 1317.[19] This destruction and death co-existed with royal suspicions about the loyalty of Gaelic friars, who were suspected of supporting Bruce. On 20 August 1316 Edward II urged the minister general to take action against them.[20] The Irish princes complained to Pope John XXII of 1317 about the recent statute enacted by the archbishop of Armagh at a council in Kilkenny to the effect that the religious houses among the English (*inter Anglicos*) should admit only Anglo-Irish

---

[13] T. M. Smallwood, 'An Unpublished Early Account of Bruce's Murder of Comyn', *The Scottish Historical Review*, 54 (1975), pp. 1–10.

[14] A. G. Little, 'Chronicles of the Mendicant Friars', in *Franciscan Essays*, II, ed. F. C. Burkitt, H. E. Goad, A. G. Little, British Society of Franciscan Studies, Extra Series, III (Manchester, 1932), pp. 85–103.

[15] *Annals of Ghent*, ed. H. Johnstone, Nelson Medieval Texts (Edinburgh, 1951), pp. 1, 86.

[16] Ibid., pp. 1, 36.

[17] Francesco da Lendinara, 'Fra Francesco da Lendinara e la storia della provincia di S.Antonio tra la fine del s. XIV e l'inizio del s. XV', ed. C. Cenci, *AFH* 55 (1962), pp. 103–92, no. 31, p. 126.

[18] John Clyn, *The Annales of Ireland by Friar John Clyn of the Convent of the Friars Minor, Kilkenny, and Thady Dowling, Chancellor of Leighlin, together with the Annals of Ross*, ed. R. Butler, pp. 11–12.

[19] *Chartularies of St. Mary's Abbey, Dublin; with the Register of Its House in Dunbrody, and Annals of Ireland*, ed. J. T. Gilbert, 2 vols, RS, LXXX, ii (London, 1884), pp. 352, 299–300.

[20] Fitzmaurice and Little, *Materials for … the Franciscan Province of Ireland*, pp. 98–9.

religious; a canon had already been accepted by the friars.[21] Continuing tensions between the two nations lay behind the decree of the 1325 general chapter that the custody of Cork should be assigned to Anglo-English members of the province.[22] Royal gifts of 3 November 1305 and 26 October 1306 unashamedly favoured the friaries inhabited by English or Anglo-Irish friars. Alms were transferred from Athlone to Cashel because there were no English friars resident at the former on 18 September 1327.[23]

The political tension experienced in the Irish province was felt elsewhere. While the English and French kings were generous towards the friars, they expected the friars' support. The absence of such support triggered retaliation by the crown. For instance, friars who supported Pope Boniface VIII rather than King Philip IV were expelled from Paris in June 1303.[24] King Edward III went one step further in dealing with his worries about the loyalty of friars ministering in sensitive areas in time of warfare. His mandate of 10 August 1333 ordered the removal of the Scottish friars, who were to be substituted by English friars.[25] During the transfer two English friars were introduced to the friary at Berwick. While the newcomers were being entertained, the Scottish friars broke open the book cupboard and collected books, chalices and vestments and carried them off.[26]

The friars' immersion in local life exposed them to the same hardships, dangers and suffering as their neighbours. This is exemplified by the immense loss of life during plagues and famines, the most virulent of which was the Black Death, which reached western Europe in 1347. First reports about the plague appear in October of that year, when some Genoese galleys, fleeing from the plague, carried it to Sicily. Michael of Piazza, a friar, witnessed the refusal of many priests to minister to the plague victims, a task which was largely undertaken by the Dominicans and Franciscans and members of other orders at Messina.[27] A confrère reports that within a short time thirty

---

[21] S. Duffy, *Robert the Bruce's Irish Wars: The Invasions of Ireland, 1306–1329* (Stroud, 2002), pp. 179–86, 182.

[22] John Clyn, *Annales*, p. 17.

[23] *Calendar of Documents relating to Ireland, Preserved in Her Majesty's Public Record Office, London, 1302–1307*, ed. H. S. Sweetman and G. F. Handcock (London, 1886), nn. 461, 578, pp. 142, 166. Fitzmaurice and Little, *Materials for . . . the Franciscan Province of Ireland*, p. 129.

[24] E. Longpré, 'Le B. Jean Duns Scot. Pour le Saint-Siège et contre le gallicanisme (25–28 juin 1303)', *France franciscaine* 11 (1928), pp. 137–62.

[25] *Rotuli Scotiae in Turri Londinensi et in Domo Capitulari Westmonasteriensi asservati*, I, ed. D. Macpherson (London, 1814), p. 258.

[26] *Chronicon de Lanercost*, p. 275.

[27] Michele da Piazza, *Cronaca 1336–1361*, ed. A. Guiffrida, Fonti per la storia di Sicilia, collana diretta da Francesco Giunta (Palermo, 1980), c. 27, pp. 82–3. Cf. S. Tramontana, 'I francescani durante la peste del 1347–8 e alcuni episodi di psicosi collectiva in Sicilia', *Francescanesimo e cultura in Sicilia (secc. XIII–XVI)*, Atti del convegno internazionale di studio nell' ottavo centenario della nascita di San Francesco d'Assisi, Palermo, 7–12 marzo 1982, and published in *Schede medievali rassegna dell'officina di studi medievali* 12/13 (1987), pp. 63–78.

of the sixty friars there were carried off by the plague.[28] The friary of Piacenza was in the infected area of the city. Bertolino Coxadocha, a friar renowned for his learning and virtues, died along with twenty-four of his confrères, nine of whom perished on a single day.[29] During the Lent 1348 only one of the 150 friars of Marseilles survived.[30] Between May and October 1348 some hundred friars died at Bologna and sixty in Florence. There were thirty deaths at Ferrara between July and September, five at Parma, ten at Modena, fifty at Venice and eighteen at Piacenza, twelve of whom died in four days.[31] The incidence of death of Santa Croce can be gauged from the number of friars attending the local chapters. There were eighty-one on 21 August 1347 and fifty-one on 14 January 1352.[32] Some twenty-five friars of Drogheda died and twenty-three at Dublin in September and October 1348.[33] The general chapter of Lyons in 1351 was notified that 13,883 friars had died since the previous chapter.[34] It is estimated that scarcely a third of the friars survived.[35]

Narratives of the friars' journeys across the seas

The Irish province produced one of the most celebrated chroniclers of the pilgrimage to the Holy Land, Simon Semeonis. Simon and Hugh le Luminour set out on 16 March 1323 and crossed the Irish Sea to Holyhead. They reached Chester on 24 March 1323, via north Wales, and made their way through England to Kent. Sailing from Dover, they reached Wissant and then headed for Paris, which was depicted as the most heavily populated city in the west. A local war prevented the friars from following the customary route to northern Italy, via Dijon, Salins and Lausanne. Instead, they travelled through Beaune and Lyons and then sailed down the Rhone. They visited the tombs of two martyred confrères in the Cordeliers of Valence on the Rhone. Mellanus of Conflans, an inquisitor, and Pachasius of Saillans had been massacred at Montélier by heretics in 1321. An additional place of interest was the shrine of St Louis of Anjou at Marseilles. Accounts were given of the shrines of Sts Columbanus, Anthony and Mark, the evangelist, at Bobbio, Padua and Venice. At Candia they saw a Franciscan bishop who had converted from Judaism.[36]

[28] *Die Chronik Johanns von Winterthur*, p. 276.
[29] A. W. Henschel, 'Document zur Geschichte des schwarzen Todes', *Archiv für die gesammte Medicin*, II, ed H. Haeser (Jena, 1841), pp. 45–57.
[30] *Knighton's Chronicle 1337–96*, ed. G. H. Martin, Oxford Medieval Texts (Oxford, 1995), pp. 96–7.
[31] C. Piana, 'Agiografia e storia in un codice dell'antico monastero di S. Charia in Modena', *StF* 52 (1955), pp. 224–35, 230.
[32] D. R. Lesnick, *Preaching in Medieval Florence: The Social World of Franciscan and Dominican Spirituality* (Athens, Georgia, 1989), pp. 210–12.
[33] John Clyn, *Annales*, pp. 35–8.
[34] William Worcestre, *Itineraries*, ed. J. H. Harvey, Oxford Medieval Texts (Oxford, 1969), pp. 94–5.
[35] *Chronica XXIV generalium ordinis minorum*, p. 544.
[36] *Itinerarium Symonis Semeonis*, nn. 1–22, pp. 24–45.

Although Simon recounted his pilgrimage to the holy places, a fuller report is supplied by Nicholas of Poggibonsi. Nicholas narrated the perils of the seas, the hardships of travels and the churches and shrines which he visited. The journey began on 1 March 1346 and took him through Florence to Bologna, where he travelled by canal to Ferrara. Thence he sailed along the river Po to Chióggia, south of Venice, where he took ship on 6 April. Shortly after the ship's departure from Pola it encountered difficulties, weathered a storm and was forced back to port for repairs. Returning to sea again, another vessel warned the captain about the pirates in the vicinity. On 1 May the ship, having deviated to Greece to avoid the raiders, found itself in the midst of another storm. While the crew fought to control the vessel, the passengers were kept below deck. The friars in particular were exhorted to pray for the ship's safety. They produced their relics of the saints and recited the litany of the Mother of God. The storm had cost the ship 150 miles, driving it back to the gulf of Venice. One casualty was a passenger, whose body was wrapped in a sheet and buried at sea; a female passenger died afterwards and was buried in a shallow grave on an island. A journey of fifty-six days brought the ship to Famagusta, whence Nicholas travelled to Nicosia and then Jaffa. Just outside Rama he visited the church at Lydda, where St George was beheaded.[37]

Nicholas was a witness to the re-establishment of the order in the Holy Land. Friars had settled at Mount Sion in 1335; news that twelve friars were living at the Holy Sepulchre reached the general chapter of 1343 at Marseilles.[38] The practice of the friars accompanying the pilgrims had begun by 1384.[39] Nicholas and his confrères were pressed for the Sultan's tribute on their arrival at Jerusalem. When their interpreter explained that the friars were unable to pay, he was flogged and the friars were taken to prison. As they were being led through the streets, Nicholas met a man for whom he carried a letter. The man settled the sum and arranged for the friars' release. Finding hospitality with their confrères on Mount Sion, they visited the holy city and lamented its debased state. The Holy Sepulchre was described in great detail. The bodies of Godfrey de Bouillon, who had retaken Jerusalem in 1099, and Baldwin, his brother and first king of the holy city, were buried in the chapel of Golgotha. Nicholas, who spent four months there, was determined to experience and narrate the liturgical celebrations of holy week.[40]

There was abundant homely detail in the narrative, which reflects the

---

[37] Fra Niccolò da Poggibonsi, *Libro d'Oltramare (1346–50)*, ed. A. Bacchi della Lega and B. Bagatti, Studium biblicum Franciscanum, II (Jerusalem, 1945), cc. 1–9, pp. 1–9.

[38] *Die Chronik Johanns von Winterthur*, p. 206.

[39] *Visit to the Holy Places of Egypt, Sinai, Palestine and Syria in 1384 by Frescobaldi, Gucci and Sigoli*, translated from the Italian by T. Bellorini and E. Hoade, Studium Biblicum Franciscanum, VI (Jerusalem, 1948), pp. 16, 127, Golubovich, *Biblioteca*, IV, pp. 427–60, 451, 453. C. Morris, 'Pilgrimage to Jerusalem in the Late Middle Ages', in *Pilgrimage: The English Experience from Becket to Bunyan*, ed. C. Morris and P. Roberts (Cambridge, 2002), pp. 141–63.

[40] Fra Niccolò da Poggibonsi, *Libro d'Oltramare (1346–50)*, cc. 10–47, pp. 9–35.

accretion of pious legends in that region. Nicholas visited the grottoes where the apostles and the Mother of God hid themselves for fear of the Jews after the crucifixion; there each apostle contributed an article of faith for the Creed. Sts John the Evangelist and Peter were accustomed to celebrate Mass there. Nicholas visited a small grotto, where the Mother of God used to wash her Son's clothes in complete privacy.[41] A church with three doors was constructed over the tomb of the Mother of God and was guarded by the Muslims, who exacted a levy from those entering. When Nicholas celebrated Mass above the tomb, numerous Muslims came to pray there. He was unable to visit the Temple of Solomon, where a mosque had been built and which was closed to Christians.[42] Bethlehem was almost in ruins. A full account was given of the church built over the birth-place of Christ. The place where St Jerome dwelled when he translated the Bible and the site of his former burial place were visited. Nicholas was present in the basilica for Christmas, when the different Christian churches commemorated the nativity.[43] Three miles outside Cairo was the place where the Mother of God fled with her Son during the persecution of Herod. When she commented on her thirst, her Son produced a fountain of water, where she drank with her husband and Son. Nicholas joined pilgrims who wished to go to the shrine of St Catherine: two were English, one from Syria and three from Constantinople.[44]

Nicholas served as a chaplain at the court of the count of Jaffa and Ascalon. James of Gubbio, who was overseas for a long period, was another confrère active there.[45] A merchant of Damietta, learning that Nicholas and his companion were friars, entertained them in his house and at his expense for twenty-four days while they awaited a ship to return them to Cyprus.[46] When they reached Venice, they intoned the *Te Deum*. The seven confrères from Toulouse, England, Burgundy, Constantinople and a Slav who set out with Nicholas all perished *en route* except Bonacorso da Massa, who had returned home earlier. On the death of these friars, Nicholas joined forces with Matthew of Todi, a brother. At Venice he met a friar who accompanied him by boat to Chióggia and thence to Ferrara in the spring of 1350.[47]

Richard FitzRalph, archbishop of Armagh (1346–1360), a critic of the friars

The friars' pastoral ministry created friction with their clerical neighbours and prompted the settlement of Pope Boniface VIII's *Super cathedram* of

[41] Ibid., cc. 64, 68, pp. 41–2, 44.
[42] Ibid., cc. 82, 86, pp. 50–1, 54.
[43] Ibid., cc. 98–111, pp. 59–66.
[44] Ibid., cc. 185, 187, 197, pp. 109, 110, 115–16.
[45] Ibid., c. 184, pp. 108–9.
[46] Ibid., cc. 184, 244, pp. 108–9, 141.
[47] Ibid., cc. 158, 264, pp. 93–4, 156–7.

18 February 1300. Boniface acknowledged the tension and conflict throughout the various ecclesiastical provinces and authorised the friars to preach in their own churches and in public places. Friars were to preach in parish churches only by the invitation of the parish priest or by the command of the bishop. The ministers provincial were required to nominate suitable candidates to preach and hear confessions and present them to the bishop for a licence; the number of confessors was to be regulated by the size of the population. Friars were given the right to bury the laity in their churches, but they were required to give the parish priest a quarter of all offerings and legacies.[48] Although Boniface and his successors felt the need to make further interventions at both local and global levels, friars were expressly licensed to preach and hear confessions according to the settlement of *Super cathedram*.[49] Richard FitzRalph, a graduate of Oxford and a priest with a wide experience of the Church in England and Ireland, became the spokesman for the secular clergy from the later 1340s.

In addition to his pastoral experience, FitzRalph had a good knowledge of the papal court in Avignon, where he had well-placed allies who shared his exasperation with the friars. He was an ideal advocate for the secular clergy.[50] He was on good terms with the friars until the last phase of his life; his homily in the church of the Cordeliers in Avignon on 4 October 1349 praised the order, which included members of his own family. Despite such a deferential beginning, he attacked the friars whose lives visibly deviated from the example and teaching of the founder. Criticism was heaped upon those who disregarded injunctions concerning poverty, obedience and the demands of residence.[51] In 1349/50 FitzRalph was a member of a theological commission invited to consider some disputed points regarding the Dominicans and Franciscans. In the case of the latter there were matters relating to the decisions taken by Popes Nicholas III and John XXII.[52] FitzRalph appeared before Pope Clement VI on 5 July 1350 to argue for the revocation of the friars' privileges in a *propositio*, which became known as *Unusquisque*. Prelates were disturbed by the friars' recent petition for a relaxation of some clauses of

---

[48] *BF*, IV, no. 179, pp. 498–500, Iohannis abbatis Victoriensis, *Liber certarum historiarum*, I, ed. F. Schneider, Scriptores rerum Germanicarum, n.s. (Hannover, 1909), pp. 358, 368.

[49] *BF*, V, nn. 4, 20, pp. 2–3, 11–14. Iohannis abbatis Victoriensis, *Liber certarum historiarum*, I, p. 371. *Inter cunctas sollicitudinis nostras* was published on 17 February 1304.

[50] A. Gwyn, 'The Sermon-Diary of Richard FitzRalph, Archbishop of Armagh', *The Proceedings of the Royal Irish Academy*, 44 section C, no. 1 (Dublin, 1937), pp. 1–57, 43–4 at 46. K. Walsh, *A Fourteenth-Century Scholar and Primate: Richard FitzRalph in Oxford, Avignon and Armagh* (Oxford, 1981).

[51] A. Gwyn, 'Richard FitzRalph, Archbishop of Armagh', *Studies, An Irish Quarterly Review* 22 (1933), pp. 389–405 at 390.

[52] 'Ricardi filii Radulphi archiepiscopi Armachani De pauperie salvatoris', in Iohannis Wycliffe, *De dominio divino libri tres*, ed. R. L. Poole (London, 1890), pp. 257–476 at 273, 277. Cf. H. Lippens, 'Le Droit nouveau des mendiants en conflit avec le droit coutumier du clergé séculier de concile de Vienne à celui de Trente', *AFH* 47 (1954), pp. 241–92.

Super cathedram. More than once FitzRalph explained that he was speaking for prelates at the curia and elsewhere. *Super cathedram*, he argued, was too lenient towards the friars.[53] A disturbing matter was the practical effect of the friars' annual visits to parishes, which undermined the work of the local priest, who knew his penitents well. A further irregularity was that husband and wife had different confessors. For twelve hundred years the practice of the church was for the faithful to be buried in the parish church where they received the sacraments. In some instances parish clerks experienced difficulties in securing the portion of the burial fees of their parishioners who chose to be interred in the friaries. As the conservator of the order's privileges he had been approached by those who complained of the friars' conduct in the matter of property and burials.[54]

Several curial cardinals provided the stimulus for FitzRalph's *De pauperie salvatoris* in 1356, which he completed in Ireland, although an eighth book was added later. Dedicated to Pope Innocent VI, the treatise addressed the theory of dominion and the theological basis of the mendicant life. The first book opened with an examination of the concept of evangelical poverty in the Rule and the more recent papal glosses of its provisions.[55] The scriptural basis of the friars' vocation was considered in the sixth book and their poverty in the seventh, noting that the order was still claiming a more perfect form of poverty than their fellow mendicants. FitzRalph was especially anxious about the friars' role as confessors. Their influence in the confessional was greater than that of the pulpit and it was the root of a range of disorders, including the burial of people in the order's churches and bequests to friaries.

By 1351 FitzRalph was back in Ireland, where his experience of the friars at Armagh, Drogheda and Dundalk gave a local focus to his growing criticism of the order. On 26 February 1354 he reiterated the traditional teaching that satisfaction and restitution were conditions for absolution and he expressly referred to confessors in religious orders who were lenient in their treatment of theft, usury and injustice. The friars were ingratiating themselves with the wealthy by granting them absolution on terms that were less than exacting; the charge was repeated in subsequent sermons. The sermon of 5 February 1355 brought the charge that the friars were dispensing their penitents from the duty of paying tithes. Additional complaints about the laxity of mendicant confessors are incorporated into FitzRalph's *Defensio curatorum*.[56]

---

[53] L. L. Hammerich, 'The Beginning of the Strife between Richard FitzRalph and the Mendicants, with an Edition of His Autobiographical Prayer and His Proposition Unusquisque', in *Det. Kgl. Danske Videnskabernes Selskab. Historisk-filologiske Meddelelser*, 26, iii (Copenhagen, 1938), pp. 53–73, 54, 73. J. Coleman, 'FitzRalph's Antimendicant "Proposicio" (1350) and the Politics of the Papal Court at Avignon', *Journal of Ecclesiastical History* 35 (1984) pp. 376–90 at 377.

[54] Hammerich, 'The Beginning of the Strife', pp. 64–70.

[55] 'Ricardi filii Radulphi archiepiscopi Armachani De pauperie salvatoris', pp. 273, 277.

[56] A. Gwyn, 'Richard FitzRalph, Archbishop of Armagh', *Studies, An Irish Quarterly Review* 25 (1936), pp. 81–96.

FitzRalph reached London on diocesan business towards the end of June 1356 and was drawn into disputes about poverty. This resulted in the friars' appeal of 10 March 1357.[57] FitzRalph's last sermon at St Paul's cross two days later responds to the appeal, but singles out the Franciscans, whose Rule is quoted to demonstrate their many lapses.[58] This criticism of the order shared some common ground with those of the reformers in the order.[59] The debates were transferred to Avignon, where FitzRalph returned to the charges against the friars with a *propositio* delivered before the pope in full consistory on 8 November 1357. Better known as the *Defensio curatorum*, this treatise condensed many of his earlier criticisms. It reaffirmed that the parish church was the natural place for confessions and burials. FitzRalph complained that each year some two thousand people in his diocese incurred the penalty of excommunication for robbery, arson and murder, but scarcely more than forty of them approached him or his penitentiary for absolution. Noting that they all communicated at Easter, FitzRalph ascertained that the others made their confession to the friars. The friars' role as confessors had enabled them to construct 'most beautiful monasteries and kingly palaces'. It was unknown for the friars to use their alms for the repair of the parish church, roads or bridges. The friars had abused their privileges as confessors, particularly in enticing the young to join their order and then not letting them speak alone to their parents.[60] FitzRalph's *De audienda confessionum* merited a reply by Roger Conway, an English friar and apologist; some thirty years later the friars were still responding to the attacks of FitzRalph.[61]

---

[57] A. Gwyn, 'Archbishop FitzRalph and the Friars', *Studies, An Irish Quarterly Review* 26 (1937), pp. 50–67 at 50, 59–60.

[58] Peterhouse Library, Cambridge, MS 223, fols. 35v–43v.

[59] Cf. W. Scase, *Piers Plowman and the New Anticlericalism*, Cambridge Studies in Medieval Literature (Cambridge, 1989), p. 49.

[60] Richard FitzRalph, 'Defensorium curatorum contra eos qui privilegiatos se dicunt', in E. Brown, ed., *Appendix ad fasciculum rerum expetendarum et fugiendarum*, II (London, 1690), pp. 466–86, 467–9.

[61] Cambridge University Library, MS Ff. I. 21, fols. 1r-260r, 260r-67v, where William Woodford's *De erroribus eiusdem Armachani* ends abruptly on the 42nd error.

CHAPTER THIRTEEN

Giovanni Boccaccio, Satire and the Friars

...the disease of galloping avarice common among the clergy, and especially among the Franciscans who do not dare to touch money.

Giovanni Boccaccio[1]

Giovanni Boccaccio's Decameron

A literary echo of many of the same charges made by Richard FitzRalph appears in Giovanni Boccaccio's *Decameron*, one of the great works of fourteenth-century literature. Written in the early 1350s, the *Decameron* is set in the Tuscan countryside where three young men and seven young women retire to await the passing of the black death. In their rustic retreat they amused themselves by recounting a hundred stories. A feature of these stories is the *persona* of the friar, who is moulded by contemporary criticisms. Although the narrators refer frequently to the mendicants generically, the Franciscans are singled out more than the other groups and always presented in an unflattering light. This portrait depicts a fraternity whose members lacked integrity, discipline and supervision; these friars bear little comparison with their saintly predecessors. The polemic deftly targets each area in which the friars had excelled in the thirteenth century.

Instead of an intelligent and engaging exposition of the Scriptures, the friars promoted superstitions and dubious cults. The devotions which they fostered were designed to attract funds. Friars sought alms for their communities and solicited offerings for the celebration of Masses. They were perceived as promoting the aggrandisement of their churches and enlargement of their premises. Instead of building up the moral life of the faithful, their preaching was largely filled with jests, quips and raillery.[2] The character of their preaching was exemplified by Cippola, a hospitaller of St Anthony. The prosperity of Certaldo in the Val d'Elsa, the birth place of the author, drew the friar to the small Tuscan town each year to collect subscriptions and alms. Cippola was warmly welcomed. Although he was illiterate, he was a lively and engaging speaker. He arrived on a Sunday in August and attended

---

[1] Boccaccio, *Decameron*, I, 6, p. 54.
[2] Ibid., X, conc., pp. 763–4. He also raises the question of homosexuality among the friars.

Mass, where he was invited to preach; people from surrounding hamlets were present. He reminded the parishioners of the custom whereby people gave alms in the form of wheat and oats, in accordance with their means, so that St Anthony would protect their livestock; particular attention was paid to the subscriptions to be collected from members of the confraternity. The people were to assemble outside the parish church at the ringing of the bell for the afternoon sermon. Cippola offered to show the people a special relic which he had brought back from the Holy Land, a feather of the archangel Gabriel. Two wags heard the announcement with a level of cynicism. They waited until the friar took his breakfast before setting out for the inn where he was staying. While the friar's coarse companion was in pursuit of a woman who worked in the inn's kitchens, they removed the putative relic, a parrot's feather. The presence of relics boosted the size of the congregation and number of the offerings. The sense of excitement and entertainment provided by contemporary sermons was captured by the narrator, who emphasises the gullibility of the crowd. Realising that the relic had been taken away, Cippola embarked upon a lengthy and detailed account of his travels and the relics he had seen and acquired. He recounted the wonderful places he had visited and the relics he had venerated, including the forelock of the Seraph which had appeared to Francis at La Verna.[3]

The story recounted by Filomena features a sanctimonious friar who was duped by a beautiful woman. The unwitting friar of good reputation was used as a mediator with a prospective lover. The prelude to the account contains a diatribe against the friars, who combined stupidity with a superior attitude towards others. A Florentine lady of some quality and beauty approached a friar, who agreed to hear her confession. Her stratagem was to report that she was being pursued by a male friend of the friar, whose assistance she sought in bringing such unwanted attentions to an end. Despite his reputation for holiness of life and his uncouthness, the friar was attracted by the lady's wealth and he recommended various charities and almsgiving, explaining his own needy plight. He failed to detect that one lie followed another. He undertook to use his influence to ensure that she was troubled no further by the suitor. At the end of the confession he solicited donations, including Mass intentions. She stuffed money into his hands and asked him to celebrate Masses for her deceased relations. When his friend visited him, the friar reproved him for his lascivious glances at the lady. The friend initially protested his innocence, but then recognised the woman's intentions. The stupidity of the friar was contrasted with the guile of the young man. The friar violated the seal of confession by disclosing the woman's words. The lady's second meeting with her confessor placed in bold relief the friars' gullibility, their thirst for money and an interest in soliciting Mass stipends. The lady returned to

---

[3] Ibid., VI, 10, pp. 451–60.

the friar again and left an unmistakable signal. Knowing the friars' reputation for avarice, she gave him a florin to celebrate Gregorian Masses. The money was gleefully accepted by the 'saintly friar', despite the prohibition on the acceptance of money. After recounting pious tales to fortify her in virtue, the friar dismissed the lady. On a subsequent visit to the friar she explained that her husband was away on business and gave directions to her bedroom. United, the lovers mocked the stupidity of the friar.[4]

The frequently repeated charge that the friars were seeking to attract burials features the duplicitous figure of Ser Cepperello, a corrupt notary and notable blasphemer of Prato, who travelled to Burgundy, where he fell mortally ill. His hosts, aware that he was not a Christian and would be denied burial in consecrated ground, went to the local friary to request the services of a confessor. Cepperello asked for the holiest and most able friar. An old friar, widely respected and a master of theology, was dispatched to the house and questioned Cepperello on chastity, honesty, avarice, temperance and patience. The confession of a number of faults elicited only a mild rebuke. When the sick man confessed that he had spat in church, the friar retorted that religious regularly did the same. Turning the tables on the sagacious friar, Cepperello castigated his confessor for the practice of spitting in church. The friar gave absolution and was misled into thinking that his penitent was a saint. He wasted no time in asking where the sick man might be buried, suggesting that he might like to be interred in the friary to benefit from the friars' intercession. Cepperello readily agreed and professed his long-standing devotion to the order. Having received the sacraments, he died shortly after Vespers. The friars were notified and that evening they celebrated a great and solemn vigil at the house. The confessor proclaimed the virtues of Cepperello and expressed his hope that miracles would be worked through his intercession. He persuaded the credulous friars to accept the body for burial in one of their chapels. The following morning they accompanied his corpse, wearing albs and copes; they carried books and followed the processional cross. In some pomp they processed from the house where he was lodging to the church for the requiem Mass.[5] During the funeral the confessor expatiated upon the virtues of the deceased and mentioned some of the matters confessed by Cepperello, regardless of the seal of confession. His commendation of the merchant was so convincing that the people believed him to be a saint and they hastened to pray at his marble tomb. The following day candles were lighted before the tomb and the trickster was venerated as a saint.[6]

The *lewed frere* was no stranger to medieval satire.[7] An observation about

---

[4]   Ibid., III, 3, pp. 200–9.
[5]   Ibid., introd., pp. 11–12.
[6]   Ibid., I, 1, pp. 25–38.
[7]   *The English Works of John Gower*, II, ed. G. C. Macaulay, Early English Text Society, Extra Series, 82 (London, 1901), VI, 138, p. 171.

the changing dispositions of the hypocritical friars stands at the beginning of the story by Pampinea, who contrasts their gentle disposition in seeking alms with their manner in the confessional. The anecdote about Berto della Massa highlights the friars' defective policy on admissions. He was a depraved scoundrel of Imola and an incorrigible liar. His reputation in the city was so bad that he decided to move elsewhere and settled in Venice, where he assumed a humble *persona* and was clothed in the habit of St Francis, taking the name of Albert of Imola. He was seen to be frugal in food and drink. He began to preach the virtues of repentance and humility so successfully that no one suspected his past. Ordained to the priesthood, he began to affect piety and intense devotion at the altar, shedding copious tears for the passion endured by the Son of God. This display of fervour impressed the Venetians, many of whom involved him in their testamentary dispositions. Some entrusted him with their money for safe-keeping and several others made him their confessor and confidential adviser. He symbolises the friars accused of abusing the sacraments to become adulterers.[8] He interrupted the confession of one of his penitents to ascertain whether she had a lover. Learning that she did not, he concocted a scheme to seduce her and was assisted by the collusion of their companion. The woman's indiscretion led to his unmasking and public humiliation. He was saved only by the intervention of some of his confrères, who escorted him back to his friary, where he was kept under lock and key and spent the remainder of his days in misery.[9]

Tebaldo degli Elisei's plans to seduce Monna Ermellina were thwarted by a friar, provoking a vitriolic outburst against the order. The confessor had painted a vivid account of the pains of hell awaiting those ensnared in adultery. On his return to Florence, Tebaldo, disguised as a pilgrim and a friar, undermined the work of the friars. He recalled the golden days of the order when friars were worthy and saintly. Contemporary friars had little in common with such men; the only link was their religious habit. Tebaldo asserted that friars' habits should be close-fitting, course and shabby as a mark of humility. Contemporary habits were ample, generously cut, smooth of texture and made from the finest fabrics. Tebaldo's testimony shows that the dress of such friars reflected their association with the papal court. Clad thus, friars paraded themselves through Florence and its *piazze*, deceiving the wealthy and other simpletons. While the first friars toiled incessantly for the salvation of souls, contemporary friars struck fear into the hearts of their penitents to procure Mass intentions and alms. Cowardice drove such men to the priesthood. Friars denounced the sin of lust in order to have easier access to women whom they try to seduce. Usury was a target of the friars' sermons

---

[8] Cf. H. Goyens, 'Speculum imperfectonis fratrum minorum compactum per venerabilem et religiosum P. Fr. Iohannem Brugman, O.F.M.', *AFH* 2 (1909), pp. 613–25 at 620–1.

[9] Boccaccio, *Decameron*, IV, 2, pp. 293–302. Cf. ibid., VII, 3, pp. 476–81; another licentious friar was Rinaldo.

so that they might be entrusted with the work of restitution. These funds were illegitimately employed for the purchase of habits, major ecclesiastical offices and bishoprics. Echoing the language of the anti-fraternal controversies, the narrator depicts friars as the new Pharisees, whose word should be followed more than their example. If they could not be chaste, they should remain within the walls of the friary. Their lascivious interests were not confined to married women. They also stood accused of having sexual relations with nuns. The popular impression that friars and nuns' contacts were not always governed by the constitutions gained some currency, which expressed itself in miniatures. In one a nun, her habit tucked up to her knees, danced to the music played by a friar.[10] Members of the laity were urged to spend their money for their own benefit rather than to finance a life of idleness for the friars in their cloisters. Tebaldo's admission to the gaol to visit Aldobrandino indicates the friars' ministry to the imprisoned.[11]

The friars had been entrusted with the inquisition in Tuscany by Pope Alexander IV (1254–61), and one of them resident in Florence was the subject of another story, which was culled from the chronicle of Giovanni Villani. Described as 'an important and rich man' (*uomo superbo e pecunioso*), the inquisitor has been identified as Peter of Aquila, who became bishop of Sant'Angeli in Naples.[12] He was on the look-out for heretics, but he was more interested in seeking out those with bulging purses. The words of a worthy man were reported to the inquisitor, who learned that the man held vast estates and a substantial sum of money. Echoing the arrest of Jesus (Matthew 26.47), the narrator tells how the friar hastened to draw up serious charges against him. In this the friar was not driven so much by a desire to curb the man's theological excesses as by the hope of material gains. He summoned the suspect and rebuked him harshly. In return, the man detected the friars' partiality for money, and arranged for coins to change hands in the hope of leniency. While there was a common avarice among the clergy, the friars were especially prone to it, despite their protestations. The narrator was surprised by the fact that major and minor theological deviancy resulted in the same punishment in the flames. The penance was subsequently commuted to the wearing of a cross, while the inquisitor pocketed the money and obliged the penitent to be present at Mass each morning at Santa Croce. The man listened attentively to the Gospel (Matthew 19.29) and castigated the friars for their greed and their neglect of the poor. He predicted that the friars would be punished severely in the next world because they had enjoyed their

---

[10] BL, Stowe MS 17, fol. 38. BL, MS Royal, 2 B. VII, fol. 176v, depicts two nuns, a monk and a barefooted Franciscan standing in a row, their hands very close.

[11] Boccaccio, *Decameron*, III, 7, pp. 229–45, 233–9.

[12] Cf. D'Alatri, *Eretici e inquisitori in Italia, studi e documenti. Il tre e il quattrocento*, 2 vols, Bibliotheca Seraphico-Capuccina, XXXI/II (Rome, 1987), Villani, *Nuova cronica*, III, lib. XIII, c. 58, pp. 429–33.

reward in this world. The lazy friars, whose vocation was to expound the Gospel, were rebuked by a man who was charged with heresy.[13]

The literary genre

These colourful narratives distracted the young from the horrors of the Black Death and amused them. Their plight called for entertainment and relief from the threat of the plague, which was ravaging Florence. Humorous anecdotes were selected to lift the spirits of the group. The raconteurs stood outside the major institutions of society and gently poked fun at local government, marriage, the clergy and religious life. The lives of the saints would have provided them with a wealth of edification, but would have focused their minds on the ultimate reality of death, a prospect that had made them flee their native city. While a utopian society affords little scope for mirth, the unpredictable and the unexpected can be a cause of laughter, even when directed against oneself. Humour is to be found in the situations in which the normal order of society is disturbed either through the failings of some or the funny experiences which people recount. Anecdotes of deception, marital infidelity, clerical failings and the vices of civic officials offer much more material for enjoyment and amusement.

The civic and ecclesiastical institutions are held up for ridicule and treated with a spirit of irreverence. There is some cynicism about the clergy, who were accused of ignorance. The narratives are peopled by corrupt officials of the Roman curia, priests conducting vendettas against each other, a priest having an affair with an abbess, a promiscuous parish priest and a lascivious provost. Famous monasteries degenerated into small communities, whose members succumbed to corruption with the connivance of abbots and prioresses. There are references to a hermit who seized the chance of sexual relations, an exceedingly wealthy abbot of Cluny and an abbot who solicited in the confessional. Civic officials did not escape criticism and the sceptre of corruption and susceptibility to bribery was implied. Powers were abused by offices of the commune, including judges.

Literature should not be employed uncritically as a historical source.[14] Like medieval hagiography, the texts require interpretation. Unless they refer to a specific historical event, these materials cannot be used indiscriminately alongside materials culled from annals, chronicles, letters and conciliar documents. Boccaccio draws upon contemporary aspects of the friars' lives. For example, Berto della Massa's change of name to Albert of Imola exemplifies the medieval practice. Cippola, probably the limiter (*lymitour*), testifies to

---

[13] Boccaccio, *Decameron*, I, 6, pp. 53–6.

[14] M. Prestwich, *The Three Edwards: War and State in England 1272–1377* (London, 1980), p. 212. C. Erickson, 'The Fourteenth-Century Franciscans and Their Critics', *FS* 35 (1975), pp. 107–35 at 107–9.

the annual visits to parishes to preach, hear confessions, seek alms and collect subscriptions from those associated with the order.[15] William Langland regarded the Franciscans among the most travelled men in medieval society.[16] This reputation, recently personified by Nicholas of Poggibonsi, enabled Cippola to indulge in tall stories about distant countries and their precious relics rather than preaching the Gospel. Complaints about the fickle friars' interest in the fortunate and the wealthy are deftly woven into the text.[17]

Neither can literary images be disregarded. Anecdotes derive credence, authority, value and colour from a historical context. Boccaccio's raconteurs speak of the friars in a way that is plausible and credible. Their image of the friar is in tune with the pleas of the internal reformers and the complaints of critics. There is a continuity between the frustrations expressed by Ubertino da Casale, Angelo Clareno, Pope John XXII, Richard FitzRalph and others. Contemporary complaints about the friars are echoed by Boccaccio. Like a cartoon, the literary expression has to be recognisable, otherwise the point is lost in a lengthy introduction of the characters.

The ten young people were not ostensibly irreligious. They foregathered in Santa Maria Novella and noted the plague's decimation of the Dominican community. Their observance of the Sabbath and the prayers to be followed on such occasions are mentioned. Indeed, religious observance of the Sabbath is given priority over the duties of the narrator, as the introduction to each day of story-telling demonstrates. The fun at the expense of priests and religious is not to be confused with an excessively critical and hostile attitude. It may represent humour, which is limited to a particular circle such as a family or a community. Scathing comments about the Church and its officials no more imply a rejection of the role of the sacraments and the spiritual life than they do of the sacrament of marriage. Despite the number of stories about matrimonial failings, the seven female raconteurs probably dreamed of their own wedding day and the formation of their own families. Although it is acceptable for members of the family to narrate humourous episodes about each other, there is a taboo on allowing one of their number to be ridiculed by others. The values of a society are sometimes cloaked in humour for the initiated and this applies particularly to anti-clericalism in a society where Christianity went unchallenged.[18] Boccaccio's image of the friar can be tested against a range of sources.

---

[15] William Langland, *The Vision of William concerning Piers the Plowman*, B text, ed. W. W. Skeat, Early English Text Society, Ordinary Series 38 (London, 1869), V, p. 139. A. Williams, 'The "Limitour" of Chaucer's Time and His "Limitacioun"', *Studies in Philology* 57 (1960), pp. 463–78.

[16] Langland, *Piers Plowman*, VIII. 14–15, p. 126.

[17] Ibid., XI. 53–8, pp. 170–1.

[18] Cf. J. M. Synge, *Plays*, ed. A. Saddlemyer (Oxford, 1969), p. 33. In his preface to *The Tinker's Wedding* on 2 December 1907, Synge considers a community's attitude to humour. I owe this reference to Professor Declan Kibert, who comments that Synge regarded satire on priests as a safety-valve, which allowed the people 'to discharge their bile against "bad apples"'.

An analysis of the texts

Friars of the thirteenth century revitalised Christendom. The combination of their fervent message and impressive example reinvigorated the Church and chided the clerical failings lampooned in the *Decameron*. By the middle of the fourteenth century the friars were losing their ascendancy in pulpit, confessional and lecture hall. While the mendicant preachers of the previous century had undergone a lengthy training for the office, Cippola, albeit a member of one of the smaller mendicant communities, was illiterate. The mendicant preacher had degenerated into a corrupt figure, whose purpose was to amuse rather than edify; he had a greater interest in attracting donations than in instructing his hearers. One of Cippola's tasks was the collection of money from members of the confraternity and from those who venerated the bogus relic. The sermon was to be an occasion of attracting money.[19] This wholly negative portrait in Boccaccio is balanced by the licences which bishops issued for friars to preach throughout the later Middle Ages; friars were appointed as preachers in dioceses, archdeaconries and deaneries. Friars were invited to preach at various occasions and were appointed to expound the Scriptures to members of the royal families and on special occasions in the life of the local Church in the middle of the fourteenth century.

The confessional supplemented the friars' work in the pulpit and offered them a forum for the propagation of the principles of Christianity. Boccaccio's mendicant confessors are respectfully introduced with a reputation for holiness of life and erudition, but the narratives show them to be naive and gullible. Confessors in Florence and Burgundy are duped by the penitent who used the friar to send messages to her prospective lover, and the unscrupulous merchant who was quite unfamiliar with confession. The confessional, which was instituted for the forgiveness of sins, was thereby corrupted into a medium for an adulterous liaison. While the friars of the thirteenth century had preached vigorously against avarice, Boccaccio accused their successors of succumbing to the same vice. The Florentine penitent acted on the friars' reputation for avarice. The same narrative depicts a friar using the confessional to solicit gifts for the order and himself. The sacrament was thereby converted into an opportunity for generating funds. Boccaccio was undoubtedly aware of instances of indiscipline by mendicant confessors. Some bishops revoked the licences given to friars appointed to hear confessions. Such instances are balanced by friars whose sacramental ministrations continued to be sought. Mendicant churches attracted queues of penitents and many noble families engaged friars as confessors. Richard FitzRalph accused the friars of being driven more by avarice than pastoral concerns in the hearing of confessions.[20]

---

[19] Cf. Langland, *Piers Plowman*, prologue, 58–60, p. 3.
[20] Richard FitzRalph, 'Defensorium curatorum', p. 479.

The suggestion that the friars were not faithful to their vow of chastity was not a new one, and it was repeated particularly in satire. Albert of Imola typifies the friar who feigned conversion, but was unable to free himself of his old failings. The office of the confessor was abused in order to seduce the Venetian woman who believed that the archangel Gabriel was in love with her. Albert's companion was aware of his proclivities and intentions, but made no effort to restrain the corrupt confessor. Similarly, Rinaldo, who pursued a Sienese woman, did not discard his old ways in his new life as a friar. He devised a scheme to ensnare the mother of his god-child. He, too, was aided and abetted by a reprobate companion, whose function was to serve as a companion and a stimulus to the fuller observance of the Rule. Here Boccaccio was on safer ground, but his inference of institutionalised deviance is harder to prove.

The charge that the friars were seeking to attract burials was a standard one, reiterated by internal reformers and the order's critics alike.[21] While Boccaccio supplies details about friars and funerals, his evidence can be tested. He presents only two men who were interred in the friars' churches and each is a disreputable character, Scannadio and Cepparello. Boccaccio's evidence is exaggerated and it is not supported by contemporary documents. The vast Italian churches confirm that many influential and powerful members of the local community were laid to rest there. Several members of royal families chose burial in the friars' churches, as the next chapter demonstrates. There were also disputes between the friars and their secular neighbours concerning burials, even to the point of exhuming bodies and re-interring them in friaries. There is no vestige of this in the *Decameron*, where the friars are reduced to burying scoundrels and reprobates.

The allegation that the friars promoted dubious cults for financial gain can be measured against other sources. In 1307 Hugh of London, a convert from Judaism aged 61, testified to the phenomenon of false cults. He informed the process of canonisation for Thomas of Cantilipe, bishop of Hereford (1275–82), that a friar of Oxford had been approached by a man who promised to make the community rich by having miracles simulated at Geoffrey of St Edmunds's tomb by himself and a team of twenty-four collaborators.[22] Urban authorities took a central role in the propagation of new cults. The commune at Udine was especially active in promoting the shrine of Odorico da Pordenone and financed his cult.[23] The friars had major

[21] Ubertino da Casale, 'Rotulus', no. 13, p. 114, points to the friars' damaging involvement in seeking funerals and burials. Cf. *Thomae Walsingham, quondam monachi S. Albani, Historia Anglicana*, ed. H. T. Riley, RS, XXVII, i (London, 1863), p. 38.

[22] A. Vauchez, *La Sainteté en occident aux derniers siècles du Moyen Age: d'après les procès de canonisation et les documents hagiographiques*, Bibliothèque des écoles françaises d'Athenes et de Rome, CCXLI (Rome, 1981), p. 650.

[23] A. Tilatti, *Odorico da Pordenone, Vita e Miracula*, Centro studi Antoniani, XLI (Padua, 2004), pp. 77–83.

shrines of international prestige at Assisi and Padua and the flow of pilgrims to these basilicas is narrated by the biographers of the two saints. In addition, members of the Second and Third Orders were also enrolled in the catalogue of saints. Many friars acquired a reputation for holiness of life and accounts of their deeds and miracles circulated. The tombs of several members of the order attracted cults and miracles were carefully documented, as in the case of Walter of Bruges, bishop of Poitiers, on 17 March 1340.[24] These manifestations of holiness in western Europe were supplemented by accounts of the martyrdom of friars toiling in the missionary territory.

The historian and the raconteur have their own intentions and objectives. The one seeks to report events in as objective a manner as possible. The other's intention is to entertain and this may lead to the truth being strained or stretched. The narrator's injection of some exaggeration was viewed as a way of vivifying and enlivening the level of humour. Boccaccio's characters are presented as the personification of goodness and integrity or neglect and corruption. In this scheme Cippola makes no attempt to preach the Gospel and the content of his homily was purely designed to loosen the purse strings in favour of the friars. The woman intent on adultery displays no compunction for her failings; the narrators would have regarded such detail as a potential distraction. There are, nonetheless, boundaries which circumscribe the work of the satirist. The failings of some men should not be exaggerated into a declaration that all are compromised by the same flaws. Boccaccio had no interest in the more positive reports about the friars, such as the missions to China and India, the missions to Persia and Bosnia, which produced new martyrs, or the heroism of the friars who ministered to the afflicted during the Black Death and contracted the plague themselves. Such accounts of heroism and single-minded dedication would not have been suitable for his brief to entertain the young.

Boccaccio's portrait of the friars encapuslates many of the complaints made by internal reformers and external critics. While its observations are not devoid of credibility, the narrators like to add spice to their stories and they succumb to exaggeration, when the writer argues from personal faults to common corruption.[25] Arnold Williams believes that Chaucer's friars cannot be taken as representatives of the mendicants as a whole. Christopher Brooke observes that, if all friars were like Chaucer's beggar, the satire would fail and the order would have withered.[26] Satirical evidence must be weighed

---

[24] Cf. *Dialogus de gestis sanctorum fratrum minorum auctore Thoma de Papia*, ed. F. M. Delorme, Bibliotheca Franciscana ascetica medii aevi, V (Quaracchi, Florence, 1923), A. Callebaut, 'Recueil de miracles et preuves du culte immémorial de S. Gautier de Bruges O.F.M., évêque de Poitiers (1279–1306)', *AFH* 5 (1912), pp. 494–519.

[25] A. M. D. Barrell, *Medieval Scotland*, Cambridge Medieval Textbooks (Cambridge, 2000), p. 53, believes that Chaucer's portrait expresses popular suspicion of the friars.

[26] A. Williams, 'Chaucer and the Friars', *Speculum*, 28 (1953), pp. 499–513 at 513. C. N. L. Brooke, *The Age of the Cloister: The Story of Monastic Life in the Middle Ages*, p. 231.

against contemporary sources. On the basis of wills, Christopher Harper-Bill's judgement is that, despite their literary image, the friars maintained their popularity.[27] Literary sources call for interpretation and are not necessarily be seen as evidence of widespread decay.

---

[27] C. Harper-Bill, *The Pre-Reformation Church in England, 1400–1530* (London, 1989), p. 73.

CHAPTER FOURTEEN

The Friars' Churches

> Even the architecture of their churches was influenced by their preaching
> mission and its success. In cities all over Europe they built large but simple
> churches with little interior adornment, the naves being little more than
> great open spaces to accommodate the crowds.
>
> Penn R. Szittya[1]

Construction

The order's first churches reflected the friars' modest role as new religious
in the neighbourhood. As they increased in number, stature and reputation, the friars attracted large numbers to their churches. In some instances,
there were three successive churches on a single site, culminating in a vast
expansive structure. By the beginning of the fourteenth century the classical
mendicant churches were under construction throughout western Europe,
especially in the more substantial cities. The completion of the church might
take a considerable length of time, sixty years or more. The solemn ceremony
of dedication marked the end of the building phase.

The link between the friars' preaching and the enlargement of their
churches was made explicit by Albertanus of Brescia in the middle of the
thirteenth century.[2] The large nave was the distinctive mark of mendicant
architecture, which was designed to maximise space for those attending
sermons. The liturgy of the Word went hand in hand with eucharistic piety
and at least six altars flanked the high altar of these churches. At a later date
side altars appeared in the nave. Contrasting the size of the friars' churches
with the parish churches, William Woodford pointed out that the former
generally had ten or twelve altars and the latter had two or three.[3] The cost
of erecting windows was borne by individuals or societies. Friars were accustomed to inscribe the donors' names on the windows, some of which were
given by guilds.[4] These churches began to rival, and in some cases surpass, the

---

[1] P. R. Szittya, *The Antifraternal Tradition in Medieval Literature* (Princeton, 1986), p. 53.
[2] Albertanus Brixiensis, *Sermones quattuor*, ed. M. Ferrari (Lonato, 1955), p. 48.
[3] Doyle, 'William Woodford', p. 179.
[4] Langland, *Piers Plowman*, III. 61 and XIV. 197–8, pp. 34, 246, *wyndowes glasen* and *Lo! how men writeth in fenestres atte freres . . .*

biggest churches in a city or town. Echoing the complaints of Ubertino da Casale, Richard FitzRalph protested that the friars built numerous sumptuous churches, cloisters, bell-towers, friaries and other fine structures.[5]

Popes and bishops aided these projects by offering indulgences to those who made donations. Influential families and citizens, some of whom sought burial in the cloister or cemetery, financed vast churches.[6] Members of the royal families of western Europe were conspicuous benefactors, especially in the construction and adornment of churches. Queen Sancia, the wife of Robert, king of Naples (1309–43), financed the building of Santa Chiara in Naples.[7] Royal gifts for the basilica of San Francesco, Assisi, are well documented. Inventories reveal a glittering array of donors, such as Pope Boniface VIII, Maria, wife of Carlo Robert, king of Hungary (1302–42), and Blanche, sister of the king of Navarre. Family loyalties to the basilica were expressed by King Robert of Naples, Queen Sancia, and their son, Charles, the duke of Calabria. Episcopal benefactors, too, gave freely to the basilica, including Cardinals Matthew de Orsini (†1305), James Colonna (†1318) and Giles Albarnoz, cardinal priest and then cardinal bishop (†1367). Ordinary friars also joined the army of benefactors, as well as those who moved in exalted circles, either as bishops or members of episcopal or papal households.[8]

The stream of offerings for the basilica in Assisi should not disguise the fact that in many instances the friars experienced difficulty in financing the construction of their churches. The manner in which they collected funds for such building did not go without criticism.[9] In some instances they depended on voluntary labour given by pious and kindly neighbours with an eye to spiritual reward. For instance, when the church in Athlone was being repaired on 27 June 1398, Benedict IX granted indulgences not merely to those who visited it, but to those who extended a helping hand for its repair.[10] Evidence, often fragmentary and salvaged from long-since perished records, points to the friars' engagement in the mechanical arts in general and construction in particular. It confirms that the friars possessed skills which were employed in the building and decoration of their new churches. The architect of San Francesco, Gargnano, was Delaio da Lodi, a friar who received sight in one eye through the intercession of St Anthony of Padua in 1301. Three years later he sculpted the bass relief between the chapel of St Anthony and

---

5   Peterhouse Library, Cambridge, MS 223, fols. 35v–43v, 41v.

6   Delorme, 'Les Cordeliers', p. 119.

7   Bihl, 'Fraticelli cuiusdam', X, no. 15, p. 366.

8   A thurible, a small glass ciborium containing relics and a mitre were donated by William de Alexandria, a member of the household of Nicholas IV, Andrew Capitanei de Assisi and Ceccus Rosane, who may once have been in the service of a bishop. Two candelabra were given by Frederick de Assisi, the sacristan, as an act of almsgiving. Cf. Alessandri and Pennacchi, 'Inventari'.

9   Langland, *Piers Plowman*, XV, 321–33, p. 272.

10 *BF*, VII, no. 254, p. 83. C. Mooney, 'Franciscan Architecture in Pre-Reformation Ireland', *The Journal of the Royal Society of Antiquaries of Ireland* 85 (1955), pp. 133–73, and 86 (1956) pp. 125–69 at 126.

the Immaculate in the friary of San Francesco at Lodi.[11] Evidence of the friars engaged in the building of friaries, especially in the Veneto, is assembled by Louise Bourdua, who amplifies such comments in her study of San Lorenzo, Vicenza.[12] She sketches the role of Nicholas, a friar active towards the middle of the century, even down to his rates of pay for his work on the two stone portals at the entrance to the church.[13] The practice of missionaries building their own churches is illustrated by Laurence of Alexandria and Peter Martelli of Provence, two non-clerical friars who were building a church in China in 1339, when they were martyred.[14]

Devotion and sacramental life of the churches

The church was a focal point in the life of the friary and the commune. The Divine Office and the sacraments were celebrated there as well as a host of public and private devotions. The friars' fervent and dignified celebration of the sacraments brought many to their churches. The large number of priests in the community ensured that Mass was celebrated several times daily both at the high altar and at the numerous side altars. This factor made Mass, confessions and the various devotional exercises more readily available than in the local parish church, which was generally served by a rector or vicar and three or four chaplains or curates. All manner of people turned to the friars for prayers, especially for funerals and anniversaries.

The friars' sermons were copied, including those by James da Tresanti, Roger de Piazza and Andrew de Pace.[15] Friars preached in their own churches, on the piazza and in the parish churches.[16] They also delivered homilies in other religious houses.[17] The Scriptures were explained on Sundays, the major feast days, Franciscan feasts and other occasions determined by the local community. Vital du Four, minister provincial of Aquitaine, preached so movingly

---

[11] P. M. Sevesi, 'Il San Francesco di Gargnano dei Frati Minori Conventuali', *MF* 52 (1952), pp. 572–80.

[12] L. Bourdua, 'I frati minori al santo nel trecento: consulenti, committenti o artisti?', *Il santo* 42 (2002), pp. 17–28 at 19.

[13] The activities of friars as builders and artists emerge from a study of the friaries of Montefalco. Bourdua, *The Franciscans and Art Patronage*, pp. 71–88, Nessi, 'Storia e arte', pp. 273–4, 308.

[14] Alessandri and Pennacchi, 'Inventari', no. 23, pp. 77, BL, MS Cotton Galba, E XIV, fol. 42v. 'Martyrium fr. minorum Almaligh an. 1339', *SF*, pp. 510–11.

[15] C. Cenci, 'Noterelle su Fr. Giacomo da Tresanti, lettore predicatore', *AFH* 86 (1993), pp. 119–28, Rogerii de Platea, O. Min., *Sermones*, ed. C. Roccaro, Officina di studi medievali, Collana franciscana, V (Palermo, 1992), D. Ciccarelli, 'Le "introductiones dominicales" di Andrea de Pace O. Min.', *Schede medievali rassegna dell'officina di studi medievali* 38 (2000), pp. 121–47. Lenten sermons preached at San Francesco, Perugia, in 1321 have been edited, while homilies delivered at San Lorenzo, Naples, during 1351 by Palmerius de Siciniano remain unedited. C. Cenci, 'Quaresimale del 1321 in S. Francesco al Prato di Perugia', *StF* 91 (1994), pp. 329–41, C. Cenci, *Manoscritti francescani della Biblioteca nazionale di Napoli*, II, SB, VIII (Grottaferrata, Rome, 1971), pp. 868–9.

[16] Hammerich, 'The Beginning of the Strife', p. 56.

[17] Cf. M. Dykmans, 'Le Dernier Sermon de Guillaume d'Alnwick', *AFH* 63 (1970), pp. 259–79.

on Christmas day 1311 at the church of the Cordeliers of Toulouse that he was instrumental in the conversion of numerous prostitutes, who subsequently committed themselves to live as a community according to the Rule of St Augustine and earned recognition from Pope John XXII.[18] The majority of friars delivered their first sermons in their own churches. Preaching remained part of the friars' role in the universities.[19] The friars' churches in the vicinity of the papal court were the venue for sermons by members of the order as well as guest preachers. Prelates were present at these sermons.[20]

Although sermons are generally closely connected with the celebration of Mass in the modern era, their medieval forerunners occurred at a time suitable for the largest number of people. Richard FitzRalph noted that, while the local curate preached only during the Mass, the friars had all day to give their sermons.[21] Bartholomew Albizi refers to a sermon which he preached in the afternoon in association with the veneration of relics in Tuscany.[22] There were evening homilies, particularly in the seasons of penance. For instance, Francesco di Marco Datini's wife and sister, Margaret and Lapa, attended sermons each evening at San Francesco, Prato, during the Lent of 1385.[23]

The friars' reputation for theological acumen and pastoral sensitivity drew the laity to their churches. Friars heard confessions throughout the week and confessors were particularly busy during Advent and Lent, when the faithful prepared for the celebration of the solemnities of Christmas and Easter. The large number of people who confessed their sins in the friars' churches during Lent, especially between Passion Sunday and Easter Sunday, became a feature of the order's apologetics.[24] The sizeable churches of the friars were deemed to be suitable venues for various types of liturgical celebration. Archbishops of York annually held ordinations in the city's mendicant churches. A general council of the Scottish Church was held at the friary of Dundee on 24 February 1310.[25]

---

[18]   H. Dedieu, 'Les Ministres provinciaux d'Aquitaine des origines à la division de l'ordre (XIIIe siecle – 1517)', *AFH* 76 (1983), pp. 129–214, 646–700 at 179–80, n. 3.

[19]   V. Doucet, 'Le Sermon de Jacques de Padoue sur S. François (Paris 1345), et son témoignage sur Alexandre de Hales', *AFH* 44 (1951), pp. 471–6.

[20]   Among those who preached in the church of the Cordeliers, Avignon, was Pierre Roger, the Benedictine cardinal priest (1339–42), the future Clement VI. Peterhouse Library, Cambridge, MS 265, fols. 140v–146v. He preached the panegyric of Cardinal Napoleon Orsini. Richard FitzRalph preached at the Cordeliers, Avignon, on 25 November 1338, 4 October 1349 and on the feast of St Martin of Tours. J. B. Schneyer, *Repertorium der lateinischen Sermones des Mittelalters: für die Zeit von 1150–1350*, Beitrage zur Geschichte der Philosophie und Theologie des Mittelalters, XLIII, v (Münster, 1973), nn. 63, 82, 83, pp. 156, 157. Cf. BL, Lansdowne, MS 393, fols. 167r–181r [177r–181r].

[21]   Hammerich, 'The Beginning of the Strife', p. 57: *ex quo fratres toto residuo diei tempore possunt predicare pro voto.*

[22]   F. Rotolo, 'La leggenda del B. Gerardo Cagnoli, O. Min. (1267–1342) di Fra Bartolomeo Albizzi, O. Min. (†1351)', *MF* 57 (1957), pp. 367–446, VII, no. 131, at 437.

[23]   I. M. Origo, *The World of San Bernardino* (New York, 1962), p. 188.

[24]   Doyle, 'William Woodford', p. 146.

[25]   *Anglo-Scottish Relations 1174–1328: Some Selected Documents*, ed. E. L. G. Stone, Oxford Medieval

Members of the Third Order were instinctively drawn to the friars' churches for their individual and corporate devotions.[26] The penitential fraternities, men and women aspiring to higher standards of the spiritual life, proliferated. Nurtured by the friars' new model of the devotional life, they have been portrayed as 'lay echoes of mendicant spirituality'.[27] They forged close links with the friars in whose churches they met on a regular basis. Numerous confraternities and guilds made their devotional homes in the friars' churches.[28] *Laudesi* groups routinely assembled in the friars' churches; their connections with Santa Croce are well documented.[29]

The order's churches were the burial places of men and women distinguished by their integrity of life and miracles. The catalogues of the order's saints, published at provincial and international levels, recorded a plethora of cults.[30] Evidence of the miracles at the shrine of Blessed Gerard Cagnoli is vividly recounted by Bartolomeo Albizzi, a friar who seems to have been the custodian of the shrine at San Francesco, Pisa.[31] San Francesco at Foligno was the resting place of seven members of the order, whose vicissitudes it reflects. Among the cults which flourished there were St Angela of Foligno (†1309), the martyrs Blessed Thomas (†1370), who was killed in Bulgaria, and Blessed Philip and James (†1377), who were slain near Bevagna.[32]

Burials

The mendicant church was a place for the interment of friars either in individual tombs or in a common grave; friars were also laid to rest in the cloister. In times of crisis and warfare it became a resting place for the slain; it served

---

Texts (Oxford, 1965), pp. 140–3.

[26] Dialta di Gualtero left 100 libre for the construction of a new chapel for the use of the Third Order in the basilica of San Francesco, Assisi, on 30 January 1343. G. Zaccaria, 'Diario storico della basilica e Sacro Convento di S. Francesco in Assisi (1220–1927)', *MF* 1963 (1963), no. 191, pp. 290–361 at 306.

[27] N. Terpstra, *Lay Confraternities and Civic Religion in Renaissance Bologna*, Cambridge Studies in Italian History and Culture (Cambridge, 1995), p. 3.

[28] G. G. Meersseman, *Ordo fraternitatis. Confraternitate e pietà dei laici nel medioevo*, 3 vols (Rome, 1977).

[29] B. Wilson, *Music and Merchants: The Laudesi Companies of Republican Florence* (Oxford, 1992), pp. 89–91, 238–9, C. Barr, *The Monophonic Lauda and the Lay Religious Confraternities of Tuscany and Umbria in the Late Middle Ages*, Early Drama, Art, and Music Monograph Series, 10 (Kalamazoo, 1988).

[30] E. Auweiller, 'De vitis sanctorum fratrum minorum provinciae Saxoniae', *AFH* 18 (1925), and 19 (1926), pp. 211–25, 46–62, 181–93, F. M. Delorme, 'Catalogus Friburgensis sanctorum fratrum minorum', *AFH* 4 (1911), pp. 544–58. R. Paciocco, *Da Francesco ai 'Catalogi sanctorum'. Livelli istituzionali e immagini agiografiche nell'ordine francescano (secoli XIII–XIV)*, Collectio Assisiensis, XX (Assisi, 1990).

[31] Cf. F. Rotolo, 'Il tratatto dei miracoli del B. Gerardo Cagnoli, O. Min. (1267–1342) di Bartolomeo Albizzi, O. Min. (†1351)', *MF* 66 (1966), pp. 128–92.

[32] L. di Fonzo, 'I beati francescani di Foligno tra santità e riforma religiosa, 1230–1860', *MF* 90 (1990), pp. 595–647 at 607–15.

a similar function for merchants who died away from home, such as Louis Bandini, a Florentine merchant interred at London.[33] Dante was buried in the friars' cemetery adjacent to San Francesco, Ravenna (†1321).[34] Testators chose their place of burial and entered a formal agreement with the friars. Mabilia's will of 15 May 1304 requested burial in San Francesco, Vicenza, before the altar of St Peter, which she had built. Funds were assigned for the decoration of the altar.[35] The privilege of burial in the friars' habit was requested by numerous testators.[36] Robert I, king of Apuglia, Sicily and Jerusalem, described as an outstanding benefactor of the order, took the habit several days before his death. His widow, Sancia, a most generous benefactress of the order, was buried in the friars' habit in 1346.[37]

Two cardinals were buried at San Francesco, Assisi. John Gaetano (†1294) was interred in the chapel of St Nicholas, which had been built by his brother and fellow cardinal, Napoleon Orsini, in 1310. The arms of Napolean appear on the stone walls of the chapel of St John the Baptist, constructed as his own place of burial. His prolonged residence at the papal court, however, led him to request burial at the Cordeliers of Avignon, in accordance with a codicil to his will of 13 February 1341. Cardinal Giles Albarnoz constructed the chapel of St Catherine, where he was buried until his removal to Toledo in 1372.[38] Several friars in episcopal orders were laid to rest in their confrères' churches. Matthew of Acquasparta, cardinal bishop, was interred at Santa Maria in Aracoeli, Rome, in 1302 and Gentile Partino da Montefiore dell'Aso, cardinal priest, in the chapel of St Louis, which he had built at San Francesco, Assisi. The latter died on 27 October 1312 and his arms were displayed above the chapel of St Martin, a chapel whose painting he had financed. Above the arch is the portrait of the benefactor kneeling before the saint. Teobaldo Pontano, *custos* of the Sacro Convento and then bishop of Assisi, founded and decorated the chapel of St Mary Magdalene, where he was buried.[39]

The construction of side altars and chapels was often associated with burials and a request for Masses to be celebrated there on a regular, sometimes daily, basis for the donor and his family and friends. These chapels were financed by particular families, whose coats of arms were exhibited there. Giorgio Vasari refers to the chapels of Santa Croce by the names of the families, who funded

[33] For example, C. L. Kingsford, *The Grey Friars of London: Their History, with the Register of Their Convent and an Appendix of Documents*, British Society of Franciscan Studies, VI (Aberdeen 1915), pp. 73, 127, 141.

[34] Boccaccio, *Opere in versi*, p. 597.

[35] Apolloni, 'Testamenti', pp. 216–23.

[36] Bihl, 'Formulae et documenta', no. 38, p. 161.

[37] John Clyn, *Annales*, p. 30. *Die Chronik Johanns von Winterthur*, pp. 254, 266.

[38] *I testamenti dei cardinali del duecento*, ed. A. P. Bagliani, Miscellanea della Società Romana di storia patria, XXV (Rome, 1980), no. 13, pp. 459–68, 466, Alessandri and Pennacchi, 'Inventari', no. 33, p. 297.

[39] A. Martindale, *Simone Martini. Complete Edition* (Oxford, 1988), pp. 19–24, Alessandri and Pennacchi, 'Inventari', no. 131, p. 321.

their construction and embellishment, rather than the saints to whom they were dedicated. The basilica became a necropolis of influential and celebrated citizens and has been described as the 'great Florentine Valhalla, the final home or memorial harbour of the native illustrious dead'.[40] While the church was under construction the friars were already receiving funds for family chapels.[41] Jane Long refers to them as 'funerary chapels', observing that they were something of a novelty in fourteenth-century Florence.[42] There is ample evidence of families entering into close relations with the friars and using the church for their own celebrations and burials.

From the thirteenth century friaries in other parts of western Europe became the resting place of members of royal families, such as Peter III, king of Aragon (†1285), who was buried in the friary at Villanuova.[43] While the kings of France were traditionally interred in St–Denis, some of their queens chose burial in the church of the Cordeliers of Paris. Joan, daughter of Henry I, king of Navarre (1270–4), was the queen of Navarre and wife of Philip IV of France. This outstanding benefactress of the order was buried there in 1305,[44] as was Philip III's widow, Marie of Brabant, in 1321.[45] Louis, the first-born son of Philip V (1316–22), died on 26 February 1316 and was entombed there, beside his maternal grandmother, Joan of Navarre. His father's heart was laid to rest in the same church, while his body was interred at St–Denis. Margaret of Bourgogne, first daughter of Robert II, duke of Burgundy, married Philip, the oldest son of Philip the Fair. Once the queen of Navarre, she died on 30 April 1315 and was buried in the church of the Cordeliers in Vernon.[46]

Decoration of the friars' churches

Despite the austerity prescribed by the constitutions of Narbonne, the vast majority of the friars' churches were decorated. Chapter houses and refectories were painted, as the example of Giotto at Santa Croce demonstrates.[47] A

---

[40] Henry James, *Italian Hours*, edited and introduced by J. Auchard, Penguin Classics (Harmondsworth, 1992), p. 268.

[41] Cenci, 'Costituzioni della provincia toscana', p. 390. A will of 5 May 1298 states that: *pro faciendo fieri unum altare pro anima.*

[42] J. C. Long, 'The Program of Giotto's Saint Francis Cycle at Santa Croce in Florence', *FS*, 52 (1992) pp. 85–133 at 85.

[43] Salimbene, *Cronica*, p. 868.

[44] *Annals of Ghent*, pp. 82–3.

[45] *Chronique Latine de Guillaume de Nangis*, I, pp. 347, and II, p. 38.

[46] Ibid., I, pp. 418, 435. *The Anonimalle Chronichle 1307 to 1334 from the Brotherton Collection MS 29*, ed. W. R. Childs and J. Taylor, Yorkshire Archaeological Society, Record Series, CXLVII (Leeds, 1991), pp. 100–1.

[47] Paintings in the chapter house of San Francesco, Siena, were mentioned by Bernardine of Siena. Bernardino da Siena, *Prediche volgari sul Campo di Siena 1427*, ed. C. Delcorno, 2 vols (Milan, 1989), p. 929. Munaldus Benemati of Assisi left the friars money to paint a picture of the Blessed Virgin in the church of Santa Chiara in 1319. Daniel Francisci Ciccoli of Assisi commissioned paintings in honour of various saints in the basilica of San Francesco where he was buried. C. Cenci, *Documentazione*

new cult frequently led to the further embellishment of the friars' churches. The flourishing devotion to Blessed Gerard Cagnoli led to his picture being painted in the churches of San Francesco at Lucca, Pistoia and Pisa.[48] At least two friars, Philip de Castello and Martin, were described as painters (*pictores*) at Assisi in 1307, 1344 and 1347; the second of these was acting on a commission from the *custos*; on the second occasion Martin was engaged to paint the refectory of San Francesco, Assisi.[49]

Giotto, the greatest artist of his generation, worked in five chapels of Santa Croce, the Baroncelli, the Bardi, the Peruzzi, the Giugni and one belonging to the Tosinghi and Spinelli families. The coronation of the Blessed Virgin was painted in the Baroncelli chapel, where the artist wrote his name and the date in gold letters. Scenes from the *vita* of St Francis were painted in the celebrated Bardi chapel. The Peruzzi chapel, whose patron saint was John the Baptist, has two portraits of the precursor of the Son of God. Two scenes from the life of St John the Evangelist adorn the same chapel. The chapel of the Giugni family, built in honour of the apostles, was decorated with scenes of martyrdom. The chapel of Tosinghi and Spinelli families was dedicated to the Assumption of the Blessed Virgin and depicted scenes from her life. Above the marble tomb of Carlo Marsuppini of Arezzo a crucifix was painted by Giotto. The Blessed Virgin and Sts John the Evangelist and Mary Magdalene stand at the foot of the cross. A tree of life was painted in the friars' refectory. John of Murrovalle summoned Giotto to Assisi to complete the work begun by Cimabue in the basilica of San Francesco. Giorgio Vasari refers to the cycle of frescoes depicting the life of the saint, the three vows and the saint in glory above the high altar in the lower church; this was directly above the tomb of St Francis. Giotto worked in both the upper and lower basilicas. On his return from Avignon in 1316 he decorated a chapel in the newly completed basilica at Padua, painted a panel for San Francesco, Verona, and a portrait of the saint for San Francesco, Pisa. Dante persuaded him to decorate the walls of San Francesco, Ravenna, with frescoes of histories. At the request of Robert, king of Naples, he adorned the walls of the convent of Santa Chiara, Naples, with scenes from the Old and New Testaments.[50]

Fresh from his work in Assisi, Pietro Lorenzetti was commissioned to

di vita assisana 1300–1530, I. 1300–1448, SB, X (Grottaferrata, Rome, 1974), pp. 65, 145–6. Peter di Bozzo left money for a picture of Beatus Onofrio in the church of San Francesco, Montefalco, on 28 June 1363. S. Nessi, *La chiesa e il convento di S. Francesco a Montefalco cronologia documentaria*, Fonti e studi francescani, X (Padua, 2002), p. 16.

48   Rotolo, 'La leggenda', III, no. 66; V, no. 90; VII, nn. 142, 144, pp. 417, 424, 441.

49   Cenci, *Documentazione di vita assisana*, p. 47, Alessandri and Pennacchi, 'Inventari', no. 85, p. 80. Zaccaria, 'Diario storico', nn. 196, 198, pp. 307–9.

50   Piccolomini, *I Commentarii*, II, c. 17, pp. 298–301, D. Norman, 'Those who pay, those who pray and those who paint: two funerary chapels', in *Siena, Florence and Padua, II: Art, Society and Religion 1280–1400, II, Case Studies*, ed. D. Norman (Yale, 1995), pp. 169–93, 169–74, Giorgio Vasari, *Le vite de' più eccellenti pittori scultori e architettori nelle redazioni del 1550 e 1568*, II, ed. R. Bettarini and P. Barocchi (Florence, 1966), pp. 98–109.

decorate the chapter house of San Francesco, Siena, where he worked with his brother, Ambrogio. The series of paintings included the crucifixion and the resurrection as well as scenes from the history of the order. The paintings were later removed and three of them were transferred to the walls of two chapels in the north transept. One of the scenes records the meeting of 1296 between Pope Boniface VIII and Louis of Anjou, who was canonised in 1317. The evolving history of the order, especially its missions in the Orient, also featured in new contracts. Ambrogio depicted the martyrdom of the four friars at Tana in 1321. This scene gained an added interest from the martyrdom of a friar from the city, Peter da Siena. A further fresco in this lost series probably recounted the martyrdom of Peter da Siena. According to Ghiberti, this series of paintings again revealed an unusually wide range of human emotions and weather conditions, including a storm with much hail, flashes of lightning and thundering earthquakes. A few fragments recently recovered from this lost scheme provide partial confirmation of Ghiberti's account.[51] The martyrdom of these friars was celebrated by the order in the aftermath of its troubled relations with Pope John XXII. Odorico da Pordenone's narrative of these miracles, featuring another local friar, James of Padua, formed the basis for the scenes of martyrdom and miracles painted in the nave of San Fermo Maggiore, Verona, and the chapter house of Il Santo, Padua.[52]

In the second half of the century wealthy families were active in commissioning the decoration of chapels in the basilica del Santo, the shrine of St Anthony at Padua, with the co-operation of the friars.[53] Documentation for the chapel of St James is comparatively plentiful. Contracts for its decoration reflect the instructions of Boniface Lupi, the patron, regarding the payment of craftsmen and the artistic scheme of the chapel and its decoration. The chapel occupied a central position and was directly opposite the shrine. The contract for the architectural and sculptural work bears the date of 12 February 1372 and stipulates which materials should be employed. Other accounts enumerate payments to the sculptor and reveal that the work was executed between 1372 and 1377. This became a funerary chapel for Lupi, his wife and his relatives from the Rossi family. It was decorated with scenes from the life and miracles of St James the Great. Details of the liturgical arrangements survive in other sources; it was to be fully furnished with everything required for the celebration of Mass, even down to a missal bearing the Lupi coat of arms. The agreement obliged the friars to celebrate three Masses on a daily basis for the souls of the benefactors in exchange for an annual payment.[54]

[51] D. Norman, *Painting in Late Medieval and Renaissance Siena* (Yale, 2003), pp. 108–11.
[52] Bourdua, *The Franciscans and Art Patronage*, pp. 46–50.
[53] Ibid., p. 147.
[54] Norman, 'Those who pay', pp. 179–93.

CHAPTER FIFTEEN

Communities of the Friars Minor Conventual

Many friars dwell in the large cities, where they have large friaries . . . . In small towns, however, few friars live.

William Woodford[1]

The province and the friary

The order was divided into provinces, which were established or dissolved by the general chapters. A province consisted of a cluster of friaries in a geographical region. In some countries there were a number of provinces, France and Italy, and in others one, such as Ireland. Foundations reflected a strong urban thrust, although several houses were established in towns. The life of each province was regulated by the triennial general chapters and more particularly by the annual chapters of provinces and custodies (see below), which selected a team of officials. Chapters addressed matters of discipline, orthodoxy and disobedience and conducted necessary negotiations with bishops and other civic and religious bodies. The differences in the size and populations of friaries within a province were reflected in the practice of holding the chapters in particular convents and not in others. The province of Aquitaine held its chapters successively at Condom, Bordeaux, Toulouse, Agen, Perigueux and Cahors.[2] There was some regional variation in the timing of the chapters, which were frequently held in conjunction with liturgical celebrations, such as Pentecost,[3] the feasts of St Anthony of Padua,[4] the octave of Sts Peter and Paul,[5] St James,[6] the Assumption of the Blessed Virgin Mary,[7] St Bartholomew,[8] the birthday of the Blessed Virgin Mary[9] and St Francis of

---

[1]   Doyle, 'William Woodford', p. 136.
[2]   Nicolaus Minorita, *Chronica*, pp. 419–20, *Processus Bernardi Delitiosi: The Trial of Fr. Bernard Délicieux, 3 September – 8 December 1319*, p. 127, Bihl, 'Statuta Aquitaniae et Franciae', IV, no. 1, p. 478.
[3]   *Chroniques de Saint-Martial de Limoges*, p. 141. The chapter of Limoges in 1305 lasted for one week.
[4]   Cenci, 'Ordinazioni', p. 30.
[5]   BL, Cotton Vespasian, B. XI, fol. 136r.
[6]   John Clyn, *Annales*, p. 14.
[7]   BL, MS Add. 7966A, fol. 27r.
[8]   John Clyn, *Annales*, p. 13.
[9]   'Chronicon provinciae Argentinensis', p. 680.

Assisi;[10] chapters also assembled on other dates, such as 1 May.[11]

The term 'custody' denotes two things. The first is a small group of friaries in a territory. There was a custody or vicariate of three friaries in Sardinia *c.* 1320. The same term was used in missionary territory: there were seventeen friaries in northern Tartary and fifteen in eastern Tartary, with the exception of India and China. The second is a provincial subdivision enjoying some regional autonomy and holding chapters. A feature of the expansion of the thirteenth century was the formation of new custodies. The number of friaries within a custody varied from one province to another, but there was a general correlation between the number of custodies and their constituent friaries. The largest number of custodies within a province was in Saxony, which had twelve custodies and eighty-eight friaries. The provinces of Aragon, Castile and St James had six custodies and thirty-five friaries, eight custodies and forty-two friaries and seven custodies and forty-one friaries respectively.

Friaries were governed by the annual chapters at custodial and provincial level.[12] The guardian exercised a delegated responsibility for the life of the community and presented friars for ordination.[13] The inventory of the friary's goods was entrusted to his keeping and he was involved in disciplinary measures taken against recalcitrant friars.[14] His powers were limited and his institution of new constitutions for the friary required the consent of his advisers.[15] The Rule was read in common each Friday, probably during the meeting of the domestic chapter, the general constitutions each month and the provincial constitutions every two months.[16] Guardians or their vicars were required to hold a weekly chapter of faults in which friars publicly confronted their failings.[17] The domestic chapter addressed the business of the community, approved contracts with benefactors and testators, and dealt with internal discipline.[18] Each community was visited annually.[19]

Every friary belonged to a custody and its members were under the authority of the guardian, who was elected by the annual provincial chapter. A conventual friary consisted of a minimum of thirteen friars in continual residence; the population of non-conventual friaries was lower.[20] The records of a provincial chapter of Tuscany on 10 May 1394 identify diverse offices,

[10] *Itinerarium Symonis Semeon*, no. 1, pp. 24–5.

[11] Cenci, 'Ordinazioni', VII, no. 12, p. 24.

[12] Cenci, 'Costituzioni della provincia toscana', IX, X, pp. 198–204.

[13] C. Piana, 'Promozioni di religiosi fracescani agli ordini sacri a Bologna (an. 1349–1508)', *AFH* 57 (1964), pp. 3–89 at 16.

[14] Cenci, 'Ordinazioni', VI, no. 25, and VII, no. 2, pp. 21, 22.

[15] Ibid., no. 3, p. 26.

[16] Chiappini, 'Communitatis responsio', p. 669. Bihl, 'Statuta generalia' (Narbonae), VII, no. 22a, p. 92. For example, Cenci, 'Ordinazioni', no. 1, p. 29.

[17] C. Cenci, 'Le costituzioni padovane del 1310', *AFH* 76 (1983), XX, no. 86, pp. 505–88 at 548.

[18] Delorme, 'Les Cordeliers', p. 117.

[19] Chiappini, 'Communitatis responsio', p. 672.

[20] Bihl, 'Statuta generalia' (Narbonae), IX, nn. 19–20, p. 295.

which reflect the stratification between the convents. Santa Croce was manifestly the principal house in the province and had a guardian, vicar, lector of the Bible, master of study, master of novices, master of the young and confessors assigned to monasteries of women. Fewer officials were appointed to the smaller friaries; Scarperia, north of Borgo San Lorenzo, had only a guardian and lector.

Guardians were sometimes entrusted with missions to restore peace between individuals or groups.[21] Evidence for the frequent change of guardians is more mixed in some provinces. Certain names recur as guardians of houses in the Irish province. Nicholas de Kilmaynan was the guardian of Dublin in 1299 and in the successive years of 1305/6, 1306/7 and 1307/8. Roger de Kilmaynan was guardian of the same friary in 1325/6 and 1326/7.[22] Adam de Callan (†1334) was the guardian of Ross for twenty-four years continuously.[23] Towards the end of the century the movement of guardians in the Veneto was more regular. Guardians were changed annually.[24] It was accepted that lectors might be sent to lecture at schools outside the province.[25]

The monk joined a particular monastery and remained there or at one of its dependent priories for life, while the friar was enrolled in a province and assigned to a custody. Apart from appointments to more specialised ministries and other tasks associated with provincial administration, friars were transferred from one custodial convent to another at the instigation of the minister provincial or the *custos*.[26] Although some friars enjoyed prolonged periods in a single friary, the movement of friars was common and is amply illustrated by the *curriculum vitae* of Francesco da Lendinara. He was appointed to the communities of Lendinara, Montagnana, Piove di Sacco, Rovigo, Padua and Vicenza; he also filled some of the major offices in the custody and was the guardian of Il Santo, Padua, *custos*, definitor of the province of Treviso, joint vicar of the province and companion of the minister provincial. He left the custody only to serve as lector at Treviso, guardian at Venice and *custos* of Verona. His sole appointment outside the province was one year as the lector at Ferrara. His experience testifies to the existence of a clerical elite who filled one influential position after another for many years.[27]

---

[21] *Chiese e conventi degli ordini mendicanti in Umbria nei secoli XIII–XIV. Inventario delle fonte archivistiche e catalogo delle informazioni documentarie. Gli archivi ecclesiastici di Città di Castello*, ed. G. Casagrande, Archivi dell'Umbria, inventari e ricerche, XIV (Perugia, 1989), I. 2. 17, p. 5.

[22] *Irish Exchequer Payments 1270–1326*, I, ed. P. Connolly (Dublin, 1998), pp. 155, 182, 189, 197, 310, 315.

[23] John Clyn, *Annales*, p. 25.

[24] Francesco da Lendinara, 'Fra Francesco', nn. 7–15, pp. 114–18.

[25] Bihl, 'Statuta generalia' (Narbonae), X, no. 17, p. 303. Cf. ibid., X, n. 3d. PAR., pp. 305–6.

[26] *Il libro della Beata Angela da Foligno*, ed. L. Thier and A. Calufetti (Grottaferrata, Rome, 1985), pp. 126–7. Angela's text was read and approved by a friar who had served as *custos* in diverse custodies.

[27] Compare also the contemporary Sienese friar Angelo Salvetti: E. Bulletti, 'Angelo Salvetti (c. 1350–1423) in documenti dell'Archivo di stato di Siena', *AFH* 54 (1961), pp. 26–93.

The admission and formation of friars

Friars' recruitment was largely local in character, as numerous prosopographical studies show. This local preponderance, especially in Italian friaries, led John of Murrovalle to take action.[28] The durability of this local monopoly, however, is reflected in the Veneto at the other end of the century. Eight friars of the twelve at Lendinara in 1382 were described as *de Lendinaria*. This local bias was accompanied by evidence of the cosmopolitan nature of the order in the person of Johannes Theotonicus.[29]

The minimum age for admission to the order was set at eighteen, although youths of fifteen might be admitted in certain circumstances.[30] Polemical exchanges focused on the recruitment of children below the age prescribed by the general constitutions. Boys as young as nine were admitted.[31] Each custody had its own friary for the reception, instruction and training of novices; where necessary, a second friary was to be designated, although in practice novices were to be found at more than two friaries in a custody.[32]

Candidates were normally admitted by ministers provincial, the *custos* or the local guardian. There was some diversity of practice about the location and timing of the ceremony of clothing. Tuscan provincial constitutions ordained that the rite of admission was to be conducted outside the church; among the appropriate venues were the sacristy and chapter house.[33] The general constitutions of 1354 decreed that the reception should take place in the chapter house in the presence of the friars.[34]

The noviciate year was a time for candidates to be schooled in the discipline of the religious life, the ideals of the order and its austerity of life, confession, prayer, the spiritual exercises, the Divine Office, the Rule and duties within the friary.[35] The instruction given to novices formed part of the internal polemic at the beginning of the century. Even though the novitiate was to last for one year, there is some evidence that the term 'novice' was applied in a wider and more monastic sense to connote the more junior members of the community. Francesco da Lendinara was clothed as a friar at San Francesco, Lendinara, in the custody of Padua in 1382. Between 1383 and 1385 he was a novice, first at Lendinara, then at Padua before returning to his native friary to complete his novitiate.[36] Before profession the friars were obliged to draw

28 Ubertino da Casale, 'Rotulus', no. 13, pp. 111–13.
29 Francesco da Lendinara, 'Fra Francesco', no. 7, pp. 114–15.
30 Bihl, 'Statuta generalia' (Narbonae), pp. 284–358, 39.
31 Francesco da Lendinara, 'Fra Francesco', no. 32, p. 127.
32 Bihl, 'Statuta generalia' (Narbonae), p. 40.
33 Cenci, 'Costituzioni della provincia toscana', I, no. 1, p. 171.
34 M. Bihl, 'Statuta generalia ordinis edita in capitulo generali an. 1354 Assisii celebrato, communiter Farineriana appellata. (Editio critica et analytica)', *AFH* 35 (1942), pp. 35–112, 177–253, at I, nn. 8–11, pp. 85, 86.
35 Chiappini, 'Communitatis responsio', pp. 668–9.
36 Francesco da Lendinara, 'Fra Francesco', nn. 7–10, pp. 114–16.

up a last will, examples of which have survived.[37]

The newly professed friars spent some years in the schools, where they followed a course leading to ordination. While the academic stratification of the order included the universities and custodial schools, most friars derived their theological formation and subsequent study from the local schools.[38] Theological studies were rooted in the close study of philosophy. The Roman province stipulated that friars should be groomed in the study of grammar, logic and philosophy. Decisions about the future studies of the individual friar were taken after that stage.[39] The experience of Francesco da Lendinara indicates the type of study available, although he offers no guidance about his theological studies, even though he became a lector. Six years after his clothing as a friar he studied the liberal arts at Bologna in 1388; it is probable that he was engaged in some earlier studies at Lendinara or Treviso. This was followed by two years at Ferrara, where he studied logic. Both a lector and a bachelor worked in the school, which numbered twenty-eight students. Francesco was ordained to the priesthood and celebrated his first Mass at Lendinara in 1392, in the second of his three years of philosophical study at Piacenza. His last year there was spent in preparation for the master's course and by 1394 he began his period of teaching as bachelor in the convent of Cesena.[40]

The centrality of biblical studies in the curriculum is reflected in the number of commentaries and copies of the sacred text in the friars' libraries. In many schools a friar was assigned to initiate students into biblical studies. For example, there was a lector of the Bible at Assisi in 1381.[41] The friars' professionalism in the search for biblical texts and commentaries inspired the *Registrum Anglie*, a device for tracing the whereabouts of books in the early fourteenth century.[42] Candidates for the priesthood were required to engage in a study of the sacraments and the principal questions of theology and canon law. Bonaventure's *Breviloquium* offers indications of the ground to be covered by those training for the ministries of the pulpit or confessional. There was a hierarchy of teaching officers, especially at the more prestigious schools. The lector was assisted by more junior confrères, *cursores* and bachelors, who were sometimes granted the services of a companion.[43] A lector

---

[37] Bihl, 'Statuta generalia' (Assisii), I, no. 10, p. 86. Cf. Cenci, *Documentazione di vita assisiana*, pp. 69–70, 94, 95.

[38] Bihl, 'Ordinationes a Benedicto XII', c. IX, nn. 1–3, pp. 346–53.

[39] A. G. Little, 'Constitutiones provinciae Romanae, anni 1316', VI, no. 4, *AFH* 18 (1925), pp. 356–73 at 368.

[40] Ibid., nn. 12–19, pp. 117–19.

[41] Cenci, *Documentazione di vita assisiana*, p. 182.

[42] *Registrum Anglie de libris doctorum et auctorum veterum*, ed. R. H. and M. A. Rouse, Corpus of British Medieval Library Catalogues (London, 1991).

[43] BIHR, Register 10, fol. 279v, Robert Brum was the *cursor sententiarum* of Newcastle on 2 October 1350. Cenci, *Documentazione di vita assisiana*, p. 134, where a *bachcalarius* had a *socius* in 1361.

and a bachelor taught at Avignon in 1328.[44] The lector was responsible for revitalising the friars' pastoral lives by lectures which the whole community was required to attend; even the hearing of confessions was suspended during the principal lectures.[45]

Although manuscripts were regarded as an index of prosperity and wealth, the friars acquired the books necessary for their ministry. Richard de Bury is a witness to the quality of the friars' libraries: 'indeed, there in the deepest poverty we found the deepest riches of wisdom treasured' (*immo ibi in altissima paupertate altissimas divitias sapientiae thesaurizatas invenimus*). A chapter of Pope Benedict XII's *ordinationes* was entitled 'On books' (*de libris*), which required an annual inventory of the libraries.[46] The implementation of this rubric is demonstrated by collections of books at Fabriano between 1348 and 1357 and inventories of libraries at Gubbio and La Verna in 1360 and 1372.[47] The large libraries of the Sacro Convento, Assisi, and Il Santo, Padua, teeming with scholastic texts, were catalogued in 1381 and 1396 respectively.[48] The friars' collection of books became the envy of several secular and religious institutions. Some friars, especially those in episcopal orders, donated their books to their confrères' libraries. The manuscripts of Matthew of Acquasparta were divided between the friars' libraries of San Fortunato, Todi, and San Francesco, Assisi.[49]

The friary and its apostolate

Friaries differed in size and importance. One exception to the trend for Dominicans to have larger communities was Majorca, a city which housed sixty-three friars and fifty Dominicans in June 1343.[50] Some thirty-one friars were present at a domestic chapter of San Francesco, Assisi, in 1368 and forty-two attended another on 19 October 1374.[51] There was some regional variation in the size of communities, as Daniel Lesnick shows in contrasting the

[44] Nicolaus Minorita, *Chronica*, pp. 179, 189.

[45] Bihl, 'Statuta Aquitaniae et Franciae', VII, nn. 3–4, p. 493.

[46] *Philobiblon Ricardi de Bury*, ed. E. C. Thomas (Oxford, 1960), p. 90. Bihl, 'Ordinationes a Benedicto XII', c. XI, nn. 1–19, pp. 355–8.

[47] Cf. E. Filippini, 'Notizie storico-bibliografiche intorno all'Archivio di S. Francesco in Fabriano, *MF* 5 (1890–2), pp. 182–5. M. Faloci-Pulignani, 'La biblioteca francescana di Gubbio', *MF* 9 (1902–5), pp. 156–63, P. S. Macherini, 'Antichi inventari della Verna', *StF*, n.s. 1 (1914–15), pp. 212–22.

[48] C. Cenci, *Bibliotheca manuscripta ad sacrum conventum Assisiensem*, 2 vols (Assisi, 1981), G. Abate and G. Luisetto, *Codici e manoscritti della Biblioteca antoniana col catalogo delle miniature*, Fonti e studi per la storia dela santo a Padova, 2 vols (Vicenza, 1975).

[49] Menestò, 'La biblioteca di Matteo d'Acquasparta', pp. 104–10. C. Cenci, 'I manoscritti del Sacro Convento d'Assisi catalogati da L. Leoni nel 1862–3', *MF* 83 (1983), pp. 245–90.

[50] Hillgarth, *Readers and Books in Majorca 1229–1550*, I, p. 10.

[51] Cenci, *Documentazione di vita assisiana*, p. 157, F. Pennacchi, 'Bullarium Franciscanum quod exstat in archivo sacri conventus S. Francisci Assisiensis (nunc apud publicam bibliothecam Assisii)', *AFH* 13 (1920), pp. 136–80, 508–86, 521–2.

average of 34.8 friars in the Gascon convents in 1289 with the 123 resident at Santa Croce in 1300.[52] Larger communities were frequently associated with the major schools, whose ranks were swollen by students from other provinces.

Each custody had its major houses, where the administrative, medical and educational resources were concentrated. These friaries, located in the main cities, were identified by provincial constitutions. The Tuscan provincial constitutions for 1362 named the friaries of Florence, Pisa, Siena, Montepulciano, Lucca, Arezzo, and Massa Marittima as the principal convents for the custodies of Florence, Pisa, Siena, Chiusi, Lucca, Arezzo and Massa Marittima, although these lists were subject to some revisions.[53] A *magnus conventus* and a *conventus solemnior* were recognised and invested with particular privileges.[54] The largest communities were located in the greater cities, as exemplified in the custody of London. While there there were eighty friars at London in 1334 and ninety in 1336, there were only twenty-four at Southampton in 1334.[55] It was estimated that the population of the four main mendicant orders in England, Ireland, Scotland and Wales was below 10,000 in the 1390s.[56]

The range of conventual buildings in a friary generally consisted of the bell-tower, cellar, cemetery, chapter house, church, cloisters, dormitory, gardens, granaries, infirmary, kitchen, library, refectory and school of theology; some friaries had the space required for the detention of disobedient friars. A variety of offices, resembling monastic structures, existed in the larger friaries. A provincial or custodial house might provide a base for officials, such as the minister provincial, *custos*, his vicar and the visitor of the Poor Clares. The larger friaries enjoyed the services of several officers: a bachelor, cantor, carpenter, cellarer, chaplain, companion for officials of the community (*socius*), confessor, cook, discreet, gardener, guardian, infirmarian, inquisitor, lector, junior lector, master of the youth, master of the professed, master of students, medical doctor, novice master, porter, procurator, sacristan, scribe, vicar and a second vicar in some cases; there was also a small number of medical doctors.[57] In the smaller convents these duties were combined. Various domestic offices were filled by the lay brothers, who remained an

---

[52] Lesnick, *Preaching in Medieval Florence*, pp. 45, 185–97.

[53] G. Abate, 'Memoriali, statuti ed atti di capitoli generali dei frati minori inediti dei secoli XIII e XIV', *MF* 33 (1933), VIII, no. 2, pp. 320–36 at 334. Cf. Cenci, 'Costituzioni della provincia toscana', VIII, no. 2, p. 196, *habeantur autem pro maioribus conventibus: in custodia clusina Clusium, in Maritima Massa et in Sardinia Castellum Castri.*

[54] Van Dijk, *Sources of the Modern Roman Liturgy*, II, no. 60, p. 352, Bihl, 'Statuta generalia' (Narbonae), XII, no. 7a, p. 317.

[55] BL, MS Cotton Nero, C. VIII, fols. 201r, 205r.

[56] Doyle, 'William Woodford', p. 176.

[57] Cf. Francesco da Lendinara, 'Fra Francesco', nn. 66–7, pp. 162–6. Cf. A. Montford, 'Dangers and Disorders: The Decline of the Dominican *Frater Medicus*', *The Journal of the Society for the Social History of Medicine* 16 (2003), pp. 169–91.

integral, albeit small, part of the community; there is sufficient evidence to challenge the questionable assertion that they became an endangered species from 1260.[58] Some friars were engaged in mechanical and manual skills, such as masons.[59] It was envisaged that they would exercise talents, such as writing, painting, weaving, gardening, tailoring, stitching, carpentry or other honest activities.[60]

Friaries in ecclesiastical, political and educational centres attracted a flow of visitors from various custodies and provinces. They provided hospitality to their confrères from other houses or provinces.[61] Franciscan bishops lodged in friaries either during their active ministry or in retirement.[62] The papal curia was a magnet for prelates exiled from their dioceses or titular bishops, some of whom were members of the order. John XXII consulted some of these prelates in March 1322 during debates about evangelical poverty.[63]

The friars' links with the Poor Clares were strongest in the provinces of the Marches of Ancona, Rome, Strasbourg and Tuscany and weakest in Apuglia, Calabria, Cologne, England, Ireland, Sicily and Touraine.[64] The appointment of Tuscan friars as confessors to the sisters and other monasteries of women in the neighbourhood of the friary points to an important sphere of activity beyond the cloister. Such friars were given accommodation by the sisters.[65] While the communities committed friars to the service of their church, they were active as preachers and confessors throughout the cities and boroughs in which their friary was located. They were invited to preach in the adjacent parish churches and they were involved in various humanitarian and religious projects. Despite the urban orientation of the movement, the friars' ministry was not circumscribed by the city walls. Friars exercised a full and fruitful apostolate in the district.

---

[58] A solitary lay brother participated in a domestic chapter at Mantua on 31 October 1353; there were four at a chapter at Vicenza on 10 January 1370.   The lay brothers of Vicenza were distinguished from the ordained friars by a testator on 14 June 1341. Apolloni, 'Testamenti', p. 233.

[59] Cenci, 'Costituzioni della Provincia Toscana', p. 389. Friar Henry, *magister lapidum*, was a beneficiary of a will of 17 February 1298. The named *fratres operarii sancti Crucis qui pro tempore fuerint* benefited from a will of 7 March 1298.

[60] S. Mencherini, 'Constitutiones generales ordinis fratrum minorum a Capitulo Perpiniani anno 1331 celebrato editae', *AFH* 2 (1909), c. 9, no. 8, pp. 269–92, 412–30, 575–99 at 414–15.

[61] Nicholas of Poggibonsi spent many days of recuperation in San Francesco, Ferrara, on his return from the Holy Land in 1350, warmly thanking the friars for their hospitality. Fra Niccolò da Poggibonsi, *Libro d'Oltramare (1346–50)*, c. 264, pp. 156–7.

[62] Walter of Bruges, bishop of Poitiers, retired to the friary in the episcopal city, where he died in 1306. Callebaut, 'Recueil de miracles', no. 1, p. 496.

[63] Peter of Bologna, bishop of Corbavia, was at the papal court in 1313, when he was one of the bishops to grant an indulgence to those visiting the small church of Santa Chiara, Montefalco; six of the ten bishops were his confrères. Montefalco, Archiv. del monastero di Santa Chiara, Pergamena, D. 38. S. Nessi, 'S. Chiara da Montefalco e il francescanesimo', *MF* 69 (1969), pp. 369–408 at 393.

[64] Golubovich, *Biblioteca*, II, pp. 250–1.

[65] B. Bughetti, 'Tabulae capitulares prov. Tusciae O. Min. (saec. XIV–XVIII)', *AFH* 10 (1917), pp. 413–97 at 416–23.

The provincial chapter drew the boundaries between friaries, within which the friars of one convent might minister without interference from a neighbouring community.[66] Each friary was to regard the places nearest to it as its own territory or *limitatio*.[67] Guardians were not permitted to send friars beyond the limits of their friary.[68] The size of the *limitatio* seems to have been related to the prestige and financial burdens shouldered by particular houses.[69] Neighbouring provinces entered into agreements about their boundaries.[70] Episcopal licences were issued to friars active inside their *limitatio*.[71] Friars went to the parishes annually to preach, hear confessions and collect alms. These preaching tours were so well entrenched in the local consciousness that testators referred to the friars' visits as 'by custom'.[72] Richard FitzRalph confirms the practice of friars visiting parishes once or twice each year.[73] The friars responsible for visiting the parishes were known as limiters and travelled with a companion.

There is evidence of friars establishing a house some miles away from their friaries. Friars paying visits to towns and villages in their *limitationes* were remembered by numerous testators, one of whom left a bed for the use of the friars visiting Certaldo.[74] This would serve as a base for friars active in adjacent archdeaconries and deaneries. Friars working away from their friary found hospitality in local religious houses or parishes, although contemporary satire shows that they also lodged with families. Visits around the *limitatio* necessitated the absence of several friars from the community for periods of some weeks, especially in the parishes more distant from the friary. Depending upon the number of foundations in the vicinity, these boundaries might stretch for more than thirty miles from the friary in some provinces. Testators from Calverley, a village between Leeds and Bradford, made bequests to the Greyfriars of Doncaster.[75] The parish of Calverley was close to the boundaries of the friaries of Doncaster and York. Boccaccio's portrait of Friar Cippola was based on the custom of friars being appointed

---

[66] J. Calamandrei, 'Constitutiones fratrum minorum observantium provinciae Thusciae ann. 1507 et 1523', *AFH* 8 (1915), pp. 189–225 at 221–5.

[67] Delorme, 'Diffinitiones... Narbonensis', no. 12, p. 503.

[68] Bihl, 'Statuta generalia' (Narbone), V, no. 4, p. 63.

[69] *Calendar of Entries in the Papal Registers relating to Great Britain and Ireland, Papal Letters*, IV, ed. J. A. Tremlow (London, 1912), pp. 516–17.

[70] M. Bihl, 'Raymundus Gaufridi, minister generalis, Parisiis 9 iunii 1292 confirmat conventionem initam inter provincias Austriae et Alemaniae Superioris de terminis eleemosynarum conquirendarum in confiniis', *AFH* 36 (1943), pp. 98–102.

[71] Cf. Little, *Franciscan Papers, Lists, and Documents*, p. 237.

[72] BIHR, Probate Register 5, fol. 132r.

[73] Hammerich, 'The Beginning of the Strife', p. 65.

[74] Cenci, 'Costituzioni della provincia toscana', p. 400, n. 91: *fr. Iacobo de Trisanti ord. Min., et si... non viveret... fratribus Minoribus de Castro florentino sive in domo sotietatis de Certaldo pro usu ipsorum fratrum venientium pro tempore ad dictum castrum de Certaldo et hospitandum ibidem.*

[75] *The Calverley Charters*, I, ed. S. Margerison and W. P. Baildon, *Publications of the Thoresby Society*, VI (Leeds, 1904), pp. 157–8, 280–1.

to work in specified archdeaconries and deaneries. These visits were necessarily co-ordinated with local mendicant communities to avoid embarrassment of friars of two orders arriving simultaneously in a parish. There was an expectation that at certain times of the year the whole community would be in residence. In addition to work in the *limitatio*, friars were engaged as confessors by nunneries and as chaplains by families.[76] A small number of friars lived at court and served as confessors.

[76] Thus William Woodford was at Framlingham Castle in Suffolk, when he commented on the 1396 condemnation of Wyclif's errors. BL, MS Royal, 8. F. XI, fols. 61r-91r.

CHAPTER SIXTEEN

The Emergence of the Observant Reform in Umbria

> We were seeking to keep the Rule in its vigour and rigour according to the will of God and the founder.
>
> Angelo Clareno[1]

Angelo's vision of renewal is encapsulated in these words. He exercised a powerful influence on those who paved the way for the reforms initiated by John de Valle, the first of three friars who established the friary at Brugliano and created a platform for the revitalisation of the order in Umbria.

An order in need of purification

Religious orders constantly seek a greater fidelity to their Rule. The friars did not escape the pain and division that visited the older orders. The friars' critics were united in their observation that the movement had fallen seriously short of its lofty ideals. A persistent charge was that friars spent too much time with the rich to the neglect of the needy. The order's large conventual buildings bore a monastic stamp, which tended to merge and confuse the insights of Sts Benedict and Francis. While the ample friaries with their double or triple cloisters gave the impression of grandeur and comfort on some of the most valuable urban sites, their churches turned friars into the rivals of the secular clergy. John Wyclif protested in the 1370s that the friars' new churches and cloisters were detrimental to the life of the parish churches, which were falling into ruin.[2] The secular clergy's objections were twofold: one, the lack of pastoral care, and two, the haemorrhaging of support from the parish church. The practice of burial in the friary merely compounded the plight of the parochial clergy, who protested that they were sometimes denied their share of the offerings prescribed by *Super cathedram*.

It was tempting to interpret the friars' success in the pulpit and confessional as a criterion of the health of the order and its contribution to the welfare of the local Church. Invitations to preach and hear confessions and the flow of alms were inadequate ways of testing its fidelity to the founder.

---

[1] Angelo Clareno, 'Epistola excusatoria', p. 524.

[2] John Wyclif, 'Fifty Heresies and Errors of the Friars', in *Select Works of John Wyclif*, III, ed. T. Arnold (Oxford, 1871), p. 380.

Increasingly gifts were bestowed not only on the friary, but also on individuals. This unhealthy development fostered the emergence of the private life and the corresponding erosion of the common life. The acceptance of private property by some friars highlighted the plight of the poor brothers who lacked benefactors.[3] There is a sense of *déjà vu* about the type and range of accusations brought against the friars during the fourteenth century. The same charges were levelled by both external and internal reformers. Richard FitzRalph quoted the words of St Francis against friars, pinpointing grave defects and gaps. His sermon at St Paul's cross, London, on 12 March 1357 contains advice pleasing to the internal reformers: the words of the Rule are not to be glossed (*verba regule non glosentur*).[4] William Langland was not a solitary voice in exhorting friars to observe the Rule they had professed.[5] However much the ministers lauded the principle of unity and abhorred schism, their ineffectiveness militated against harmony. Following the turmoil of the 1320s, the order entered a period of reappraisal of its domestic and apostolic endeavours.

The sense of dismay occasioned by the friars' conduct ran in tandem with a renewed interest in the varied sources on the life of Francis, his writings and the views of those associated with him. While the 1260s saw the withdrawal of the earlier biographies of the saint, invaluable sources survived in the friars' libraries and the archives in Assisi. The polemical exchanges in the first decade of the fourteenth century brought to life newly available sources, principally in the writings of Ubertino da Casale. Ubertino used important information about the founder in a manuscript in the library of the Sacro Convento and quires which he believed to have been copied by Leo on the subject of the saint's intention.[6] He and Angelo Clareno had privileged access to a rich oral tradition circulating among those associated with the saint and his followers. Copies of Francis's complete writings were becaming available to the friars of the fourteenth century.[7] New materials included the *Scripta Leonis*, a text which was brought to completion, and the *Speculum perfectionis*, which bears the date of 1318.[8] This literature was not confined to the group of friars clamouring for reform and penetrated even the gen-

---

[3] Bihl, 'Statuta generalia' (Assisii), IV, no. 12, p. 99.
[4] Peterhouse Library, Cambridge, MS 223, fols. 35v–43v, 40r.
[5] Langland, *Piers Plowman*, XX. 246, p. 378: *but lyveth after yore rewle*.
[6] Ubertino da Casale, 'Declaratio', *ALKG*, III, pp. 162–95, 168, 178.
[7] Cf. K. Esser and R. Oliger, *La Tradition manuscrite des Opuscules de Saint François d'Assise: préliminaries de l'édition critique*, Subsidia Scientifica Francisacalia cura Instituti Historici Capuccini, 3 (Rome, 1972).
[8] Nimmo, *Reform and Division in the Franciscan Order*, pp. 309–52. Cf. A. G. Little, 'Description of Franciscan Manuscript, Formerly in the Phillipps Library, Now in Possession of A. G. Little', in *Collectanea Franciscana*, I, ed. A. G. Little, M. R. James and H. M. Bannister, British Society of Franciscan Studies, V (Abderdeen, 1914), pp. 9–113, E. Menestò, 'La *Compilatio Avenionensis*: una raccolta di testi francescani della prima metà del XIV secolo', *Studi medievali* 16 (2003), pp. 1423–1541, for a collection of miscellaneous texts associated with the founder and his circle.

eral curia. Gerald Odonis had passages read from old biography (*leggenda vecchia*) in the refectory at Avignon.[9] The recovery of old sources and the transcription of newly available texts, incorporating the order's oral tradition, focused on the saint and his vision for the order. They placed in bold relief the chasm between the founder and the conduct of friars who were no strangers to quarrels and litigation. These literary sources kindled a deeper dissatisfaction with the state of the order and its level of observance. They nurtured aspirations for standards consonant with the ideals of the founder. These varied sources and the personal knowledge of Angelo Clareno kept alive the vision of reform. In the 1330s there were shoots of renewal in the province of St Francis, the birthplace of the order.

Polemical exchanges acted as a spur to reform among the Community at different stages in the century.[10] It is difficult to gauge the appetite for reform between 1325 and 1350 and caution should be exercised about estimates of how well the Rule was observed. The liberty and independence enjoyed by some communities under Pope Celestine V remained the reformers' model. The torch of literal observance flickered in the minds of men like Prince Philip of Majorca, who was deeply influenced by Angelo Clareno. In the autumn of 1328 he petitioned Pope John XXII to permit an autonomous form of life governed by the Rule and Testament. The inhabitants of the proposed new friaries would beg for alms and engage in manual work. The prince regarded his plans as analogous to the Cistercian renewal of the Rule of St Benedict. The timing of the petition was not propitious because it was made in the aftermath of the dismissal of Michael of Cesana. The prince's proposal was rejected by Pope John XXII on 26 January 1331.[11]

The Umbrian expression of this Observant reform was rooted in a particular perception of the Franciscan vocation and distanced itself from the main direction of the order for the previous hundred years. It breathed the air of Leo, Rufino and Angelo rather than that of Salimbene. The retreat from the cities and the round of pastoral activities was a salient feature of the movement. This version of the order's heritage focused on the life of the early communities of Rivo Torto and the Portiuncula. The hermitage was the place in which the Franciscan character would be reforged. The vicissitudes of the Benedictine order and its innumerable reforms reflect the orientation of the reformers and supplied a precedent. The monks who withdrew from Molesme in 1098 to settle at Cîteaux, known as the 'new monastery' (*novum monasterium*), wanted to revive the spirit of St Benedict by returning to what they perceived as the central features of the Rule. In so doing they gave birth to a new reform, which spread rapidly in the middle of the twelfth century.[12]

[9]   Cf. F. M. Delorme, 'Les Flores Sancti Francisci', *MF* 43 (1943), pp. 171–8.

[10] 'Chronicon provinciae Argentinensis', p. 681, Glassberger, *Chronica*, p. 199.

[11] *BF*, V, no. 894, p. 490.

[12] *The Ecclesiastical History of Orderic Vitalis*, IV, ed. M. Chibnall, Oxford Medieval Texts (Oxford,

The reinvigoration of the Franciscan life encountered similar friction and tension with the proponents of the established form of religious life. Polemical exchanges ensued.

John de Valle

Angelo Clareno was instrumental in the life of John de Valle, whom he numbers among the persecuted friars.[13] John is revered as one of the founders of the Observant reform. Entering the order in 1325 at San Francesco, Foligno, he nurtured hopes of observing the Rule in all its simplicity and vigour. It is unclear whether he entered the order as a priest. For around nine years he lived in the friaries of the Umbrian province and enjoyed a good reputation with its officials. The support of his minister provincial was pivotal to the petition to settle in a hermitage. Having received a sympathetic hearing from the minister provincial, John approached the minister general. The respect in which he was held in the Umbrian province augmented his chances of success, allaying fears about his future conduct. His obedience was not challenged and assurances that he wished to live within the confines of the order rather than making a bid for independence were accepted. Uniformity of dress was maintained by his decision to wear the habit of his confrères rather than the divisive one worn by reformers. Furthermore, he was immune from the influence of the little brothers of the poor life (*Fraticelli de paupere vita*), the successors of Angelo Clareno and the Spiritual friars. This zealous group, active in Umbria and other provinces of Italy, was tainted with heresy. The application met with success and in 1334 John and four friars settled at Brugliano in the mountains bordering Umbria and the Marches. Here a primitive form of the observance was followed and the seed was planted which in later times was to flower into the Observance. Little is known about the life of the friars dwelling in that inhospitable region.

John's manner of life established two principles which distinguished the Umbrian movement. First, renewal was based on the restoration of an ascetic and disciplined life within the hermitage, which was so prominent a feature in the life of the founder. John was consciously harking back to an aspect of the friars' life which had been jettisoned in the move to the cities. Secondly, the reform afforded a position of leadership to those friars who were not ordained. Ironically, this revived their influence for the first time since the coup against Elias of Cortona in 1239. The reform movement placed its emphasis on a communal life of poverty, manual labour and contemplation. The minister general's permission to live a more austere life within the confines of the order harked back to the establishment of separate friaries three decades earlier in Provence. Mariano of Florence sees John as a pivotal

1973), pp. 324–7.
13 *Liber chronicarum sive tribulationum ordinis minorum*, V, no. 233, pp. 520–1.

figure in the reform and states that Brugliano was an exceedingly inhospitable settlement (*asperrimus locus*), seven miles from Foligno. John lived there in the pure and literal observance of the Rule in great perfection. He was the origin of the Observant reform and the source of its dissemination.[14]

Many of John's ideas about the nature of the reform are a matter of conjecture and several questions remain unanswered. How did he envisage the relationship between his small community and the other friaries of the Umbrian province? Were sympathetic members of the province invited to spend time at the hermitage? Did John celebrate Mass for people living in the mountainous region? How did he view the *fraticelli de paupere vita* who were active in nearby Marches of Ancona? Was his intention to live by the Rule alone with a few friars? Or did he harbour aspirations for the growth and enlargement of the movement? The intentions of the minister provincial of Umbria also remain unknown. He was well disposed towards John, conducted visitations and was a medium for appointments to the hermitage. The reasons for the minister general's permission for the foundation are also open to various interpretations, including Nimmo's hypothesis that Gerald Odonis deployed the incipient Observants to nullify the influence of the *fraticelli* in that region.[15]

The community at Brugliano undoubtedly assuaged the fears of the general curia and the local minister provincial, who probably regarded it as a laudable expression of renewal. Were friars from Brugliano established at the Carceri, the friary on Monte Subasio above Assisi, in 1340 by the minister general in place of the expelled *fraticelli*?[16] Friars who followed a stricter observance were viewed in respectful terms by the general chapter of Venice in 1346. The chapter decreed that those who wished to live in the austerity of penance and the observance of the highest poverty should be treated benevolently and favourably by the ministers in the Community's friaries. They deserved respect and admiration as exemplars of life and luminaries. The same encouragement was to be extended to friars dwelling in hermitages. Ministers were to ensure that friars permitted to live in hermitages were secure and proven in their religious vocation and not liable to create disturbance. References to hermitages raise the question of whether the friary at Brugliano was extending its ideals to other centres or did it denote currents of reform?[17] Regulations for the hermitages were issued by William Fariner, the minister general.[18]

One of the reasons for the successful life of the community at Brugliano

[14] Directio periodici, p. 641.

[15] Ibid., pp. 377–8.

[16] *Chronica XXIV Generalium ordinis minorum*, p. 530.

[17] F. M. Delorme, 'Acta capituli generalis anno 1346 Venetiis celebrati', *AFH* 5 (1912), VI, no. 45, pp. 698–709, 707–8.

[18] R. Pratesi, 'Una lettera enciclica del ministro generale Guglielmo Farinier (25 gennaio 1349)', *AFH* 50 (1957) pp. 348–63 at 361.

was the trust that the minister provincial of Umbria reposed in John and the life that he was leading. This confidence had been crucial in paving the way for what might have been deemed an experiment, at least in the later 1330s. It had also enabled the ministers general and provincial to hold their nerve, when Pope Clement VI issued his warning on 29 November 1343, the anniversary of the confirmation of the Rule by Pope Honorius III. The pope referred to men who claimed to be living the Rule to the letter, but were in effect damaging the order's unity.[19] John died at Brugliano in 1351 and there are references to his virtues in life and miracles in death.[20]

Gentile da Spoleto

A position of leadership was already being taken by Gentile da Spoleto, a lay brother, before the death of John de Valle. He, too, had lived at San Francesco, Foligno, a friary closely associated with the movement for renewal. Perhaps buoyed by the growth in numbers, Gentile turned his mind to expansion and he petitioned the papal court for privileges to safeguard their form of religious life. He made representations to Pope Clement VI, perhaps through his own family connections. The pope granted the reformers four hermitages in the dioceses of Assisi and Spoleto, the Carceri, La Romita, Monteluce and Giano, on 13 December 1350. Twelve friars were to occupy each place and they were to be selected by the minister provincial of Umbria either from existing friars or from others prepared to adopt this way of life. They were to live 'simply, in pristine purity'; no superior of the order was allowed to interfere with them. Permission was given for the admission of novices as well as those who transferred from the Community's friaries.[21] The first of these friaries was a hermitage dear to St Francis, who had spent periods of retreat there. Moreover, the friary brought the reform movement close to the cradle of the order, the city of Assisi. The papal licence, however, exceeded the terms by which John de Valle had lived at Brugliano and the petition to the papal court rather than a request to the minister general rankled with the friars, reviving memories of the strategy of the earlier reformers, who bypassed the ministers provincial and general, and appealed directly to the popes.

News of Gentile's approach to the papal court and the allocation of further hermitages to the group created a predictable reaction. First, unlike John de Valle, Gentile neglected to collaborate with the appropriate authorities at local and international levels. His pre-emptive move revived memories of the disputes associated with Ubertino da Casale and Angelo Clareno and quickly polarised opinion. Secondly, the expansion of the reform was per-

---

[19] *BF*, VI, no. 245, p. 139.

[20] *Da Francesco ai 'Catalogi sanctorum'*, pp. 137, 165.

[21] *BF*, VI, no. 558, pp. 245–6.

ceived by some as the birth of a new threat to the unity and harmony of the order at a tense moment in its history, coming so soon after the trauma of the 1320s. While the members of the Umbrian province may have been happy to have one hermitage given to the reformers, they might have looked askance at the emergence of a further four friaries. The Community's response to the implications of the papal bull was articulated by Arnaldus da Sarnano, minister provincial of Aquitaine and author of the *Chronicle of the Tweny-four Generals*. He claimed that he had been deceived by Gentile and his followers, who had petitioned Pope Clement VI for the four hermitages. The more damaging perception was that Gentile was engineering a division within the order. The reformers' criticism of the order rubbed salt in the wounds. The reformers, it was alleged, had accused the Community of living the Rule in a manner which had been glossed and modified through papal declarations. Reformers were smeared by the traditional accusation that they had adopted different habits and accepted apostates and others unsuitable for the religious life.[22] A greater sympathy for the reformers' aspirations was shown by Mariano of Florence, who enjoyed the benefit of hindsight. He depicted Gentile as 'the disciple of the holy brother John de Valle'. Gentile petitioned the pope for the four hermitages that would be colonised by groups of a dozen friars, who wished to observe the Rule in all its purity.[23] What seemed like the moment of the Observants riumph signalled the opposite.

The concerns voiced by Arnaldus da Sarnano gained the ascendant and galvanised the minister general to produce new constitutions at the general chapter of Assisi in 1354. The ministers were instructed to take action against the sect within the order. Under the rubric of poverty and the ban on the reception of money, the constitutions stipulated that, although some friars had sought stricter levels of observance, the friars were to live in unity, according to the decision of the minister provincial and *custos*.[24] Gentile's rejection of the new general constitutions reflects the hardening of opinion on both sides. The reformers' refusal played into the hands of their critics, who appeared to be vindicated in their charges of factionalism and possibly heresy. The good will generated by John de Valle was dissipated in the welter of accusations and counter-charges. The reform movement was seen to be distancing itself from the order and indulging in polemics.

Gentile declared that he and his followers could no longer live under the jurisdiction of the ministers. His refusal to accept the new constitutions prompted an investigation by William Fariner, the minister general (1348–57), and Cardinal Giles Albarnoz. Nicholas Glassberger reports that in 1355 the minister general and the cardinal pursued Gentile and two of his followers, who were imprisoned in the friary at Orvieto on the cardinal's authority. The

---

[22] *Chronica XXIV generalium ordinis minorum*, p. 547.
[23] *Directio periodici*, pp. 302–3.
[24] Bihl, 'Statuta generalia' (Assisii), II, no. 14, III, no. 23, pp. 89, 95–6.

permission granted to Gentile was fully revoked by Pope Innocent VI on 18 August 1355.[25] The reforms were suppressed through the influence of the cardinal, who was the papal legate in Italy.[26] Even in the dissolution of the reform there was division among Gentile's followers. While he and one other were incarcerated, the rump of the movement was reintegrated into the life of the order. His recourse to the pope in 1350 may have arisen from an excessive insecurity about the protection of Brugliano and its plans for expansion in Umbria. Gentile was eventually released from the friary of Orvieto and was permitted to return to Brugliano, where he died in 1362. This raises the question of the status of the latter friary in the years following the suppression of 1355.

Paoluccio dei Trinci da Foligno

Born at Foligno in 1309, Paoluccio was a member of one of the leading families in the city, and through the maternal line was closely related to the Orsini family of Rome.[27] He was the nephew of Paolo dei Trinci, bishop of Foligno, who had been engaged in the presentation of the petition of Prince Philip of Majorca at the papal court in 1340. Aged 14, Pauluccio entered the order at Foligno. He was deeply attached to the ideal of asceticism and simplicity. Like Gentile, he was not a priest. At an unknown date he attached himself to the reformers in the wake of John de Valle's foundation. The years following his return to Foligno in around 1355 were undoubtedly difficult and he experienced a certain amount of personal hostility and some violence. After one particularly severe punishment his father removed him and established him in a tower in his own garden. There he devoted himself to prayer that the friars might accept some measure of reform. He gained the respect and admiration of the community. Nimmo regards this as an essential element in the restoration of good will towards the reformers; Paoluccio's qualities recreated the conditions that had obtained in 1334. A form of observance which was supported by the ministers seems to have offered the more secure path.[28]

Paoluccio still dreamed of the restoration of the movement of reform. A new minister general was elected at the general chapter of Assisi in 1367, Thomas Frignani da Modena, a master of theology from Bologna and minister provincial there. The following year the friary of Foligno hosted the provincial chapter of Umbria under the presidency of Thomas Racani d'Amelia, the new minister provincial. Frignani attended the provincial chapter and held an interview with Paoluccio as well as with other members of the influential

---

[25] *BF*, VI, no. 683, pp. 291–2, Glassberger, *Chronica*, p. 189.
[26] Directio periodici, p. 303.
[27] M. Faloci-Pulignani, 'Il Beato Paoluccio Trinci da Foligno', *MF* 6 (1896), pp. 97–128.
[28] Nimmo, *Reform and Division in the Franciscan Order*, p. 395.

Trinci family. He listened to Paoluccio's aspirations and gave him permission to go back to Brugliano with some volunteers to live with greater rigour the unglossed Rule. Within a short time he regretted this permission and attempted to revoke it. Members of the Trinci family, however, bound him to his decision to allow Paoluccio to return to Brugliano. He was, however, subsequently delated to the Roman curia and suspended from the office of minister general. One of the allegations was that the concession to Paoluccio was dangerous. Among his accusers were William, the Franciscan bishop of Narni, and Thomas Racani. One of Frignani's defenders was the celebrated poet, Petrarch, who wrote to Pope Urban V on 1 January 1369. Frignano was publicly exonerated in St Peter's basilica in the presence of numerous prelates, clerics and religious in 1370. One of the three cardinals appointed to hear the charges was the future Pope Gregory XI (1370–8), who was determined to protect the friars of strict observance.[29] One of the beneficiaries of Frignano's vindication was the friary of Brugliano. The reformers were given renewed approval by the cardinals' commission. This was a bitter pill for the critics of Brugliano to swallow.[30]

Despite some teething troubles, Paoluccio gained a reputation for integrity and holiness; it was not long before admirers and disciples made their way to the hermitage. The movement spread quite rapidly in comparison with the earlier settlement in the hills. Within four years the number of friars had grown to populate an additional ten hermitages attached to Brugliano by 28 July 1373. The new establishments included the four hermitages which had been granted to the reformers in 1350. Communities were formed at La Scarzuola, Greccio, Fonte Colombo and Poggi Bustone. The other foundations were made at Stroncone, Montegiove in the province of Umbria and four houses in the province of Rome. The group was spreading beyond Umbria and moving southwards and eastwards. Hermitages associated with St Francis were passing into the hands of the new reform.[31]

About 1373 a pivotal event occurred in the Umbrian province. Another branch of the heretical group (the *fraticelli de opinione*), clinging to the ideals of St Francis and perpetuating Michael of Cesena's opposition to Pope John XXII, harassed the community of friars at Perugia. The Perugian friary sought assistance from Paoluccio and his confrères, whom they temporarily accommodated at the abandoned hermitage of San Francesco al Monte. Paoluccio and his brethren went to Perugia, where they publicly routed the *fraticelli*, through disputaiton and the power of their own example. This resulted in the *fraticelli* being driven from the city. This work raised the profile of the reformers, who were held in high esteem and grew in number. The chronicler

[29] Cf. *BF*, VI, no. 1337a, pp. 533–4.
[30] A. Callebaut, 'Thomas de Frignano, ministre général et ses défenseurs: Pétraque, Philippe de Cabassol et Philippe de Maizières, vers 1369–70', *AFH* 10 (1917), pp. 239–49.
[31] M. Faloci-Pulignani, 'Il Beato Paoluccio Trinci da Foligno', pp. 106–7, 113.

links this apostolate with the admission of several men, including scholars and doctors, to the Observant family. One of them was Marco da Bergamo, a doctor of civil and canon law, who acquired a reputation for sanctity.[32] The reformers' role in the expulsion of the *fraticelli* was to change the ministers' perception of them in a twofold manner. First, it laid to rest the frequently repeated mantra that the reformers were theologically suspect, prone to disobedience, disorder and heresy. At a stroke this age-old weapon was destroyed on the streets of Perugia. Secondly, it demonstrated that there could be a positive and fruitful partnership between the urban-based communities and their confrères who dwelled in hermitages. This new spirit of respect and mutual collaboration expressed itself in the donation of San Francesco al Monte to the reformers. The friary was half a mile from Perugia and it was a site sanctified by many of the followers of St Francis, especially Giles of Assisi.

An even greater benefit was Paoluccio's close ties with the religious authorities in the order and the Church at large. The good will of the local minister provincial was already expressed in the donation of San Francesco al Monte in 1374. He was one of the signatories in the transfer of the land to the new occupants of the hermitage. Another signatory was the minister general, Leonardo Rossi da Giffoni (1373–8) who subsequently became a cardinal. The partnership of a supportive minister provincial of Umbria and minister general effectively safeguarded and protected the reform. It was the first time the reformers enjoyed such confidence and good will from the ministers. Allied to this strong support was papal backing. On 22 June 1374 Pope Gregory IX instructed the bishop of Orvieto to protect the Observants.[33]

The 1380s saw further development and new powers and privileges conferred upon Paoluccio and his followers. The friary of San Damiano just outside Assisi passed to them on 12 September 1380.[34] Paoluccio, 'father of the Observant friars', was instituted as the minister provincial of Umbria's commissary for the reformed hermitages from 1380. William Hast, the minister provincial, authorised Paoluccio to admit novices to the reform movement in 1384. Three years later Paoluccio's deteriorating health prompted him to appoint John de Stroncone as his commissary and co-adiutor. He sent John to Florence to negotiate a foundation, which was made at Fiesole in 1391.[35] Increasing infirmity obliged Paoluccio to leave Brugliano in 1390 and return to San Francesco, Foligno, where he died on 17 September 1391 and was interred in a chapel of the convent close to the martyrs, Philip and James.[36] In 1390 three more foundations were added in the Marches. John

[32] *Directio periodici*, p. 307.
[33] *BF*, VI, no. 1337a, pp. 533–4.
[34] L. Bracaloni, *Storia di San Damiano in Assisi*, 2nd edn (Todi, 1926), pp. 149–50.
[35] *Directio periodici*, pp. 701–2.
[36] Di Fonzo, 'I beati francescani', pp. 616–21.

of Stroncone received the historic hermitage of Il Colombaio, near Siena, and was the guardian there when Bernardine of Siena was admitted in 1402 for the completion of his novitiate.[37] A papal brief of 23 March 1403 for the foundation of two more communities referred to John of Stroncone as vicar of the minister general for the reformed houses in Tuscany and Umbria.[38] Paoluccio had observed the Rule in a pure and literal form. Several friars were admitted and new friaries were established and there were new manifestations of holiness. Mariano of Florence saw in the new community at Brugliano a step towards the partition of the order.[39]

While the Umbrian reform gathered impetus, there were parallel movements in France and Spain, coinciding with the beginning of the Great Schism. New groups arose in the provinces of Touraine around 1390, Santiago in 1392 and Castile in 1394. Although these independent groups advanced at a modest level in their early years, the movement in Umbria first and then Tuscany laid the foundations for the ministry of Bernardine of Siena.[40]

[37]   C. Piana, 'I processi di canonizzazione su la vita di S. Bernardino da Siena', *AFH* 44 (1951), VII, no. 1, pp. 87–160, 383–435 at 144.

[38]   *BF*, VII, no. 454, pp. 164–5.

[39]   Directio periodici, p. 305.

[40]   D. Nimmo, 'The Genesis of the Observance', in *Il rinnovamento del francescanesimo l'osservanza: atti dell' XI convengo internazionale, Assisi, 20–1–22 ottobre 1983*, Società internazionale di studi francescani (Assisi, 1985), pp. 107–47 at 109–12, 132–6.

CHAPTER SEVENTEEN

The Preaching of St Bernardine of Siena

> Bernardine travelled virtually throughout the whole of Italy preaching and carrying out other good deeds.
>
> Angelo of Philippi de Bonnisignis[1]

John de Stroncone linked the reformers of Brugliano and Bernardine of Siena, whom he received at Colombaio in 1402. Bernardine's impact upon the fledgling community resembled that of Bernard of Clairvaux on the growth of the Cistercians. He preached in several regions of Italy and his visits are better documented than those of St Francis.

Bernardine's vocation

Bernardine was born into the old and noble Sienese family of the Albizzeschi at the Tuscan city of Massa Marittima on 8 September 1380, the year of the death of St Catherine of Siena. His parents were Tollo degli Albizzeschi, *podestà* of the city, and Nera degli Avveduti, a native of the city. It was the Sienese custom to baptise sons on the day of their birth.[2] By the age of six Bernardine was orphaned. For five years he was brought up by his maternal aunt, Diana, who communicated her piety to him. At eleven, he passed into the care of his father's brother and sister-in-law at Siena, who supervised his education. These studies laid the foundation on which he built in later years. Bernardine was already well versed in grammar, poetry, rhetoric, canon law and the Scriptures.[3] He frequently visited Tobia, his cousin, a member of the Third Order. A concern for the needy marked his life. At eighteen he joined the confraternity of the Mother of God in the hospital of Santa Maria della Scala in Siena, a decision whose ripples would have an effect on the next stage of his life. This group combined austerity of life with care of the poor.[4]

---

[1] Piana, 'I processi', XVII, no. 3, p. 401.

[2] F. Doelle, 'Sermo S. Iohannis de Capistrano O.F.M. ineditus de S. Bernardino Senensi O.F.M.', *AFH* 6 (1913), pp. 76–90, 85.

[3] F. van Ortroy, 'Vie de S. Bernardin de Sienne par Léonard Benvoglienti', *Analecta Bollandiana* 21 (1902), nn. 1–2, pp. 53–80 at 59–60, Piana, 'I processi', II, nn. 1–3, III, nn. 1–3, VIII, no. 3, pp. 131–8, 138–40, 149.

[4] Van Ortroy, 'Vie de S. Bernardin', nn. 2–3, 8, 12, pp. 59–61, 63–4, 66–7.

The plague which raged throughout Italy in 1400 took its toll on Siena and terrified its citizens. The climate of intense fear was heightened by the deaths of fifty priests and 120 helpers at the hospital of Santa Maria della Scala, where an average of twelve patients died daily. People were afraid to cross the piazza where the hospital stood and helpers were scarce. Bernardine and twelve friends went there and ministered to the sick and dying. Heedless of personal danger, he was indefatigable in his nursing from morning until night. Estimates of the duration of the epidemic range from two months and some days to five months and eight days. When it subsided, Bernardine parried the suggestion that he might join the Augustinian hermits at Lecceto, south of San Miniato, because he was responsible for an elderly paternal aunt, Bartholomea, whom he tended until her death. Then he decided to pursue the life of a hermit and established an oratory on his own property.[5]

Drawn to the Franciscan ideals, Bernardine sought the counsel of the elderly John Ristori (Ristauri) da Siena, who had spent thirty years in Bosnia. Ristori successfully vouched for his young friend and steered his formal application through the meeting of the community's council on 6 September 1402. Bernardine's good reputation in the city and his devotion to St Francis and his order ensured his acceptance by the community at San Francesco, Siena.[6] Two days later, on his twenty-second birthday, Bernardine was admitted as a novice and clothed by Ristori after matins.[7] The new recruit was given the name of Bernardine in honour of the celebrated abbot of Clairvaux, an outstanding propagator of Marian devotion.[8] The friary, however, did not provide Bernardine with the values and atmosphere which he sought. Contemporary estimates of his stay there range from two months to a few days before his move to Colombaio on Monte Amiata in the diocese of Chiusi. The Observant friary, to the south of Siena and above Seggiano, was the home of friars who observed the poverty prescribed by the Rule; such communities were something of a rarity at the beginning of the fifteenth century.[9] It is unclear why Bernardine did not proceed directly to Colombaio instead of the urban friary of Siena. The early biographers link his knowledge of the reform with his desire to join it. Despite Bernardine's departure from San Francesco, he maintained cordial relations with the friars. Friars of San Francesco testified to his virtues and the efficacy of his sermons, noting that he celebrated Mass and preached there on numerous occasions.[10]

John de Stroncone was in a position to reply to the novice's questions

[5]   Ibid., nn. 14, 20–1, p. 68, 71–2. Doelle, 'Sermo S. Iohannis', p. 87, Piana, 'I processi', V, nn. 1–3, pp. 140–3.

[6]   Van Ortroy, 'Vie de S. Bernardin', no. 24, p. 73, Piana, 'I processi', p. 99, n. 2.

[7]   Piana, 'I processi', VII, pp. 144–9, Van Ortroy, 'Vie de S. Bernardin', no. 24, p. 73.

[8]   *Prediche volgari sul Campo di Siena 1427*, p. 683.

[9]   F. van Ortroy, 'Vie inédite de S. Bernardin de Sienne par un frère mineur, son contemporain', *Analecta Bollandiana* 25 (1906), no. 5, pp. 304–38 at 309–10, and 'Vie de S. Bernardin', no. 25, p. 74.

[10] Piana, 'I processi', XI, no. 3, XVII, no. 3, pp. 160, 401.

about the heroes of the reform movement in Umbria and its establishment in Tuscany. The asceticism and discipline of the Observants matched his own ideals and vision. He served God with self-abnegation and fervour. He helped to create a revival of the apostolic life under the Rule, which had been lost and become extinct, making his profession on 8 September 1403.[11] For the remainder of his life he adopted the greatest poverty and habitually avoided contact with money. He lived in great austerity and did not eat meat, eggs or cheese.[12] He was ordained priest and celebrated his first Mass on 8 September 1404 and in the same year was licensed to preach. A year after his profession Bernardine asked the rector of the hospital of Santa Maria della Scala for the use of the oratory of Beato Onofrio della Capriola, a hermitage close to Siena. Recalling Bernardine's heroism during the plague, the rector entrusted the property to the friars. The site was formally accepted by John de Stroncone and a party of friars was established there, where they constructed a modest friary and church dedicated to Santa Maria de Capriola.[13] Bernardine's strong Marian devotion may have led to this dedication. He exhorted his confrères to observe the Rule and to live to good purpose.[14] He refused to touch coins given as alms for the construction of the new friary. He was content and was allowed to work among the poor and to beg his bread from door to door.[15] La Capriola, known locally as the *convento dell' Osservanza*, is only a few miles north-west of Siena and overlooks the city. He remained there until 1417, returning on many occasions, especially for his homilies in the city, and there he compiled the Latin sermons which occupy nine volumes in the Quaracchi edition.[16] In a passage reminiscent of the early biographers' witness to the excellence of the observance at the Portiuncula, Pius II attests that the most saintly friars were appointed to La Capriola.[17] The friars' church there was constructed from 1423 to 1430 and consecrated on 12 September 1452.

Bernardine's early years in the reform demonstrated its regional emphases. Whereas Gentile da Spoleto and Paoluccio dei Trinci were not ordained, Bernardine was ordained within a year of his profession. His biographers and the witnesses at the cause of canonisation display no embarrassment about this. Moreover, ordination to the priesthood was dovetailed with the ministry of preaching, a role from which John de Valle had withdrawn in 1334. The office of the pulpit was closely connected with that of priestly status. Bernardine's

---

[11] Van Ortroy, 'Vie de S. Bernardin', no. 31, p. 78.

[12] Doelle, 'Sermo S. Iohannis', p. 88. Van Ortroy, 'Vie de S. Bernardin', no. 31, p. 78, Piana, 'I processi', XXIV, no. 3, p. 413.

[13] Piana, 'I processi', VII, no. 1, XVI, no. 3, XVII, no. 3, pp. 144, 398, 400.

[14] Ibid., I, no. 1, XXIII, no. 3, pp. 128, 412.

[15] Ibid., XXIV, no. 3, p. 414, Van Ortroy, 'Vie de S. Bernardin', nn. 25–6, pp. 74–5.

[16] *S. Bernardini Senensis ordinis fratrum minorum opera omnia studio et cura PP. Collegii S. Bonaventurae ad fidem codicum edita*, 9 vols (Quaracchi, Florence, 1950–65).

[17] Piccolomini, *I Commentarii*, IV, c. 14, pp. 694–5.

sermons signal the Italian Observants' engagement with urban communities.[18] His visits to the large centres of population should not distract attention from his sermons in towns and villages. The new element was that at the end of the sermon Bernardine returned to the hermitage.

Bernardine's itinerant preaching

For around forty years Bernardine was an indefatigable preacher whose fame spread throughout Italy. Homilies in Assisi, Florence, Milan, Padua, Perugia, Rome, Siena, Venice and in many other cities brought him praise and fame. Preaching tours were made in the face of some ill health and hostility on account of his propagation of devotion to the Holy Name of Jesus. Some Augustinian and Dominican friars were disturbed by this cult, fearing that it was liable to misinterpretation and superstition; they accused him of heresy and delated him to Pope Martin V, who cleared him.[19] Andrew di Francesco da Siena heard him speaking about vices and virtues at the convent of San Francesco, Siena, and the city's *piazza del campo*. Masseo de Florence, who had heard Bernardine's sermons in Siena, Florence and Bologna, remarked that he detested vices and extolled the virtues more than any other contemporary preacher. This was a feature of his sermons in other cities, including Asciano, Rome, Venice and Viterbo.[20] The broad appeal of Bernardine's preaching was emphasised by the presence of famous theologians, skilled doctors, lawyers and religious, as well as nobles, merchants, rustics, mercenaries and prostitutes.[21]

Bernardine steeped himself in the study of Christian literature. He worked hard to prepare his sermons by day and by night.[22] He travelled throughout Italy on foot, including journeys from Siena to Padua.[23] His following was reminiscent of that of Berthold of Regensberg in the 1250s. Bernardine was at Ferrara in 1408 and during the great plague of 1415–17. In the same period, probably 1416, he was at Mantua. The following year he was at Milan, where he enjoyed much success and fostered devotion to the holy name of Jesus, offering for veneration the wax tablet inscribed with the name of Jesus.[24]

[18] Cf. L. McAodha, 'The Nature and Efficacy of Preaching according to St. Bernardine of Siena', *FS* 27 (1967), pp. 221–48.

[19] Piana, 'I processi', XXVII, nn. 2–3, pp. 417–26, E. Longpré, 'S. Bernardin de Sienne et le nom de Jésus (écrits polémiques)', *AFH* 29 (1936), pp. 443–77.

[20] Piana, 'I processi', IX, no. 3, XXVII, no. 3, pp. 154–5, 420. *Le prediche volgari (Florence 1424)*, ed. C. Cannarozzi, 2 vols (Pistoia, 1934), II, p. 1.

[21] Van Ortroy, 'Vie inédite de S. Bernardino', no. 10, p. 313.

[22] Doelle, 'Sermo S. Iohannis', p. 89, Piana, 'I processi', XXVII, no. 3, p. 420.

[23] Piana, 'I processi', II, no. 3, p. 135.

[24] D. Pacetti, 'La predicazione di S. Bernardino in Toscana. Con documenti inediti estratti dagli atti del processo di canonizzazione', *AFH* 33 (1940), pp. 268–318, at 280. 291 and 34 (1941), pp. 261–83. B. de Gaiffier, 'Le Mémoire d'André Biglia sur la prédication de Saint Bernardin de Sienne', *Analecta Bollandiana* 53 (1935), nn. 4, 8, pp. 308–58, 315, 319.

Bernardine was already an experienced preacher when in 1417 he was transferred from La Capriola to Fiesole, where he met John of Capistrano and James of the Marches, who would become his close collaborators. During the meditation after the morning offices a novice of Fiesole arose and urged Bernardine to go to Lombardy as a preacher. Despite the guardian's rebuke to the junior member of the community, Bernardine read this as a divine sign and secured the necessary permissions to betake himself to Lombardy.[25] Although he had already preached in several cities, thereafter he was constantly active in the diverse cities of Italy. He preached twice at Padua between 1413 and 1417 and was back there in 1443, at the instigation of the vicar general of the order, when he delivered sixty-five sermons from Ash Wednesday to the second Sunday of Easter. The sermons were recorded and then translated into Latin by Daniel de Purçillis. The manuscript includes accounts of the prodigies which occurred there during his earlier sermons and the manner of his departure from Il Santo, Padua, for Vicenza.[26] The promotion of peace within and between communities was a salient feature of Bernardine's preaching in numerous cities. He was credited with the restoration of harmony at Assisi, Bologna, Brescia, Florence, Massa Marittima, Milan, Perugia, Rome, Siena, Vicenza and many other cities, towns and villages. More than a hundred reconciliations were effected at Massa Marittima during Lent 1444. He did the same at Pavia. Another dimension of this preaching was Bernardine's sensitivity towards the poor and debtors. When Filippo M. Visconti, the duke of Milan, sent five hundred gold pieces in alms, Bernardine graciously received them and deployed the money to liberate paupers and debtors from prison in 1423.[27]

The pattern for these sermons was reflected by the city of Perugia, where Bernardine preached several times. The diary of Antonio dei Veghi records the impact of his sermons from 19 September 1425 until the end of October. After celebrating Mass he preached in the city's *piazza maggiore*. The following day it was decreed that shops would not open and people would not work during the time of the sermon. Six days later Bernardine urged the men and women of the district to bring objects of vanity and sources of distraction to San Francesco within the next fortnight and in October these were to be burned on the piazza in front of the episcopal residence. These sermons bore fruit in the reformation of conduct and the extinction of factions, the pacification of souls and the bonfire of games and female vanities. On 23 September Bernardine preached in the piazza in the presence of a crowd estimated at more than three thousand people. Vices and sins were assailed

---

[25] Van Ortroy, 'Vie inédite de S. Bernardino', no. 13, pp. 315–16.

[26] S. Tosti, 'Di alcuni codici delle prediche di S. Bernardino da Siena con un saggio di quelle inedite', *AFH* 12 (1919), pp. 187–263 at 218–23, 254–63. Cf. D. Gallo, 'San Bernardino da Siena a Padova: predicazione, devozione civica e culto', *Il santo* 38 (1998), pp. 341–54.

[27] Piana, 'I processi', X, nn. 1–3, XXIV, no. 3, pp. 155–9, 413.

and he offered instruction on the conduct of a Christian life. His influence extended to fifteen of the city's statutes, the *statuta sancti Bernardini*, which were enacted on 4 November 1425. These focus on cupidity, blasphemy against God and his saints, proscribed games, usury, sodomites and access to the nuns' convents.[28] Two years later, 19 February 1427, he returned to the city and preached to a large crowd on the piazza of San Francesco on the Thursday, Friday and Saturday, and again, in extreme cold, on the Sunday and Monday. He was there again on 28 September 1438, when he preached on the piazza. A chronicler observed that on this occasion Bermardine targeted ingratitude and sodomy. He returned to the city again on 10 August 1441, the feast of the city's patron saint, San Lorenzo, and preached about justice and the assumption of the Mother of God.[29]

The people of Tuscany featured among those healed at Bernardine's intercession and they were the first to hear his sermons. He preached for more than forty consecutive days at Prato and accomplished good things there. Eye-witnesses reported that the churches were too small for the large congregation in 1424. Each morning he preached from the piazza in front of San Francesco to huge crowds, whose numbers have been estimated at between four and eight thousand. His last sermon, on 12 June, the Monday of Pentecost, propagated devotion to the holy name. He showed the people the holy monogram YHS. One witness attests that people were liberated from demons. On 11 September 1424 Bernardine preached in San Francesco, Lucca, and for two hours he addressed a huge crowd in the piazza di San Martino, outside the city's cathedral. He promoted peace in the midst of the city's wars with the Florentines.[30] He preached at Volterra in December 1424 outside the church of San Francesco. As soon as he had completed his sermons in Siena on 10 June 1425, he went to Asciano where he preached a course of sermons in the church of San Francesco. A document of 15 June from the Signoria of Siena commanded the *podestà* of Asciano to permit Bernardine to preach wherever he pleased and to allow the people of the neighbourhood to attend his sermons.[31] Bernardino preached the Lenten sermons in the church of San Francesco, Arezzo, in 1428. The civic authorities commented on the fruit of the friar's preaching and drew attention to his influence in the destruction of Fontetecta, a pagan site outside the city, where diabolical works and idolatrous rituals were perceived as a threat to the Christian community.[32]

---

[28] Cf. M. Bigaroni, 'San Bernardino a Todi', *StF* 73 (1976), pp. 109–25.

[29] Cf. A. Fantozzi, 'Documenta Perusina de S. Bernardino Senensi', *AFH* 15 (1922), pp. 103–54, 406–70, D. Pacetti, 'La predicazione di S. Bernardino da Siena a Perugia e ad Assisi nel 1425', *CF* 9 (1939), pp. 494–520, and 10 (1940), pp. 5–28 at 161–88, S. Nessi, 'La confraternita di S. Girolamo in Perugia', *MF* 67 (1967), pp. 78–115 at 79–80. The commune took a close interest in the death and incipient cult of Bernardine, whom they honoured in a variety of ways, issuing documents from 5 June 1444.

[30] Pacetti, 'La predicazione', pp. 301–15.

[31] Ibid., pp. 285–9.

[32] Ibid., 34 (1941), pp. 261–83, 261–71.

Regrettably the extant sources provide no details about the rituals enacted there. His last Lenten sermons were preached in Massa Marittima in 1444. They were delivered daily at San Francesco in the city of his birth. Barnabas of Siena reports that the impact of these sermons was the radical extirpation of fierce hostilities in the city and the restoration of the love of Christ and peace and harmony.[33] Bernardine's sermons in Florence and Siena are among the best documented and in each case the civic authorities invited him to preach there and re-establish peace.

Sermons in Florence (1424, 1425) and Siena (1425, 1427)

When he arrived in Florence in Lent 1424, Bernardine was conscious of the influence of Manfred of Vercelli, the controversial Dominican preacher, who had been there from 1419 to 1423.[34] On the first Sunday he asked parents to bring children from the age of five to the sermons in the following week.[35] Chroniclers expatiated on the impressive results of those sermons, which were held at Santa Croce. Sometimes Bernardine announced the themes to be addressed in the sermons so that people might select the days to be present. Sermons were delivered each morning and on the last day Bernardine preached both in the morning and evening. Sundays provided him with his best attendances, when he announced the themes for the coming week's homilies.[36] By the 1420s his sermons were major religious and social events and they would continue for a month or more. They lasted for two or three hours.[37] The number of people in attendance was put at more than forty thousand by Masseo de Florence, a friar of Santa Croce and an eye-witness to the events which took place on the piazza in 1424.[38]

The church and piazza of Santa Croce were filled by large crowds of citizens and people from the neighbourhood on 9 April, Passion Sunday, for a sermon on the sins and self-indulgence which stone Christ. People were invited to discard items of vanity and superstition. A vast bonfire, known as the devil's castle, was constructed in the piazza, which held four hundred backgammon tables, several baskets full of dice, over four thousnad packs of playing cards and a large supply of items of personal vanity. At the end of the sermon Bernardine descended the steps of the pulpit inside the church and made his way to the piazza in the company of friars to preside over the bonfire.[39] A cloth barrier separated the sexes at these sermons. Despite such

---

[33] Ibid., pp. 271–7. Piana, 'I processi', X, no. 1, p. 156, n. 1.

[34] C. L. Polecritti, *Preaching Peace in Renaissance Italy: Bernardine of Siena and His Audience* (Washington, 2000), p. 25.

[35] *Le prediche volgari* (Florence, 1424), I, p. 66.

[36] Ibid., II, p. 72.

[37] Ibid., I, p. 451: *venite a udire el predicatore, due or tre ore che vi diletta!*

[38] Piana, 'I processi', XII, no. 3, p. 386, n. 2.

[39] Tosti, 'Di alcuni codici', pp. 187–94.

arrangements, it was not easy to ensure strict partition so that the people might listen attentively to the celebrated preacher. Bernardine narrated that, while he was preaching at Verona, a soldier refused to stand with the men and defiantly remained on the women's side. The soldier noisily announced that because he was not permitted to stand where he pleased, he would go gambling. Bernardine told his audience that the man had subsequently lost an arm in a fight, a handicap which he attributed to the man's stubbornness.[40] The Florentines' predilection for building chapels rather than showing forth fruits of true penitence was deplored.[41]

The Florentines entreated Bernardine to return the following Lent, as he promised in his last sermon in 1424. On his second visit the sermons lasted from 4 February to 15 March 1425. The extant manuscripts contain only forty sermons preached once again in Santa Croce. The themes included the occult judgements of God, how God governs the world, the prodigal son, the battle against demonic forces, the seven mortal sins, how Jesus cast the demon out of the man who was deaf and dumb and the gravity of mendacity.[42] On Palm Sunday he preached on the knowledge of this world and its *mores*. The succeeding days of holy week were occasions for sermons on the state of the soul and the love of God, the justice of the soul, the spiritual condition and its superiority over the secular, the passion of the Lord and preparation for the reception of the Body of Christ.[43] Sermons on the holy name frequently occurred in collections and this theme informs homilies delivered on Monday and Saturday of Easter week and the following Monday in 1425.[44]

At the end of his Florentine sermons Bernardine, yielding to the magistrates' entreaties, returned to Siena, where he delivered a lengthy series of homilies in the spring of 1425, which feature in contermporary correspondence.[45] He preached daily at Siena in April and May 1425, 21 and 29 April excepted. Sermons between 20 April and 2 May took place in the cloister of San Francesco and the piazza of San Francesco. A sermon on that piazza was captured by Sano di Pietro, whose painting is in the Museo dell' Opera del Duomo in Siena; the local artist depicts several friars listening to the saint, who carries a crucifix. Giacomo Nannis de Griffulis of Siena reports that from 3 May the size of the crowds necessitated the transfer of the sermons to the *piazza del campo* in front of the *palazzo pubblico*. One witness estimated that crowds of thirty thousand attended the sermon, which was accompanied by

---

[40] *Le prediche volgari (Florence, 1424)*, I, pp. 423–4.

[41] *Le prediche volgari (Florence, 1425)*, ed. C. Cannarozzi, in 3 vols (Pistoia, 1940), I, p. 89.

[42] Tosti, 'Di alcuni codici', pp. 194–9.

[43] B. Bughetti, 'Il Codice bernardiniano contenente gli schemi del santo in volgare per la quaresima di Firenze 1425 (Siena, Osservanza, Museo Castelli, n. 28)(a)', *AFH* 34 (1941), pp. 185–235.

[44] Ibid., nn. 65, 70, 72, pp. 196–7.

[45] S. Tosti, 'De praedicatione S. Bernardini Senensis in patria civitate, anno 1425', *AFH* 8 (1915), pp. 678–80.

a bonfire of vanities.[46] On 16 May the sermon was held in the great hall of the lords of the city, perhaps on account of the weather, and four days later the rain forced Bernardine to preach in the evening instead of the morning. Some of the sermons were associated with solemn processions. One such took place on 28 May and was vividly described by Giacomo Nannis de Griffulis of Siena, the author of a Latin text of the cycle of sermons, who supplied details of the date and venue. The day began with the Mass on the piazza and then a sermon on the holy name, after which the monogram was shown to the people for veneration. Then came the solemn procession, which moved first to the cathedral. The claim of contemporary witnesses that thirty thousand people were present on bended knee should be informed by the late medieval inclination to exaggerate the size of the crowds attending the sermons. On the vigil of Corpus Christi Bernardine exhorted the people to have the name of Jesus posted on their principal municipal building, the palace of the lords, for the protection of the building and the city. The city's statutes were accordingly modified and a huge YHS emblem, the symbol of the holy name of Jesus, was placed above the main portal of the *palazzo pubblico*, where it is visible to visitors in the twenty-first century.[47]

One manuscript contains forty-five sermons preached during the late summer of 1427.[48] The sermons, beginning on 15 August and continuing throughout September, were recorded by an eye-witness.[49] The first was painted by Neroccio di Bartolomeo and Sano di Pietro. The latter reproduces the various ranks of Sienese society, the *signori* of the council and the assembled population, male and female. A pulpit was erected in the piazza del campo. Bernardine carried the tablet bearing the sacred monogram, YHS. Exhorting the Sienese citizens to a warm devotion, Bernardine reminded them that the Mother of God was the city's celestial patron. He also confirmed that he was preaching at the request of the civic authorities.[50] Leonard Benvoglienti was present at the sermon on 8 September, the birthday of the Mother of God. Bernardine explained his special enthusiasm for that feast. On that feast he had been born, baptised, clothed as a friar and professed, and celebrated Mass for the first time, and he wished to die on that day.[51] This declaration, with few variants, occurs near the beginning of the sermon, a day which marked the silver jubilee of his admission as a novice.[52] Pope Martin V sent Bernardine to Siena to pacify the city. The friar reconciled several estranged parties

[46] Tosti, 'Di alcuni codici delle prediche di S. Bernardino da Siena con un saggio di quelle inedite', p. 203, Piana, 'I processi', XII, no. 3, p. 386.
[47] Tosti, 'Di alcuni codici', pp. 198–207. Cf. G. Milanesi, ed., *Documenti per la storia dell'arte Senese* (Siena, 1854), II, pp. 128–30.
[48] Tosti, 'Di alcuni codici', pp. 215–18.
[49] Origo, *The World of San Bernardino*, p. 12.
[50] *Prediche volgari sul Campo di Siena 1427*, pp. 102–3, 110.
[51] Van Ortroy, 'Vie de S. Bernardin', no. 11, p. 66.
[52] *Prediche volgari sul Campo di Siena 1427*, p. 683.

on numerous occasions and peace was made on the *piazza del campo* and in the hall of the priors. The names of the individuals who had been reconciled with each other were identified by witnesses at the cause of canonisation.[53] His penultimate sermon focused on the love and seraphic ardour of St Francis and commented on the saint's legacy for Siena, including membership of the Third Order.[54] His concentration on the apostolate of the pulpit was so absorbing that he laid aside every other occupation, including the hearing of confessions.[55] He believed that sermons were so important that it was better for someone to be absent from Mass than the sermon.[56] Death came at the friary of Aquila on 20 May 1444.

Bernardine was one of the most outstanding preachers of the fifteenth century. His popularity did much to boost and then increase the reform movement throughout Italy. His relatively early canonisation on 24 May 1450 confirmed the new vitality of the Observant reform, which was reviving the conditions of the halcyon days of the order in the middle of the thirteenth century 1450. The reform movement had a persuasion and momentum which could not be ignored. It challenged the other friars to reform themselves for the unity of the order. Failure to respond to this stimulus created the conditions for the promulgation of *Ut sacra ordinis minorum religio* by Pope Eugene IV, signalling the division which increasingly marked the order founded by St Francis.

---

[53] Piana, 'I processi', X, nn. 1–3, pp. 155–9.
[54] *Prediche volgari sul Campo di Siena 1427*, pp. 931, 1315–44.
[55] Ibid., p. 803.
[56] Ibid., p. 149.

CHAPTER EIGHTEEN

Towards Division, 1400–1446

Ut sacra confirmed the authority of the Observant Vicars General, and effectively divided the Observants from the Conventuals.

Marie Richards[1]

Growth of the Observant family

An anonymous biographer of Bernardine presented him as the providential instrument for the renewal of the order, which was perceived as having lapsed from the pristine fervour of St Francis.[2] New signs for optimism lay in the approximately twenty-five friaries in the Observant reform at the beginning of the fifteenth century. This figure was augmented greatly through the influence of Bernardine, whose preaching brought many to religious life. Julian of Siena testified that more than a hundred of his fellow citizens had taken the habit. One estimate was that Bernardine's preaching had led more than twenty thousand to the religious life. The witnesses supply no information about women converted to the numerous communities of Poor Clares in Tuscany and Umbria.

Mark di Leonard of Bologna saw many impressive men seeking admission to the order. The names of several recruits to the order were supplied by the witnesses to the cause of canonisation. Many usurers were converted and made fitting restitution; a number became Observants and some of them were named. Recruits included many who had been regarded as vain laymen before taking the habit and living laudably as friars. Vocations included men who became the best preachers, such as Silvester de Radiconduli, Louis di Pietro Lantani and numerous others. While some converts gained a good reputation as confessors, others were drawn into Bernardine's inner circle as *socii*. Anthony Bonaventure de Rossi, a noble of Siena, attested that Bernardine's influence on the nascent fraternity was central and that he was the foundation and dynamo for the dissemination of the Observant ideal.[3]

Bernardine constructed or had friaries built in many cities. Pride of

---

[1] M. Richards, 'The Conflict between Observant and Conventual Reformed Franciscans in Fifteenth-Century France and Flanders', *FS* 50 (1990), pp. 263–81 at 267.

[2] Van Ortroy, 'Vie inédite de S. Bernardino', no. 12, p. 314.

[3] Piana, 'I processi', XV, nn. 1–3, pp. 390–4.

place went to La Capriola, which the friars built with their own hands, as the painting of Giacomo da Lodi in the church of San Francesco at Lodi depicts. Bernardine took a close interest in the establishment of the friary at Massa Marittima. New friaries were established at Agguzano, Bagni di San Casciano, Cetona, Monte Orsaio, Vetrata near Massa, Scansani and several places in Italy. From 1414 the Observants were established at Giacchherino, near Pistoia, perhaps as a result of Bernardine's preaching there or in its vicinity.[4] Some transfiliations were associated with his preaching. After his sermons at Poggibonsi the convent of San Francesco was granted to the Observants in 1438.[5] Louis di Pietro Lantani had heard that many places (*loca*) and friaries had been established through the preaching and industry of Bernardine, especially in the province of Milan, hitherto closed to the reform movement. Paul di Christophero de Montutiis of Siena was with Bernardine in Lombardy where many different friaries were constructed. Estimates of the size of the reform movement in the life of Bernardine vary from thirty-eight to two hundred friaries. Some of these friaries had previously belonged to the *fraticelli de opinione*.[6] One biographer attests that Bernardine enlarged the Observant family to number over three hundred friaries, either built or reformed.[7] The papal role in sanctioning the formation of new communities and the responsibilities of Bernardine is demonstrated by Pope Martin V's letter of 5 June 1426, which authorised him to receive four places for the Observants.[8]

As in Umbria and then Tuscany, the progress of the reform in France and Spain was initially slow. It was, however, interspersed with periods of rapid expansion in France between 1406 and 1408 and in Spain between 1408 and 1417. Such reforms received vital support from a number of ministers provincial and general sympathetic to the new ideals. For example, the reform at Mirebeau was supported by the Avignonese minister general and the minister provincial of Touraine, who removed unreformed friars. This positive policy persisted for some fifteen years. Giovanni Bardolini, the Avignonese minister general, laid down guidelines for the reformed friary at Séez on 5 September 1404. The friars were encouraged to fulfil their vows faithfully, to show contempt for worldly things and above all to love one another. Some four years later the minister general installed a reformed community at St-Omer in place of the unreformed friars.[9] Some of the crucial judgements about the life of the reformers were made by Pope Benedict XIII (1394–1417), who encouraged the minister general to reform the order as early as 11 April 1404 and

---

[4] Pacetti, 'La predicazione', p. 291.

[5] Ibid., pp. 289–90.

[6] Piana, 'I processi', XVI, nn. 1–3, 394–400. Ibid., XV, no. 1, p. 391.

[7] Van Ortroy, 'Vie de S. Bernardin', no. 31, p. 78.

[8] *BF*, VII, no. 1715, pp. 655–6.

[9] F. Gratien, 'Les Débuts de la réforme des cordeliers en France et Guillaume Josseaume (1390–1436)', *Études franciscaines* 31 (1914), pp. 415–39 at 431–4.

was sympathetic to the plight of the reformers. Reformers in the provinces of Burgundy, France and Touraine were exempted from the jurisdiction of the ministers on 26 April 1407 and on 13 May 1408, when Benedict appointed Thomas de Curte as their vicar general. Benedict used the formal title *pro regulari observantia* ('for observance of the Rule') on 17 August 1414 in founding a reformed settlement at Castile.[10] These permissions were bitterly resented by the Conventuals and positions became even more polarised.

The Conventuals protested to Alexander V (1409–10), their confrère, who had been elected as pope at the council of Pisa. He ruled on 24 September 1409 that the Observants should live in obedience to the minister general.[11] Feeling that their room for manoeuvre was restricted, the French reformers published their grievances in a letter to the University of Paris on 8 February 1410, explaining their ideals. They had nothing to do with money, either personally or through an intermediary; they enjoyed the mere use of material things, which was defined in terms of *usus pauper*; they did not store food, but begged their food daily; their clothing was poor; they did not ride horses and wore shoes only in cases of necessity; women were excluded from the cloisters; friars all ate together in a refectory, sharing the same food, and they slept in a dormitory. They defined themselves in terms of a return to the halcyon days of the order.[12] The university, which had its own grievances against the new mendicant pope, found in favour of the reformers. Their declaration on 13 June of the same year referred to the institution of a vicar general by Pope Benedict XIII with the approval of the minister general. The friary of St-Omer and all similar friaries should be free to live in peace under the direction of the vicar general.[13] This decision gave the early Observants a propaganda tool to be wielded against their critics and would-be oppressors.

The Observant movement in Italy was gaining ground, as is reflected in the acquisition of Santa Maria degli Angeli. Antonio Vinitti da Perèto, minister general, ceded the psychologically important friary to the reformers in 1415, granting them one of the most sacred places in the order. Mariano of Florence explains that the transfer coincided with the increase in the number of Observant friaries. At that time there were scarcely thirty friaries or *loca* in Italy and about two hundred friars. The chronicler then emphasises the impact of Bernardine of Siena, John of Capistrano, James of the Marches and Albert da Sarteano. These four pillars of the Observance were instrumental in the diffusion of the ideal throughout Italy and its implantation in Bohemia, Germany and Hungary.[14]

[10] *BF*, VII, nn. 962, 1022, 1047, 1126, 1128, pp. 327, 350–1, 361–2, 387–90.

[11] Ibid., no. 1187, pp. 417–18.

[12] L. Oliger, 'De relatione inter observantium querimonias Constantienses (1415) et Ubertini Casalensis quoddam scriptum', *AFH* 9 (1916), pp. 3–41.

[13] *Chartularium universitatis Parisiensis*, IV, no. 1886, p. 181.

[14] *Directio periodici*, pp. 706–7. M. Bigaroni, 'Passagio del convento di S. Maria della Porziuncola all'Osservanza', *StF* 84 (1987), pp. 201–15.

A shifting balance of power

Encouraged by the verdict of the Parisian masters, the French reformers turned to a higher court. Their uneasy relations with the Conventuals moved the disparate groups to take a momentous step. During the period of vacancy following the deposition of John XXIII, the anti-pope, at the council of Constance on 29 May 1415, they appealed to the council through the ambassadors of the French king and in the presence of Jordan Orsini, cardinal protector and the other cardinals. Sigismund, holy Roman emperor (1410–37), was present and acknowledged the justice of their petition. The matter was considered by the minister general as well as masters and discreets of the Conventuals and friars from the three provinces of northern France. The nineteenth session of the council responded on 23 September 1415 with this declaration: 'there is promulgated at this session an ordinance between the Friars Minor of the strict observance and others of the common life, to put an end to the discords which have arisen in certain provinces'. The approbation which greeted the petition was contained in a fuller text of the same date explaining the new arrangements. Nicholas Rudolph was appointed the first vicar for the Observants in the provinces of France, Touraine and Burgundy.[15] Mariano of Florence attests that the fearful and timid friars, who had been scattered throughout France, were emboldened to seek permission for the vigorous continuance of the reform movement, which had begun in some friaries in the provinces of Touraine, Burgundy and Italy. Moreover, a vicar provincial was appointed.[16] This decision was a milestone in the French Observants' quest for protection and some form of independence.

While the Conventuals invested immense energy in seeking the repeal of the conciliar decree, the Observants were expanding and moving into new provinces. The Observants were introduced to southern Germany in 1426 at the behest of Mathilda, wife of Louis III, ruler of the Rhine Palatinate. She arranged the appointment of reformers from Tours as her confessors and chaplains. Despite initial obstruction from the Conventuals, a reformed friary was established at Heidelberg.[17] By 1427 the Observants were making inroads in the island of Sicily with foundations at Agrigento, Messina and Palermo.[18] They reached southern France relatively late and were invited to form communities, beginning at Montpellier in 1435.[19] One expression of

---

[15] *Decrees of the Ecumenical Councils*, ed. N. Tanner (London, 19990), I, p. 433, *BF*, VII, no. 1362, pp. 493–5, Glassberger, *Chronica*, pp. 256–61.

[16] Directio periodici, p. 706.

[17] P. L. Nyphus, 'The Observant Reform Movement in Southern Germany', *FS* 32 (1972), pp. 154–67 at 163–4.

[18] D'Alatri, 'Gli insediamenti osservanti in Sicilia nel corso del quattrocentro', *Schede medievali rassegna dell'officina di studi medievali* 32/33 (1997), pp. 41–50.

[19] R. Pratesi, 'L'introduzione della regolare osservanza nella Francia meridionale', *AFH* 50 (1957), pp. 178–94 at 181, 192–4.

the steady expansion of the reform was the transfer of several friaries from the Conventuals to the Observants.[20] In some instances the urban or borough authorities were agents of renewal, preferrring to support a more zealous religious community. This led to the replacement of the Conventuals by the Observants.[21] A striking development was the transfer of large urban friaries to the reformers, a fact which would have important implications for the future of the movement. San Francesco at Lucca passed to the Observants in 1454 and thus the friars were once more content to minister to urban communities. On occasion, transfers were attributed to the lax lifestyle of the Conventual communities. The future Pius II (1458–64), an admirer of Bernardine, cited that as the reason for the transfer of the friary of Tivoli.[22]

The transfer of a friary from the jurisdiction of the Conventuals to the Observants entailed the removal of one group of friars and the installation of another; the ejected Conventual friars were assigned to other convents by their ministers. Such transfers were not unfailingly conducted in a peaceful manner and there is evidence of Conventual opposition to a new regime. When the friary of Mirebeau was seized by the Conventuals, the matter was brought before the parliament of Poitiers at the instigation of Guillaume Josseaume at Poitiers on 16 June 1421.[23] The Tuscan convent of Cetona, whose foundation stretched back to 1212, joined the reform movement in 1440. Six years later, however, the Conventuals tried to regain it, but Pope Eugene IV thwarted them. The convent of San Processo was briefly in the hands of the Observants in 1400 and passed to them again in 1440, but five years later it returned to the Conventuals. The citizens of Castello in Umbria entreated Bernardine to reform their local friary. Accordingly, he dispatched a dozen friars there to replace the Conventuals.[24]

On 7 May 1420 Pope Martin V permitted friars in the provinces of France, Burgundy and Touraine to adopt a strict observance of the Rule; no legislation of recent years should in any way interfere with the decrees of the council of Constance.[25] Papal impatience for reform is personified by Martin, whose mind was inclining towards the conclusion reached by the Parisian masters and the council of Constance. The general chapter at Forlì provided him with a platform for the implementation of his views. He wrote to the capitulars on 14 April 1421 and underlined the urgent need to elect a suitable minister general, who would lead the order both by word and example.

---

[20] For example, the convent of San Francesco, Candia, passed to the reformers in 1420. G. Hofmann, 'La biblioteca scientifica del monastero di San Francesco a Candia nel medio evo', *Orientalia Christiana periodica* 8 (1942), p. 317–60.

[21] Glassberger, *Chronica*, pp. 316, 318–20.

[22] Piccolomini, *I Commentarii*, V, no. 27, pp. 986–9.

[23] Gratien, 'Les débuts', pp. 434–9.

[24] B. Bughetti, 'Documenta inedita de S. Bernardino Senensi, O.F.M. (1430–45)', *AFH* 29 (1936), pp. 478–500 at 481–2, 492–3.

[25] *BF*, VII, no. 1448, p. 534.

Discipline and rectitude of life were necessary qualities at a time when many abandoned the Rule and constitutions. Spiritual concerns had been rejected by the friars, who lived in the manner of their secular neighbours and brought the order into contempt. The chapter elected Angelo Salvetti on 10 May 1421. The former minister provincial of Tuscany was intending to reform the order, but died before he could achieve it.[26] He spent much of his time at Rome, although in the late summer he began a visitation of some ultramontane provinces. The following year he was in Geneva and reported on his visits to Germany. Abuses concerning money or alms were to be corrected.[27]

The unsuitability of Salvetti's successor galvanised Pope Martin V to seize the initiative. He convened a general chapter to be held in Assisi at Pentecost 1430 under the presidency of John Cerventes, the Spanish cardinal priest, an advocate of reform.[28] This was one of the last opportunities for the implementation of a reform which would keep the order together. The minister general was, however, the first casualty of this programme. Anthony de Massa was deposed on the grounds that he had not combated laxity in the order. William de Casale, the vicar general, was elected. William was a man who was sensitive to the aims of the Observants. The papal constitutions were read at the general chapter and then published for both parts of the order. The minister general took the lead in solemnly swearing to uphold these new ordinances and moved the whole order to do the same. This seemed like a moment of conciliation and optimism after the last fifteen years of discord and party strife. John of Capistrano undertook to prepare an exposition of the constitutions in the form of a commentary on the Rule.[29]

William de Casale was the minister general of the whole order. The growing strength of the Observants is reflected in their augmented share in the government of the order. William appointed John of Capistrano as his commissary or representative and the visitor for the provinces of southern Italy in 1430. He also granted a range of special commissions to Bernardine of Siena on 1 October 1430.[30] He appointed him as his vicar general for the Observants on 22 July 1438, a decision which was ratified by Pope Eugene IV on 1 September of that year.[31] In addition, some Observants now served as ministers provincial. For example, Albert da Sarteano was elected as the minister provincial in the province of St Anthony of Padua.

Nonetheless, the hopes of the general chapter and its immediate aftermath did not stand the test of time. The joint visitation of the order by William de Casale and John of Capistrano was eventually abandoned. Within the space

[26] Directio periodici, p. 709.
[27] Bulletti, 'Angelo Salvetti', pp. 80–1, R. Pratesi, 'Angelo Salvetti, ministro generale O.F.M. (10 maggio 1421 – 6 ottobre 1423)', *AFH* 54 (1961), pp. 94–113, Glassberger, *Chronica*, pp. 274–7.
[28] *BF*, VII, no. 1888, p. 735.
[29] Glassberger, *Chronica*, pp. 289–90, Directio periodici, p. 713.
[30] Bughetti, 'Documenta inedita de S. Bernardino Senensi', pp. 481–2.
[31] *BF*, n.s. I, no. 385, pp. 177–8.

of two months the minister general himself was seeking absolution from the oath which he had sworn at the chapter. Moreover, these dispensations were granted by a pope who had earlier displayed some irritation with the Conventuals' slowness to initiate reform. Martin's *Ad perpetuam rei memoriam* of 27 July 1430 interpreted anew and modified the constitutions enacted by that year's general chapter. On 23 August 1430 *Ad statum*, which was addressed to the minister general, permitted the friars, through their proctors, to retain and enjoy any kind of property, real or personal, on condition that it legally belonged to the holy see. Similarly, the ministers who had bound themselves at the chapter joined the queue for dispensations from the observance of the Martinian constitutions. This shameful spectacle punctured John of Capistrano's hopes for reconciliation and reform.[32] Thereafter some form of partition was inevitable, although on 1 March 1439 Pope Eugene IV instructed Bernardine and Albert da Sarteano to pacify an Observant who was agitating for a division in the order.[33]

Ut sacra *and the ground rules for parallel communities*

The Conventuals' reluctance to embrace radical reform was accompanied by resentment at the measure of independence enjoyed by the Observants; renewal occupied a lower place on their agenda. The ruling of the council of Constance was regarded as a pivotal moment in the history of the Observants. The Conventuals perceived it as a threat and spent a disproportionate amount of time seeking its repeal. Led by the minister general, they made another unsuccessful effort at the council of Basle in 1435.[34] As on earlier occasions, the pope refused to accede to their request. *Ut sacra ordinis minorum religio* was issued by Pope Eugene IV in 1446;[35] a weighty factor in the background to the bull was the prestige and widespread influence of Bernardine of Siena and John of Capistrano, particularly at the papal court from the later 1420s. Despite the charges of heresy brought by Augustinian friars and the Dominicans, Bernardine was ably assisted by John of Capistrano. He was vindicated and continued to propagate devotion to the holy name. Invited to deliver a series of sermons in St Peter's basilica, his reputation was enhanced and this led to offers of bishoprics, beginning with Siena in 1427.[36] Bernardine and John of Capistrano worked closely with the pope on a number of fronts and enjoyed his confidence and favour. Together with Albert da Sarte-

[32] *BF*, VII, nn. 1892, 1893, pp. 737–9, Glassberger, *Chronica*, p. 290.

[33] Bughetti, 'Documenta inedita de S. Bernardino Senensi', pp. 490–1.

[34] Glassberger, *Chronica*, pp. 293–8, C. Schmitt, 'La Réforme de l'observance discutée au concile de Bâle', *AFH* 83 (1990), pp. 369–404 and 84 (1991), pp. 3–50.

[35] Variant dates of 11 January, 22 June and 23 July 1446 are given by Luke Wadding, Nicholas Glassberger and the editor of *Bullarium Franciscanum*.

[36] Piana, 'I processi', XXIV, no. 3, XXIX, no. 3, pp. 414, 427, 428. Offers from Ferrara, Milan, Urbino and other cities were declined.

ano and James of the Marches, they were important figures in the promotion of papal policies. John's indefatigable ministry against heretics, whether among the *fraticelli de opinione* or bodies outside the Church, had made him an indispensable ally of Popes Martin V and Eugene IV. The papal registers for this period chart the number of new foundations made by the Observants in different provinces. Licences for such new friaries were issued on 14, 16 and 18 March 1444, 24 October 1444, 19 January 1445, 23 April 1445 and 9 February 1446.[37] There is no comparable evidence of expansion on the part of the Conventuals.

The death of William de Casale on 22 February 1442 gave Eugene one last opportunity to intervene, just as Pope Martin V had done at Assisi twelve years earlier. He believed that the order's unity could be saved only through the election of Albert da Sarteano. He made known his support for the candidacy of Albert, whom he appointed as vicar general on 1 September 1442 for the reform of the order in the provinces north of the Alps. He invested Albert with special responsibility for the forthcoming general chapter at Padua.[38] During the chapter the Conventuals showed that they did not share the papal confidence. They ejected Albert from the hall and elected Anthony Rusconi, the minister provincial of Milan. This show of defiance cost them dearly and convinced Eugene that the order could not survive in its present form. A greater autonomy was required by the Observants in order to safeguard their ideals and the pope was disposed to confer this. To that end he confirmed the minister general's letter which instituted vicars general for the Observants on 1 August 1443.[39]

The growing ascendancy of the Observants was demonstrated by a special mark of favour, signalling papal approval. Aracoeli was the traditional home of the general curia on the Capitol, a church closely associated with the rich tradition of the order and the scene of general chapters. Pope Eugene IV entrusted this church to the Observants; *Ad ea* of 6 January 1445 required the departure of the Conventuals and the installation of the Observants; Mariano of Florence adds that the church was entrusted to John of Capistrano.[40] The Conventuals later established themselves at the ancient basilica of Santi Apostoli in 1463, thanks to Cardinal John Bessarion. Although Pope Eugene IV became aware of strong opposition to his plans, he wrote to the two vicars general of the Observants on 31 October 1445. He reminded them that their term of office would end in the following summer and instructed them to convene the friars in chapter for the election of a vicar general for Italy and one for beyond the Alps.[41] He issued *Ut sacra* the following year.

[37]   *BF*, n.s., I, nn. 767, 771, 772, 823, 858, 905, 962, pp. 361–2, 363–4, 387, 410–11, 440, 472.
[38]   Ibid., nn. 605–6, 614, pp. 284–6, 289–91.
[39]   Glassberger, *Chronica*, pp. 307–8. *BF*, n.s.,I, no. 705, pp. 332–4.
[40]   Ibid., nn. 846–7, pp. 398–9. Directio periodici, p. 123.
[41]   *BF*, n.s. I, no. 948, p. 466.

John of Capistrano and John de Maubert were provided as the vicars general. The election of the vicars was to be determined by the Observants at their chapters and the minister general was obliged to confirm the decision within three days. The office of vicar general was perceived as a permanent one, which could not be undermined by the machinations of the Conventuals. The machinery of Observant government was installed and regulated by provincial and general chapters. Eugene convened the chapter of the Observants to be held at Aracoeli and was present for the meeting, a clear indication of his preference for the Observant cause.[42] The pope reminded the minister general, Anthony Rusconi, not to interfere in affairs of the Observants, except in matters which had been agreed at Siena.[43] The Conventuals held their general chapter at Montpellier and this was a less important event.

One exception to the triumphal march of the Observants was the outlook of St Colette of Corbie (1381–1447), a Poor Clare and the founder of the Colettan reform which began in France and led to the renewal of some communities of friars and the foundation of others.[44] She was in correspondence with William de Casale, who was supportive of her aims for reform.[45] At the instigation of her confessor, Henry of Baume, who had previously been at Mirebeau, Colette was unwavering in her determination that her renewal should remain outside the jurisdiction of the Observants. She favoured a connection with the reformed Conventuals and obedience to the ministers. The Colettans lived side by side with the Observants and relations were sometimes strained; there were disputes as early as 1427.[46] Between 1443 and 1446 John de Maubert, vicar general for the northern provinces, endeavoured to bring the Colettans under the jurisdiction of the Observant vicars. He informed Peter of Vaux, Colette's confessor, of his desire to bring the two branches of the reform together before his death, although he recognised that there were some personal animosities in many cities.[47] The Observants of France and the Colettans had grown in parallel between 1412 and 1446 and made their own foundations. What John de Maubert had hoped to achieve by persuasion was imposed by Pope Eugene IV's *Dum praeclara merita* on 9 February 1447.[48] Eugene's death gave the Colettans an opportunity to reassert their desire to live under obedience to the minister general.[49]

[42] Glassberger, *Chronica*, pp. 316–17, *BF*, n.s. 1, no. 1007, pp. 497–500.

[43] *BF*, n.s. 1, nn. 1, no. 994, pp. 489–90.

[44] Nimmo, *Reform and Division in the Franciscan Order*, pp. 443–51.

[45] U. d'Alençon, 'Lettres inédites de Guillaume de Casal à Sainte Colette de Corbie et notes pour la biographie de cette Sainte', *Études franciscaines* 19 (1908), pp. 460–81, 668–91, and 'Documents sur la réforme de Ste. Colette en France', *AFH* 2 (1909), pp. 447–56, 600–12 and 3 (1910), pp. 82–97.

[46] H. Lippens, 'Deux épisodes du litige séculaire entre les Clarisses-Colettines et les Pères Observants au sujet de leurs privilèges respectifs (XVe et XVI s)', *AFH* 41 (1948), pp. 282–95.

[47] Richards, 'The Conflict', pp. 263–81, J. Goyens, 'Trois lettres inédites de Fr. Jean Maubert, vicaire général des observants ultramontains a Fr. Pierre da Xaux', *AFH* 5 (1912), pp. 85–8.

[48] *BF*, n.s. 1, no. 1046, pp. 526–7.

[49] Richards, 'The Conflict', pp. 267–8.

Just as the friars of the 1240s and 1250s saw the order evolve and develop in ways unforeseen by the founder and first friars, the Observants were not circumscribed by the eremitical experiences of Brugliano. The permissions in favour of the reformers envisaged a form of life suitable for a few men intent on observing the Rule literally. There seems to have been no expectation that this would remain anything other than a small body of fervent and zealous men possessed of a tender conscience in matters pertaining to the Rule and constitutions. John de Valle and Paoluccio dei Trinci da Foligno undoubtedly reflected on the fate of the early Spirituals. This prompted them to disarm potential critics by co-operating with the ministers; this was the kernel of the reform of Brugliano and it was perceived a *sine qua non* for progress. The modest increase in numbers from the 1370s seemed to be containable, offering no threat to the unity of the order.

The Observant family was gradually transformed from a relatively small number of friars to a sizeable cohort of men determined to rekindle the Franciscan flame. While Bernardine of Siena and John of Capistrano continued to foster good relations with the minister general and the local minister provincials, they were *de facto* leaders of a large number of men spreading throughout Italy. Foundations followed in the wake of the preaching tours and they produced disciples who attained fame as preachers of high renown. The city was the natural location for their sermons and this focus re-established friaries in urban centres. Moreover, there were separate shoots of reform in France and Spain, where the friars were successful in obtaining a measure of independence from the ministers. Exemptions were granted to the reformers who wished to safeguard their vision against the Conventuals, who were deeply perturbed by the prospect of division.

The frustrations and suspicions experienced in France and Spain demanded a solution: reform or the acceptance of the phenomenon of the Observants. Moreover, moral leadership of the order was draining from the Conventuals. The Observants were markedly different; they were zealous and conspicuously poor. The combined effects of the steady growth in the number of Observant convents and the remarkable impact of the preaching of Bernardine of Siena and John of Capistrano posed an administrative headache. Ministers could no longer appeal to unenforceable constitutions. By the 1440s they could not dismiss the Observants as misguided and theologically suspect. The reformers could not be swatted aside, the fate of Gentile da Spoleto. The growth in the number of reformers and the transfiliation of friaries left the ministers with little option but to reform the order.

Ut sacra divided the Observants from the Conventuals and gave the minister general the token approval of the vicars general. It caused resentment, bitterness and a sense of apprehension.[50] Raphael Huber believed that *Ut*

---

[50] C. Piana, 'Lettera inedita di S. Bernardino da Siena ed altra corrispondenza per la storia del pulpito di S. Petronio a Bologna nel' 400', *AFH* 47 (1954), p. 54–87 at 62–4.

sacra and the first general chapter of the Observants in 1446 at Araceoli made the division of the order inevitable.[51] The bull confirmed that the order could no longer remain as a single family. The order had survived many crises in its history of almost 240 years. All these storms had been weathered. The friars had regrouped and resumed their traditional ministries. The unity of the order under the authority of the minister general was envisaged by St Francis and approved by Pope Honorius III. *Ut sacra* inaugurated a new era and recognised the differences between the two groups of friars. Its solution caused heartache, paving the way for the emergence of two orders which would develop along their own lines, as the last chapter will indicate.

---

[51] R. M. Huber, *A Documented History of the Franciscan Order (1182–1517)* (Milwaukee, 1944), p. 369.

CHAPTER NINETEEN

Observants and Conventuals, 1420–1456

Thus in 1446 ... the Franciscans ... divided into two communities, parallel to, and independent of, one other.

Duncan Nimmo[1]

The consolidation of the Observant movement

The Observants enjoyed papal favour and began to promulgate provincial statutes from 1448.[2] Their leaders, Albert da Sarteano (†1450), John of Capistrano (†1456) and James of the Marches (†1476), were influential figures, whose sermons attracted large audiences; they were connected with the foundation of new communities.[3] Unlike Bernardine, all three travelled to other countries in response to the needs of the Church and the reform. Their growing influence was vital for the implantation of the reform on Italian soil and beyond it. They made the Italian movement one of the wonders of fifteenth-century Europe.[4] The preaching of the Observant friars was instrumental in making peace in cities, several of which enthusiastically sought their assistance.[5] The disciples of the four pillars of the Observance became illustrious preachers and took positions of leadership in the reform movement in the second half of the century. Matthew d'Agrigento, a celebrated preacher, was a leader of the reform in Sicily in the 1420s, whose ministry was praised by Bernardine, his master.[6] Michael da Carcano da Milano's vocation was associated with a sermon delivered by Albert da Sarteano in the piazza

---

[1] Nimmo, *Reform and Division in the Franciscan Order*, p. 634.

[2] L. Oliger, 'Statuta observantium provinciae S. Angeli in Apulia a. 1448 et tabula congregationis observantium Cismontanorum a. 1467', *AFH* 8 (1915), pp. 92–105. M. Bihl, 'Statuta generalia observantium Ultramontanorum an. 1451 Barcinonae condita. Eorum textus editur; de eorum methodo, indole etc. disseritur ... (subditur eorumdem index specialis)', *AFH* 38 (1945), pp. 106–97, M. Bihl, 'Statuta provincialia fr. minorum observantium Thusciae ann. 1457 et 1518', *AFH* 8 (1915), pp. 146–88.

[3] For example, *BF*, n.s. 1, nn. 246, 248, pp. 114–16. James was instituted as an inquisitor in Hungary and Austria on 22 August 1436. Three days later he was licensed to receive two houses in Bohemia, three in Hungary and three in Austria.

[4] Nimmo, 'The Genesis of the Observance', p. 131.

[5] Polecritti, *Preaching Peace in Renaissance Italy*, p. 4.

[6] D'Alatri, 'Gli insediamenti osservanti in Sicilia nel corso del quattrocento', pp. 42–3. Bernardino da Siena, *Prediche volgari sul Campo di Siena 1427*, p. 157.

of Milan cathedral in 1440. He preached in several cities of Italy, beginning with his Lenten sermons in his native Milan.[7] One of the most gifted preachers of the reform was Robert of Lecce, who was dubbed a second St Paul.[8] John of Capistrano communicated with Observants in Spain and Burgundy.[9] He laboured in Austria, Bohemia, Germany, Hungary and Poland. The son of a soldier, he was a judge before he was drawn to the reform when it was still in its infancy. The link between the foundations of the Observant reform at Brugliano and its flowering in the fifteenth century is recorded by Mariano of Florence, who unites John de Stroncone and John of Capistrano in 1414. The pioneer of the Observant movement received into the reform a man who would be a towering figure, an ardent reformer and an outstanding preacher.[10]

John of Capistrano was entrusted with a position of leadership and on 9 September 1422 he and other friars were licensed to receive five new friaries in the province of Abruzzo.[11] Similar permissions were given by Popes Eugene IV and Nicholas V between 13 October 1435 and 4 May 1453.[12] The making of peace between cities was a salient feature in his ministry. For instance, he effected a reconciliation between Ortona and Lanciano in 1427.[13] His preaching was associated with the reinvigoration of the order. Enea Piccolomini, the future Pope Pius II (1458–64), prevailed upon Pope Nicholas V (1447–55) to send John to Germany to revitalise the order. He later heard John preaching at Vienna in 1451.[14] John was soon drafted into the campaign against the *fraticelli de opinione*; Pope Martin V granted him

[7] P. M. Sevesi, 'Il Beato Michele da Carcano da Milano O.F.M.', *AFH* 3 (1910), pp. 448–63, 633–63, and 4 (1911), pp. 24–49, 456–81.

[8] *Directio periodici*, p. 125, expresses the reformers' sense of betrayal on account of his defection to the Conventuals in 1452. Robert's integrity and vanity were questioned and the quest for high office was presented as one of the reasons for his decision to throw in his lot with the Conventuals. Relations were undoubtedly exacerbated by his actions against the Observants, particularly his moves to secure the repeal of *Ut sacra*. Cf. O. V. Ravaioli, 'Testimonianze della predicazione di Roberto da Lecce a Padova', in *Predicazione francecana e societa veneta nel quattrocento: committenza, ascolto, ricezione: Atti del II Convegno internazionale di studi francescani, Padova, 26-7-28 marzo 1987*, Centro studi Antoniani, XVI (Padua, 1995), pp. 185–220.

[9] H. Lippens, 'Saint Jean de Capistran en mission aux États Bourguignons, 1442–1143. Essai de reconstitution de ses voyages et negociations a l'aide de documents inedits', *AFH* 35 (1942), pp. 113–42, 242–95.

[10] *Directio periodici*, p. 706.

[11] *BF*, VII, no. 1534, pp. 576–7. Records of John's sermons are less well preserved than those of Bernardine. A. Chiappini, 'La produzione letteraria di S. Giovanni da Capestrano', *MF* 25 (1925), pp. 54–103.

[12] *BF*, n.s. I, nn. 195, 716, 726, 727, 843, 858, 1322, 1325, 1337, 1554, 1600, 1658, pp. 95–6, 340–1, 346, 396–7, 410, 675–6, 677, 686–7, 775–6, 798–9, 824–5.

[13] H. D'Agostino, 'Instrumentum pacis a S. Ioanne Capistranensi inter Ortonenses et Lancianenses conciliatae, 1427', *AFH* 17 (1924), pp. 219–36. A. Sacchetti Sassetti, 'Giacomo della Marca paciere a Rieti', *AFH* 50 (1957), pp. 75–82.

[14] Piccolomini, *I Commentarii*, I, c. 20, pp. 108–9.

the faculty of preaching against them on 27 May 1427.[15] Pope Eugene IV gave him a commission to extirpate that heresy on 1 May 1432. A similar directive was issued on 3 July 1447.[16] John was appointed to the inquisition at Venice on 9 August 1437.[17] He was also employed on diplomatic business for the pope and undertook journeys to Armenia, Naples and the Holy Land. Shortly after the decisive battle for the defence at Belgrade he endeavoured to rouse Christendom in response to the fall of Constantinople on 29 May 1453. Following the successful battle for the defence of Hungary and western Europe he died at Ilok on 23 October 1456.

As a lawyer John stressed the vow of obedience and was critical of members of the reform who exalted their own views above those of the papal interpretations of the Rule. He shared common ground with earlier commentators on the Rule who accepted the papacy's right to interpret the Rule and the order's place in the Church. In 1431 when Philip Berbegal, a Spanish Observant, asserted the supremacy of the Rule over those who wished to gloss it, John produced his own authoritative commentary. The Rule, he maintained, was not sacrosanct. It was derived from the Church, not *vice versa*. He stressed that the founder promised obedience and reverence to the pope and his successors. Thus, it was the pope who approved the Rule. Ordained friars were bound to the recitation of the Divine Office and they required episcopal permission for their sermons. The office of cardinal protector was instituted for the orthodoxy of the order.[18] Nicholas of Osimo, a minister provincial, compiled an exposition of the Rule in 1440, summarising anew the friars' vocation. The chapters of the Rule were each glossed in their turn. Mention was made of the papal declarations regarding the Rule, especially those issued by Nicholas III and Clement V. This was an explanation of the Observant interpretation of the Rule, especially in such matters as poverty, the possession of money and the use of the alms given to the friars.[19]

An element in the polemical exchanges between the Observants and Conventuals was that the former lacked an intellectual rigour. Mindful of these allegations, Bernardine of Siena established a school of theology for the friars at Perugia in 1440. John of Capistrano sent out a circular letter in 1444, promoting theological study. The first sermon on study opens in a traditional way with a quotation from James 1.17 regarding the divine source of all gifts. He argued against the zealots who regarded the Rule and study

[15] *BF*, VII, no. 1710, pp. 653–4. Cf. L. Oliger, 'De Dialogo contra fraticellos S. Iacobi de Marchia', *AFH* 4 (1911), pp. 3–23.

[16] *BF*, n.s. 1, nn. 63, 1076, pp. 39, 544.

[17] *BF*, n.s. 1, no. 311, pp. 145–6.

[18] L. Oliger, 'Documenta inedita ad historiam fraticellorum spectantia', *AFH* 3 (1910), pp. 253–79, 505–29, 680–99, 4 (1911), pp. 3–23, 688–712, 5 (1912), pp. 74–84, and 6 (1913), pp. 267–90, 515–30, 710–47 at 716–20, for a partial transcription of the letter.

[19] A. Wilmart, 'Le Commentaire de Nicolas d'Osimo sur la regle de saint François', *Analecta Reginensia*, Studi e testi, LIX (Rome, 1933), pp. 301–10.

as incompatible. The link between study and the path to sanctification was reinforced through a lengthy quotation from the penultimate section of St Bonaventure's prologue to the *Breviloquium*. Clerics were informed that a threefold knowledge was necessary for the exercise of their office – an immersion in the Scriptures, secular literature and arts. Friars were reminded that St Francis authorised St Anthony to embark upon theological study for the benefit of the friars. John attested that it was the intention of Pope Eugene IV and his own that suitable friars should be appointed to give themselves to theological study.[20]

John's views were reinforced by James of the March's sermon, which may have been preached at the general chapter at Florence in 1449.[21] Five years earlier James had founded a substantial library of more than 180 volumes close to Monteprandone, his native city. This fine collection of manuscripts displayed the reformers' educational credentials. The first catalogue was drawn up on 15 June 1444 and the second two years later. The customary biblical and patristic texts were present. Scholastic theology was represented by Anselm, Bernard of Clairvaux, Peter Lombard, Richard of St Victor, Pope Innocent III and Peter of Tarantasia, Thomas Aquinas, Nicholas Trivet, Gregory of Rimini and Nicholas of Lyra. Franciscan authors included Alexander of Hales, Jean de la Rochelle, Bonaventure, Jacopone da Todi, John of Wales, John Duns Scotus, Alexander of Alexandria, Hugh of Newcastle, Francis of Meyronnes, Francis of Rimini and Astesano da Asti. There were several volumes of canon law, including the decretals and their glosses and the writings of Raymund of Pennafort and Ostiensis. The collection also included works of poetry and classical philosophy. James had purchased some of the volumes and copied others by hand.[22]

The Observant reform reached Ireland and houses were formed in several Gaelic areas. A vicariate was established in 1460, though there were earlier currents of reform. In addition to the new foundations after that date, more than half of the Conventual houses joined the Observant family.[23] In the same decade the new movement reached Scotland. Pope Pius II wrote to the vicar general north of the Alps on 9 June 1463 and commented on the devotion of Queen Mary of Gueldres, widow of James II, and the people, who had requested the introduction of the Observants. The queen was credited with the Observants' introduction, as her grandson, James IV, would later affirm. The vicar general was licensed to erect, found and build three or four friaries

[20] A. Chiappini, 'S. Iohannis de Capistrano sermones duo ad studentes et epistola circularis de studio promovendo inter observantes', *AFH* 11 (1918), pp. 97–131 at 104, 116–17, 124, 128–31.

[21] N. Dal-Gal, 'Sermo S. Iacobi de Marchia: De excellentia ordinis S. Francisci (ex codice autographo)', *AFH* 4 (1911), pp. 303–13.

[22] G. Pagnani, 'Alcuni codici della libreria di S. Giacomo della Marca scoperti recentemente', *AFH* 45 (1952), pp. 171–92, and xlviii (1955), pp. 131–46, D. Pacetti, 'La libreria di San Bernardino da Siena e le sue vicende attraverso cinque secoli', *StF* 62 (1965), pp. 3–43.

[23] Cf. Ó Clabaigh, *The Franciscans in Ireland*.

there and receive two or three of the friaries maintained by the Conventuals.[24] In contrast to the vigorous developments in neighbouring Ireland and Scotland, the reformers did not reach England until 1482. Pope Sixtus IV, a Conventual, acceded to the request of King Edward IV and on 4 January 1481 authorised the foundation at Greenwich.[25] Historians have attributed the late arrival of the Observants to the high levels of communal discipline and good conduct of the Conventuals, the only members of the order in England. Another factor was the crown's wish to impress the Spanish royal family with its reforming credentials by introducing the Observant reform to England.[26]

The English province of the Friars Minor Conventual

Between 1420 and 1456 the friars of England exercised their traditional apostolates, which they seem to have carried out in a satisfactory manner. No new foundations had been made since the friary at Aylesbury in 1387. While the number of friars was smaller than it had been during the thirteenth and early fourteenth centuries, the population remained steady and in the second half of the fifteenth century the registers of ordinations imply a measure of vitality and new energy in some custodies.[27] No friaries were suppressed and the conventual range of buildings were not transferred to any other order. Cries for reform were few. The once rich archives and ample libraries of the province did not survive the religious and political revolution of the sixteenth century and this robs historians of fuller details.

Roger Dowe's term as minister provincial ended in controversy and there were some disturbances, which the extant records do not explain. He was removed from office by the minister general on 1 October 1431. Hugh David and John Wynchilse, proctors of the order at Rome, were appointed as vicars of the province and were instructed to summon Roger and certain

---

[24] *BF*, n.s. 2, no. 1117, p. 578, I. B. Cowan and D. E. Easson, eds., *Medieval Religious Houses Scotland*, 2nd edn (London, 1957, 1976), p. 129.

[25] *BF*, n.s. 3, no. 1389, pp. 696–7, A. G. Little, 'Introduction of the Observant Friars into England', *Proceedings of the British Academy* 10 (1921–3), pp. 455–71, A. G. Little, 'Introduction of the Observant Friars into England: A Bull of Alexander VI', *Proceedings of the British Academy* 27 (1941), pp. 155–66, A. R. Martin, 'The Grey Friars of Greenwich', *The Archaeological Journal* 80 (1923), pp. 81–114.

[26] K. D. Brown, 'Wolsey and Ecclesiastical Order: The Case of the Franciscan Observants', in *Cardinal Wolsey: Church, State and Art*, ed. S. J. Gunn and P. G. Lindley (Cambridge, 1991), pp. 219–38 at 223. He comments that the English Observance was overwhelmingly an early Tudor creation, and that Henry VII's role in securing the transfer of the three former Conventual friaries in 1499 and the foundation of the friary at Richmond represented his attempt to imitate the Cisnerian reform movement of contemporary Spain.

[27] M. Robson, 'The Grey Friars in York, c. 1450–1530', *The Religious Orders in Pre-Reformation England*, Studies in the History of Medieval Religion, XVIII, ed. J. G. Clark (Woodbridge, 2002), pp. 109–19.

friars who would confirm or annul his removal from office.[28] One sign of some relaxation of Conventual discipline is the papal dispensation to hold benefices, although it is unclear whether all the recipients found benefices. George Courtenay, John Haxay, Robert Mersey and Thomas Joyes obtained licences between 24 September 1440 and 24 April 1443 respectively; in some instances the applications were supported by members of the aristocracy such as the duke of Gloucester in whose service Thomes Joyes had spent many years.[29] Further licences were issued in the 1450s, including Thomas Cliffe who was dispensed on 30 November 1453. He was admitted to the prebendal church of Swarkiston on 14 April 1486 in the archdeaconry of Derby, but he resigned before 7 August 1487.[30] An example of a shorter tenure is provided by Thomas de Richmond, who received a dispensation on 25 February 1457. He was presented as rector of the parish of St Cuthbert in Peasholme, York, on 24 December of that year. He was described as being from the convent of the order of friars minor of the city of York when he was appointed as the archbishop's penitentiary in the county town and as a confessor in the archdeaconry of York on 16 August 1458.[31]

One gauge of the order's fidelity was its witness to evangelical poverty. In the 1390s William Woodford attested that few friaries of the English province were not in debt.[32] Wills constituted a major source of financial support for the friars and were a barometer on their lifestyle. Benefactors included members of the aristocracy, prelates, parochial clergy and the local community. The foreign merchants and members of the nobility who brought to the country a strong affection for the order are represented by Lucia Visconti, countess of Kent and widow of Edmund de Holland. She left a thousand crowns to each mendicant house in London in her will of 31 May 1424. The same sum was left to the Poor Clares of Aldgate and the mendicant houses of Milan.[33] The *custos* and *subcustos* of London received 20s. each from Hugh Halsham, a soldier who had fought at Agincourt, whose will was drawn up on 7 February 1441. Each doctor of theology in the friary received one mark (13s. 4d.) and each priest half a mark. Deacons received quarter of a mark and every other member of the community attending his funeral was given an eighth of a mark, including subdeacons and acolytes.[34]

[28]   *BF*, n.s. 1, no. 27, pp. 20–1.
[29]   *Calendar of Entries in the Papal Registers relating to Great Britain and Ireland, Papal Letters*, IX, ed. J. A. Tremlow (London, 1912), pp. 103, 264, 271, 410. *BF*, n.s. 1, nn. 492, 601, 641, 662, pp. 238, 283, 303, 312.
[30]   *BF*, n.s. 1, no. 1717, p. 851. Lichfield Record Office, B/A/1/12, fols. 75r, 77r.
[31]   *BF*, n.s. 2, no. 256, p. 134, BIHR, Register 20, fols. 10v, 199r.
[32]   Doyle, 'William Woodford', p. 178: *nam pauci sunt conventus in Anglia de Ordine Minorum qui non sunt indebtitati et pauperes, pecuniam non habentes.*
[33]   *The Register of Henry Chichele, Archbishop of Canterbury 1414–1443*, II, ed. E. F. Jacob, 4 vols, Canterbury and York Society, XLII, XLV, XLVI, XLVII (Oxford, 1937, 1943, 1945, 1947), pp. 278–83.
[34]   Ibid., pp. 608–9.

The sum of £20 was given to the Greyfriars of Dorchester by Humphrey Stafford, knight of Hoke in Dorset, on 4 December 1442. Half of the money was for the endowment of a daily Mass at the altar of the Holy Trinity for the benefit of himself and his brother, John, the bishop of Bath and Wells. Ralph Hoby, a friar and theologian, received four marks. Although Sir Humphrey was buried in the Benedictine abbey of Abbotsbury, Dorset, he donated an organ to his chapel, probably the chapel of Holy Trinity, in the friary in return for prayers for himself, his forebears, heirs and friends.[35] Joan, widow of Sir Thomas Fooge, requested burial beside her husband in Canterbury cathedral. She made gifts to the city's mendicants, including the sum of 20s. for the guardian and community of the Greyfriars; each friar was given an additional sum of 12d. when this will was compiled on 20 May 1420.[36] The register of Henry Chichele, archbishop of Canterbury (1414–43), contains gifts to only four named friars. Although relatively few friars' names recur three or four times in the extant wills in other dioceses, there is nothing comparable to the volume of bequests given to the friars of Bologna in the thirteenth century; the names of some friars appear in the more than one edited will.

Limiters solicited alms throughout the territory of each convent, and there are instances of their being robbed. Richard Wintworth on 21 December 1447 left quarter of a mark to the mendicant limiters visiting Everton, Nottinghamshire.[37] The alms associated with suffrages offer a welcome insight into the influence and levels of observance among the friars. Revenue associated with the friars' churches came in the form of regular collections, money for candles, stipends for Masses, deposits or payments in full from those who wished to be interred in the conventual church or cemetery. Fees of varying sizes were paid by those who invited friars to preach on special occasions and by religious houses and private households which engaged a friar as confessor. The other evidence, however, is more fragmentary. Friars visited the homes of the gentry and the aristocracy, as extant account books reveal.[38] Monastic houses continued to provide the friars with another regular supply of alms. Friars begged alms from the monasteries within their *limitatio*.[39] Wheat was provided for the Greyfriars of Richmond between 1446 and 1458 by the Cistercians of Fountains Abbey, which recorded a payment of 5s. to the order in 1456/7.[40]

---

[35] Ibid., pp. 620–4.

[36] Ibid., pp. 202–3.

[37] BIHR, Probate Register 2, fol. 198rv.

[38] Cf. F. Swabey, *Medieval Gentlewoman: Life in a Widow's Household in the Later Middle Ages* (Stroud, Gloucestershire, 1999). National Archives, C47/4/8b, fols. 3r–26v, for an example from the early fifteenth century.

[39] *Two Compotus Rolls of Saint Augustine's Abbey, Bristol* (for 1491–2 and 1511–12), ed. G. Beachcroft and A. Sabin, Bristol Record Society' Publications, IX (Bristol, 1938), p. 73.

[40] *Memorials of the Abbey of St. Mary of Fountains*, III, ed. J. T. Fowler, Surtees Society, CXXX

The friars opened to the neighbours various degrees of spiritual kinship with the order. Through letters of fraternity and other forms of association the laity enjoyed some of the friars' spiritual privileges in the form of intercession.[41] John Tentirden, citizen and ironmonger of London, left alms to the London Greyfriars in his will of 1458.[42] Annual subscriptions to the friary are implied by the funds collected by Boccaccio's Friar Cipolla. The perception that the friars were poor persisted until the dissolution. Innumerable testators frequently listed the friars in conjunction with the paupers and prisoners. The recognition of the friars' poverty prompted the city council of York on 21 January 1478 to award them an annual pension of 20s., which was still being paid on the eve of the suppression of the friary in September 1538.[43] Evidence concerning the friars' diet is in stark contrast to the image of the lax religious.[44]

Although many of the finest preachers of the fifteenth century belonged to the Observant wing of the order, the Conventuals' ranks included several fine exponents of the Word of God.[45] English friars preached at a variety of venues, from the cathedral to the parish church or chapel belonging to the local borough.[46] The friars' annual sermons in parish churches and chapels within their *limitatio* were mentioned by testators at Batley and Leeds on 23 July 1435 and on 27 June 1448 respectively.[47]

(Durham, 1918), pp. 19, 161.

[41] R. N. Swanson, 'Mendicants and Confraternity in Late Medieval England', *The Religious Orders in Pre-Reformation England*, pp. 121–41, H. Lippens, 'De Litteris confraternitatis apud Fratres Minores ab Ordinis initio ad annum usque 1517', *AFH* 32 (1939), pp. 49–88.

[42] A. G. Little, 'Franciscan Letters of Confraternity', *The Bodleian Library Record* 5 (1954–6), pp. 13–25, 19.

[43] *York Civic Records*, II, ed. A. Raine, Yorkshire Archaeological Society, Record Series, CIII (Wakefield, 1941), pp. 30–1, 33–4.

[44] Cf. P. L. Armitage, B. West *et al.* 'Faunal Evidence from a Late Medieval Garden Well of the Greyfriars, London', *Transactions of the London and Middlesex Archaeological Society* 36 (1985), pp. 107–36.

[45] Directio periodici, p. 710, under the year 1424.

[46] Cf. D. Gallo, 'Predicatori francescani nella cattedrale di Padova durante il quattrocento', in *Predicazione francecana e societa veneta nel quattrocento. Comitenza, ascolto, ricezione: Atti del II Convegno internazionale di studi francescani*, pp. 145–83, 174–80. Friars were accustomed to preach regularly in the cathedrals of Salisbury and Exeter. C. Wordsworth, *Ceremonies and Processions of the Cathedral Church of Salisbury* (Cambridge, 1901), p. 154, the *comperta in visitacione*, AD 1475: *Inspeximus quod xx sunt sermones numero, quorum novem computantur et assignantur ex consuetudine fratribus minoribus et predicatoribus*... N. Orme, *Exeter Cathedral – As it was 1050–1550* (Exeter, 1986), pp. 25, 106, n. 15. The Paston letters and papers disclose that John Brackley (†1464/5), a friar of Norwich and the confessor to Sir John Fastolf, preached at St Paul's Cathedral, London, and Norwich Cathedral priory. *Paston Letters and Papers of the Fifteenth Century*, ed. N. Davis, Early English Text Society, Supplementary Series 20–21, 2 vols (Oxford, 2004 [1971–6]), II, nn. 617, 635, 705, pp. 222, 240, 332. William Russell, guardian of the London Greyfriars, delivered a controversial sermon at St Paul's Cross, London, on 28 January 1425. *The Register of Henry Chichele*, III, pp. 104–5, 108, 110, 118–38, 141–2, 147, 151–7, 175–7. Cf. also 178–9, 181–2, 186, 193–4.

[47] R. B. Cook, 'Wills of Leeds and District', *Publications of the Thoresby Society* 22 (1915), pp. 235–64, 238–9. W. Brigg, 'Testamenta Leodiensia', *Publications of the Thoresby Society* 2 (1891), pp. 98–110 at 100–1.

Friars were invited to address special congregations, especially during Advent and Lent.[48] Throughout the later Middle Ages friars preached in the royal chapels, a practice which continued until the dissolution of the province in 1539. The crown's account books furnish details of a group of friars invited to preach at court. By the fifteenth century the friars invited to preach at court were generally drawn from the ranks of the Oxbridge theologians or senior officials of the English province.[49]

A special licence was extended to some friars to cross both the boundaries of their *limitatio* and custody as itinerant preachers. Margery Kempe attests that people used to follow William Melton from town to town for his homilies. His sermons on the passion moved her to tears in the church of St James, a chapel of ease of St Margaret, King's Lynn, around 1420.[50] A friar of this name was a famous preacher whose sermons recommended the Corpus Christi play to the citizens of York. He protested that some citizens and visitors for the festival joined in revelry, drunkenness, clamour, singing and other improprieties. They paid little attention to the divine offices of the day and they lost the benefit of the indulgences granted by Pope Urban IV. He persuaded the people that the play should be on one day and the procession on another so they might attend church.[51] A Friar Melton, a Franciscan, preached in Bury St Edmunds on the feast of St Ethelreda on the Sunday before the feast of St Michael.[52]

Melton's sermons on the decalogue, the Mother of God and divine mercy in 1430 and 1431 were entered in the sermon diary of Nicholas Philip, a friar associated with King's Lynn. This text reveals that its author was accustomed to preach in various parts of England between 1430 and 1436 and that he

---

[48] The monks of Westminster Abbey invited Robert Kyry to preach on Good Friday in 1450; two of Kyry's confrères preached there in the 1470s. B. Harvey, 'A Novice's Life at Westminster Abbey in the Century before the Dissolution', *The Religious Orders in Pre-Reformation England*, pp. 51–73 at 53n. Homilies by friars were also given there on Good Friday in 1474 and 1477 by William Goddard and an unnamed bachelor of theology.

[49] Thomas (or John) Kyry (Kery), John Fulford and Thomas Burton preached before Henry VI on the first three Sundays of Lent in 1442, that is, on 18 and 25 February and 4 March. National Archives, E 101/409/9, fol. 32v. William Grene, a bachelor of theology, preached an Easter sermon before the same king on 10 February 1448, the first Sunday of Lent. National Archives, E 101/410/1, fol. 23v. William Goddard and Thomas (John) Kyry (Kery), preached before the royal family on the first Sunday of Lent and on Palm Sunday in 1452, that is, 14 March and 18 April. National Archives, E 101/409/9, fol. 32v, E. 101/410, 6, fol. 34v. Goddard preached again on the second Sunday of Lent, 5 March 1452.

[50] *The Book of Margery Kempe*, ed. S. B. Meech, with notes by H. E. Allen, Early English Text Society, Ordinary Series 212 (Oxford, 1940), pp. 148–69, 321.

[51] *York Memorandum Book, II (1388–1493)*, ed. M. Sellars, Surtees Society CXXV (York, 1915), pp. 156–9.

[52] Only one of the sermons from this notebook was expressly attributed to this friar, although no subsequent authors are mentioned in the two-year cycle of sermons. R. L. Homan, 'Old and New Evidence of the Career of William Melton, O.F.M.', *FS* 49 (1989), pp. 25–33. Gonville and Caius College Library, Cambridge, MS 356, fol. 3.

collected materials for his sermons. He was at King's Lynn in 1432, where he did some writing. The text covers 177 folios and features sermons which were preached at Newcastle, Oxford and Lichfield. The homilies were prepared for the various Sundays and feast days of the liturgical year; additional sermons were prepared for synods, the dedication of churches, burials, processions and treated the decalogue. There were five sermons for Easter Sunday. While the vast majority of the sermons were preached to the laity, three were devoted to the visitation of friaries and two for the profession of novices. Nicholas Philip may have been associated with Friars Melton and Holbeche on their preaching tours. Bars of music appear in folio 90 and may reflect the role of the friars as minstrels, a term which their founder had applied to them more than two centuries earlier.[53] Music was a medium for the friars' message; two centuries earlier St Francis had depicted his disciples as the Lord's ministrels. Friars are credited with the spread of the Christmas carol in England, Italy and Spain.[54] An artistic reflection of their activities is a miniature of barefooted friar playing a guitar.[55]

[53] A. J. Fletcher, *Preaching, Politics and Poetry in Late-Medieval England* (Dublin, 1998), pp. 40–57, 45–6, 50–1.

[54] R. H. Robbins, 'The Earliest Carols and the Franciscans', *Modern Language Notes* 53 (1938), pp. 239–45, R. H. Robbins, 'Friar Herebert and the Carol', *Anglia*, 75 (1957), pp. 194–8.

[55] BL, MS Royal, 2 B. VII, fol. 177r, depicts a nun with a psalter and a Franciscan. Cf. D. L. Jeffrey, *The Early English Lyric and Franciscan Spirituality* (Lincoln, Nebraska, 1975).

CONCLUSION

This study began with the vision and ideals of one of the most attractive saints of the Middle Ages and it ends with his followers' bitter and painful division. The Observants and the Conventuals moved towards the formal and definitive separation which was effected by Leo X's *Ite vos* on 29 May 1517. The formation of parties representing groups of friars appears in the earliest hagiography and it mars the historiography of the order. These positions became more polarised. By the 1290s differences of opinion could no longer be held in check, no matter how much the general curia lauded the vow of obedience and the unity of the order. At a critical time the ministers were slow to comprehend that they, too, were accountable for their administration. They failed to grasp the reformers' aspirations and were prone to label them as troublesome and disobedient. They defaulted on the trust implicit in the solemn utterances of the vows by neglecting to establish and maintain a manner of life consonant with the tenets of the poor saint of Assisi. They consistently underestimated the growing strength of the Observants, who occupied the moral high ground increasingly in the 1430s and 1440s. The Observants' policies carried the day and led to Leo X's settlment in 1517. Nonetheless, the thirst for reform quickly manifested itself in the birth of the Capuchins (1525–9). New movements of reform appeared in the early twentieth century and others have emerged from the three main branches of the order. St Francis's ecumenical appeal spawned groups outside the Catholic Church. His imitation of the poor and naked Christ is as attractive today as it was in 1206. His voluntary poverty and abandonment to divine providence are challenging and offer an alternative to the restless quest for absolute security. Since the idyllic days of the first fraternity at Rivo Torto and then the Portiuncula the same vision has fuelled a succession of reform movements, whose fruits are conspicuous today.

SELECT BIBLIOGRAPHY

Manuscripts

Assisi, Biblioteca comune, MS 325
Cambridge
    Peterhouse Library, MS 223
    University Library, MS Ff.I.21
London
    BL, MS Cotton Galba, MS E XIV
    BL, Cotton Nero, MS C.VIII
    BL, Cotton Vespasian, MS B.XI
    BL, MS Royal 3.B.XII
    BL, MS Royal, 7.E.II
    BL, MS Add. 7966A
    BL, MS Add. 14251
    Corporation of London, Records Office, Letter Book M
    National Archives, E101/397/7
    National Archives, E 101/409/9
    National Archives, E 101/410/1
York
    BIHR, Probate Registers 1, 2, 5
    BIHR, Episcopal Register 10

Primary printed sources

Abate, G., 'Memoriali, statuti ed atti di capitoli generali dei fratri minori inediti dei secoli XIII e XIV', *MF* 33 (1933), pp. 320–36.
—— 'S. Rosa da Viterbo, Terziaria francescana (1233–1251), Fonti storiche della vita et loro revisione critica', *MF* 52 (1952), pp. 133–278.
Acta Franciscana e tabulariis Bononiensibus deprompta, ed. B. Giordani, Analecta Franciscana, IX (Quaracchi, Florence, 1927).
Alexander of Hales, *Summa fratris Alexandri studio et cura PP. Collegii S. Bonaventurae ad fidem codicum edita*, 6 vols (Quaracchi, Florence, 1924–1948, 1979).
Angela of Foligno, *Complete Works*, translated with an introduction by P. Lachance, Classics of Western Spirituality (New York, 1993).
Angelo da Clareno, 'Epistola excusatoria ad papam de falso impositis et fratrum calumniis', *ALKG*, I, pp. 521–33.
—— *Expositio super regulam fratrum minorum di Frate Angelo Clareno*, ed. G. Boccalli, Pubblicazioni della Biblioteca francescana, Chiesa Nuova-Assisi, VII (Assisi, 1994).
—— *Liber chronicarum sive tribulationum ordinis minorum di Frate Angelo Clareno*, ed. G. Boccali, Pubblicazioni della Biblioteca francescana, Chiesa Nuova-Assisi, 8 (Assisi, 1998).

S. Antonii Patavini, O. Min. doctoris evangelici Sermones dominicales et festivi ad fidem codicum recogniti, ed. B. Costa, L. Frasson, I. Luisetto, P. Marangon, 3 vols (Padua, 1979).

Beguin, B., *L'Anonyme de Pérouse: un temoin de la fraternité franciscaine primitive*, Textes franciscains (Paris, 1979).

Bernardine of Siena, *Le prediche volgari (Florence 1424)*, ed. C. Cannarozzi, 2 vols (Pistoia, 1934).

——*Le prediche volgari (Florence 1425)*, ed. C. Cannarozzi, 3 vols (Florence, 1940).

——*Le prediche volgari (Siena 1425)*, ed. C. Cannarozzi, 2 vols (Florence, 1958).

——*Prediche volgari sul Campo di Siena 1427*, ed. C. Delcorno, 2 vols (Milan, 1989).

——*S. Bernardini Senensis ordinis fratrum minorum opera omnia studio et cura PP. Collegii S. Bonaventurae ad fidem codicum edita*, 9 vols (Quaracchi, Florence, 1950–1965).

Bihl, M., 'Ordinationes a Benedicto XII pro fratribus minoribus promulgatae per bullam 28 Novembris 1336', *AFH* 30 (1938), pp. 309–90.

——'Statuta generalia ordinis edita in capitulo generali an. 1354 Assisii celebrato, communiter Farineriana appellata. (Editio critica et analytica)', *AFH* 35 (1942), pp. 35–112, 177–253.

——'Statuta generalia ordinis edita in capitulis generalibus celebratis Narbonae an. 1260, Assisii an. 1279 atque Parisiis an. 1292. (Editio critica et synoptica. Index specialis)', *AFH* 34 (1941), pp. 13–94, 284–358.

Bonaventure, *Doctoris Seraphici S. Bonaventurae S.R.E. episcopi cardinalis opera omnia edita studio et cura PP. Collegii a S. Bonaventura ad plurimos codices MSS emendata anecdotis aucta prolegomenis scholiis notisque illustrata*, 10 vols (Quaracchi, Florence, 1882–1902).

——*Sancti Bonaventurae Sermones dominicales*, ed. J. Bougerol, Bibliotheca Franciscana scholastica medii aevi, XXVII (Grottaferrata, Rome, 1977).

——*The Soul's Journey into God, The Tree of Life, The Life of St. Francis*, trans. and intr. E. Cousins, The Classics of Western Spirituality (New York, 1978).

——*St. Bonaventure's Writings concerning the Franciscan Order*, transl. and intr. D. Monti, Works of Saint Bonaventure (New York, 1994).

Bougerol, J. G., 'Sermons de maîtres franciscains du XIIIe siècle', *AFH* 81 (1988), pp. 17–49.

Bozon, Nicholas, *Nine Verse Sermons by Nicholas Bozon: The Art of the Anglo-Norman Poet and Preacher*, ed. B. J. Levy, Medium Aevum Monographs, New Series, XI (Oxford, 1981).

Callebaut, A., 'Le Sermon historique d'Eudes de Châteauroux à Paris, le 18 mars 1229. Autour de l'origine de la grève universitaire et de l'enseignement des mendicants', *AFH* 28 (1935), pp. 81–114.

Cenci, C., *Bibliotheca manuscripta ad Sacrum Conventum Assisiensem*, 2 vols (Assisi, 1981).

——'Costituzioni della provincia toscana tra i secoli XIII e XIV', *StF* 79 (1982), pp. 369–409, and 80 (1983), pp. 171–206.

——'De fratrum minorum constitutionibus praenarbonensibus', *AFH* 83 (1990), pp. 50–95.

——*Documentazione di vita assisana 1300–1530, I. 1300–1448*, SB, X (Grottaferrata, Rome, 1974).

——'Fra Francesco da Lendinara e la storia della provincia di S. Antonio tra la fine del s. XIV e l'inizio del s. XV', *AFH* 55 (1962), pp. 103–92.

Cenci, C., 'Vestigia constitutionum praenarbonensium', *AFH* 97 (2004), pp. 61–98.

Chiappini, A., 'S. Iohannis de Capistrano sermones duo ad studentes et epistola circularis de studio promovendo inter observantes', *AFH* 11 (1918), pp. 97–131.

Chronicon de Lanercost MCCI–MCCCXLVI, ed. J. Stevenson (Edinburgh, 1839).

Clyn, Fra John, and Thady Dowling, *The Annales of Ireland by Friar John Clyn of the Convent of the Friars Minor, Kilkenny, and Thady Dowling, Chancellor of Leighlin, together with the Annals of Ross*, ed. R. Butler (Dublin, 1839).

Dal-Gal, N., 'Sermo S. Iacobi de Marchia: De excellentia ordinis S. Francisci (ex codice autographo)', *AFH* 4 (1911), pp. 303–13.

Davy, M. M., *Les Sermons universitaires parisiens de 1230–1231*, Études de philosophie médiévale, XV (Paris, 1931).

Delorme, F. M., 'Diffinitones capituli generalis O.F.M. Narbonensis (1260)', *AFH* 3 (1910), pp. 491–504.

—— 'Les Cordeliers dans le Limousin aux XIIIe–XVe siècle', *AFH* 32 (1939), pp. 201–59 and 33 (1940), pp. 114–60.

Doelle, F., 'Sermo S. Iohannis de Capistrano O.F.M. ineditus de S. Bernardino Senensi O.F.M.', *AFH* 6 (1913), pp. 76–90.

Doucet, V., 'Angelus Clarinus, Ad Alvarum Pelagium, Apologia pro vita sua', *AFH* 39 (1946), pp. 63–200.

—— 'Le Sermon de Jacques de Padoue sur S. François (Paris 1345), et son témoignage sur Alexandre de Halès', *AFH* 44 (1951), pp. 471–76.

Doyle, E., 'William Woodford, O.F.M.: His Life and Works together with a Study and Edition of His *Responsiones contra Wiclevum et Lollardos*', *FS* 43 (1983), pp. 17–187.

Expositio quatuor magistrorum super regulam fratrum minorum (1241–1242), ed. L. Oliger, Storia e letteratura raccolta di studi e testi, XXX (Rome, 1950).

Faral, E., 'Les "Responsiones" de Guillaume de Saint-Amour', *Archives d'histoire doctrinale et littéraire du Moyen Age* 18 (1951), pp. 337–94.

Faloci-Pulignani, M., 'Il Beato Paoluccio Trinci da Foligno', *MF* 6 (1896), pp. 97–128.

Flood, D., 'John of Wales's *Commentary on the Franciscan Rule*', *FS* 60 (2002), pp. 93–138.

Fontes Francescani, ed. E. Mensetò, S. Brufani *et al.*, Medioevo francescano, Collana diretta da Enrico Menestò, Testi II (Assisi, 1995).

Gieben, S., 'Robert Grosseteste on Preaching, with the Edition of the Sermon "Ex rerum initiatarum" on Redemption', *CF* 37 (1967), pp. 100–41.

Giuliano da Spira, *Officio ritmico e Vita secunda*, ed. V. Gamboso, Fonti agiografiche antoniane, II (Padua, 1985).

Golubovich, G., *Biblioteca bio-bibliografica della Terra Santa e dell'oriente francescano*, 5 vols (Quaracchi, Florence, 1906–27).

Golubovich, H., 'Disputatio Latinorum et Graecorum seu relatio apocrisariorum Gregorii IX de gestis Nicaeae in Bithynia et Nymphaeae in Lydia 1234', *AFH* 12 (1919), pp. 418–70.

Goyens, J., 'Trois lettres inédites de Fr. Jean Maubert, vicaire général des observants ultramontains a Fr. Pierre da Xaux', *AFH* 5 (1912), pp. 85–8.

Guerrini, P., 'Gli statuti di una antica congregazione francescana di Brescia', *AFH* 1 (1908), pp. 544–68.

Henniges, D., 'Vita Sanctae Elisabeth, landgraviae Thuringiae, auctore anonymo, nunc primum in lucem edita', *AFH* 2 (1909), pp. 240–68.

Heysse, A., 'Ubertini da Casali opusculum "Super tribus sceleribus"', *AFH* 10 (1917), pp. 103–74.

Hugonis de Digna Declaratio in Regulam S. Francisci, ed. D. Flood, SB, XIV (Grotta-ferrata, Roma, 1979).

Iacopone da Todi, *Laude*, ed. F. Mancini, Scrittori d' Italia, CCLVII (Bari, 1974).

Il libro della Beata Angela da Foligno, ed. L. Thier and A. Calufetti (Grottaferrata, Rome, 1985).

Itinerarium Symonis Semeonis ab Hybernia ad Terram Sanctam, ed. M. Esposito, Scrip-tores Latini Hiberniae, IV (Dublin, 1960).

'Itinerarium Willelmi de Rubruc', *SF*, pp. 145–332.

Iunctae Bevegnatis, *Legenda de vita et mirculis Beatae Margaritae de Cortona*, ed. F. Iozzelli, Bibliotheca Franciscana ascetica medii aevi, XIII (Grottaferrata, Rome, 1997).

Jacopone da Todi, *The Lauds*, transl. S. and E. Hughes, The Classics of Western Spirituality (London, 1982).

Jean de la Rochelle, *Summa de anima*, ed. J. Bougerol (Paris, 1995).

John Duns Scotus, *Four Questions on Mary*, transl. and intr. A. B. Wolter (Santa Barbara, 1988).

Jordan of Giano, *Chronica Fratris Jordani*, ed. H. Boehmer, Collection d'études et de documents sur l'histoire religieuse et littéraire du Moyen Age, VI (Paris, 1908).

Legenda Latina Sanctae Clarae virginis Assisiensis, ed. G. Boccalli, Pubblicazioni della biblioteca francescana, Chiesa Nuova-Assisi, XI (Assisi, 2001).

Liber exemplorum ad usum predicantium, saeculo XIII compositus a quodam fratre minore Anglico de provincia Hiberniae, ed. A. G. Little, British Society of Franciscan Studies, I (Aberdeen, 1908).

Liber miraculorum e altri testi medievali, ed. V. Gamboso, Fonti agiografiche antoniane, V (Padua, 1997).

Libro delle nuove e strane e meravigliose cose. Volgarizzamento italiano del secolo XIV, dell'Itinerarium di Odorico da Pordenone Omin, ed. A. Andreose, Centro studi Anto-niani, XXXIII (Padua, 2000).

The Life of Saint Douceline Beguine of Provence, Library of Medieval Women, translated from the Occitan by K. Garay and M. Jeay (Woodbridge, 2001).

Little, A. G., 'Constitutiones provinciae Romanae, anni 1316', *AFH* 18 (1925), pp. 356–73.

—— 'Definitiones capitulorum generalium ordinis fratrum minorum, 1260–1282', *AFH* 7 (1914), pp. 676–82.

Marsh, Adam, *The Letters of Adam Marsh*, ed. and translated by Hugh Lawrence, 2 vols, Oxford Medieval Texts (Oxford, 2006).

McElrath, D., ed., *Franciscan Christology*, Franciscan Institute Publications, Franciscan Sources, no. I (New York, 1980).

Monumenta Franciscana, ed. J. S. Brewer and R. Howlett, 2 vols, RS, IV (London, 1858 and 1882).

Fra Niccolò da Poggibonsi, *Libro d'Oltramare (1346–1350)*, ed. A. Bacchi della Lega and B. Bagatti, Studium biblicum Franciscanum, II (Jerusalem, 1945).

Nicolaus Minorita, *Chronica. Documentation on Pope John XXII, Michael of Cesena and The Poverty of Christ with Summaries in English. A Source Book*, ed. G. Gál and D. Flood, The Franciscan Institute (New York, 1996).

Oliger, L., 'Liber exemplorum fratrum minorum saeculi XIII (excerpta e cod. Ottob. lat. 522)', *Antonianum* 2 (1927), pp. 203–76.

Oliger, L., 'Statuta observantium provinciae S. Angeli in Apulia a. 1448 et tabula congregationis observantium Cismontanorum a. 1467', *AFH* 8 (1915), pp. 92–105.

Pecham, Fra John, *Fratris Johannis Pecham quondam archiepiscopi Cantuariensis tractatus tres de paupertate*, ed. C. L. Kingsford, A. G. Little and F. Tocco, British Society of Franciscan Studies, II (Aberdeen 1910). Includes 'Tractatus contra Fratrem Robertum Kilwardby, O.P.', pp. 91–147, and 'Defensio fratrum mendicantium', pp. 148–91.

Peter Olivi's Rule Commentary, Edition and Presentation, ed. D. Flood, Veröffentlichungen des Instituts für europäische Geschichte Mainz, LXVII (Weisbaden, 1972).

Piana, C., 'I processi di canonizzazione su la vita di S. Bernardino da Siena', *AFH* 44 (1951), pp. 87–160, 383–435.

Pieper, L., 'A New Life of St. Elizabeth of Hungary: The Anonymous Franciscan', *AFH* 93 (2000), pp. 29–78.

Processus Bernardi Delitiosi: The Trial of Fr. Bernard Délicieux, 3 September – 8 December 1319, ed. A. Friedlander, Transactions of the American Philosophical Society, 86, pt. 1 (Philadelphia, 1996).

Robert Grosseteste, *De cessatione legalium*, ed. R. C. Dales and E. B. King, Auctores Britannici medii aevi, VII (London, 1986).

——*De decem mandatis*, ed. R. C. Dales and E. B. King, Auctores Britannici medii aevi, X (London, 1987).

——*Hexaëmeron*, ed. Dales and S. Gieben, Auctores Britannici medii aevi, VI (London, 1982).

——*Opera Roberti Grosseteste Lincolniensis*, I, ed. J. McEvoy, Corpus Christianorum, continuatio mediaevalis, CXXX (Turnhout, 1995).

——*Roberti Grosseteste episcopi quondam Lincolniensis Epistolae*, ed. H. R. Luard, RS, XXV (London, 1861).

——*Templum Dei*, edited from MS 27, Emmanuel College, Cambridge, by Joseph Goering and F. A. C. Mantello, Toronto Medieval Latin Texts (Toronto, 1984).

Rotolo, F., 'Il tratatto dei miracoli del B. Gerardo Cagnoli, O. Min. (1267–1342) di Fra Bartolomeo Albizzi, O. Min. (†1351)', *MF* 66 (1966), pp. 128–92.

——'La Leggenda del B. Gerardo Cagnoli, O. Min.(1267–1342) di Fra Bartolomeo Albizzi, O. Min. (†1351)', *MF* 57 (1957), pp. 367–446.

Registrum Anglie de libris doctorum et auctorum veterum, ed. R. H. and M. A. Rouse, Corpus of British Medieval Library Catalogues (London, 1991).

Sacrum commercium sancti Francisci cum domina Paupertate, ed. S. Brufani, Medioevo francescano, Collana diretta da Ernesto Menestò, Testi, I (Assisi, 1990).

Salimbene de Adam, *Cronica*, ed. G. Scalia, Scrittori d'Italia, CCXXXII/III (Bari, 1966). Republished by Corpus Christianorum, continuatio mediaevalis, CXXV, CXXVa, 2 vols (Turnhout, 1998/99).

Sartori, A., *Archivio sartori, documenti di storia e arte francescana, II/2, La provincia del Santo dei fratri minori conventuali*, a cura di P. Giovanni Luisetto (Padua, 1986).

Scripta Leonis, Rufini et Angeli sociorum S. Francisci. The Writings of Leo, Rufino and Angelo Companions of St. Francis, ed. R. B. Brooke, Oxford Medieval Texts (Oxford, 1970).

Sevesi, P. M., 'Documenta hucusque inedita saeculi XIII pro historia almae fratrum minorum provinciae Mediolanensis [seu Lombardiae]', *AFH* 2 (1909), pp. 561–74.

——'Il Beato Michele da Carcano da Milano O.F.M.', in *AFH* 3 (1910), pp. 448–63, 633–63, and 4 (1911), pp. 24–49, 456–81.

Sources of the Modern Roman Liturgy: The Ordinals by Haymo of Faversham and Related Documents (1243–1307), ed. S. J. P. Van Dijk, 2 vols, Studia et documenta Franciscana cura fratrum minorum in Austria, Belgio, Germania, Neerlandia edita (Leiden, 1963).

Le Speculum laicorum: édition d'une collection d'exempla, composée en Angleterre à la fin du XIIIe siècle, ed. J. Th. Welter (Paris, 1914).

La Tabula exemplorum secundum ordinem alphabeti: recueil d'exempla compilé en France à la fin du XIIIe siècle, ed. J. Th. Welter, Thesaurus exemplorum, III (Paris, 1926).

Thomas of Eccleston, *Tractatus Fr. Thomae vulgo dicti de Eccleston de adventu fratrum minorum in Angliam*, Collection d'études et de documents, VII, ed. A. G. Little (Paris, 1909), and Thomas of Eccleston, *Fratris Thomae vulgo dicti de Eccleston Tractatus de adventu fratrum minorum in Angliam*, ed. A. G. Little (Manchester, 1951).

Van Ortroy, F., 'Vie inédite de S. Bernardin de Sienne par un frère mineur, son contemporain', *Analecta Bollandiana* 25 (1906), pp. 304–38.

Visconti, Federico, *Les Sermons et la visite pastorale de Federico Visconti archevêque de Pise (1253–1277)*, ed. N. Bériou, Sources et documents d'histoire du moyen âge publiés par l'école française de Rome, III (Rome, 2001).

Vita del 'Dialogus' e 'Benignitas', ed. V. Gamboso, Fonti agiografiche antoniane, III (Padua, 1986).

Vita prima o 'Assidua', ed. V. Gamboso. Fonti agiografiche antoniane, I (Padua, 1981).

Vite 'Raymundina' e 'Rigaldina', ed. V. Gamboso, Fonti agiografiche antoniane, IV (Padua, 1992).

Vorreux, D., 'Un sermon de Philippe le chancelier en faveur des frères mineurs de Vauvert', *AFH* 68 (1975), pp. 3–22.

Wilmart, A., 'Le Commentaire de Nicolas d'Osimo sur la regle de saint François', in *Analecta Reginensia*, Studi e testi, LIX (Rome, 1933), pp. 301–10.

Secondary printed sources

Andrews, F., *The Early Humiliati*, Cambridge Studies in Medieval Life and Thought, 4th Series, XLIII (Cambridge, 1999).

Backman, C. R., 'Arnau de Vilanova and the Franciscan Spirituals in Sicily', *FS* 50 (1990), pp. 3–29.

Bartoli-Langeli, F., 'Il manifesto francescano di Perugia del 1322 alle origini dei fraticelli "de opinione"', *Picenum Seraphicum* 11 (1974), pp. 204–61.

Bériou, N., *L'Avènement des maîtres de la parole: la prédication à Paris à XIII siècle*, 2 vols, Collection des études augustiniennes (Paris, 1998).

Bougerol, J., *Introduction à l'étude de S. Bonaventure*, Bibliothèque de théologie, série 1, Théologie dogmatique, II (Paris, 1961).

—— 'Le origini e la finalità dello studio nell'ordine francescano', *Antonianum* 53 (1978), pp. 405–22.

Bourdua, L., 'Friars, Patrons, and Workshops at the Basilica del Santo, Padua', *The Church and the Arts*, ed. D. Wood, Studies in Church History, XXVIII (Oxford, 1992), pp. 131–41.

—— 'I frati minori al santo nel trecento: consulenti, committenti o artisti?', *Il santo*, 42 (2002), pp. 17–28.

—— *The Franciscans and Art Patronage in Late Medieval Italy* (Cambridge, 2004).

Brady, I. C., 'Sacred Scripture in the Early Franciscan School', in *La sacra scrittura e i francescani*, Pontificium Athenaeum Antonianum, Studium Biblicum Franciscanum (Rome, 1973), pp. 65–82.

—— 'The Distinctions of Lombard's Book of Sentences and Alexander of Hales', *FS* 25 (1965), pp. 90–116.

—— 'The Writings of Saint Bonaventure regarding the Franciscan Order', *MF* 75 (1975), pp. 89–112.

Brooke, R. B., *Early Franciscan Government: Elias to Bonaventure*, Cambridge Studies in Medieval Life and Thought, n.s., VII (Cambridge, 1959).

—— 'Recent Work on St Francis of Assisi', *Analecta Bollandiana* 100 (1982), pp. 653–76.

—— *The Coming of the Friars*, Historical Problems: Studies and Documents, XXIV (London, 1975).

—— *The Image of St Francis in the Thirteenth Century* (Cambridge, 2006).

Brown, K. D., 'Wolsey and Ecclesiastical Order: The Case of the Franciscan Observants', in *Cardinal Wolsey: Church, State and Art*, ed. S. J. Gunn and P. G. Lindley (Cambridge, 1991), pp. 219–38.

Bulletti, E., 'Angelo Salvetti (c.1350–1423) in documenti dell'Archivo di stato di Siena', *AFH* 54 (1961), pp. 26–93.

Burr, D., *Olivi and Franciscan Poverty: The Origins of the Usus Pauper Controversy* (Philadelphia, 1989).

—— *The Persecution of Peter Olivi*, Transactions of the American Philosophical Society, n.s., 66v (Philadelphia, 1976).

—— *The Spiritual Franciscans: From Protest to Persecution in the Century after Saint Francis* (Pennsylvania, 2001).

Burton, J., *Monastic and Religious Orders in Britain, 1000–1300*, Cambridge Medieval Texbooks (Cambridge, 1994).

Callebaut, A., 'Les Provinciaux de la province de France au XIIIe siècle. Notes, documents, et études', *AFH* 10 (1917), pp. 289–356.

—— 'Thomas de Frignano, ministre général et ses défenseurs: Pétraque, Philippe de Cabassol et Philippe de Maizières, vers 1369–70', *AFH* 10 (1917), pp. 239–49.

Callus, D. A., ed., *Robert Grosseteste Scholar and Bishop: Essays in Commemoration of the Seventh Centenary of His Death* (Oxford, 1955).

Campbell, J., 'Le Sommaire de l'enquête pour la canonisation de S. Elzéar de Sabran, TOF (†1323)', *MF* 73 (1973), pp. 438–73.

Casagrande, G., *Religiosità penitenziale e città al tempo dei comuni*, Bibliotheca Seraphico-Capuccina, XLVIII (Rome, 1995).

Cenci, C., *Manoscritti francescani della Biblioteca nazionale di Napoli*, II, SB, VIII (Grottaferrata, Rome, 1971).

—— 'I Gonzaga e i frati minori dal 1365 al 1430', *AFH* 58 (1965), pp. 3–47, 201–79.

—— 'I manoscritti del Sacro Convento d'Assisi catalogati da L. Leoni nel 1862–63', *MF* 83 (1983), pp. 245–90.

—— 'Noterelle su Fr. Giacomo da Tresanti, lettore predicatore', *AFH* 86 (1993), pp. 119–28.

—— 'Quaresimale del 1321 in S. Francesco al Prato di Perugia', *StF* 91 (1994), pp. 329–41.

—— 'San Pietro Pettinaio presentato da un predicatore senese contemporaneo', *StF* 87 (1990), pp. 5–30.

Chiappini, A., 'La produzione letteraria di S. Giovanni da Capestrano', *MF* 25 (1925), pp. 54–103.

Ciccarelli, D., 'Le "introductiones dominicales" di Andrea de Pace O. Min.', *Schede medievali rassegna dell'officina di studi medievali* 38 (2000), pp. 121–47.

Cook, W. R., 'Fraternal and Lay Images of St. Francis in the Thirteenth Century', in *Popes, Teachers and Canon Law in the Middle Ages*, ed. J. Ross Sweeney and S. Chodorow (Ithaca, 1989), pp. 263–89.

—— 'The St. Francis Dossal in Siena. An Important Interpretation of the Life of Francis of Assisi', *AFH* 87 (1994), pp. 3–20.

Cotter, F. J., *The Friars Minor in Ireland: From Their Arrival to 1400*, ed. R. A. McKelvie, Franciscan Institute Publications, History Series, VII (New York, 1994).

Courtenay, W. J., *Adam Wodeham: An Introduction to His Life and Writings*, Studies in Medieval and Reformation Thought, XXI (Leiden, 1978).

—— *Schools and Scholars in Fourteenth-Century England* (Princeton, 1987).

—— 'The Instructional Programme of the Mendicant Convents at Paris in the Early Fourteenth Century', in *The Medieval Church: Universities, Heresy and the Religious Life. Essays in Honour of Gordon Leff*, ed. P. Biller and R. B. Dobson, Studies in Church History, Subsidia, XI (Woodbridge, 1999), pp. 77–92.

—— 'The Parisian Franciscan Community in 1303', *FS* 53 (1993), pp. 155–73.

Cresi, D., 'Statistica dell'ordine minoritico all'anno 1282', *AFH* 56 (1963), pp. 157–62.

Cusato, M. F., 'Talking about Ourselves: The Shift in Franciscan Writing from Hagiography to History (1235–1247)', *FS* 58 (2000), pp. 37–75.

—— 'Whence the "Community"?' *FS* 60 (2002), pp. 39–92.

D'Alatri, M., *Eretici e inquisitori in Italia, studi e documenti, il duecento & il tre e il quattrocento*, 2 vols, Bibliotheca Seraphico-Capuccina, XXXI (Rome, 1986–7).

—— 'Gli insediamenti osservanti in Sicilia nel corso del Quattrocentro', in *Schede medievali rassegna dell'officina di studi medievali* 32/33 (1997), pp. 41–50.

—— *I frati penitenti di San Francesco nella società del due e trecento*, Istituto Storico dei Cappuccini (Rome, 1977).

—— *Il movemento francescano della penitenza nella società medioevale*, Atti del terzo convegno di Studi francescani, Padova, 1979 (Rome, 1980).

D'Alençon, U., 'Documents sur la réforme de Ste. Colette en France', *AFH* 2 (1909), pp. 447–56, 600–12 and 3 (1910), pp. 82–97.

D'Avray, D. L., 'Sermons to the Upper Bourgeoise by a Thirteenth-Century Franciscan', in *The Church in Town and Countryside*, ed. D. Baker, Studies in Church History, XVI (Oxford, 1979), pp. 187–99.

—— *The Preaching of the Friars: Sermons Diffused from Paris before 1300* (Oxford, 1985).

Dedieu, H., 'Les Ministres provinciaux d'Aquitaine des origines à la division de l'ordre (XIIIe siecle – 1517)', *AFH* 76 (1983), pp. 129–214, 646–700.

Di Fonzo, L., 'I beati francescani di Foligno tra santità e riforma religiosa, 1230–1860', *MF* 90 (1990), pp. 595–647.

Doucet, V., 'The History of the Problem of the Authenticity of the Summa', *FS* 7 (1947), pp. 26–41, 274–312.

Douie, D. L., *Archbishop Pecham* (Oxford, 1952).

—— *The Nature and the Effect of the Heresy of the Fraticelli* (Manchester, 1932).

—— 'St.Bonaventura's Part in the Conflict between Seculars and Mendicants in Paris', in *S. Bonaventura 1274–1974*, II, ed. J. Bougerol *et al.* (Grottaferrata, Roma, 1973), pp. 585–612.

Duval-Arnould, L., 'La Constitution "Cum inter nonnullos" de Jean XXII sur la pauvreté du Christ et des Apôtres: rédaction préparatoire et rédaction définitive',

AFH 77 (1984), pp. 406–20.

Emery, R. W., *The Friars in Medieval France: A Catalogue of the French Mendicant Convents, 1200–1500* (New York, 1962).

Erickson, C., 'The Fourteenth-Century Franciscans and Their Critics', *FS* 35 (1975), pp. 107–35.

Faral, E., 'Les "responsiones" de Guillaume de Saint-Amour', *Archives d'histoire doctrinale et littéraire du Moyen Age* 18 (1951), pp. 337–94.

Fennessy, I., 'Castledermot and the Franciscans', *Journal of the County Kildare Archaeological Society and Surrounding Districts* 18 (1992–9), pp. 542–64.

Fitzmaurice, E. B., and A. G. Little,, *Materials for the History of the Franciscan Province of Ireland A.D. 1230–1450*, British Society of Franciscan Studies, X (Manchester, 1920).

Fleming, J. V., *An Introduction to the Franciscan Literature of the Middle Ages* (Chicago, 1977).

Fletcher, A. J., *Preaching, Politics and Poetry in Late-Medieval England* (Dublin, 1998).

Francis of Assisi, Early Documents, The Saint, The Founder and the Prophet, 3 vols, ed. R. J. Armstrong, J. A. W. Hellmann and W. J. Short (New York, 1999/2001).

Freed, J. B., *The Friars and German Society in the Thirteenth Century*, The Mediaeval Academy of America, LXXXVI (Cambridge, Mass., 1977).

Geanakoplos, D. J., 'Bonaventura, the Two Mendicant Orders and the Greeks at the Council of Lyons', *The Orthodox Churches and the West*, ed. D. Baker, Studies in Church History, XIII (Oxford, 1976), pp. 183–211.

Ginther, J. R., *Master of the Sacred Page: A Study of the Theology of Robert Grosseteste, ca. 1229/30–1235* (Aldershot, 2004).

——'Theological Education at the Oxford Studium in the Thirteenth Century: A Reassment of Robert Grosseteste's Letter to the Oxford Theologians', *FS* 55 (1998), pp. 83–104.

Glorieux, P., 'Le Conflit de 1252–1257 à la lumiere du memoire de Guillaume de Saint-Amour', *Recherches de théologie ancienne et médiévale* 24 (1957), pp. 364–72.

Gratien de Paris, *Histoire de la fondation et de l'évolution de l'ordre des Frères Mineurs au XIII siècle*, Bibliotheca Seraphico-Capuccina, XXIX (Rome, 1926).

Gratien, F., 'Les Débuts de la réforme des cordeliers en France et Guillaume Josseaume (1390–1436)', *Études franciscaines* 31 (1914), pp. 415–39.

Gwyn, A., 'Archbishop FitzRalph and the Friars', *Studies, An Irish Quarterly Review* 26 (1937), pp. 50–67.

——'Richard FitzRalph, archbishop of Armagh', *Studies, An Irish Quarterly Review* 25 (1936), pp. 81–96.

Hammerich, L. L., 'The Beginning of the Strife between Richard FitzRalph and the Mendicants, with an Edition of His Autobiographical Prayer and His Proposition Unusquisque', *Det. Kgl. Danske Videnskabernes Selskab. Historisk-filologiske Meddelelser* 26, iii (Copenhagen, 1938).

Harkins, C., 'The Authorship of a Commentary on the Franciscan Rule Published among the Works of St. Bonaventure', *FS* 29 (1969), pp. 157–248.

Havely, N., *Dante and the Franciscans: Poverty and the Papacy in the Commedia* (Cambridge, 2004).

Hayes, Z., *The Hidden Center: Spirituality and Speculative Christology in St. Bonaventure* (New York, 1981).

Henquinet, F. M., 'Clair de Florence, O.F.M., canoniste et pénitencier pontifical vers le milieu du XIII siècle', *AFH* 32 (1939), pp. 3–48.

Henquinet, F. M., 'Le Canoniste Fr. Mainfroid de Tortona O.F.M., disciple d'Alexandre de Halès et de Jean de la Rochelle', *AFH* 33 (1940), pp. 221–5.

Homan, R. L., 'Old and New Evidence of the Career of William Melton, O.F.M.', *FS* 49 (1989), pp. 25–33.

Humphreys, K. W., *The Book Provisions of the Medieval Friars 1215–1400*, Studies in the History of Libraries and Librarianship, I (Amsterdam, 1964).

Jackson, P., trans. and introd., *The Mission of Friar William of Rubruck: His Journey to the Court of the Great Khan Möngke 1253–1255*, The Hakluyt Society, 2nd series, CLXXIII (London, 1990).

Jeffrey, D. L., *The Early English Lyric and Franciscan Spirituality* (Lincoln, Nebraska, 1975).

Kingsford C. L., *The Grey Friars of London: Their History, with the Register of Their Convent and an Appendix of Documents*, British Society of Franciscan Studies, VI (Aberdeen, 1915).

Lambert, M. D., *Franciscan Poverty: The Doctrine of the Absolute Primacy of Christ and the Apostles in the Franciscan Order 1210–1323* (New York, 1998).

Lawrence, C. H., 'The English Parish and Its Clergy in the Thirteenth Century', *The Medieval World*, ed. P. Linehan and J. L. Nelson (London, 2001), pp. 648–70.

—— 'The Letters of Adam Marsh and the Franciscan School at Oxford', *Journal of Ecclesiastical History* 42 (1991), pp. 218–38.

—— *The Friars: The Impact of the Early Mendicant Movement on Western Society*, The Medieval World (London, 1994).

Le Goff, J., 'Apostolat mendiant et fait urbain dans la France médiévale: l'implantation des ordres mendiants. Programme-questionnaire pour une enquête', *Annales économies sociétés civilisations* 23 (1968), pp. 335–52.

—— 'Ordres mendiants et urbanisation dans la France médiévale: État de "enquête"', *Annales économies sociétés civilisations* 25 (1970), pp. 924–46.

Lemaitre, J.-L., 'L'"obituaire" des cordeliers de Rodez', *AFH* 87 (1994), pp. 31–63.

Lesnick, D. R., *Preaching in Medieval Florence: The Social World of Franciscan and Dominican Spirituality* (Athens, Georgia, 1989).

Little, A. G., *Franciscan Papers, Lists and Documents* (Manchester, 1943).

—— 'Introduction of the Observant Friars into England', *Proceedings of the British Academy* X (1921–1923), pp. 455–71.

—— 'Introduction of the Observant Friars into England: A Bull of Alexander VI', *Proceedings of the British Academy* 27 (1941), pp. 155–66.

—— *The Grey Friars in Oxford*, Oxford Historical Society, XX (Oxford, 1892).

Little, L. K., *Religious Poverty and the Profit Economy in Medieval Europe* (London, 1978).

Long, J. C., 'The Program of Giotto's Saint Francis Cycle at Santa Croce in Florence', *FS* 52 (1992) pp. 85–133.

Maier, C. T., *Crusade Propaganda and Ideology: Model Sermons for the Preaching of the Cross* (Cambridge, 2000).

—— *Preaching the Crusades: Mendicant Friars and the Cross in the Thirteenth Century*, Cambridge Studies in Medieval Life and Thought (Cambridge, 1994).

McAodha, L., 'The Holy Name of Jesus in the Preaching of St. Bernardine of Siena', *FS* 29 (1969), pp. 37–65.

McEvoy, J., 'Robert Grosseteste's Greek Scholarship: A Survey of Present Knowledge', *FS* 56 (1998), pp. 255–64.

McEvoy, J., *The Philosophy of Robert Grosseteste* (Oxford, 1982).

—— 'Robert Grosseteste and the Reunion of the Church', *CF* 45 (1975), pp. 39–84.

Millett, B., 'The Friars Minor in County Wicklow, Ireland, 1260–1982', *AFH* 77 (1984), pp. 110–36.

Mincuzzi, R., 'Santa Rosa da Viterbo, penitente del XIII secolo', *Analecta tertii ordinis regularis Sancti Francisci*, 31 (2000), pp. 7–120.

Mooney, C., 'The Franciscans in County Mayo', *Journal of the Galway Archaeological and Historical Society* 28 (1958–9), pp. 42–69.

Moorman, J. R. H., *A History of the Franciscan Order: From Its Origins to the Year 1517* (Oxford, 1968).

—— *The Grey Friars of Cambridge 1225–1538* (Cambridge, 1952).

—— *The Franciscans in England 1224–1974* (Oxford, 1974).

—— *The Sources for the Life of S. Francis of Assisi* (Manchester, 1940).

Nimmo, D., *Reform and Division in the Medieval Franciscan Order: From Saint Francis to the Foundation of the Capuchins*, Bibliotheca Seraphico-Capuccina, XXXIII (Rome, 1987).

Nold, P., *Pope John XXII and His Franciscan Cardinal: Bertrand de la Tour and the Apostolic Poverty Controversy*, Oxford Historical Monographs (Oxford, 2003).

Norman, D., 'Those who pay, those who pray and those who paint: two funerary chapels', *Siena, Florence and Padua, II: Art, Society and Religion 1280–1400, II, Case Studies*, ed. D. Norman (Yale, 1995), pp. 169–93.

Nyphus, P. L., 'The Observant Reform Movement in Southern Germany', *FS* 32 (1972), pp. 154–67.

O'Carroll, M., ed., *Robert Grosseteste and the Beginnings of a British Theological Tradition*, Bibliotheca Seraphico-Capuccina, LXIX (Rome, 1983).

Ó'Clabaigh, C. N., *The Franciscans in Ireland, 1400–1534. From Reform to Reformation* (Dublin, 2002).

Osborne, K. B., ed., *The History of Franciscan Theology* (New York, 1994).

Pacetti, D., 'La predicazione di S. Bernardino da Siena a Perugia e ad Assisi nel 1425', *CF* 9 (1939), pp. 494–520, and 10 (1940), pp. 5–28, 161–88.

—— 'La Predicazione di S. Bernardino in Toscana. Con Documenti inediti estratti dagli atti del processo di canonizzazione', *AFH* 33 (1940), pp. 268–318, 291 and 34 (1941), pp. 261–83.

Parsons, A., 'Bernardine of Feltre and the Montes Pietatis', *FS* 1 (1941), pp. 11–32.

Paton, B., *Preaching Friars and the Civic Ethos: Siena, 1380–1480*, Westfield Publications in Medieval Studies, VII (London, 1992),

Polecritti, C. L., *Preaching Peace in Renaissance Italy: Bernardine of Siena and His Audience* (Washington, 2000).

Pratesi, R., 'L'introduzione della regolare osservanza nella Francia meridionale', *AFH* 50 (1957), pp. 178–94.

Raedts, P., *Richard Rufus of Cornwall and the Tradition of Oxford Theology*, Oxford Historical Monographs (Oxford, 1987).

Richards, M., 'The Conflict between Observant and Conventual Reformed Franciscans in Fifteenth-Century France and Flanders', *FS* 50 (1990), pp. 263–81.

Robson, M., 'Franciscan Bishops *in partibus infidelium* Ministering in Medieval England', *Antonianum* 78 (2003), pp. 547–73.

—— 'Franciscan Lectors at Christ Church Cathedral Priory, Canterbury, 1275–1314', *Archaeologia Cantiana (Kent Archaeological Society)* 112 (1993), pp. 261–81.

Robson, M., *St Francis of Assisi: The Legend and the Life* (London, 1997).

—— *The Franciscans in the Medieval Custody of York*, Borthwick Institute of Historical Research, University of York, Borthwick Papers, CXIII (York, 1997).

—— 'The Grey Friars in York, *c.* 1450–1530', *The Religious Orders in Pre-Reformation England*, Studies in the History of Medieval Religion, XVIII, ed. J. G. Clark (Woodbridge, 2002), pp. 109–119.

Roest, B., *A History of Franciscan Education (c.1210–1517)*, Education and Society in the Middle Ages and Renaissance, XI (Leiden, 2000).

—— 'Franciscan Educational Perspectives: Reworking Monastic Traditions', in *Medieval Monastic Education*, ed. G. Ferzoco and C. Muessig (Leicester, 2000), pp. 168–81.

—— *Franciscan Literature of Religious Instruction before the Council of Trent*, Medieval and Early Modern Studies, 117 (Leiden, 2005).

—— 'The Role of Lectors in the Religious Formation of Franciscan Friars, Nuns and Tertiaries', *Studio e studia: le scuole degli mendicanti tra XIII e XIV secolo*, Societa internazionale di studi francescani, Atti del XXIX convegno internazionale, 2001 (Spoleto, 2002), pp. 83–115.

Röhrkasten, J., 'Local Ties and International Connections of the London Mendicants', *Mendicants, Military Orders, and Regionalism in Medieval Europe*, ed. J. Sarnowsky (Aldershot, 1999), pp. 145–83.

—— 'Londoners and London Mendicants in the Late Middle Ages', *Journal of Ecclesiastical History* 47 (1996), pp. 446–77.

—— 'Mendicants in the Metropolis: The Londoners and the Development of the London Friaries', in *Thirteenth Century England VI*, ed. M. Prestwich (Woodbridge, 1997), pp. 61–75.

—— *The Mendicant Houses of Medieval London 1221–1539*, Vita Regularis Ordnungen und Deutungen religiosen Lebens im Mittelalter, 21 (Münster, 2004).

—— 'The Origin and Early Development of the London Mendicant Houses', in *The Church in the Medieval Town*, ed. T. R. Slater and G. Rosser (Aldershot, 1998), pp. 76–99.

Sacchetti Sassetti, A., 'Giacomo della Marca paciere a Rieti', *AFH* 50 (1957), pp. 75–82.

Schmitt, C., 'La Réforme de l'observance discutée au concile de Bâle', *AFH* 83 (1990), pp. 369–404 and 84 (1991), pp. 3–50.

Scocca, F., 'Santità femminile nel terzo ordine francescano. Alcune figure emblematiche', *Analecta tertii ordinis regularis Sancti Francisci* 34 (2003), pp. 179–98.

Sheehan, M. W., 'The Religious Orders 1220–1370', *The History of the University of Oxford, I, The Early Oxford Schools*, ed. J. I. Catto (Oxford, 1984), pp. 193–223.

Southern, R. W., *Robert Grosseteste: The Growth of an English Mind in Medieval Europe* (Oxford, 1986).

Swanson, J., *John of Wales: A Study of the Works and Ideas of a Thirteenth-Century Friar*, Cambridge Studies in Medieval Life and Thought, fourth series (Cambridge, 1989).

Szittya, P. R., *The Antifraternal Tradition in Medieval Literature* (Princeton, 1986).

Thomson, W. R., *Friars in the Cathedral: The First Franciscan Bishops 1226–1261*, The Pontifical Institute of Mediaeval Studies, Studies and Texts, 33 (Toronto, 1975).

Tilatti, A., *Odorico da Pordenone, Vita e Miracula* Centro studi Antoniani, 41 (Padua, 2004).

Van Dijk, S. J. P., and J. Hazelden Walker, *The Origins of the Modern Roman Liturgy: The Liturgy of the Papal Court and the Franciscan Order in the Thirteenth Century* (London, 1960).

Voorvelt, G. P.C. and B. P. van Leeuwen, 'L'Evangéliaire de Baltimore. Étude critique sur le missel que saint François aurait consulte', *CF* 59 (1989), pp. 261–321.

Walsh, K., *A Fourteenth-Century Scholar and Primate: Richard FitzRalph in Oxford, Avignon and Armagh* (Oxford, 1981).

Watt, J. A., *The Church and the Two Nations in Medieval Ireland*, Cambridge Studies in Medieval Life and Thought, 3rd series, 3 (Cambridge, 1970).

—— 'The Papacy', in *The New Cambridge Medieval History, V, c. 1198–c. 1300*, pp. 107–63.

Welter, J. Th., *L'Exemplum dans la littérature religieuse et didactique du Moyen Age*, Bibliotheque d'histoire ecclesiastique de France (Paris, 1927).

INDEX